Peer Review of the Automatic Exchange of Financial Account Information 2021

OECD
BETTER POLICIES FOR BETTER LIVES

Please cite this publication as:
OECD (2021), *Peer Review of the Automatic Exchange of Financial Account Information 2021*, OECD Publishing, Paris, *https://doi.org/10.1787/90bac5f5-en*.

ISBN 978-92-64-35288-9 (print)
ISBN 978-92-64-46897-9 (pdf)

Photo credits: Cover © OECD with cover illustration by Renaud Madignier.

Corrigenda to publications may be found on line at: *www.oecd.org/about/publishing/corrigenda.htm*.

Foreword

The OECD hosted Global Forum on Transparency and Exchange of Information for Tax Purposes (the Global Forum) provides a multilateral response to tackle offshore tax evasion. It brings together over 160 jurisdictions dedicated to improving transparency and the exchange of information for tax purposes.

The Global Forum promotes and ensures the effective implementation of two complementary international standards: the exchange of information on request (EOIR) and the automatic exchange of financial account information (AEOI), both of which provide for closer co-operation between tax authorities worldwide so that they can obtain information necessary to ensure tax compliance.

The OECD developed the Standard for Automatic Exchange of Financial Account Information in Tax Matters (AEOI Standard) in 2014, working with G20 countries. It provides for the annual exchange of a predefined set of information on financial accounts held by individuals and entities resident in a foreign jurisdiction, between tax authorities. The Global Forum has been supporting, monitoring and reviewing the implementation of the AEOI Standard since its inception. It has published detailed yearly reports on the implementation of the AEOI Standard by all participating jurisdictions since exchanges commenced in 2017.

This report builds on the report published in 2020 to present updated results of the peer reviews conducted by the Global Forum with respect to the domestic and international legal frameworks put in place by the first 102 jurisdictions to implement the AEOI Standard. It also provides details of the peer reviews being conducted by the Global Forum with respect to the effectiveness of the implementation of the AEOI Standard in practice. The detailed results of these peer reviews are expected to be published in 2022.

This document was approved by the AEOI Peer Review Group on 11 October 2021 and adopted by the AEOI Peers on 5 November 2021. It was prepared for publication by the Secretariat of the Global Forum on Transparency and Exchange of Information for Tax Purposes.

Table of contents

Foreword 3

Abbreviations and acronyms 8

Executive summary 9

1 Monitoring the implementation of the AEOI Standard 11
- The AEOI commitment process 12
- Monitoring the timeliness of delivery 12
- Peer reviews of the quality of implementation 16
- Note 16

2 Peer reviews of the AEOI Standard's implementation 17
- Global Forum AEOI peer reviews: covering all key areas 18
- Peer reviews of the AEOI legal frameworks 18
- Peer reviews of the effectiveness in practice of AEOI implementation 26
- Notes 31

3 Jurisdiction-specific reports 32
- Andorra 33
- Anguilla 36
- Antigua and Barbuda 39
- Argentina 43
- Aruba 47
- Australia 52
- Austria 55
- Azerbaijan 58
- The Bahamas 61
- Bahrain 65
- Barbados 68
- Belgium 72
- Belize 75
- Bermuda 79
- Brazil 82
- British Virgin Islands 85
- Brunei Darussalam 89
- Bulgaria 92
- Canada 95

Cayman Islands	99
Chile	102
China (People's Republic of)	105
Colombia	108
Cook Islands	111
Costa Rica	114
Croatia	118
Curaçao	121
Cyprus	126
Czech Republic	129
Denmark	132
Dominica	135
Estonia	138
Faroe Islands	142
Finland	145
France	148
Germany	151
Ghana	155
Gibraltar	159
Greece	162
Greenland	165
Grenada	168
Guernsey	172
Hong Kong (China)	175
Hungary	178
Iceland	182
India	185
Indonesia	188
Ireland	191
Isle of Man	194
Israel	197
Italy	201
Japan	204
Jersey	208
Korea	211
Kuwait	214
Latvia	217
Lebanon	221
Liechtenstein	224
Lithuania	227
Luxembourg	230
Macau (China)	233
Malaysia	237
Malta	240
Marshall Islands	243
Mauritius	246
Mexico	249
Monaco	252
Montserrat	255
Nauru	258

Netherlands 261
New Zealand 265
Niue 268
Norway 271
Pakistan 274
Panama 277
Poland 281
Portugal 285
Qatar 288
Romania 291
Russia 296
Saint Kitts and Nevis 300
Saint Lucia 303
Saint Vincent and the Grenadines 307
Samoa 311
San Marino 314
Saudi Arabia 317
Seychelles 320
Singapore 323
Sint Maarten 326
Slovak Republic 328
Slovenia 331
South Africa 334
Spain 337
Sweden 340
Switzerland 343
Trinidad and Tobago 347
Turkey 349
Turks and Caicos Islands 352
United Arab Emirates 356
United Kingdom 359
Uruguay 362
Vanuatu 366

Annex A. Assessments carried out under the Staged Approach 369

Annex B. Details of the exchange agreements in place 371

Annex C. The AEOI Terms of Reference 386

FIGURES

Figure 2.1. Overall determinations at a glance 23

Figure A A.1. The Staged Approach to the AEOI assessment process 369

TABLES

Table 1.1. Jurisdictions that have exchanged information in 2020 and 2021 13
Table 1.2. Jurisdictions that have not yet exchanged information because their legal implementation is ongoing 16
Table 1.3. Jurisdictions that have not yet exchanged information because their technical implementation is ongoing 16
Table 1.4. Jurisdictions committed to commencing exchanges from 2022 onwards 16
Table 2.1. The determinations 21
Table 2.2. Overview of the determinations on the legal frameworks for the assessed jurisdictions 24

Abbreviations and acronyms

AEOI	Automatic Exchange of Information
AEOI Standard	The Standard for Automatic Exchange of Financial Account Information in Tax Matters
AML	Anti-Money Laundering
APRG	AEOI Peer Review Group
CR	Core Requirement
CRS	Common Reporting Standard
CRS MCAA	CRS Multilateral Competent Authority Agreement
CTS	Common Transmission System
FATCA	Foreign Account Tax Compliance Act
FATF	Financial Action Task Force
G20	The Group of Twenty
Global Forum	Global Forum on Transparency and Exchange of Information for Tax Purposes
KYC	Know Your Customer
Model CAA	Model Competent Authority Agreement
OECD	Organisation for Economic Co-operation and Development
SR	Sub-requirement

Executive summary

Ensuring taxpayers pay the tax that is due is crucial to maintaining public finances and reinforcing the public's trust in the tax system. In this regard, governments have long sought to ensure that taxpayers with offshore financial activities continue to meet their domestic tax obligations. This has become increasingly challenging as the financial sector has become progressively global in nature and of heightened importance as jurisdictions work to address the impacts of the COVID-19 pandemic.

The key tool available to governments to ensure the correct payment of tax with respect to offshore income and assets is the exchange of information between tax authorities. A very significant and recent milestone in this regard was the development by the OECD, working with G20 countries, of the Standard for Automatic Exchange of Financial Account Information in Tax Matters (AEOI Standard).

The AEOI Standard built upon the pre-existing and ongoing exchange of information on request, to provide a common multilateral framework for the domestic collection and international exchange of information on Financial Accounts between tax authorities on an automatic basis.

In this regard the AEOI Standard provides a common approach to ensuring that Financial Institutions report information to their domestic tax authorities in relation to Financial Accounts held by foreign tax residents or, in certain cases, held by Entities controlled by foreign tax residents (defined as Controlling Persons). Tax authorities then exchange that information with the tax authority from the jurisdiction where the Account Holder/Controlling Person is resident. This allows tax authorities to verify whether taxpayers are properly declaring their international financial affairs and paying the tax that is due to their domestic tax authorities.

Recognising its huge potential, 120 jurisdictions have so far committed to exchange information under the AEOI Standard and more are expected. Furthermore, the vast majority of these jurisdictions have already introduced the necessary legal frameworks and technical solutions, and are collecting the information from their Financial Institutions and exchanging it with their exchange partners. The key task now is ensuring that the AEOI Standard operates effectively in practice and that its potential benefits are realised.

The Global Forum therefore monitors the global implementation of the AEOI Standard and carries out peer reviews to assess the quality of its implementation. It has already reviewed the domestic and international legal frameworks for the first 100 jurisdictions that committed to exchange information automatically from 2017 or 2018, and published the results in 2020. Since then, several jurisdictions have addressed the recommendations made. Their reviews and the conclusions drawn have been updated accordingly and are included in this report. This report also includes the review of the legal frameworks for the two jurisdictions that committed to commence exchanging information from 2019.

The Global Forum is also carrying out peer reviews to ensure that the exchanges are operating effectively in practice. This includes ensuring that Reporting Financial Institutions comply with the requirements and that the information is prepared, formatted and transmitted in accordance with the requirements. These reviews are ongoing, with the results expected to be published in 2022.

This report is structured as follows:

- Chapter 1 provides the latest results of the monitoring process to track the timeliness of the delivery of all of the commitments to implement the AEOI Standard.
- Chapter 2 sets out details of the peer reviews that have been conducted so far, along with: (i) a summary of the results of the reviews of the AEOI legal frameworks, including the updated determinations made with respect to each jurisdiction, and (ii) a summary of the reviews in relation to effectiveness in practice, including the key issues identified.
- Chapter 3 presents the updated analysis and results of each jurisdiction's peer review with respect to its legal frameworks implementing the AEOI Standard, including the specific recommendations made.
- Annex A details the staging of the various reviews (the "Staged Approach").
- Annex B provides information on all the exchange agreements that are in place with respect to the AEOI Standard, including those activated through multilateral frameworks, as well as bilateral agreements.
- Annex C contains the AEOI Terms of Reference, which provides the basis for the AEOI reviews.

The information in this report is up to date as of 10 November 2021. Further information and updates are available on the AEOI Portal (www.oecd.org/tax/automatic-exchange) and the relevant communication channels that each jurisdiction has in place domestically.

1 Monitoring the implementation of the AEOI Standard

In response to the international community's demand to advance global transparency and exchange of information for tax purposes, demonstrated by the calls from the G20, the OECD developed the AEOI Standard in 2014. All members of the Global Forum, aside from developing countries that did not host a financial centre, were asked to commit to automatically exchanging financial information under the AEOI Standard by 2017 or 2018. This section contains the latest information on the timeliness of the implementation of the AEOI Standard by all jurisdictions.

Following a call by the G20, the OECD, working with G20 countries, developed the AEOI Standard in 2014. The Global Forum was immediately tasked by the G20 with monitoring the implementation of the AEOI Standard worldwide. As a first step the Global Forum put in place a commitment process to facilitate the widespread application of the AEOI Standard, based on a level playing field.

The AEOI commitment process

As soon as the AEOI Standard was developed, the Global Forum recognised the potential benefits of its rapid and widespread implementation, alongside its existing standard of exchange of information on request (EOIR). The Global Forum therefore immediately put in place a process to promote the global implementation of the AEOI Standard. Consequently, all Global Forum members, except for developing countries that did not host a financial centre, were asked to commit to:

- implement the AEOI Standard;
- exchange information with all Interested Appropriate Partners (all jurisdictions interested in receiving information from a jurisdiction and that meet the expected standards in relation to confidentiality and data safeguards); and
- commence exchanges in 2017 or 2018.

Forty-nine "early adopter" jurisdictions quickly committed to exchange information under the AEOI Standard in 2017 and a further 51 jurisdictions in 2018. Another 20 jurisdictions have since committed to implementing the AEOI Standard in time to start exchanging by 2024. This includes 14 developing countries not asked to commit to the AEOI Standard to a specific timeline, but that want to access the benefits the AEOI Standard has to offer. It also includes a further three jurisdictions identified through the Global Forum's "jurisdiction of relevance" process established to maintain a level playing field, which subsequently voluntarily committed to implement the AEOI Standard.

Further details on the individual commitments made are contained in the tables 1.1 to 1.3 below.

Monitoring the timeliness of delivery

The Global Forum has since monitored the timeliness of the delivery of each aspect of the implementation process. The key milestones relate to:

- putting in place a domestic legislative framework to require Financial Institutions to collect and report the information for exchange that is in accordance with the detailed due diligence and reporting rules contained in the AEOI Standard;
- putting in place an international legal framework permitting the automatic exchange of information with a jurisdiction's Interested Appropriate Partners. This includes an underlying legal basis and an administrative agreement containing the details of the exchanges – the vast majority of jurisdictions are using the multilateral Convention on Mutual Administrative Assistance in Tax Matters (the Convention) along with the CRS Multilateral Competent Authority Agreement (or CRS MCAA)[1]; and
- a technical infrastructure to receive the information from Financial Institutions and to process and transmit it to a jurisdiction's exchange partners. All jurisdictions use the Common Transmission System (CTS), developed and procured by the OECD and managed by the Global Forum.

Further details on each jurisdiction's timeliness in meeting these milestones are contained in the tables 1.2 to 1.4 below.

Delivery of the commitments

Table 1.1 presents details of the exchanges that took place in 2020 and 2021. The widespread delivery of the exchanges shows that the overwhelming majority of jurisdictions implemented the necessary legal and technical frameworks, in accordance with their commitments.

97% of the jurisdictions have delivered on their commitment to exchange information under the AEOI Standard.

Table 1.1. Jurisdictions that have exchanged information in 2020 and 2021

Jurisdiction	Year of commitment to first exchanges	Number of partners to which the data relating to 2019 was sent in 2020	Number of partners to which the data relating to 2020 was sent in 2021
1. Albania[1, 6]	2021	59	69
2. Andorra	2018	69	60
3. Anguilla	2017	52	55
4. Antigua and Barbuda[2]	2018	30	-
5. Argentina	2017	71	76
6. Aruba	2018	66	64
7. Australia	2018	70	72
8. Austria	2018	68	71
9. Azerbaijan[6]	2018	48	63
10. Bahamas	2018	56	58
11. Bahrain	2018	59	63
12. Barbados	2018	61	64
13. Belgium	2017	72	77
14. Belize	2018	64	63
15. Bermuda	2017	60	64
16. Brazil	2018	69	76
17. British Virgin Islands	2017	67	65
18. Brunei Darussalam	2018	33	41
19. Bulgaria	2017	71	72
20. Canada	2018	57	66
21. Cayman Islands	2017	70	73
22. Chile	2018	69	72
23. China (People's Republic of)	2018	69	75
24. Colombia	2017	70	77
25. Cook Islands	2018	68	68
26. Costa Rica	2018	69	71
27. Croatia	2017	70	75
28. Curaçao	2018	66	51
29. Cyprus	2017	72	74
30. Czech Republic	2017	66	74
31. Denmark	2017	73	76
32. Dominica[3]	2018	-	1
33. Ecuador[6]	2021	N/A	44
34. Estonia	2017	69	73
35. Faroe Islands	2017	67	73
36. Finland	2017	70	77
37. France	2017	68	71

Jurisdiction	Year of commitment to first exchanges	Number of partners to which the data relating to 2019 was sent in 2020	Number of partners to which the data relating to 2020 was sent in 2021
38.Including New Caledonia	*2020*	*29*	*33*
39. Germany	2017	68	74
40. Ghana[6]	2019	64	62
41. Gibraltar	2017	69	72
42. Greece	2017	69	74
43. Greenland	2018	69	77
44. Grenada	2018	65	61
45. Guernsey	2017	70	73
46. Hong Kong (China)	2018	50	67
47. Hungary	2017	72	71
48. Iceland	2017	67	70
49. India	2017	68	72
50. Indonesia	2018	69	72
51. Ireland	2017	73	77
52. Isle of Man	2017	68	75
53. Israel	2018	61	67
54. Italy	2017	71	75
55. Japan	2018	70	75
56. Jersey	2017	69	72
57. Kazakhstan[2]	2021	N/A	-
58. Korea	2017	70	74
59. Kuwait	2019	67	62
60. Latvia	2017	69	75
61. Lebanon[2]	2018	50	-
62. Liechtenstein	2017	68	75
63. Lithuania	2017	70	70
64. Luxembourg	2017	72	77
65. Macau (China)	2018	60	67
66. Malaysia	2018	65	68
67. Malta	2017	73	73
68. Marshall Islands	2018	59	60
69. Mauritius	2018	69	74
70. Mexico	2017	67	73
71. Monaco	2018	63	65
72. Montserrat[2]	2017	60	-
73. Nauru	2018	69	73
74. Netherlands	2017	68	70
75. New Zealand	2018	66	73
76. Nigeria[6]	2020	25	63
77. Norway	2017	71	75
78. Oman	2020	28	28
79. Pakistan[6]	2018	57	61
80. Panama	2018	63	66
81. Peru[6]	2020	15	45
82. Poland	2017	71	74
83. Portugal	2017	71	76
84. Qatar	2018	49	58
85. Romania	2017	67	71
86. Russia	2018	63	68
87. Saint Kitts and Nevis	2018	57	59

Jurisdiction	Year of commitment to first exchanges	Number of partners to which the data relating to 2019 was sent in 2020	Number of partners to which the data relating to 2020 was sent in 2021
88. Saint Lucia	2018	65	68
89. Saint Vincent and the Grenadines[4]	2018	-	-
90. Samoa	2018	64	65
91. San Marino	2017	68	71
92. Saudi Arabia	2018	68	74
93. Seychelles	2017	63	25
94. Singapore	2018	66	70
95. Slovak Republic	2017	68	77
96. Slovenia	2017	72	78
97. South Africa	2017	68	76
98. Spain	2017	71	78
99. Sweden	2017	70	73
100. Switzerland	2018	66	72
101. Turkey	2018	34	55
102. Turks and Caicos Islands[5]	2017	63	58
103. United Arab Emirates	2018	68	70
104. United Kingdom	2017	70	72
105. Uruguay	2018	70	74
106. Vanuatu	2018	53	52

Notes: The number of exchanges jurisdictions undertake each year tend to increase due to the expansion of exchange networks. However, fluctuations are observed in some cases due to technical issues when sending the information. This can lead to rejections by exchange partners of the information sent. In such cases, jurisdictions are expected to address the issues and send/re-send the information.

The United States has undertaken automatic information exchanges pursuant to FATCA from 2015 and entered into intergovernmental agreements (IGAs) with other jurisdictions to do so. The Model 1A IGAs entered into by the United States acknowledge the need for the United States to achieve equivalent levels of reciprocal automatic information exchange with partner jurisdictions. They also include a political commitment to pursue the adoption of regulations and to advocate and support relevant legislation to achieve such equivalent levels of reciprocal automatic exchange.

1. Albania voluntarily committed to 2021, but started exchanges in 2020.
2. These jurisdictions are delayed in undertaking the exchanges that should have taken place in 2021. They are expected to carry out the exchanges in the near future.
3. Dominica was delayed in undertaking the exchanges that should have taken place in 2018, 2019 and 2020. It has been able to commence exchanges with one partner so far in 2021 and is expected to carry out the remaining exchanges in the near future.
4. Due to technical difficulties, Saint Vincent and the Grenadines was delayed in undertaking the exchanges that should have taken place in 2020 and 2021.
5. Due to technical difficulties, the Turks and Caicos Islands was delayed in undertaking the exchanges that should have taken place in 2019.
6. These jurisdictions are developing countries that were not asked to commit to implementing the AEOI Standard to a particular timeline, but did so voluntarily.

While recognising the widespread successes in the fulfilment of the commitments made, some jurisdictions have not yet delivered. A fully effective AEOI Standard requires a level playing field and the Global Forum therefore continues to work closely with these jurisdictions to facilitate the delivery of their commitments.

Table 1.2 shows the jurisdictions that are late in putting in place the necessary legal frameworks to implement the AEOI Standard, namely **Sint Maarten** and **Trinidad and Tobago**.

Table 1.2. Jurisdictions that have not yet exchanged information because their legal implementation is ongoing

Jurisdiction	Year of commitment to first exchanges	Status
1. Sint Maarten	2018	Domestic and international legal frameworks not in place
2. Trinidad and Tobago	2018	Domestic and international legal frameworks not in place

Table 1.3 shows the jurisdictions that have in place the legal frameworks to implement the AEOI Standard but that have not put in place the technical requirements for exchange, namely **Niue**.

Table 1.3. Jurisdictions that have not yet exchanged information because their technical implementation is ongoing

Jurisdiction	Year of commitment to first exchanges	Status
1. Niue	2018	Has not linked into the CTS

Commitments to commence exchanges in the future

A further twelve jurisdictions are committed to starting exchanges in the coming years. These are set out in Table 1.4 below.

Table 1.4. Jurisdictions committed to commencing exchanges from 2022 onwards

Year of commitment to first exchanges	Jurisdiction
2022	Jamaica[1], Kenya[1], Maldives[1], Morocco[1]
2023	Jordan[2], Moldova[1], Montenegro[2], Thailand[2], Uganda[1], Ukraine[1]
2024	Georgia[1], Rwanda[1]

1. Developing countries that do not host a financial centre and that were not asked to commit to a specific date to exchange information, but that have done so voluntarily.
2. Jordan, Montenegro and Thailand were identified through the Global Forum process aimed at identifying jurisdictions of relevance for the implementation of the AEOI Standard and subsequently voluntarily committed to implement the AEOI Standard.

Peer reviews of the quality of implementation

While the timeliness of implementation is critical, the full potential benefits of the AEOI Standard will only be delivered if the requirements are implemented in a complete and effective manner.

To ensure this, Global Forum conducts peer reviews with respect to the quality of the implementation of all aspects of the AEOI Standard. Chapter 2 contains further details in this regard.

Note

[1] Details on each of the agreements in place can be found in Annex B.

2 Peer reviews of the AEOI Standard's implementation

In addition to monitoring the timeliness of each jurisdiction's implementation of the AEOI Standard, the Global Forum conducts peer reviews to ensure the implementation is both complete and effective. This chapter provides an overview of the methodology used for the peer reviews and a summary of the findings so far.

In order to ensure that the implementation of the AEOI Standard is both complete and effective, the Global Forum conducts peer reviews in relation to all of the key areas of the AEOI Standard. These are conducted in accordance with the agreed Terms of Reference for the AEOI reviews, which are contained in Annex C of this report.

Global Forum AEOI peer reviews: covering all key areas

Properly implementing the AEOI Standard requires various legal, technical and operational aspects to be put in place and for them to operate effectively in practice. The Global Forum therefore conducts peer review processes specifically designed for each of the requirements in the AEOI Terms of Reference. The various processes are as follows:

- **Confidentiality and data safeguards**: The information exchanged, which is sensitive taxpayer information, must be properly safeguarded and used only for the purpose for which it was exchanged or subsequently authorised, in accordance with the international treaty framework. The Global Forum therefore conducts reviews of the legal and operational arrangements jurisdictions have in place before they commence exchanging information. Assistance is given where needed. The Global Forum again reviews the legal and operational arrangements in place once exchanges are underway, to ensure the requirements are met on an ongoing basis. The Global Forum also has a mechanism to react to breaches of confidentiality or the safeguarding of data.
- **Domestic and international legal frameworks**: Financial Institutions must be required to conduct the due diligence and reporting requirements and there must be a legal basis to exchange the information. The Global Forum therefore conducts peer reviews of the domestic legislative frameworks and the international legal frameworks to ensure they are complete. The detailed results, updated to reflect the most recent changes, are set out in this report.
- **Effectiveness in practice**: Not only must the legal frameworks be in place, but they must be implemented and operate effectively in practice. The Global Forum is therefore currently reviewing each jurisdiction's implementation of the AEOI Standard in practice, including the frameworks and activities taken to ensure compliance by Financial Institutions and the exchanges in practice. A summary of the initial findings are included in this report. The detailed results are expected to be published in 2022.

The Global Forum conducts these reviews in stages, mirroring the timings of the implementation process. This ensures that issues are identified early, supporting the effectiveness of the AEOI Standard during the implementation process. Further details on the staging of the various reviews (the "Staged Approach") are available in Annex A.

Peer reviews of the AEOI legal frameworks

This report includes updated information on the results of the peer reviews of the legal frameworks put in place to implement the AEOI Standard that were first published in 2020, including determinations on the extent to which each jurisdiction has put the necessary frameworks in place.

What is new in this report?

Since the publication of the report in 2020, 13 jurisdictions requested a reassessment of their legal frameworks to reflect the actions they have taken to address the recommendations made: Australia, Azerbaijan, Czech Republic, Dominica, Estonia, Faroe Islands, Israel, Liechtenstein, Macau (China),

Romania, Slovak Republic, South Africa and Spain. This report therefore includes updated analysis and conclusions to reflect the most up-to-date situation in these jurisdictions.

Analysis and conclusions have also been included in this report for jurisdictions that committed to commence exchanges from 2019, in accordance with the agreed review timetable. These jurisdictions are: Ghana and Kuwait.

What is reviewed

The AEOI Terms of Reference group the requirements with respect to the legal frameworks into two Core Requirements. These are set out below:

- **Core Requirement 1**: Jurisdictions should have a domestic legislative framework in place that requires all Reporting Financial Institutions to conduct the due diligence and reporting procedures in the CRS, and that provides for the effective implementation of the CRS as set out therein.
- **Core Requirement 2**: Jurisdictions should have exchange relationships in effect with all Interested Appropriate Partners as committed to and that provide for the exchange of information in accordance with the Model CAA.

Annex C reproduces the AEOI Terms of Reference, including the detailed Sub-Requirements.

How it is reviewed

For each of review processes in relation to the AEOI legal frameworks, the following steps are conducted:

- The Global Forum Secretariat conducts an initial in-depth analysis of the legal texts and drafts proposed recommendations where issues are identified.
- The analysis and draft recommendations are sent to all AEOI Peers[1] for input, which is included as appropriate.
- The analysis and proposed recommendations is sent to the AEOI Peer Review Group (APRG)[2] for approval.
- The approved analysis and recommendations are submitted to all AEOI Peers for adoption.

Details specific to each peer review process of the legal frameworks are set out below.

Peer reviews in relation to Core Requirement 1

Core Requirement 1 in the AEOI Terms of Reference refer to the detailed due diligence and reporting procedures that Financial Institutions must follow, as specified in the AEOI Standard. These are standardised procedures to ensure that Financial Institutions report the correct information on Financial Accounts and their Account Holders to the tax authority in a uniform manner. It is therefore crucial that each jurisdiction properly reflects these requirements in its domestic legislative framework. The specific elements reviewed are as follows:

- **The due diligence and reporting rules and the framework to enforce the requirements**: This includes a review of how each jurisdiction has: (i) defined the scope of Reporting Financial Institutions, (ii) defined the scope of Financial Accounts that must be reviewed, (iii) implemented the detailed due diligence procedures that must be applied to identify Reportable Accounts, (iv) defined the information that must be reported and (v) provided for a legal framework to enforce the requirements.
- **The jurisdiction-specific Non-Reporting Financial Institutions and Excluded Accounts**: This consists of a specific review to ensure that the Non-Reporting Financial Institutions and Excluded

Accounts provided for by each jurisdiction meet the requirements of the AEOI Standard and pose a low-risk of use for tax evasion.

- **Related legal frameworks**: Where jurisdictions rely on non-AEOI legal frameworks to implement the AEOI Standard, these are also reviewed. More specifically, some jurisdictions have cross-referenced pre-existing legislative provisions defining "beneficial owners" to define Controlling Persons with respect to the AEOI Standard and/or provisions to enforce the due diligence and reporting requirements. Where this is the case, then the legislative frameworks referred to are also reviewed to the extent they are relevant for the implementation of the AEOI Standard.

Peer reviews in relation to Core Requirement 2

Core Requirement 2 in the AEOI Terms of Reference contains requirements with respect to both the contents of the international agreements used to exchange the information and the scope of the network of exchange relationships. These requirements are also essential to ensure effective exchange, based on a level playing field. The particular processes conducted are as follows:

- **Ensuring exchange networks are complete**: It is ensured that each jurisdiction's exchange network includes all of their Interested Appropriate Partners (i.e. those jurisdictions interested in receiving information from a jurisdiction and that meet the expected standards in relation to confidentiality and data safeguards). This includes facilitating jurisdictions in putting agreements in place and the provision of a peer review mechanism that jurisdictions may trigger if they become concerned about delays in a particular potential partner putting in place an exchange agreement with them.
- **The contents of the exchange agreements**: The contents of the exchange agreements put in place are reviewed to ensure their provisions are in accordance with the requirements.

Drawing conclusions

Once the Global Forum completes the reviews of the legal frameworks, it draws conclusions with respect to the extent to which each jurisdiction is considered to have the required legal frameworks "in place". This culminates in determinations being issued.

The proposed conclusions and determinations are made by an AEOI Assessment Panel of 14 experts drawn from AEOI Peer jurisdictions with a mandate of analysing the results of the peer reviews and preparing a short report on each jurisdiction. The AEOI Assessment Panel consults each Assessed Jurisdiction in relation to its report before submitting the reports to the APRG for discussion and approval. The reports are then sent to all AEOI Peers for adoption prior to publication. The jurisdiction-specific reports are presented in Chapter 3.

The determinations made with respect to each Core Requirement and the overall determination are either: "**In Place**", "In Place But **Needs Improvement**" or "**Not In Place**". Further details on how to interpret each of these determinations are set out in Table 2.1 below.

Table 2.1. The determinations

Determination	Description
In Place	A jurisdiction's legal framework is determined as being "**In Place**" where the review of its legal framework does not identify any gaps that need to be addressed in order for the legal framework to be in accordance with the AEOI Terms of Reference. This is the case where the peer review processes have not resulted in any recommendations. It is possible, although unusual, for a legal framework to be determined to be In Place even where there is a recommendation. This is only the case where the gap is viewed as so minor that it would have a highly limited impact on the operation of the AEOI Standard.
In Place But **Needs Improvement**	A jurisdiction's legal framework is determined as being "In Place But **Needs Improvement**" where the review of its legal framework concludes that the legal framework is in place but certain aspects need improvement in order for it to be fully in accordance with the AEOI Terms of Reference. This is the case where the peer review processes have identified one or more deficiencies material to the proper functioning of elements of the AEOI Standard. The determination of In Place But Needs Improvement is therefore a broad category. It includes jurisdictions with one recommendation, as well as jurisdictions with multiple recommendations. In all cases, the deficiencies are viewed collectively as material to the proper functioning of certain elements of the AEOI Standard, but not to its overall operation.
Not In Place	A jurisdiction's legal framework is determined as being "**Not In Place**" where the review of its legal framework shows that the legal framework needs to be significantly improved in order to be in accordance with the AEOI Terms of Reference. At the extreme, this is the case where a jurisdiction has not implemented the relevant legal framework. More commonly, this is where the peer review processes have resulted in recommendations viewed collectively as having a material impact on the overall operation of the AEOI Standard. It is important to note, aside from the jurisdictions that have not implemented a legal framework, a determination of Not In Place does not mean that a jurisdiction's legal framework is not in effect. In fact, several aspects of that legal framework are likely to be in place as required. The determination instead means that the impact of the deficiencies found are viewed as creating a material risk to the overall proper functioning of the AEOI Standard (e.g. a jurisdiction's legal framework to enforce the due diligence requirements is substantively incomplete).

Overall compliance remains high and improving

Even prior to the publication of the AEOI peer review report in 2020, many jurisdictions were quick to address the issues raised to ensure a complete implementation of the required legal frameworks. Sixty-four jurisdictions brought amendments into effect to address the recommendations made and requested a reassessment by the Global Forum. Overall, over 450 recommendations were addressed, including over 50 jurisdiction-specific exclusions being removed as they were found to insufficiently meet the requirements.

Since the publication of the AEOI peer review report in 2020, a further 13 jurisdictions requested a reassessment of their legal framework to reflect the actions they have taken to address the recommendations made. Their actions resulted in a further 66 recommendations being addressed, including the removal of 17 jurisdiction-specific exclusions. In terms of the conclusions, the amendments resulted in four jurisdictions (Czech Republic, Liechtenstein, Slovak Republic and South Africa) achieving an upgrade both to their determination in relation to CR1 and their overall determination, from "In Place But **Needs Improvement**" to "**In Place**" and one jurisdiction (Azerbaijan) achieving an upgrade both to its determination in relation to CR1 and its overall determination, from **"Not In Place**" to "In Place But **Needs Improvement**". Furthermore, one jurisdiction (Dominica) achieved an upgrade in its determination, in relation to CR1 and their overall determination, from **"Not In Place**" to "**In Place**". These amendments are reflected in this report.

With respect to the two jurisdictions that committed to commence exchanges from 2019 (i.e. the two new reviews in this report), Ghana and Kuwait, they received a determination of "In Place" for CR2. With respect to CR1, Ghana received a determination of "In Place But **Needs Improvement**" and Kuwait received a determination of "**Not In Place**". Their determinations for CR1 were also mirrored in their overall determinations.

In terms of the overall picture, there continues to be a very high level of compliance of the legal frameworks put in place to implement the AEOI Standard with the AEOI Terms of Reference. Of the 102 jurisdictions committed to commencing exchanges by 2019, virtually all of them (100) have an international legal framework that is fully in accordance with the AEOI Terms of Reference. The Global Forum has therefore issued them with a determination of **"In Place" for CR2**. Furthermore, the majority of jurisdictions (59) have domestic legislative frameworks that are also fully in accordance with the AEOI Terms of Reference. The Global Forum has therefore issued these jurisdictions with a determination of **"In Place" for CR1**. **Fifty-nine jurisdictions therefore received an overall determination of "In Place"**.

By far the next largest group of jurisdictions (32) are those for which the Global Forum issued a determination of "**In Place" for CR2** and "In Place But **Needs Improvement" for CR1.** Their peer review reports include one or more recommendations to amend their domestic legislative framework in order for it to be fully consistent with the AEOI Terms of Reference. Consequently, **32 jurisdictions received an overall determination of "**In Place But **Needs Improvement"**. In total, 89% of the jurisdictions now have domestic and international legal frameworks that are fully or substantially in place, up from 88% in 2020. This demonstrates a generally high level of compliance with the Terms of Reference.

> Following the actions taken, 89% of the jurisdictions have now been determined to have domestic and international legal frameworks that are fully or substantially in accordance with the AEOI Terms of Reference

Of the remaining jurisdictions (12), 10 have implemented a domestic legislative framework which contains many of the requirements, but that include significant deficiencies. The remaining two jurisdictions have not yet implemented a domestic legal framework. **Twelve jurisdictions have therefore received an overall determination of "Not In Place"**. Figure 2.1 summarise the distribution of the peer review results.

Figure 2.1. Overall determinations at a glance

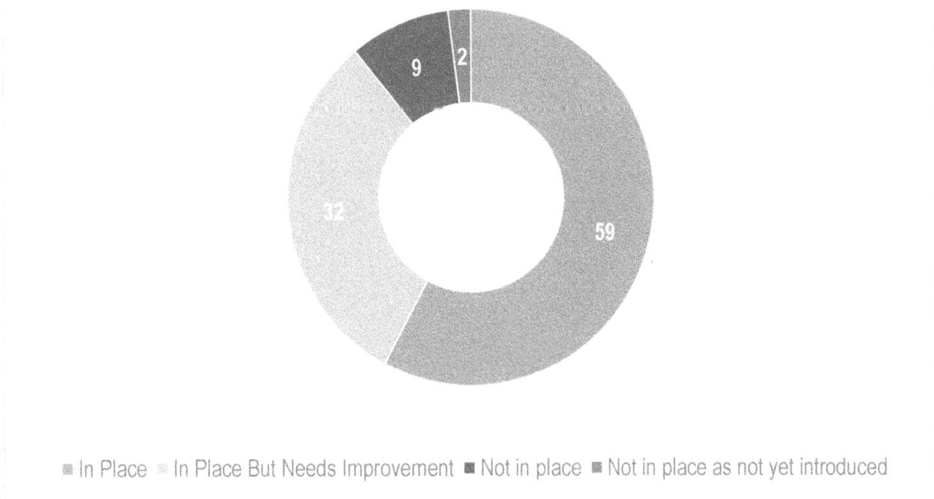

The main need for improvement remains the jurisdiction-specific exclusions and the enforcement frameworks

As set out last year, while there is a generally high level of compliance with the requirements, there are some commonalities in relation to the issues where recommendations are made. Some of these are highlighted below.

The most common issues relate to the following:

- There are several instances where the Global Forum has found that the jurisdiction-specific Non-Reporting Financial Institutions and Excluded Accounts are not in accordance with to the requirements of the AEOI Standard. This is the largest category of remaining recommendations.
- Perhaps of even greater significance are the issues found with respect to the legislative provisions to enforce the requirements. This includes powers to address avoidance of the due diligence and reporting requirements, the ability to impose sanctions on Account Holders and Controlling Persons for submitting false self-certifications and having record-keeping obligations that cover the full scope of the records required to be kept under the AEOI Standard. Such recommendations represent the next largest category of issues. Their significance is shown by the fact that all of the jurisdictions with legal frameworks that have been determined to be "**Not In Place**" have multiple recommendations with respect to their enforcement frameworks.
- Several more specific recommendations have also been made in cases where jurisdictions have summarised the detailed definitions in the AEOI Standard with the omission of relevant details that are needed to ensure their full and proper operation.

The Global Forum continues to work with the jurisdictions concerned to assist them in addressing the issues where recommendations have been made.

Jurisdiction-specific conclusions

Table 2.2 contains a summary of the determinations made with respect to legal frameworks introduced by each jurisdiction to implement the AEOI Standard. Further details on the analysis and reasons for the determinations for each jurisdiction can be found in Chapter 3.

Table 2.2. Overview of the determinations on the legal frameworks for the assessed jurisdictions

Jurisdiction	Core Requirement 1 (domestic legal framework)	Core Requirement 2 (international legal framework)	Overall determination
Andorra	In Place But **Needs Improvement**	**In Place**	In Place But **Needs Improvement**
Anguilla	**In Place**	**In Place**	**In Place**
Antigua and Barbuda	In Place But **Needs Improvement**	**In Place**	In Place But **Needs Improvement**
Argentina	In Place But **Needs Improvement**	**In Place**	In Place But **Needs Improvement**
Aruba	**Not In Place**	**In Place**	**Not In Place**
Australia	In Place But **Needs Improvement**	**In Place**	In Place But **Needs Improvement**
Austria	**In Place**	**In Place**	**In Place**
Azerbaijan	In Place But **Needs Improvement**	**In Place**	In Place But **Needs Improvement**
Bahrain	**In Place**	**In Place**	**In Place**
Barbados	In Place But **Needs Improvement**	**In Place**	In Place But **Needs Improvement**
Belgium	In Place But **Needs Improvement**	**In Place**	In Place But **Needs Improvement**
Belize	**Not In Place**	**In Place**	**Not In Place**
Bermuda	**In Place**	**In Place**	**In Place**
Brazil	**In Place**	**In Place**	**In Place**
British Virgin Islands	In Place But **Needs Improvement**	**In Place**	In Place But **Needs Improvement**
Brunei Darussalam	**In Place**	**In Place**	**In Place**
Bulgaria	**In Place**	**In Place**	**In Place**
Canada	In Place But **Needs Improvement**	**In Place**	In Place But **Needs Improvement**
Cayman Islands	**In Place**	**In Place**	**In Place**
Chile	In Place But **Needs Improvement**	**In Place**	In Place But **Needs Improvement**
China	**In Place**	**In Place**	**In Place**
Colombia	**In Place**	**In Place**	**In Place**
Cook Islands	**In Place**	**In Place**	**In Place**
Costa Rica	**Not In Place**	**In Place**	**Not In Place**
Croatia	In Place But **Needs Improvement**	**In Place**	In Place But **Needs Improvement**
Curaçao	**Not In Place**	**In Place**	**Not In Place**
Cyprus	**In Place**	**In Place**	**In Place**
Czech Republic	**In Place**	**In Place**	**In Place**
Denmark	**In Place**	**In Place**	**In Place**
Dominica	**In Place**	**In Place**	**In Place**
Estonia	In Place But **Needs Improvement**	**In Place**	In Place But **Needs Improvement**
Faroe Islands	In Place But **Needs Improvement**	**In Place**	In Place But **Needs Improvement**
Finland	**In Place**	**In Place**	**In Place**
France	**In Place**	**In Place**	**In Place**
Germany	In Place But **Needs Improvement**	**In Place**	In Place But **Needs Improvement**

Jurisdiction	Core Requirement 1 (domestic legal framework)	Core Requirement 2 (international legal framework)	Overall determination
Ghana	In Place But **Needs Improvement**	**In Place**	In Place But **Needs Improvement**
Gibraltar	**In Place**	**In Place**	**In Place**
Greece	**In Place**	**In Place**	**In Place**
Greenland	**In Place**	**In Place**	**In Place**
Grenada	**Not In Place**	**In Place**	**Not In Place**
Guernsey	**In Place**	**In Place**	**In Place**
Hong Kong (China)	**In Place**	**In Place**	**In Place**
Hungary	In Place But **Needs Improvement**	**In Place**	In Place But **Needs Improvement**
Iceland	**In Place**	**In Place**	**In Place**
India	In Place But **Needs Improvement**	**In Place**	In Place But **Needs Improvement**
Indonesia	**In Place**	**In Place**	**In Place**
Ireland	**In Place**	**In Place**	**In Place**
Isle of Man	**In Place**	**In Place**	**In Place**
Israel	**Not In Place**	**In Place**	**Not In Place**
Italy	**In Place**	**In Place**	**In Place**
Japan	In Place But **Needs Improvement**	**In Place**	In Place But **Needs Improvement**
Jersey	**In Place**	**In Place**	**In Place**
Korea	**In Place**	**In Place**	**In Place**
Kuwait	**Not In Place**	**In Place**	**Not In Place**
Latvia	In Place But **Needs Improvement**	**In Place**	In Place But **Needs Improvement**
Lebanon	**In Place**	**In Place**	**In Place**
Liechtenstein	**In Place**	**In Place**	**In Place**
Lithuania	**In Place**	**In Place**	**In Place**
Luxembourg	**In Place**	**In Place**	**In Place**
Macau (China)	**Not In Place**	**In Place**	**Not In Place**
Malaysia	**In Place**	**In Place**	**In Place**
Malta	**In Place**	**In Place**	**In Place**
Marshall Islands	**In Place**	**In Place**	**In Place**
Mauritius	**In Place**	**In Place**	**In Place**
Mexico	In Place But **Needs Improvement**	**In Place**	In Place But **Needs Improvement**
Monaco	In Place But **Needs Improvement**	**In Place**	In Place But **Needs Improvement**
Montserrat	**In Place**	**In Place**	**In Place**
Nauru	**In Place**	**In Place**	**In Place**
Netherlands	In Place But **Needs Improvement**	**In Place**	In Place But **Needs Improvement**
New Zealand	**In Place**	**In Place**	**In Place**
Niue	**In Place**	**In Place**	**In Place**
Norway	**In Place**	**In Place**	**In Place**

Jurisdiction	Core Requirement 1 (domestic legal framework)	Core Requirement 2 (international legal framework)	Overall determination
Pakistan	**In Place**	**In Place**	**In Place**
Panama	In Place But **Needs Improvement**	**In Place**	In Place But **Needs Improvement**
Poland	In Place But **Needs Improvement**	**In Place**	In Place But **Needs Improvement**
Portugal	**In Place**	**In Place**	**In Place**
Qatar	**In Place**	**In Place**	**In Place**
Romania	**Not In Place**	**In Place**	**Not In Place**
Russia	In Place But **Needs Improvement**	**In Place**	In Place But **Needs Improvement**
Saint Kitts and Nevis	**In Place**	**In Place**	**In Place**
Saint Lucia	In Place But **Needs Improvement**	**In Place**	In Place But **Needs Improvement**
Saint Vincent and the Grenadines	In Place But **Needs Improvement**	**In Place**	In Place But **Needs Improvement**
Samoa	**In Place**	**In Place**	**In Place**
San Marino	**In Place**	**In Place**	**In Place**
Saudi Arabia	**In Place**	**In Place**	**In Place**
Seychelles	In Place But **Needs Improvement**	**In Place**	In Place But **Needs Improvement**
Singapore	**In Place**	**In Place**	**In Place**
Sint Maarten	**Not In Place**	**Not In Place**	**Not In Place**
Slovak Republic	**In Place**	**In Place**	**In Place**
Slovenia	**In Place**	**In Place**	**In Place**
South Africa	**In Place**	**In Place**	**In Place**
Spain	**In Place**	**In Place**	**In Place**
Sweden	**In Place**	**In Place**	**In Place**
Switzerland	In Place But **Needs Improvement**	**In Place**	In Place But **Needs Improvement**
The Bahamas	In Place But **Needs Improvement**	**In Place**	In Place But **Needs Improvement**
Trinidad and Tobago	**Not In Place**	**Not In Place**	**Not In Place**
Turkey	**In Place**	**In Place**	**In Place**
Turks and Caicos Islands	In Place But **Needs Improvement**	**In Place**	In Place But **Needs Improvement**
United Arab Emirates	**In Place**	**In Place**	**In Place**
United Kingdom	**In Place**	**In Place**	**In Place**
Uruguay	In Place But **Needs Improvement**	**In Place**	In Place But **Needs Improvement**
Vanuatu	**In Place**	**In Place**	**In Place**

Peer reviews of the effectiveness in practice of AEOI implementation

Having complete legal frameworks is not sufficient to ensure that the AEOI Standard is effective and delivers the potential benefits it has to offer. It must also be ensured that the requirements are being effectively implemented in practice. The Global Forum has therefore commenced its peer reviews to assess the effectiveness in practice of each jurisdiction's implementation of the AEOI Standard.

What is reviewed

Similarly to the legal frameworks, the AEOI Terms of Reference group the requirements with respect to effectiveness in practice into the same two Core Requirements. These are set out below:

- **Core Requirement 1**: Jurisdictions should ensure that in practice Reporting Financial Institutions correctly implement the due diligence and reporting procedures, which includes a requirement for jurisdictions to have in place an administrative framework to ensure the effective implementation of the CRS.
- **Core Requirement 2**: Jurisdictions should exchange the information effectively in practice, in a timely manner, including by sorting, preparing, validating and transmitting it in accordance with the AEOI Standard.

Annex C reproduces the AEOI Terms of Reference, including the detailed Sub-Requirements.

How it is reviewed

For the reviews of effectiveness in practice, the following procedures are followed:

- Each jurisdiction provides a detailed description of the operational frameworks they have in place to ensure the effective implementation of the AEOI Standard. This information is provided in accordance with agreed detailed questionnaires covering all aspects of the AEOI Terms of Reference. Information on the activities they have undertaken is also provided, as well as the outcomes achieved.
- All AEOI Peers are invited to provide input in relation to their experiences in relation to the exchanges in practice and any issues experienced when trying to utilise the information received from each of their exchange partners. Input is also provided on the level of co-operation experienced with each jurisdiction when seeking to follow- up and with them to address such issues.
- The AEOI Assessment Panel, comprised 13 of experts from AEOI Peer jurisdictions, analyses the information provided and other relevant information such as that found in the public domain, and follows up with each jurisdiction and its exchange partners with respect to any omissions or uncertainties. Once a complete as possible view of the situation in each jurisdiction is established, the AEOI Assessment Panel prepares a short report on each jurisdiction.
- The reports are provided to each jurisdiction for comment before they are submitted to the APRG for discussion and approval. They are then sent to all AEOI Peers for adoption before being published.

During 2021, the process set out above has taken place, although the reports are not for publication at this stage. This is to provide early transparency to jurisdictions in relation to the issues identified and to provide time for actions to be taken to address them, given the AEOI Standard is relatively new. The process will be repeated in 2022 to reflect the most up to date information before the reports are published.

Details specific to each part of the peer review process in relation to effectiveness in practice are set out below.

Peer reviews in relation to Core Requirement 1

The AEOI Terms of Reference refer to jurisdictions ensuring that, in practice, Reporting Financial Institutions are effectively implementing the detailed due diligence and reporting procedures specified in the AEOI Standard. Various specific requirements in relation to the required framework are set out, such as the elements of the administrative compliance framework that must be put in place. Some of the key elements are referred to below.

- **Having an effective administrative framework to ensure compliance**: This includes: (i) developing a compliance strategy based on a risk assessment that takes into account a range of relevant information sources, (ii) procedures to ensure that Reporting Financial Institutions are reporting information as required, and (iii) verification procedures to ensure that the information being reported is complete and accurate, including accessing the records maintained by Reporting Financial Institutions. Various other specific aspects are mentioned, including the need for effective enforcement mechanisms.
- **International collaboration to ensure effectiveness**: There are also provisions in the AEOI Standard to provide for collaboration between exchange partners to address errors or non-compliance by Reporting Financial Institutions.

In practice, reviewing the implementation of these requirements has involved the following two steps:

- The first step is obtaining a clear view of all of the aspects of each jurisdiction's plans, policies and procedures put in place to ensure the effective implementation of the AEOI Standard by Reporting Financial Institutions, as well as the actions taken and the outcomes achieved. In this regard there are several key criteria that the AEOI Assessment Panel seeks to establish are being delivered. For example, a jurisdiction's approach should be based on a jurisdiction-specific strategy that takes into account the domestic context, such as the nature of the financial sector and relevant issues and risks. This strategy should also be refined over time to ensure its ongoing effectiveness. As part of this strategy, the first broad set of actions that are expected to be taken by jurisdictions on an ongoing basis is a comparison between the list of Financial Institutions that reported information, with other information sources. This is in order to identify any Reporting Financial Institutions that are incorrectly not reporting. The other information sources used should include lists of regulated entities as well as information sources relevant to identifying non-regulated Reporting Financial Institutions. Then, if any entities are identified that should be reporting and that are not, follow-up actions are expected to be taken to ensure that reporting takes place as well as ongoing compliance. The second broad set of expected actions relate to ensuring that the information that is reported is complete and accurate. This involves developing and implementing a compliance strategy that includes an analysis of the information reported, compliance checks and in-depth reviews, including the inspection of the records held by Reporting Financial Institutions. Again, if non-compliance is identified then action should be taken to ensure compliance on an ongoing basis. In this regard dissuasive penalties should be applied where appropriate. Details of the relevant policies and procedures as well as the maturity, scale and frequency of their application are examined, as well as details of the types of issues identified and the follow-up actions taken.
- The second step is complementing the analysis with information on the experience of each jurisdiction's exchange partners. This includes whether the jurisdiction's exchange partners have identified any errors or suspected non-compliance by Reporting Financial Institutions when processing and analysing the information received. Of relevance is also if such issues have been raised with the jurisdiction and, if so, whether follow-up actions are being taken and whether the issues have yet been resolved.

Where deficiencies or areas for improvement are identified, then recommendations are made.

Peer reviews in relation to Core Requirement 2

The AEOI Terms of Reference also contain requirements in relation to the processing of the information reported by Reporting Financial Institutions and its subsequent transmission to exchange partners. Some of the key elements are below.

- **Preparing and validating the information**: Once reported by Reporting Financial Institutions, the information must be sorted, prepared and validated in accordance with the technical requirements set out in the AEOI Standard (e.g. the CRS XML Schema).
- **Using secure channels to exchange the information**: It is of vital importance that the information is kept safe while it is being transmitted. This is ensured through the use of the Common Transmission System which utilises industry leading security standards and which is used by all jurisdictions.
- **Timeliness in the exchanges and follow-up**: The timeliness of the exchanges are also reviewed, including the timeliness of any response to follow-up from a jurisdictions' partners, including the provision of additional or amended information as necessary.

In practice, reviewing the implementation of these requirements has involved obtaining detailed information from each jurisdiction's exchange partners on a range of relevant areas. These include qualitative descriptions of any issues experienced with the preparation and format of the information received from the jurisdiction in question, as well as information on the numbers of rejections of files due to the requirements not being met. Similarly, details in relation to the timeliness of the exchanges as well as the timeliness of the provision of new or amend information in response to follow-up enquiries are examined. Where such issues are reported by a jurisdiction's exchange partners then there is engagement with both sides to the exchange relationship to identify the underlying causes and what needs to be done.

Again, where deficiencies or areas for improvement are identified, then recommendations are made.

Initial findings of the review processes

The timeline for the peer reviews in relation to the effectiveness in practice of the implementation of the AEOI Standard was designed to allow issues to be identified early and to provide time for them to be addressed, before the final conclusions are drawn and the results published. This was to recognise that the AEOI Standard is still relatively new and that the expectations in relation to ensuring its effectiveness in practice would evolve as the relevant experience grows. A summary of the initial findings of the review process is provided below.

Core Requirement 1: Ensuring Reporting Financial Institutions correctly implement the due diligence and reporting procedures

To date it is clear that a very significant number of jurisdictions have already diligently reflected on how it can be best ensured that the AEOI Standard operates effectively in their domestic context, taking into account jurisdiction-specific risks identified, and developing and implementing suitable compliance strategies. These include appropriate policies and procedures to both ensure that Reporting Financial Institutions report information as required and that the information they report is complete and accurate.

As a first step, this generally includes communication and outreach activities to ensure that Reporting Financial Institutions are aware of their obligations and have channels to ask any questions they have to resolve remaining uncertainties. This is to help ensure compliance upfront. This is generally complemented by the provision of guidance or answers to frequently asked questions. The overwhelming majority of jurisdictions have already carried out such activities.

Most jurisdictions have also taken action to verify that all Reporting Financial Institutions are reporting information as required. This generally incudes cross-checking the Financial Institutions that report information against regulatory lists, the FFI list for US FATCA purposes and other relevant sources of information, such as tax filings. Where there are discrepancies, then jurisdictions are taking action to ensure that the relevant obligations are being complied with and that information is being reported as required.

With respect to making sure that the information being reported is complete and accurate, greater variation has been observed in the level of the maturity of implementation so far. A very large number of jurisdictions have implemented desk-based checks to identify potential non-compliance, and many have also commenced in depth reviews, including on-site visits and the inspection of the records held by Reporting Financial Institutions. Furthermore, jurisdictions are often carrying out dedicated checks to follow-up on issues raised by their exchange partners, to ensure that self-certifications are being obtained as required and to follow-up on the reporting of undocumented accounts. There are also many examples where enforcement frameworks have already been activated to address non-compliance and to ensure the requirements are being complied with on an ongoing basis. Where such activities have not yet taken place, jurisdictions often have detailed plans to commence them and the activities are expected to commence in the coming months. In other cases, implementation is far less mature and jurisdictions are still reflecting on the broad frameworks to be put in place. These jurisdictions have significant work to do in order to deliver what is required. It is noted that the implementation of some of these activities has often been impacted by the COVID-19 pandemic. This is an area where significant further progress in implementation is expected in the coming months and the Global Forum is providing assistance where needed.

Core Requirement 2: Exchanging the information effectively in practice and in a timely manner

When it comes to the exchange of the information and ensuring that the technical and timing requirements are being met, the vast majority of jurisdictions are performing well. Furthermore, where issues have arisen, the vast majority of jurisdictions are reacting effectively, engaging with their exchange partners and identifying and addressing the underlying issues.

There are some instances of jurisdictions experiencing systematic issues with how they prepare the information to send. They are generally reviewing their systems and processes accordingly, to ensure that the issues are fixed in time for future exchanges.

Next steps

Under the agreed methodology, each step of the review process will be repeated during 2022 to develop an up to date picture of the implementation of the AEOI Standard across all jurisdictions. This will allow jurisdictions to provide any updates in relation to the activities they have undertaken, including in response to the issues identified so far, as well as for their exchange partners to provide further input in relation to their experience with exchanging information in practice.

The current process will culminate in 2022 with the AEOI Peers adopting the peer reviews for all jurisdictions committed to commence exchanges from 2017 or 2018, including ratings on the effectiveness of each jurisdiction's implementation of the AEOI Standard in practice. These will be included in next year's published report.

Notes

[1] All jurisdictions committed to implementing the AEOI Standard and that have passed domestic legislation to that effect.

[2] A peer review group of the Global Forum consisting of 34 members which replaced the former AEOI Group (www.oecd.org/tax/transparency/documents/aprg-members.pdf).

3 Jurisdiction-specific reports

Andorra

Overall findings

Andorra's legal framework implementing the AEOI Standard is in place but needs improvement in order to be fully consistent with the requirements of the AEOI Terms of Reference. While Andorra's international legal framework to exchange the information with all of Andorra's Interested Appropriate Partners (CR2) is consistent with the requirements, its domestic legislative framework requiring Reporting Financial Institutions to conduct the due diligence and reporting procedures (CR1) has deficiencies significant to the proper functioning of an element of the AEOI Standard. More specifically, Andorra's legal framework includes jurisdiction-specific Excluded Accounts that are not in accordance with the AEOI Standard.

The methodology used for the peer reviews and that therefore underpins this report is outlined in Chapter 2.

Overall determination on the legal framework: In Place But **Needs Improvement**

Conclusions on the legal framework

General context

Andorra commenced exchanges under the AEOI Standard in 2018.

In order to provide for Reporting Financial Institutions to collect and report the information to be exchanged, Andorra:

- enacted Law 19/2016, of 30 November 2016, on automatic exchange of information in tax matters as amended by Law 29/2017, Law 30/2017, and Law 19/2018;
- introduced Decree of 2 August 2017, Decree of 7 February 2018, Decree of 3 October 2018 and Decree of 16 January 2019;
- introduced the Ministerial Order of 7 February 2018;
- issued further guidance, which is not legally binding; and
- made reference to the Law 14/2017, of 22 June, on the prevention and fight against money laundering and terrorist financing with respect to the identification of Controlling Persons.

Under this framework Reporting Financial Institutions were required to commence the due diligence procedures in relation to New Accounts from 1 January 2017. With respect to Preexisting Accounts, Reporting Financial Institutions were required to complete the due diligence procedures on High Value Individual Accounts by 31 December 2017 and on Lower Value Individual Accounts and Entity Accounts by 31 December 2018.

With respect to the exchange of information under the AEOI Standard, Andorra:

- is a Party to the Convention on Mutual Administrative Assistance in Tax Matters and activated the associated CRS Multilateral Competent Authority Agreement in time for exchanges in 2018; and
- has in place an agreement with the European Union.

Detailed findings

The detailed findings for Andorra are below, organised per Core Requirement (CR) and sub-requirement (SR), as extracted from the AEOI Terms of Reference (www.oecd.org/tax/transparency/documents/aeoi-terms-of-reference.pdf).

CR1 Domestic legal framework: Jurisdictions should have a domestic legislative framework in place that requires all Reporting Financial Institutions to conduct the due diligence and reporting procedures in the CRS, and that provides for the effective implementation of the CRS as set out therein.

Determination: In Place But **Needs Improvement**

Andorra's domestic legislative framework is in place and contains most of the key aspects of the CRS and its Commentary requiring Reporting Financial Institutions to conduct the due diligence and reporting procedures, but it needs improvement in relation to the scope of Financial Accounts required to be reported (SR 1.2). More specifically, Andorra provides for several jurisdiction-specific Excluded Accounts that are not in accordance with the requirements.

SR 1.1 Jurisdictions should define the scope of Reporting Financial Institutions consistently with the CRS.

Andorra has defined the scope of Reporting Financial Institutions in its domestic legislative framework in accordance with the CRS and its Commentary.

Recommendations:

No recommendations made.

SR 1.2 Jurisdictions should define the scope of Financial Accounts and Reportable Accounts consistently with the CRS and incorporate the due diligence procedures to identify them.

Andorra has defined the scope of the Financial Accounts that are required to be reported in its domestic legislative framework and incorporated the due diligence procedures that must be applied to identify them in a manner that is largely consistent with the CRS and its Commentary. However, deficiencies have been identified. More specifically, Andorra provides for four jurisdiction-specific Excluded Accounts that are not in accordance with the requirements. The definition of Financial Accounts, including the provision of Excluded Accounts, is material to the proper functioning of the AEOI Standard.

Recommendations:

Andorra should amend its domestic legislative framework to remove four entries from its jurisdiction-specific list of Excluded Accounts as they do not meet the requirements because they are not subject to regulation as a savings or investment vehicle. The entries are: i) accounts linked to insurance contracts or any other contractual arrangement for pension plans or other social welfare instruments; ii) accounts linked to insurance contracts or any other arrangement for savings products for purposes other than retirement; iii) operative current accounts exclusively used for payments associated with ownership or usage of a residence in Andorra; and iv) custodial accounts holding Andorran Government public debt securities with an average balance not exceeding USD 50 000.

SR 1.3 Jurisdictions should incorporate the reporting requirements contained in Section I of the CRS into their domestic legislative framework.

Andorra has incorporated the reporting requirements in its domestic legislative framework in accordance with the CRS and its Commentary.

Recommendations:

No recommendations made.

SR 1.4 Jurisdictions should have a legislative framework in place that allows for the enforcement of the requirements of the CRS in practice.

Andorra has a legislative framework in place to enforce the requirements in accordance with the CRS and its Commentary.

Recommendations:

No recommendations made.

CR2 International legal framework: Jurisdictions should have exchange relationships in effect with all Interested Appropriate Partners as committed to and that provide for the exchange of information in accordance with the Model CAA.

Determination: In Place

Andorra's international legal framework to exchange the information is in place, is consistent with the Model CAA and its Commentary and provides for exchange with all of Andorra's Interested Appropriate Partners (i.e. all jurisdictions that are interested in receiving information from Andorra and that meet the required standard in relation to confidentiality and data safeguards). (SRs 2.1 – 2.3)

SR 2.1 Jurisdictions should have exchange agreements in effect with all Interested Appropriate Partners that permit the automatic exchange of CRS information.

Andorra has exchange agreements that permit the automatic exchange of CRS information in effect with all its Interested Appropriate Partners.

Recommendations:

No recommendations made.

SR 2.2 Such an exchange agreement should be put in place without undue delay, following the receipt of an expression of interest from an Interested Appropriate Partner.

Andorra put in place its exchange agreements without undue delay.

Recommendations:

No recommendations made.

SR 2.3 Jurisdictions should ensure that the exchange agreements in effect provide for the exchange of information in accordance with the requirements of the Model CAA.

Andorra's exchange agreements provide for the exchange of information in accordance with the requirements of the Model CAA.

Recommendations:

No recommendations made.

Comments by the assessed jurisdiction

Since 2009, Andorra has initiated a transformative process to meet its commitments to transparency and meeting international standards of exchange of tax information, and has also consolidated a modern national tax and economic regulatory framework to be equivalent to those of our neighbouring countries. While it has been a challenging task, Andorra has had notable success in such a short period of time and Andorra has done it with the conviction that this was the only path to follow. The outcome of the evaluation contained in this report confirms this commitment.

Andorra's priority is to be as competitive as possible in a globalized economy, with full commitment to transparency and compliance with international standards, while continuing to improve the legal framework and ensuring a level playing field.

Anguilla

Overall findings

Anguilla's legal framework implementing the AEOI Standard is in place and is consistent with the requirements of the AEOI Terms of Reference. This includes Anguilla's domestic legislative framework requiring Reporting Financial Institutions to conduct the due diligence and reporting procedures (CR1) and its international legal framework to exchange the information with all of Anguilla's Interested Appropriate Partners (CR2).

The methodology used for the peer reviews and that therefore underpins this report is outlined in Chapter 2.

Overall determination on the legal framework: In Place

Conclusions on the legal framework

General context

Anguilla initially intended to commence exchanges under the AEOI Standard in 2017 but due to the impact of the hurricanes in the region instead commenced exchanging in 2018.

In order to provide for Reporting Financial Institutions to collect and report the information to be exchanged, Anguilla:

- enacted the Tax Information Exchange (International Cooperation) Act;
- introduced the International Tax Compliance (CRS) Regulations; and
- issued further guidance (referred to as Guidance Notes), which is not legally binding.

Under this framework Reporting Financial Institutions were required to commence the due diligence procedures in relation to New Accounts from 1 July 2016. With respect to Preexisting Accounts, Reporting Financial Institutions were required to complete the due diligence procedures on High Value Individual Accounts by 31 December 2016 and on Lower Value Individual Accounts and Entity Accounts by 31 December 2017.

With respect to the exchange of information under the AEOI Standard, Anguilla:

- has the Convention on Mutual Administrative Assistance in Tax Matters in place[1] and activated the associated CRS Multilateral Competent Authority Agreement in time for exchanges in 2018; and
- put in place three bilateral agreements.[2]

Detailed findings

The detailed findings for Anguilla are below, organised per Core Requirement (CR) and sub-requirement (SR), as extracted from the AEOI Terms of Reference (www.oecd.org/tax/transparency/documents/aeoi-terms-of-reference.pdf).

CR1 Domestic legal framework: Jurisdictions should have a domestic legislative framework in place that requires all Reporting Financial Institutions to conduct the due diligence and reporting procedures in the CRS, and that provides for the effective implementation of the CRS as set out therein.

Determination: In Place

Anguilla's domestic legislative framework is in place and contains all of the key aspects of the CRS and its Commentary requiring Reporting Financial Institutions to conduct the due diligence and reporting procedures (SRs 1.1 – 1.3). It also provides for a framework to enforce the requirements (SR 1.4).

SR 1.1 Jurisdictions should define the scope of Reporting Financial Institutions consistently with the CRS.

Anguilla has defined the scope of Reporting Financial Institutions in its domestic legislative framework in accordance with the CRS and its Commentary.

Recommendations:

No recommendations made.

SR 1.2 Jurisdictions should define the scope of Financial Accounts and Reportable Accounts consistently with the CRS and incorporate the due diligence procedures to identify them.

Anguilla has defined the scope of the Financial Accounts that are required to be reported in its domestic legislative framework and incorporated the due diligence procedures that must be applied to identify them in accordance with the CRS and its Commentary.

Recommendations:

No recommendations made.

SR 1.3 Jurisdictions should incorporate the reporting requirements contained in Section I of the CRS into their domestic legislative framework.

Anguilla has incorporated the reporting requirements in its domestic legislative framework in accordance with the CRS and its Commentary.

Recommendations:

No recommendations made.

SR 1.4 Jurisdictions should have a legislative framework in place that allows for the enforcement of the requirements of the CRS in practice.

Anguilla has a legislative framework in place to enforce the requirements in accordance with the CRS and its Commentary.

Recommendations:

No recommendations made.

CR2 International legal framework: Jurisdictions should have exchange relationships in effect with all Interested Appropriate Partners as committed to and that provide for the exchange of information in accordance with the Model CAA.

Determination: In Place

Anguilla's international legal framework to exchange the information is in place, is consistent with the Model CAA and its Commentary and provides for exchange with all of Anguilla's Interested Appropriate Partners (i.e. all jurisdictions that are interested in receiving information from Anguilla and that meet the required standard in relation to confidentiality and data safeguards). (SRs 2.1 – 2.3)

SR 2.1 Jurisdictions should have exchange agreements in effect with all Interested Appropriate Partners that permit the automatic exchange of CRS information.

Anguilla has exchange agreements that permit the automatic exchange of CRS information in effect with all its Interested Appropriate Partners.

Recommendations:

No recommendations made.

SR 2.2 Such an exchange agreement should be put in place without undue delay, following the receipt of an expression of interest from an Interested Appropriate Partner.

Anguilla put in place its exchange agreements without undue delay.

Recommendations:

No recommendations made.

SR 2.3 Jurisdictions should ensure that the exchange agreements in effect provide for the exchange of information in accordance with the requirements of the Model CAA.

Anguilla's exchange agreements provide for the exchange of information in accordance with the requirements of the Model CAA.

Recommendations:

No recommendations made.

Comments by the assessed jurisdiction

No comments made.

Notes

[1] Through a territorial extension by the United Kingdom.

[2] With Guernsey, the Isle of Man and the United Kingdom.

Antigua and Barbuda

Overall findings

Antigua and Barbuda's legal framework implementing the AEOI Standard is in place but needs improvement in order to be fully consistent with the requirements of the AEOI Terms of Reference. While Antigua and Barbuda's international legal framework to exchange the information with all of Antigua and Barbuda's Interested Appropriate Partners (CR2) is consistent with the requirements, its domestic legislative framework requiring Reporting Financial Institutions to conduct the due diligence and reporting procedures (CR1) has deficiencies significant to the proper functioning of elements of the AEOI Standard. Most significantly, Financial Account is not defined in accordance with the AEOI Standard and there are no sanctions on Account Holders and Controlling Persons for the provision of false self-certifications.

The methodology used for the peer reviews and that therefore underpins this report is outlined in Chapter 2.

Overall determination on the legal framework: In Place But **Needs Improvement**

Conclusions on the legal framework

General context

Antigua and Barbuda commenced exchanges under the AEOI Standard in 2018.

In order to provide for Reporting Financial Institutions to collect and report the information to be exchanged, Antigua and Barbuda:

- enacted the Automatic Exchange of Financial Account Information Act 2016 (No. 11 of 2016);
- enacted the Automatic Exchange of Financial Account Information (Amendment) Act 2017 (No. 39 of 2017); and
- introduced the Automatic Exchange of Financial Account Information Regulations 2017, (Statutory Instrument No. 18 of 2017).

Under this framework Reporting Financial Institutions were required to commence the due diligence procedures in relation to New Accounts from 1 January 2017. With respect to Preexisting Accounts, Reporting Financial Institutions were required to complete the due diligence procedures on High Value Individual Accounts by 31 December 2017 and on Lower Value Individual Accounts and Entity Accounts by 31 December 2018.

With respect to the exchange of information under the AEOI Standard, Antigua and Barbuda is a Party to the Convention on Mutual Administrative Assistance in Tax Matters and activated the associated CRS Multilateral Competent Authority Agreement in time for exchanges in 2018.

Detailed findings

The detailed findings for Antigua and Barbuda are below, organised per Core Requirement (CR) and sub-requirement (SR), as extracted from the AEOI Terms of Reference (www.oecd.org/tax/transparency/documents/aeoi-terms-of-reference.pdf).

CR1 Domestic legal framework: Jurisdictions should have a domestic legislative framework in place that requires all Reporting Financial Institutions to conduct the due diligence and reporting procedures in the CRS, and that provides for the effective implementation of the CRS as set out therein.

Determination: In Place But **Needs Improvement**

Antigua and Barbuda's domestic legislative framework is in place and contains most of the key aspects of the CRS and its Commentary requiring Reporting Financial Institutions to conduct the due diligence and reporting procedures, but it needs improvement in relation to the scope of Financial Accounts required to be reported (SR 1.2), the reporting requirements (SR 1.3) and the framework to enforce the requirements (SR 1.4). Most significantly, Financial Account is not defined in accordance with the requirements and there are no sanctions on Account Holders and Controlling Persons for the provision of false self-certifications.

SR 1.1 Jurisdictions should define the scope of Reporting Financial Institutions consistently with the CRS.

Antigua and Barbuda has defined the scope of Reporting Financial Institutions in its domestic legislative framework in accordance with the CRS and its Commentary.

Recommendations:

No recommendations made.

SR 1.2 Jurisdictions should define the scope of Financial Accounts and Reportable Accounts consistently with the CRS and incorporate the due diligence procedures to identify them.

Antigua and Barbuda has defined the scope of the Financial Accounts that are required to be reported in its domestic legislative framework and incorporated the due diligence procedures that must be applied to identify them in a manner that is largely consistent with the CRS and its Commentary. However, a deficiency has been identified. More specifically, Antigua and Barbuda's domestic legislative framework omits several key details of the definition of Financial Account, which is material to the proper functioning of the AEOI Standard.

Recommendations:

Antigua and Barbuda should amend its domestic legislative framework to define Financial Account in accordance with the AEOI Standard, rather than defining it by exclusion as is currently the case (i.e. an account that is not (a) a retirement or pension account; (b) a non-retirement tax favoured account; (c) a term life insurance contract; (d) a estate account; (e) a depository account due to not-returned over payments and (g) a low risk excluded account).

SR 1.3 Jurisdictions should incorporate the reporting requirements contained in Section I of the CRS into their domestic legislative framework.

Antigua and Barbuda has incorporated the reporting requirements in its domestic legislative framework in accordance with the CRS and its Commentary. While a deficiency has been identified with respect to the timing of the measurement of the balance of a Reportable Account, given the account is still required to be reported along with its balance, the deficiency is considered to be relatively minor and its impact not to be material.

Recommendations:

Antigua and Barbuda should amend its domestic legislative framework to specify that Reporting Financial Institutions should always report the balance or value of a Reportable Account as at the end of the calendar year.

SR 1.4 Jurisdictions should have a legislative framework in place that allows for the enforcement of the requirements of the CRS in practice.

Antigua and Barbuda has a legislative framework in place to enforce the requirements in a manner that is largely consistent with the CRS and its Commentary. However, deficiencies have been identified. Most significantly, Antigua and Barbuda's legislative framework does not impose sanctions for the provision of false self-certifications by Account Holders and Controlling Persons. This is a key element of the required enforcement framework and is therefore material to the proper functioning of the AEOI Standard.

Recommendations:

Antigua and Barbuda should amend its domestic legislative framework to include sanctions on Account Holders and Controlling Persons for providing false self-certifications.

Antigua and Barbuda should amend its domestic legislative framework to require Reporting Financial Institutions to maintain records of self-certifications for at least five years from the deadline to report the information, rather than five years from the date when an account is closed.

CR2 International legal framework: Jurisdictions should have exchange relationships in effect with all Interested Appropriate Partners as committed to and that provide for the exchange of information in accordance with the Model CAA.

Determination: In Place

Antigua and Barbuda's international legal framework to exchange the information is in place, is consistent with the Model CAA and its Commentary and provides for exchange with all of Antigua and Barbuda's Interested Appropriate Partners (i.e. all jurisdictions that are interested in receiving information from Antigua and Barbuda and that meet the required standard in relation to confidentiality and data safeguards). (SRs 2.1 – 2.3)

SR 2.1 Jurisdictions should have exchange agreements in effect with all Interested Appropriate Partners that permit the automatic exchange of CRS information.

Antigua and Barbuda has exchange agreements that permit the automatic exchange of CRS information in effect with all its Interested Appropriate Partners.

Recommendations:

No recommendations made.

SR 2.2 Such an exchange agreement should be put in place without undue delay, following the receipt of an expression of interest from an Interested Appropriate Partner.

Antigua and Barbuda put in place its exchange agreements without undue delay.

Recommendations:

No recommendations made.

SR 2.3 Jurisdictions should ensure that the exchange agreements in effect provide for the exchange of information in accordance with the requirements of the Model CAA.

Antigua and Barbuda's exchange agreements provide for the exchange of information in accordance with the requirements of the Model CAA.

Recommendations:

No recommendations made.

Comments by the assessed jurisdiction

Antigua and Barbuda has conducted remedial action and submitted legislative amendments to the Automatic Exchange of Financial Account Information Act 2016 as amended and the Automatic Exchange of Financial Account Information Regulations 2017, in accordance with the stated recommendations. Accordingly, the said amendments will be subjected to the Parliamentary process of debate and passage in 2020.

Argentina

Overall findings

Argentina's legal framework implementing the AEOI Standard is in place but needs improvement in order to be fully consistent with the requirements of the AEOI Terms of Reference. While Argentina's international legal framework to exchange information with all Argentina's Interested Appropriate Partners (CR2) is consistent with the requirements, its domestic legislative framework requiring Reporting Financial Institutions to conduct the due diligence and reporting procedures (CR1) has deficiencies significant to the proper functioning of elements of the AEOI Standard. More specifically, Argentina's legal framework has deficiencies related to the scope of Reporting Financial Institutions and the due diligence procedures to identify Reportable Accounts. Moreover, Argentina's domestic legal framework does not impose sanctions on Account Holders and Controlling Persons for the provision of a false self-certification.

The methodology used for the peer reviews and that therefore underpins this report is outlined in Chapter 2.

Overall determination on the legal framework: In Place But **Needs Improvement**

Conclusions on the legal framework

General context

Argentina commenced exchanges under the AEOI Standard in 2017.

In order to provide for Reporting Financial Institutions to collect and report the information to be exchanged, Argentina:

- relies on Section 7 of the Decree No. 618/1997;
- enacted the AFIP General Resolution No. 4.056/2017 and amendments, that replaced the AFIP General Resolution 3.826/2015;
- introduced the FIU Resolutions 121, 229 and 230; and
- issued further guidance, which is not legally binding.

Under this framework Reporting Financial Institutions were required to commence the due diligence procedures in relation to New Accounts from 1 January 2016. With respect to Preexisting Accounts, Reporting Financial Institutions were required to complete the due diligence procedures on High Value Individual Accounts by 31 December 2016 and on Lower Value Individual Accounts and Entity Accounts by 31 December 2017.

Following the initial Global Forum peer review, Argentina made various amendments to its legislative framework to address issues identified, the last of which was effective from 14 February 2019.

With respect to the exchange of information under the AEOI Standard, Argentina is a Party to the Convention on Mutual Administrative Assistance in Tax Matters and activated the associated CRS Multilateral Competent Authority Agreement in time for exchanges in 2017.

Detailed findings

The detailed findings for Argentina are below, organised per Core Requirement (CR) and sub-requirement (SR), as extracted from the AEOI Terms of Reference (www.oecd.org/tax/transparency/documents/aeoi-terms-of-reference.pdf).

CR1 Domestic legal framework: Jurisdictions should have a domestic legislative framework in place that requires all Reporting Financial Institutions to conduct the due diligence and reporting procedures in the CRS, and that provides for the effective implementation of the CRS as set out therein.

Determination: In Place But **Needs Improvement**

Argentina's domestic legislative framework is in place and contains most of the key aspects of the CRS and its Commentary requiring Reporting Financial Institutions to conduct the due diligence and reporting procedures, but it needs improvement in relation to the scope of Reporting Financial Institutions required to report information (SR 1.1), the due diligence procedures required to identify Reportable Accounts (SR 1.2) and the framework to enforce the requirements (SR 1.4). More specifically, Argentina's legal framework provides for some jurisdiction-specific Non-Reporting Financial Institutions that do not meet the requirements, does not fully incorporate the due diligence procedures for the purposes of identifying if a Controlling Person of a Passive NFE is a Reportable Person and does not impose sanctions on Account Holders and Controlling Persons for the provision of false self-certifications.

SR 1.1 Jurisdictions should define the scope of Reporting Financial Institutions consistently with the CRS.

Argentina has defined the scope of Reporting Financial Institutions in its domestic legislative framework in a manner that is largely consistent with the CRS and its Commentary. However, deficiencies have been identified. More specifically, Argentina has provided for six jurisdiction-specific Non-Reporting Financial Institutions that are not in accordance with the requirements. The definition of Reporting Financial Institution, including the provision of Non-Reporting Financial Institutions, is material to the proper functioning of the AEOI Standard.

Recommendations:

Argentina should amend its domestic legislative framework to remove six entities from its jurisdiction-specific list of Non-Reporting Financial Institutions as they are Non-Financial Entities and should therefore be treated as such under the AEOI Standard. The entries are: i) Property Insurance; ii) Insurance on the Income related to the Labour Risk Law and Life Insurance; iii) Health Insurance and Personal Accidents Insurance that do not provide the creation of Savings Reserve; iv) Marketable Securities Broker Agents; v) Foreign Exchange Brokers; and vi) Foreign Exchange Houses, Agencies and Offices.

SR 1.2 Jurisdictions should define the scope of Financial Accounts and Reportable Accounts consistently with the CRS and incorporate the due diligence procedures to identify them.

Argentina has defined the scope of the Financial Accounts that are required to be reported in its domestic legislative framework and incorporated the due diligence procedures that must be applied to identify them in a manner that is largely consistent with the CRS and its Commentary. However, a deficiency has been identified. More specifically, Argentina does not specify that Reporting Financial Institutions may only rely on a self-certification by the Account Holder or its Controlling Person for the purposes of determining whether the Controlling Person is a Reportable Person.

Recommendations:

Argentina should amend its domestic legislative framework to specify that, for New Entity Accounts, Reporting Financial Institutions may only rely on a self-certification provided by a Passive NFE Account Holder or its Controlling Person to determine whether the Controlling Person is a Reportable Person.

SR 1.3 Jurisdictions should incorporate the reporting requirements contained in Section I of the CRS into their domestic legislative framework.

Argentina has incorporated the reporting requirements in its domestic legislative framework in accordance with the CRS and its Commentary.

Recommendations:

No recommendations made.

SR 1.4 Jurisdictions should have a legislative framework in place that allows for the enforcement of the requirements of the CRS in practice.

Argentina has a legislative framework in place to enforce the requirements in a manner that is largely consistent with the CRS and its Commentary. However, a deficiency has been identified. More specifically, Argentina's legislative framework does not impose sanctions for the provision of false self-certifications by Account Holders and Controlling Persons. This is a key element of the required enforcement framework and is therefore material to the proper functioning of the AEOI Standard.

Recommendations:

Argentina should amend its domestic legislative framework to include sanctions on Account Holders and Controlling Persons for the provision of a false self-certification.

CR2 International legal framework: Jurisdictions should have exchange relationships in effect with all Interested Appropriate Partners as committed to and that provide for the exchange of information in accordance with the Model CAA.

Determination: In Place

Argentina's international legal framework to exchange the information is in place, is consistent with the Model CAA and its Commentary and provides for exchange with all of Argentina's Interested Appropriate Partners (i.e. all jurisdictions that are interested in receiving information from Argentina and that meet the required standard in relation to confidentiality and data safeguards). (SRs 2.1 – 2.3)

SR 2.1 Jurisdictions should have exchange agreements in effect with all Interested Appropriate Partners that permit the automatic exchange of CRS information.

Argentina has exchange agreements that permit the automatic exchange of CRS information in effect with all its Interested Appropriate Partners.

Recommendations:

No recommendations made.

SR 2.2 Such an exchange agreement should be put in place without undue delay, following the receipt of an expression of interest from an Interested Appropriate Partner.

Argentina put in place its exchange agreements without undue delay.

Recommendations:

No recommendations made.

SR 2.3 Jurisdictions should ensure that the exchange agreements in effect provide for the exchange of information in accordance with the requirements of the Model CAA.

Argentina exchange agreements provide for the exchange of information in accordance with the requirements of the Model CAA.

Recommendations:

No recommendations made.

Comments by the assessed jurisdiction

In addition to GR 4056/2017 and its amendment -GR 4422/2019- which address the recommendations previously made in the report; in December 2020, GR 4888/2020 was published in order to amend said resolutions and comply with the observations made in the report regarding the excluded subjects in Annex II. Therefore, the following entities were removed from the jurisdiction specific list of Non-Reporting Financial Institutions: i) Property Insurance; ii) Insurance on the Income related to the Labour Risk Law and Life Insurance; iii) Health Insurance and Personal Accidents Insurance that do not provide the creation of Savings Reserve; iv) Foreign Exchange Brokers; and v) Foreign Exchange Houses, Agencies and Offices.

As regards the recommendation made to point SR 1.2, GR 4888/2020 modified Annex IV of GR 4056 so that in the case of New Entity Accounts, the Reporting Financial Institutions may only rely on a self-certification provided by a Passive NFE Account Holder or its Controlling Person for determining whether the Controlling Person is a Reportable Person.

At present, the AFIP has a registry of reporting entities, and is also working on bilateral agreements with the different regulatory bodies of those entities to implement joint actions.

Argentina will therefore be requesting re-assessment to reflect these changes in its report.

Aruba

Overall findings

Aruba's legal framework implementing the AEOI Standard is not in place in accordance with the requirements of the AEOI Terms of Reference. While Aruba's international legal framework to exchange the information with all of Aruba's Interested Appropriate Partners (CR2) is consistent with the requirements, its domestic legislative framework requiring Reporting Financial Institutions to conduct the due diligence and reporting procedures (CR1) has significant deficiencies in areas that are fundamental to the proper functioning of the AEOI Standard. Most significantly, Aruba's legislative framework does not set out some of the key due diligence timelines, does not properly identify all of the relevant Financial Institutions and lacks sanctions under its enforcement framework.

The methodology used for the peer reviews and that therefore underpins this report is outlined in Chapter 2.

Overall determination on the legal framework: Not In Place

Conclusions on the legal framework

General context

Aruba commenced exchanges under the AEOI Standard in 2018.

In order to provide for Reporting Financial Institutions to collect and report the information to be exchanged, Aruba:

- enacted Ordinance No. 74 of 2017;
- introduced State Decree No. 76 of 2017;
- issued further guidance, which is not legally binding; and
- relies on its legal framework implementing the FATF Recommendations for the purposes of the identification of Controlling Persons under the AEOI Standard.

Under this framework Reporting Financial Institutions were required to commence the due diligence procedures in relation to New Accounts from 1 January 2017. With respect to Preexisting Accounts, the non-binding guidance states that the review of High Value Individual Accounts should be completed in time for the 2018 reporting deadline and by 31 December 2018 in the cases of Lower Value Individual Accounts and Entity Accounts.

With respect to the exchange of information under the AEOI Standard, Aruba has the Convention on Mutual Administrative Assistance in Tax Matters in place[1] and activated the associated CRS Multilateral Competent Authority Agreement in time for exchanges in 2018.

Detailed findings

The detailed findings for Aruba are below, organised per Core Requirement (CR) and sub-requirement (SR), as extracted from the AEOI Terms of Reference (www.oecd.org/tax/transparency/documents/aeoi-terms-of-reference.pdf).

CR1 Domestic legal framework: Jurisdictions should have a domestic legislative framework in place that requires all Reporting Financial Institutions to conduct the due diligence and reporting procedures in the CRS, and that provides for the effective implementation of the CRS as set out therein.

Determination: Not In Place

Aruba's domestic legislative framework is not in place as required as it does not contain several key aspects of the CRS and its Commentary. Significant deficiencies have been identified in relation to the scope of Reporting Financial Institutions required to report information (SR 1.1), the scope of Financial Accounts required to be reported and the due diligence procedures to be applied (SR 1.2) and the framework to enforce the requirements (SR 1.4). Most significantly, the due diligence provisions in Aruba's legislative framework do not include some key dates determining the application of the due diligence obligations, the procedures and evidence that may be relied upon for the determination of the status of Financial Institutions depart from those set out in the AEOI Standard and there are no sanctions in the enforcement framework.

SR 1.1 Jurisdictions should define the scope of Reporting Financial Institutions consistently with the CRS.

Aruba has defined the scope of Reporting Financial Institutions in its domestic legislative framework in a manner that is largely consistent with the AEOI Standard and its Commentary. However, deficiencies have been identified. More specifically, Aruba's legislative framework:

- classifies certain entities as Non-Reporting Financial Institutions that are not in accordance with the requirements set out in the AEOI Standard; and
- does not specify the date as of when Qualified Credit Card Issuers that are treated as Non-Reporting Financial Institutions are required to implement policies requiring the returning of overpayments made.

The scope of Reporting Financial Institutions, including the specification of Non-Reporting Financial Institutions, is material to the proper functioning of the AEOI Standard.

Recommendations:

Aruba should amend its domestic legislative framework to remove the classification of: (i) entities with shareholders, participants or controlling persons from one single family or a very limited group; and (ii) Trust Office Foundation (or STAK) as Non-Financial Entities without regard to the requirements to be classified as such.

Aruba should amend its domestic legislative framework to require Qualified Credit Card Issuers to implement policies with respect to the returning of overpayments from a specified date in order to be treated as Non-Reporting Financial Institutions.

Aruba should amend its domestic legislative framework to remove two entries from its jurisdiction-specific list of Non-Reporting Financial Institutions as they do not meet the requirements with respect to legally defined thresholds on contributions and limited options of withdrawal. The entries are: (i) Cooperative Savings and Credit Associations; and (ii) Customs and Savings and Credit Associations.

SR 1.2 Jurisdictions should define the scope of Financial Accounts and Reportable Accounts consistently with the CRS and incorporate the due diligence procedures to identify them.

Aruba has not defined the scope of the Financial Accounts that are required to be reported in its domestic legislative framework and has not incorporated the due diligence procedures that must be applied to identify them in a manner that is consistent with the AEOI Standard and its Commentary as significant deficiencies have been identified. More specifically, Aruba's legislative framework:

- does not specify the date as of when the Qualified Credit Card Issuers need to implement policies for the returning of overpayments, which is required for Depository Accounts due to not-returned overpayments to be treated as Excluded Accounts;
- does not follow the conditions set out in the AEOI Standard for when Reporting Financial Institutions can use existing classifications as Documentary Evidence with respect to Preexisting Entity Accounts;
- does not specify the date on which a Preexisting Entity Account is first to be identified; and
- does not specify the dates by when the due diligence procedures on High and Lower Value Preexisting Individual Accounts as well as Preexisting Entity Accounts are to be completed; the non-binding guidance indicates that these procedures should be completed in time for 2018 reporting deadline in the case of High Value Individual Accounts and by 31 December 2018 in the cases of Lower Value Individual Accounts and Entity Accounts.

The scope of Financial Accounts and the due diligence procedures to identify them are material to the proper functioning of the AEOI Standard.

Recommendations:

Aruba should amend its domestic legislative framework to require Qualified Credit Card Issuers to implement policies with respect to the returning of overpayments from a specified date in order for Depository Accounts due to not-returned overpayments to be treated as Excluded Accounts.

Aruba should amend its domestic legislative framework to require Reporting Financial Institutions to only use Documentary Evidence in relation to the due diligence procedures for Preexisting Entity Accounts in accordance with the conditions in the AEOI Standard.

Aruba should amend its domestic legislative framework to specify the date on which a Preexisting Entity Account is first to be identified using the USD 250 000 balance or value threshold.

Aruba should amend its legislative framework to specify the completion dates for the reviews of: (i) Preexisting High Value Individual Accounts; (ii) Preexisting Lower Value Individual Accounts; and (iii) Preexisting Entity Accounts.

SR 1.3 Jurisdictions should incorporate the reporting requirements contained in Section I of the CRS into their domestic legislative framework.

Aruba has incorporated the reporting requirements in its domestic legislative framework in accordance with the CRS and its Commentary. While a deficiency has been identified with respect to the reporting of the currency denomination, it is considered to be relatively minor as the CRS XML Schema will compel the reporting of a currency type.

Recommendations:

Aruba should amend its domestic legislative framework to require Reporting Financial Institutions to identify the currency in which each account is denominated.

SR 1.4 Jurisdictions should have a legislative framework in place that allows for the enforcement of the requirements of the CRS in practice.

Aruba does not have a legislative framework in place to enforce the requirements in a manner that is consistent with the CRS and its Commentary as significant deficiencies have been identified. More specifically, Aruba's legislative framework:

- does not include rules to prevent Financial Institutions, persons or intermediaries from adopting practices intended to circumvent the due diligence and reporting procedures as required;

- does not contain provisions imposing sanctions on Account Holders and Controlling Persons for the provision of a false self-certification;
- does not impose sanctions on Reporting Financial Institutions for failing to apply the due diligence procedures (they are restricted to failing to report the relevant information); and
- allows self-certifications to be obtained after the opening of the account in circumstances beyond those that are permitted.

These are key elements of the required enforcement framework and are therefore material to the proper functioning of the AEOI Standard.

Recommendations:

Aruba should amend its domestic legislative framework to include rules to prevent Financial Institutions, persons and intermediaries from adopting practices intended to circumvent the due diligence and reporting procedures.

Aruba should amend its domestic legislative framework to include sanctions on Account Holders and Controlling Persons for the provision of a false self-certification.

Aruba should amend its domestic legislative framework to include sanctions for failure to comply with the due diligence and reporting procedures in accordance with the AEOI Standard.

Aruba should amend its domestic legislative framework to limit the circumstances when it is permissible to obtain a valid self-certification after the opening of a New Account in accordance with the requirements.

CR2 International legal framework: Jurisdictions should have exchange relationships in effect with all Interested Appropriate Partners as committed to and that provide for the exchange of information in accordance with the Model CAA.

Determination: In Place

Aruba's international legal framework to exchange the information is in place, is consistent with the Model CAA and its Commentary and provides for exchange with all of Aruba's Interested Appropriate Partners (i.e. all jurisdictions that are interested in receiving information from Aruba and that meet the required standard in relation to confidentiality and data safeguards). (SRs 2.1 – 2.3)

SR 2.1 Jurisdictions should have exchange agreements in effect with all Interested Appropriate Partners that permit the automatic exchange of CRS information.

Aruba has exchange agreements that permit the automatic exchange of CRS information in effect with all its Interested Appropriate Partners.

Recommendations:

No recommendations made.

SR 2.2 Such an exchange agreement should be put in place without undue delay, following the receipt of an expression of interest from an Interested Appropriate Partner.

Aruba put in place its exchange agreements without undue delay.

Recommendations:

No recommendations made.

SR 2.3 Jurisdictions should ensure that the exchange agreements in effect provide for the exchange of information in accordance with the requirements of the Model CAA.

Aruba's exchange agreements provide for the exchange of information in accordance with the requirements of the Model CAA.

Recommendations:

No recommendations made.

Comments by the assessed jurisdiction

No comments made.

Note

[1] Through a territorial extension by the Netherlands.

Australia

Overall findings

Australia's legal framework implementing the AEOI Standard is in place but needs improvement in order to be fully consistent with the requirements of the AEOI Terms of Reference. While Australia's international legal framework to exchange the information with all of Australia's Interested Appropriate Partners (CR2) is consistent with the requirements, its domestic legislative framework requiring Reporting Financial Institutions to conduct the due diligence and reporting procedures (CR1) has a deficiency significant to the proper functioning of an element of the AEOI Standard. More specifically, Australia's legal framework includes a category of jurisdiction-specific Excluded Account that is not in accordance with the AEOI Standard.

The methodology used for the peer reviews and that therefore underpins this report is outlined in Chapter 2.

Overall determination on the legal framework: In Place But **Needs Improvement**

Conclusions on the legal framework

General context

Australia commenced exchanges under the AEOI Standard in 2018.

In order to provide for Reporting Financial Institutions to collect and report the information to be exchanged, Australia:

- enacted the Tax Laws Amendment (Implementation of the Common Reporting Standard) Act 2015 (TLA(ICRS) 2015); and
- issued further guidance, which is not legally binding.

Under this framework Reporting Financial Institutions were required to commence the due diligence procedures in relation to New Accounts from 1 July 2017. With respect to Preexisting Accounts, Reporting Financial Institutions were required to complete the due diligence procedures on High Value Individual Accounts by 31 July 2018 and on Lower Value Individual Accounts and Entity Accounts by 31 July 2019 and 31 July 2018 respectively.

Following the initial Global Forum peer review, Australia made various amendments to its legislative framework to address issues identified, the last of which was effective from 18 December 2020.

With respect to the exchange of information under the AEOI Standard, Australia:

- is a Party to the Convention on Mutual Administrative Assistance in Tax Matters and activated the associated CRS Multilateral Competent Authority Agreement in time for exchanges in 2018; and
- put in place a bilateral agreement.[1]

Detailed findings

The detailed findings for Australia are below, organised per Core Requirement (CR) and sub-requirement (SR), as extracted from the AEOI Terms of Reference (www.oecd.org/tax/transparency/documents/aeoi-terms-of-reference.pdf).

CR1 Domestic legal framework: Jurisdictions should have a domestic legislative framework in place that requires all Reporting Financial Institutions to conduct the due diligence and reporting procedures in the CRS, and that provides for the effective implementation of the CRS as set out therein.

Determination: In Place But **Needs Improvement**

Australia's domestic legislative framework is in place and contains most of the key aspects of the CRS and its Commentary requiring Reporting Financial Institutions to conduct the due diligence and reporting procedures, but it needs improvement in relation to the scope of Financial Accounts required to be reported (SR 1.2). More specifically, Australia's legislative framework provides for a category of jurisdiction-specific Excluded Account that does not meet all the requirements.

SR 1.1 Jurisdictions should define the scope of Reporting Financial Institutions consistently with the CRS.

Australia has defined the scope of Reporting Financial Institutions in its domestic legislative framework in accordance with the CRS and its Commentary.

Recommendations:

No recommendations made.

SR 1.2 Jurisdictions should define the scope of Financial Accounts and Reportable Accounts consistently with the CRS and incorporate the due diligence procedures to identify them.

Australia has defined the scope of the Financial Accounts that are required to be reported in its domestic legislative framework and incorporated the due diligence procedures that must be applied to identify them in a manner that is largely consistent with the CRS and its Commentary. However, a deficiency has been identified. More specifically, Australia provides for a jurisdiction-specific Excluded Account that is not in accordance with the requirements, as it does not provide for effective penalties for withdrawals that do not meet the criteria of the account. The definition of Financial Accounts, including the provision of Excluded Accounts, is material to the proper functioning of the AEOI Standard.

Recommendations:

Australia should amend its domestic legislative framework to remove the Scholarship Plans from its jurisdiction-specific list of Excluded Accounts, as they do not meet the requirements in the AEOI Standard, such as by not having penalties for withdrawals from the accounts for non-educational purposes.

SR 1.3 Jurisdictions should incorporate the reporting requirements contained in Section I of the CRS into their domestic legislative framework.

Australia has incorporated the reporting requirements in its domestic legislative framework in accordance with the CRS and its Commentary.

Recommendations:

No recommendations made.

SR 1.4 Jurisdictions should have a legislative framework in place that allows for the enforcement of the requirements of the CRS in practice.

Australia has a legislative framework in place to enforce the requirements in accordance with the CRS and its Commentary.

Recommendations:

No recommendations made.

CR2 International legal framework: Jurisdictions should have exchange relationships in effect with all Interested Appropriate Partners as committed to and that provide for the exchange of information in accordance with the Model CAA.

Determination: In Place

Australia's international legal framework to exchange the information is in place, is consistent with the Model CAA and its Commentary and provides for exchange with all of Australia's Interested Appropriate Partners (i.e. all jurisdictions that are interested in receiving information from Australia and that meet the required standard in relation to confidentiality and data safeguards). (SRs 2.1 – 2.3)

SR 2.1 Jurisdictions should have exchange agreements in effect with all Interested Appropriate Partners that permit the automatic exchange of CRS information.

Australia has exchange agreements that permit the automatic exchange of CRS information in effect with all its Interested Appropriate Partners.

Recommendations:

No recommendations made.

SR 2.2 Such an exchange agreement should be put in place without undue delay, following the receipt of an expression of interest from an Interested Appropriate Partner.

Australia put in place its exchange agreements without undue delay.

Recommendations:

No recommendations made.

SR 2.3 Jurisdictions should ensure that the exchange agreements in effect provide for the exchange of information in accordance with the requirements of the Model CAA.

Australia's exchange agreements provide for the exchange of information in accordance with the requirements of the Model CAA.

Recommendations:

No recommendations made.

Comments by the assessed jurisdiction

No comments made.

Note

[1] With Singapore. Australia has also activated a relationship under the CRS MCAA with Singapore.

Austria

Overall findings

Austria's legal framework implementing the AEOI Standard is in place and is consistent with the requirements of the AEOI Terms of Reference. This includes Austria's domestic legislative framework requiring Reporting Financial Institutions to conduct the due diligence and reporting procedures (CR1) and its international legal framework to exchange the information with all of Austria's Interested Appropriate Partners (CR2).

The methodology used for the peer reviews and that therefore underpins this report is outlined in Chapter 2.

Overall determination on the legal framework: In Place

Conclusions on the legal framework

General context

Austria commenced exchanges under the AEOI Standard in 2018.

In order to provide for Reporting Financial Institutions to collect and report the information to be exchanged, Austria:

- enacted the Common Reporting Standard Act (Federal Law Gazette I Nr 115/2015);
- issued further guidance, which is legally binding; and
- made reference to the Beneficial Owners Register Act for the purposes of the identification of Controlling Persons under the AEOI Standard.

Under this framework Reporting Financial Institutions were required to commence the due diligence procedures in relation to New Accounts from 1 October 2016. With respect to Preexisting Accounts, Reporting Financial Institutions were required to complete the due diligence procedures on High Value Individual Accounts by 31 December 2017 and on Lower Value Individual Accounts and Entity Accounts by 31 December 2018.

Following the initial Global Forum peer review, Austria made various amendments to its legislative framework to address issues identified, the last of which was effective from 24 April 2020.

With respect to the exchange of information under the AEOI Standard, Austria:

- is a Party to the Convention on Mutual Administrative Assistance in Tax Matters and activated the associated CRS Multilateral Competent Authority Agreement in time for exchanges in 2018;
- has in place European Directive 2011/16/EU on Administrative Cooperation in the Field of Taxation as amended by Directive 2014/107/EU; and
- has in place European Union agreements with five European third countries.[1]

Detailed findings

The detailed findings for Austria are below, organised per Core Requirement (CR) and sub-requirement (SR), as extracted from the AEOI Terms of Reference (www.oecd.org/tax/transparency/documents/aeoi-terms-of-reference.pdf).

CR1 Domestic legal framework: Jurisdictions should have a domestic legislative framework in place that requires all Reporting Financial Institutions to conduct the due diligence and reporting procedures in the CRS, and that provides for the effective implementation of the CRS as set out therein.

Determination: In Place

Austria's domestic legislative framework is in place and contains all of the key aspects of the CRS and its Commentary requiring Reporting Financial Institutions to conduct the due diligence and reporting procedures (SRs 1.1 – 1.3). It also provides for a framework to enforce the requirements (SR 1.4).

SR 1.1 Jurisdictions should define the scope of Reporting Financial Institutions consistently with the CRS.

Austria has defined the scope of Reporting Financial Institutions in its domestic legislative framework in accordance with the CRS and its Commentary.

Recommendations:

No recommendations made.

SR 1.2 Jurisdictions should define the scope of Financial Accounts and Reportable Accounts consistently with the CRS and incorporate the due diligence procedures to identify them.

Austria has defined the scope of the Financial Accounts that are required to be reported in its domestic legislative framework and incorporated the due diligence procedures that must be applied to identify them in accordance with the CRS and its Commentary.

Recommendations:

No recommendations made.

SR 1.3 Jurisdictions should incorporate the reporting requirements contained in Section I of the CRS into their domestic legislative framework.

Austria has incorporated the reporting requirements in its domestic legislative framework in accordance with the CRS and its Commentary.

Recommendations:

No recommendations made.

SR 1.4 Jurisdictions should have a legislative framework in place that allows for the enforcement of the requirements of the CRS in practice.

Austria has a legislative framework in place to enforce the requirements in accordance with the CRS and its Commentary.

Recommendations:

No recommendations made.

CR2 International legal framework: Jurisdictions should have exchange relationships in effect with all Interested Appropriate Partners as committed to and that provide for the exchange of information in accordance with the Model CAA.

Determination: In Place

Austria's international legal framework to exchange the information is in place, is consistent with the Model CAA and its Commentary and provides for exchange with all of Austria's Interested Appropriate Partners (i.e. all jurisdictions that are interested in receiving information from Austria and that meet the required standard in relation to confidentiality and data safeguards). (SRs 2.1 – 2.3)

SR 2.1 Jurisdictions should have exchange agreements in effect with all Interested Appropriate Partners that permit the automatic exchange of CRS information.

Austria has exchange agreements that permit the automatic exchange of CRS information in effect with all its Interested Appropriate Partners.

Recommendations:

No recommendations made.

SR 2.2 Such an exchange agreement should be put in place without undue delay, following the receipt of an expression of interest from an Interested Appropriate Partner.

Austria put in place its exchange agreements without undue delay.

Recommendations:

No recommendations made.

SR 2.3 Jurisdictions should ensure that the exchange agreements in effect provide for the exchange of information in accordance with the requirements of the Model CAA.

Austria's exchange agreements provide for the exchange of information in accordance with the requirements of the Model CAA.

Recommendations:

No recommendations made.

Comments by the assessed jurisdiction

No comments made.

Note

[1] Andorra, Liechtenstein, Monaco, San Marino and Switzerland.

Azerbaijan

Overall findings

Azerbaijan's legal framework implementing the AEOI Standard is in place but needs improvement in order to be consistent with the requirements of the AEOI Terms of Reference. While Azerbaijan's international legal framework to exchange the information with all of Azerbaijan's Interested Appropriate Partners (CR2) is consistent with the requirements, its domestic legislative framework requiring Reporting Financial Institutions to conduct the due diligence and reporting procedures (CR1) has deficiencies significant to the proper functioning of the AEOI Standard. More specifically, Azerbaijan does not fully incorporate some of the due diligence procedures and there is a deficiency relating to the enforcement framework.

The methodology used for the peer reviews and that therefore underpins this report is outlined in Chapter 2.

Overall determination on the legal framework: In Place But **Needs Improvement**

Conclusions on the legal framework

General context

Azerbaijan commenced exchanges under the AEOI Standard in 2018.

In order to provide for Reporting Financial Institutions to collect and report the information to be exchanged, Azerbaijan:

- enacted Limits and Regulations for provision of information on financial transactions carried out by legal entities and individuals of foreign states in the territory of Azerbaijan to the competent authorities of those countries approved by the Cabinet of Ministers in the decision No. 211 as amended on 22 June, 2018 and 15 September, 2021; and
- made reference to the Law of the Republic of Azerbaijan on the Prevention of the Legalisation of Criminally Obtained Funds or Other Property and the Financing of Terrorism (AML law), for the purposes of the identification of Controlling Persons under the AEOI Standard.

Under this framework Reporting Financial Institutions were required to commence the due diligence procedures in relation to New Accounts from 1 July 2017. Reporting Financial Institutions were required to complete the due diligence procedures on all Preexisting Accounts by 30 June 2018.

With respect to the exchange of information under the AEOI Standard, Azerbaijan is a Party to the Convention on Mutual Administrative Assistance in Tax Matters and activated the associated CRS Multilateral Competent Authority Agreement in time for exchanges in 2018.

Detailed findings

The detailed findings for Azerbaijan are below, organised per Core Requirement (CR) and sub-requirement (SR), as extracted from the AEOI Terms of Reference (www.oecd.org/tax/transparency/documents/aeoi-terms-of-reference.pdf).

CR1 Domestic legal framework: Jurisdictions should have a domestic legislative framework in place that requires all Reporting Financial Institutions to conduct the due diligence and reporting procedures in the CRS, and that provides for the effective implementation of the CRS as set out therein.

Determination: In Place But **Needs Improvement**

Azerbaijan's domestic legislative framework is in place and contains many of the key aspects of the CRS and the Commentary requiring Reporting Financial Institutions to conduct the due diligence and reporting procedures, but it needs improvement in relation to the due diligence procedures to be applied (SR 1.2) and the framework to enforce the requirements (SR 1.4). Most significantly, Azerbaijan's legislative framework sets a threshold for the identification of Controlling Persons that differs from the one defined in its legal framework implementing the Financial Action Task Force (FATF) Recommendations.

SR 1.1 Jurisdictions should define the scope of Reporting Financial Institutions consistently with the CRS.

Azerbaijan has defined the scope of Reporting Financial Institutions in its domestic legislative framework in accordance with the CRS and its Commentary.

Recommendations:

No recommendations made.

SR 1.2 Jurisdictions should define the scope of Financial Accounts and Reportable Accounts consistently with the CRS and incorporate the due diligence procedures to identify them.

Azerbaijan has defined the scope of the Financial Accounts that are required to be reported in its domestic legislative framework and incorporated the due diligence procedures that must be applied to identify them in a manner that is largely consistent with the CRS and its Commentary. However, a deficiency has been identified. More specifically, Azerbaijan's legislative framework sets a threshold for the identification of Controlling Persons that differs from the one defined in its AML law.

This element of the due diligence procedures is material to the proper functioning of the AEOI Standard.

Recommendations:

Azerbaijan should amend its domestic legislative framework to ensure that the approach to determine Controlling Persons under the AEOI Standard is aligned to its approach to determine beneficial owners under its domestic AML/KYC Procedures.

SR 1.3 Jurisdictions should incorporate the reporting requirements contained in Section I of the CRS into their domestic legislative framework.

Azerbaijan has incorporated the reporting requirements in its domestic legislative framework in accordance with the CRS and its Commentary.

Recommendations:

No recommendations made.

SR 1.4 Jurisdictions should have a legislative framework in place that allows for the enforcement of the requirements of the CRS in practice.

Azerbaijan has a legislative framework in place to enforce the requirements in a manner that is largely consistent with the CRS and its Commentary. However, a deficiency has been identified. More specifically, Azerbaijan's legislative framework does not contain provisions imposing sanctions on Account Holders and Controlling Persons for the provision of a false self-certification. This is a key element of the required enforcement framework and is therefore material to the proper functioning of the AEOI Standard.

Recommendations:

Azerbaijan should amend its domestic legislative framework to include sanctions on Account Holders and Controlling Persons for the provision of a false self-certification.

CR2 International legal framework: Jurisdictions should have exchange relationships in effect with all Interested Appropriate Partners as committed to and that provide for the exchange of information in accordance with the Model CAA.

Determination: In Place

Azerbaijan's international legal framework to exchange the information is in place, is consistent with the Model CAA and its Commentary and provides for exchange with all of Azerbaijan's Interested Appropriate Partners (i.e. all jurisdictions that are interested in receiving information from Azerbaijan and that meet the required standard in relation to confidentiality and data safeguards). (SRs 2.1 – 2.3)

SR 2.1 Jurisdictions should have exchange agreements in effect with all Interested Appropriate Partners that permit the automatic exchange of CRS information.

Azerbaijan has exchange agreements that permit the automatic exchange of CRS information in effect with all its Interested Appropriate Partners.

Recommendations:

No recommendations made.

SR 2.2 Such an exchange agreement should be put in place without undue delay, following the receipt of an expression of interest from an Interested Appropriate Partner.

Azerbaijan put in place its exchange agreements without undue delay.

Recommendations:

No recommendations made.

SR 2.3 Jurisdictions should ensure that the exchange agreements in effect provide for the exchange of information in accordance with the requirements of the Model CAA.

Azerbaijan's exchange agreements provide for the exchange of information in accordance with the requirements of the Model CAA.

Recommendations:

No recommendations made.

Comments by the assessed jurisdiction

No comments made.

The Bahamas

Overall findings

The Bahamas' legal framework implementing the AEOI Standard is in place but needs improvement in order to be fully consistent with the requirements of the AEOI Terms of Reference. While The Bahamas' international legal framework to exchange the information with all of The Bahamas' Interested Appropriate Partners (CR2) is consistent with the requirements, its domestic legislative framework requiring Reporting Financial Institutions to conduct the due diligence and reporting procedures (CR1) has deficiencies significant to the proper functioning of elements of the AEOI Standard. Most significantly, a jurisdiction-specific Non-Reporting Financial Institution is provided for that does not meet the requirements and incorrect values may be reported in relation to certain Controlling Persons of trusts.

The methodology used for the peer reviews and that therefore underpins this report is outlined in Chapter 2.

Overall determination on the legal framework: In Place But **Needs Improvement**

Conclusions on the legal framework

General context

The Bahamas commenced exchanges under the AEOI Standard in 2018.

In order to provide for Reporting Financial Institutions to collect and report the information to be exchanged, The Bahamas:

- enacted the Automatic Exchange of Financial Account Information Act 2016 (amended in 2017 and in 2019);
- introduced the Automatic Exchange of Financial Account Information Regulations 2017 (amended in 2017); and
- issued further guidance, which is not legally binding.

Under this framework Reporting Financial Institutions were required to commence the due diligence procedures in relation to New Accounts from 1 July 2017. With respect to Preexisting Accounts, Reporting Financial Institutions were required to complete the due diligence procedures on High Value Individual Accounts by 31 December 2017 and on Lower Value Individual Accounts and Entity Accounts by 31 December 2018.

Following the initial Global Forum peer review, The Bahamas made various amendments to its legislative framework to address issues identified, the last of which was effective from 30 April 2019.

With respect to the exchange of information under the AEOI Standard, The Bahamas is a Party to the Convention on Mutual Administrative Assistance in Tax Matters and activated the associated CRS Multilateral Competent Authority Agreement in time for exchanges in 2018.

Detailed findings

The detailed findings for The Bahamas are below, organised per Core Requirement (CR) and sub-requirement (SR), as extracted from the AEOI Terms of Reference (www.oecd.org/tax/transparency/documents/aeoi-terms-of-reference.pdf).

CR1 Domestic legal framework: Jurisdictions should have a domestic legislative framework in place that requires all Reporting Financial Institutions to conduct the due diligence and reporting procedures in the CRS, and that provides for the effective implementation of the CRS as set out therein.

Determination: In Place But **Needs Improvement**

The Bahamas' domestic legislative framework is in place and contains many of the key aspects of the CRS and its Commentary requiring Reporting Financial Institutions to conduct the due diligence and reporting procedures, but it needs improvement in some areas relating to the scope of Reporting Financial Institutions required to report information (SR 1.1) and the reporting requirements (SR 1.3). Most significantly, a jurisdiction-specific Non-Reporting Financial Institution is provided for that does not meet the requirements and incorrect values may be reported with respect to certain Controlling Persons of trusts.

SR 1.1 Jurisdictions should define the scope of Reporting Financial Institutions consistently with the CRS.

The Bahamas has defined the scope of Reporting Financial Institutions in its domestic legislative framework in a manner that is largely consistent with the CRS and its Commentary. However, a deficiency has been identified. More specifically, The Bahamas provides for a jurisdiction-specific Non-Reporting Financial Institution that is not in accordance with the requirements. The scope of Reporting Financial Institution, including the provision of Non-Reporting Financial Institutions, is material to the proper functioning of the AEOI Standard, which may materially impact the proper functioning of the AEOI Standard.

Recommendations:

The Bahamas should amend its domestic legislative framework to remove Bahamas Executive Entities from its list of categories of jurisdiction-specific Non-Reporting Financial Institutions, as they do not meet the requirements of the AEOI Standard.

SR 1.2 Jurisdictions should define the scope of Financial Accounts and Reportable Accounts consistently with the CRS and incorporate the due diligence procedures to identify them.

The Bahamas has defined the scope of the Financial Accounts that are required to be reported in its domestic legislative framework and incorporated the due diligence procedures that must be applied to identify them in accordance with the CRS and its Commentary.

Recommendations:

No recommendations made.

SR 1.3 Jurisdictions should incorporate the reporting requirements contained in Section I of the CRS into their domestic legislative framework.

The Bahamas has incorporated the reporting requirements in its domestic legislative framework in a manner that is largely consistent with the CRS and its Commentary. However, deficiencies have been identified. Most significantly, The Bahamas has guidance advising that in the case of a Reportable Person who is a settlor of an irrevocable trust, or a protector or any other natural person exercising ultimate effective control over any trust (revocable or irrevocable), the account balance attributable to them is zero if that person has no beneficial interest in the trust. The reporting of account balance or value is a key element of the reporting requirements and is therefore material to the proper functioning of the AEOI Standard.

Recommendations:

The Bahamas should amend its domestic legislative framework to ensure that lodging a notification of reporting in another jurisdiction is not a substitute for reporting on Reportable Accounts maintained in The Bahamas in the limited circumstances where reporting may be required in both jurisdictions.

The Bahamas should amend its domestic legislative framework to require the account balance or value with respect to all Controlling Persons of a trust holding a Reportable Account to be reported in accordance with the AEOI Standard.

SR 1.4 Jurisdictions should have a legislative framework in place that allows for the enforcement of the requirements of the CRS in practice.

The Bahamas has a legislative framework in place to enforce the requirements in accordance with the CRS and its Commentary.

Recommendations:

No recommendations made.

CR2 International legal framework: Jurisdictions should have exchange relationships in effect with all Interested Appropriate Partners as committed to and that provide for the exchange of information in accordance with the Model CAA.

Determination: In Place

The Bahamas' international legal framework to exchange the information is in place, is consistent with the Model CAA and its Commentary and provides for exchange with all of The Bahamas' Interested Appropriate Partners (i.e. all jurisdictions that are interested in receiving information from The Bahamas and that meet the required standard in relation to confidentiality and data safeguards). (SRs 2.1 – 2.3)

SR 2.1 Jurisdictions should have exchange agreements in effect with all Interested Appropriate Partners that permit the automatic exchange of CRS information.

The Bahamas has exchange agreements that permit the automatic exchange of CRS information in effect with all its Interested Appropriate Partners.

Recommendations:

No recommendations made.

SR 2.2 Such an exchange agreement should be put in place without undue delay, following the receipt of an expression of interest from an Interested Appropriate Partner.

The Bahamas put in place its exchange agreements without undue delay.

Recommendations:

No recommendations made.

SR 2.3 Jurisdictions should ensure that the exchange agreements in effect provide for the exchange of information in accordance with the requirements of the Model CAA.

The Bahamas' exchange agreements provide for the exchange of information in accordance with the requirements of the Model CAA.

Recommendations:

No recommendations made.

Comments by the assessed jurisdiction

The Bahamas is in the process of making amendments to the second schedule of the Automatic Exchange of Financial Account Information Regulations 2017.

Bahrain

Overall findings

Bahrain's legal framework implementing the AEOI Standard is in place and is consistent with the requirements of the AEOI Terms of Reference. This includes Bahrain's domestic legislative framework requiring Reporting Financial Institutions to conduct the due diligence and reporting procedures (CR1) and its international legal framework to exchange the information with all of Bahrain's Interested Appropriate Partners (CR2).

The methodology used for the peer reviews and that therefore underpins this report is outlined in Chapter 2.

Overall determination on the legal framework: In Place

Conclusions on the legal framework

General context

Bahrain commenced exchanges under the AEOI Standard in 2018.

In order to provide for Reporting Financial Institutions to collect and report the information to be exchanged, Bahrain:

- transposed the Multilateral Competent Authority Agreement on Automatic Exchange of Financial Account Information (MCAA) and the Multilateral Convention on Mutual Administrative Assistance in Tax Matters (MAC) into its domestic law; and
- enacted the CBB Common Reporting Standard (CRS) Directive OG/53/2017, the CBB CRS Directive OG/212/2017, the CBB CRS Directive OG/277/2018, and the MOICT circular FAEI/90/HR/2018.

Under this framework Reporting Financial Institutions were required to commence the due diligence procedures in relation to New Accounts from 1 July 2017. With respect to Preexisting Accounts, Reporting Financial Institutions were required to complete due diligence procedures on High Value Individual Accounts by 31 December 2017 and on Lower Value Individual Accounts and Entity Accounts by 31 December 2018.

With respect to the exchange of information under the AEOI Standard, Bahrain is a Party to the Convention on Mutual Administrative Assistance in Tax Matters and activated the associated CRS Multilateral Competent Authority Agreement in time for exchanges in 2018.

Detailed findings

The detailed findings for Bahrain are below, organised per Core Requirement (CR) and sub-requirement (SR), as extracted from the AEOI Terms of Reference (www.oecd.org/tax/transparency/documents/aeoi-terms-of-reference.pdf).

CR1 Domestic legal framework: Jurisdictions should have a domestic legislative framework in place that requires all Reporting Financial Institutions to conduct the due diligence and reporting procedures in the CRS, and that provides for the effective implementation of the CRS as set out therein.

Determination: In Place

Bahrain's domestic legislative framework is in place and contains all of the key aspects of the CRS and its Commentary requiring Reporting Financial Institutions to conduct the due diligence and reporting procedures (SRs 1.1 – 1.3). It also provides for a framework to enforce the requirements (SR 1.4).

SR 1.1 Jurisdictions should define the scope of Reporting Financial Institutions consistently with the CRS.

Bahrain has defined the scope of Reporting Financial Institutions in its domestic legislative framework in accordance with the CRS and its Commentary.

Recommendations:

No recommendations made.

SR 1.2 Jurisdictions should define the scope of Financial Accounts and Reportable Accounts consistently with the CRS and incorporate the due diligence procedures to identify them.

Bahrain has defined the scope of the Financial Accounts that are required to be reported in its domestic legislative framework and incorporated the due diligence procedures that must be applied to identify them in accordance with the CRS and its Commentary.

Recommendations:

No recommendations made.

SR 1.3 Jurisdictions should incorporate the reporting requirements contained in Section I of the CRS into their domestic legislative framework.

Bahrain has incorporated the reporting requirements in its domestic legislative framework in accordance with the CRS and its Commentary.

Recommendations:

No recommendations made.

SR 1.4 Jurisdictions should have a legislative framework in place that allows for the enforcement of the requirements of the CRS in practice.

Bahrain has a legislative framework in place to enforce the requirements in accordance with the CRS and its Commentary.

Recommendations:

No recommendations made.

CR2 International legal framework: Jurisdictions should have exchange relationships in effect with all Interested Appropriate Partners as committed to and that provide for the exchange of information in accordance with the Model CAA.

Determination: In Place

Bahrain's international legal framework to exchange the information is in place, is consistent with the Model CAA and its Commentary and provides for exchange with all of Bahrain's Interested Appropriate Partners (i.e. all jurisdictions that are interested in receiving information from Bahrain and that meet the required standard in relation to confidentiality and data safeguards). (SRs 2.1 – 2.3)

SR 2.1 Jurisdictions should have exchange agreements in effect with all Interested Appropriate Partners that permit the automatic exchange of CRS information.

Bahrain has exchange agreements that permit the automatic exchange of CRS information in effect with all its Interested Appropriate Partners.

Recommendations:

No recommendations made.

SR 2.2 Such an exchange agreement should be put in place without undue delay, following the receipt of an expression of interest from an Interested Appropriate Partner.

Bahrain put in place its exchange agreements without undue delay.

Recommendations:

No recommendations made.

SR 2.3 Jurisdictions should ensure that the exchange agreements in effect provide for the exchange of information in accordance with the requirements of the Model CAA.

Bahrain's exchange agreements provide for the exchange of information in accordance with the requirements of the Model CAA.

Recommendations:

No recommendations made.

Comments by the assessed jurisdiction

No comments made.

Barbados

Overall findings

Barbados' legal framework implementing the AEOI Standard is in place but needs improvement in order to be fully consistent with the requirements of the AEOI Terms of Reference. While Barbados' international legal framework to exchange the information with all of Barbados' Interested Appropriate Partners (CR2) is consistent with the requirements, its domestic legislative framework requiring Reporting Financial Institutions to conduct the due diligence and reporting procedures (CR1) has deficiencies significant to the proper functioning of elements of the AEOI Standard. Most significantly, Barbados' legal framework includes categories of jurisdiction-specific Non-Reporting Financial Institutions that are not in accordance with the AEOI Standard and there are some deficiencies with respect to the enforcement framework.

The methodology used for the peer reviews and that therefore underpins this report is outlined in Chapter 2.

Overall determination on the legal framework: In Place But **Needs Improvement**

Conclusions on the legal framework

General context

Barbados commenced exchanges under the AEOI Standard in 2018.

In order to provide for Reporting Financial Institutions to collect and report the information to be exchanged, Barbados:

- enacted Section 83 of the Income Tax Act of Barbados; and
- introduced the Income Tax (Automatic Exchange of Information) Regulations 2017.

Under this framework Reporting Financial Institutions were required to commence the due diligence procedures in relation to New Accounts from 1 July 2017. With respect to Preexisting Accounts, Reporting Financial Institutions were required to complete the due diligence procedures on High Value Individual Accounts by 31 December 2017 and on Lower Value Individual Accounts and Entity Accounts by 31 December 2018.

With respect to the exchange of information under the AEOI Standard, Barbados is a Party to the Convention on Mutual Administrative Assistance in Tax Matters and activated the associated CRS Multilateral Competent Authority Agreement in time for exchanges in 2018.

Detailed findings

The detailed findings for Barbados are below, organised per Core Requirement (CR) and sub-requirement (SR), as extracted from the AEOI Terms of Reference (www.oecd.org/tax/transparency/documents/aeoi-terms-of-reference.pdf).

CR1 Domestic legal framework: Jurisdictions should have a domestic legislative framework in place that requires all Reporting Financial Institutions to conduct the due diligence and reporting procedures in the CRS, and that provides for the effective implementation of the CRS as set out therein.

Determination: In Place But **Needs Improvement**

Barbados' domestic legislative framework is in place and contains most of the key aspects of the CRS and its Commentary requiring Reporting Financial Institutions to conduct the due diligence and reporting procedures, but it needs improvement in relation to the scope of Reporting Financial Institutions required to report information (SR 1.1) and the framework to enforce the requirements (SR 1.4). Most significantly, Barbados' legislative framework provides for three jurisdiction-specific Non-Reporting Financial Institutions that are not in accordance with the requirements, does not provide for sanctions on Account Holders and Controlling Persons for the provision of a false self-certification and sets out non-recurring record keeping obligations with respect to the reportable accounts subject to annual reporting.

SR 1.1 Jurisdictions should define the scope of Reporting Financial Institutions consistently with the CRS.

Barbados has defined the scope of Reporting Financial Institutions in its domestic legislative framework in a manner that is largely consistent with the CRS and its Commentary. However, deficiencies have been identified. More specifically, Barbados provides for three jurisdiction-specific Non-Reporting Financial Institutions that are not in accordance with the requirements. The definition of Reporting Financial Institutions, including the provision of Non-Reporting Financial Institutions, is material to the proper functioning of the AEOI Standard.

Recommendations:

Barbados should amend its domestic legislative framework to remove three entries from its jurisdiction-specific list of Non-Reporting Financial Institutions as they do not meet the requirements. The entries are: (i) the Co-operative Credit Union League Ltd; (ii) the Agency for Micro Enterprise Development Ltd (Fund Access); and (iii) the Enterprise Growth Fund Ltd.

SR 1.2 Jurisdictions should define the scope of Financial Accounts and Reportable Accounts consistently with the CRS and incorporate the due diligence procedures to identify them.

Barbados has defined the scope of the Financial Accounts that are required to be reported in its domestic legislative framework and incorporated the due diligence procedures that must be applied to identify them in accordance with the CRS and its Commentary.

Recommendations:

No recommendations made.

SR 1.3 Jurisdictions should incorporate the reporting requirements contained in Section I of the CRS into their domestic legislative framework.

Barbados has incorporated the reporting requirements in its domestic legislative framework in accordance with the CRS and its Commentary. While a deficiency has been identified with respect to the reporting of the account number, it is considered to be relatively minor as an account number or functional equivalent is required to be reported.

Recommendations:

Barbados should amend its domestic legislative framework to require Reporting Financial Institutions to always report an account number when one exists, rather than a functional equivalent.

SR 1.4 Jurisdictions should have a legislative framework in place that allows for the enforcement of the requirements of the CRS in practice.

Barbados has a legislative framework in place to enforce the requirements in a manner that is largely consistent with the CRS and its Commentary. However, deficiencies have been identified. More specifically, Barbados' legislative framework:

- does not impose sanctions on Account Holders and Controlling Persons for the provision of a false self-certification; and
- does not include rules requiring Reporting Financial Institutions to keep records in accordance with the requirements.

These are key elements of the required enforcement framework and are therefore material to the proper functioning of the AEOI Standard.

Recommendations:

Barbados should amend its domestic legislative framework to include sanctions on Account Holders and Controlling Persons for the provision of a false self-certification.

Barbados should amend its domestic legislative framework to require Reporting Financial Institutions to maintain records for at least five years from the deadline to report the information, rather than five years from the end of the calendar year for which the record was made.

CR2 International legal framework: Jurisdictions should have exchange relationships in effect with all Interested Appropriate Partners as committed to and that provide for the exchange of information in accordance with the Model CAA.

Determination: In Place

Barbados' international legal framework to exchange the information is in place, is consistent with the Model CAA and its Commentary and provides for exchange with all of Barbados' Interested Appropriate Partners (i.e. all jurisdictions that are interested in receiving information from Barbados and that meet the required standard in relation to confidentiality and data safeguards). (SRs 2.1 – 2.3)

SR 2.1 Jurisdictions should have exchange agreements in effect with all Interested Appropriate Partners that permit the automatic exchange of CRS information.

Barbados has exchange agreements that permit the automatic exchange of CRS information in effect with all its Interested Appropriate Partners.

Recommendations:

No recommendations made.

SR 2.2 Such an exchange agreement should be put in place without undue delay, following the receipt of an expression of interest from an Interested Appropriate Partner.

Barbados put in place its exchange agreements without undue delay.

Recommendations:

No recommendations made.

SR 2.3 Jurisdictions should ensure that the exchange agreements in effect provide for the exchange of information in accordance with the requirements of the Model CAA.

Barbados' exchange agreements provide for the exchange of information in accordance with the requirements of the Model CAA.

Recommendations:

No recommendations made.

Comments by the assessed jurisdiction

No comments made.

Belgium

Overall findings

Belgium's legal framework implementing the AEOI Standard is in place but needs improvement in order to be fully consistent with the requirements of the AEOI Terms of Reference. While Belgium's international legal framework to exchange information with all Belgium's Interested Appropriate Partners (CR2) is consistent with the requirements, its domestic legislative framework requiring Reporting Financial Institutions to conduct the due diligence and reporting procedures (CR1) has a deficiency significant to the proper functioning of an element of the AEOI Standard. More specifically, a deficiency has been identified in Belgium's enforcement framework.

The methodology used for the peer reviews and that therefore underpins this report is outlined in Chapter 2.

Overall determination on the legal framework: In Place But **Needs Improvement**

Conclusions on the legal framework

General context

Belgium commenced exchanges under the AEOI Standard in 2017.

In order to provide for Reporting Financial Institutions to collect and report the information to be exchanged, Belgium:

- enacted *"Loi du 16 décembre 2015 réglant la communication des renseignements relatifs aux comptes financiers, par les institutions financières belges et le SPF Finances, dans le cadre d'un échange automatique de renseignements au niveau international et à des fins fiscales"*; and
- issued further guidance, which is legally binding.

Under this framework Reporting Financial Institutions were required to commence the due diligence procedures in relation to New Accounts from 1 January 2016. With respect to Preexisting Accounts, Reporting Financial Institutions were required to complete the due diligence procedures on High Value Individual Accounts by 31 December 2016 and on Lower Value Individual Accounts and Entity Accounts by 31 December 2017.

Following the initial Global Forum review, Belgium amended its legislative framework to address issues identified, effective from 1 January 2018.

With respect to the exchange of information under the AEOI Standard, Belgium:

- is a Party to the Convention on Mutual Administrative Assistance in Tax Matters and activated the associated CRS Multilateral Competent Authority Agreement in time for exchanges in 2016;
- has in place European Directive 2011/16/EU on Administrative Co-operation in the Field of Taxation as amended by Directive 2014/107/EU; and
- has in place agreements with five European third countries[1]

Detailed findings

The detailed findings for Belgium are below, organised per Core Requirement (CR) and sub-requirement (SR), as extracted from the AEOI Terms of Reference (www.oecd.org/tax/transparency/documents/aeoi-terms-of-reference.pdf).

CR1 Domestic legal framework: Jurisdictions should have a domestic legislative framework in place that requires all Reporting Financial Institutions to conduct the due diligence and reporting procedures in the CRS, and that provides for the effective implementation of the CRS as set out therein.

Determination: In Place But **Needs Improvement**

Belgium's domestic legislative framework is in place and contains most of the key aspects of the CRS and its Commentary requiring Reporting Financial Institutions to conduct the due diligence and reporting procedures, but it needs improvement in relation to the framework to enforce the requirements (SR 1.4). More specifically, Belgium does not have rules to prevent the circumvention of the due diligence and reporting procedures.

SR 1.1 Jurisdictions should define the scope of Reporting Financial Institutions consistently with the CRS.

Belgium has defined the scope of Reporting Financial Institutions in its domestic legislative framework in accordance with the CRS and its Commentary.

Recommendations:

No recommendations made.

SR 1.2 Jurisdictions should define the scope of Financial Accounts and Reportable Accounts consistently with the CRS and incorporate the due diligence procedures to identify them.

Belgium has defined the scope of the Financial Accounts that are required to be reported in its domestic legislative framework and incorporated the due diligence procedures that must be applied to identify them in accordance with the CRS and its Commentary.

Recommendations:

No recommendations made.

SR 1.3 Jurisdictions should incorporate the reporting requirements contained in Section I of the CRS into their domestic legislative framework.

Belgium has incorporated the reporting requirements in its domestic legislative framework in accordance with the CRS and its Commentary.

Recommendations:

No recommendations made.

SR 1.4 Jurisdictions should have a legislative framework in place that allows for the enforcement of the requirements of the CRS in practice.

Belgium has a legislative framework in place to enforce the requirements in a manner that is largely consistent with the CRS and its Commentary. However, a deficiency has been identified. More specifically, Belgium's legislative framework does not include rules to prevent Financial Institutions, persons or intermediaries from adopting practices intended to circumvent the due diligence and reporting procedures. This is a key element of the required enforcement framework and is therefore material to the proper functioning of the AEOI Standard.

Recommendations:

Belgium should amend its domestic legislative framework to include rules to prevent Financial Institutions, persons or intermediaries adopting practices intended to circumvent the due diligence and reporting procedures.

CR2 International legal framework: Jurisdictions should have exchange relationships in effect with all Interested Appropriate Partners as committed to and that provide for the exchange of information in accordance with the Model CAA.

Determination: In Place

Belgium's international legal framework to exchange the information is in place, is consistent with the Model CAA and its Commentary and provides for exchange with all of Belgium's Interested Appropriate Partners (i.e. all jurisdictions that are interested in receiving information from Belgium and that meet the required standard in relation to confidentiality and data safeguards).

SR 2.1 Jurisdictions should have exchange agreements in effect with all Interested Appropriate Partners that permit the automatic exchange of CRS information.

Belgium has exchange agreements that permit the automatic exchange of CRS information in effect with all its Interested Appropriate Partners.

Recommendations:

No recommendations made.

SR 2.2 Such an exchange agreement should be put in place without undue delay, following the receipt of an expression of interest from an Interested Appropriate Partner.

Belgium put in place its exchange agreements without undue delay.

Recommendations:

No recommendations made.

SR 2.3 Jurisdictions should ensure that the exchange agreements in effect provide for the exchange of information in accordance with the requirements of the Model CAA.

Belgium's exchange agreements provide for the exchange of information in accordance with the requirements of the Model CAA.

Recommendations:

No recommendations made.

Comments by the assessed jurisdiction

No comments made.

Note

[1] Andorra, Liechtenstein, Monaco, San Marino and Switzerland.

Belize

Overall findings

Belize's legal framework implementing the AEOI Standard is not in place in accordance with the requirements of the AEOI Terms of Reference. While Belize's international legal framework to exchange the information with all of Belize's Interested Appropriate Partners (CR2) is consistent with the requirements, Belize's domestic legislative framework requiring Reporting Financial Institutions to conduct the due diligence and reporting procedures (CR1) has significant deficiencies in areas that are fundamental to the proper functioning of the AEOI Standard. More specifically, deficiencies have been identified in Belize's enforcement framework and in other key areas.

The methodology used for the peer reviews and that therefore underpins this report is outlined in Chapter 2.

Overall determination on the legal framework: Not In Place

Conclusions on the legal framework

General context

Belize commenced exchanges under the AEOI Standard in 2018.

In order to provide for Reporting Financial Institutions to collect and report the information to be exchanged, Belize:

- enacted the Mutual Administrative Assistance in Tax Matters Act; and
- introduced the Mutual Administrative Assistance in Tax Matters (Automatic Exchange of Financial Account Information) Regulations, Statutory Instrument No 52 of 2017.

Under this framework Reporting Financial Institutions were required to commence the due diligence procedures in relation to New Accounts from 1 January 2017. With respect to Preexisting Accounts, Reporting Financial Institutions were required to complete the due diligence procedures on High Value Individual Accounts by 31 December 2017 and on Lower Value Individual Accounts and Entity Accounts by 31 December 2018.

With respect to the exchange of information under the AEOI Standard, Belize is a Party to the Convention on Mutual Administrative Assistance in Tax Matters and activated the associated CRS Multilateral Competent Authority Agreement in time for exchanges in 2018.

Detailed findings

The detailed findings for Belize are below, organised per Core Requirement (CR) and sub-requirement (SR), as extracted from the AEOI Terms of Reference (www.oecd.org/tax/transparency/documents/aeoi-terms-of-reference.pdf).

CR1 Domestic legal framework: Jurisdictions should have a domestic legislative framework in place that requires all Reporting Financial Institutions to conduct the due diligence and reporting procedures in the CRS, and that provides for the effective implementation of the CRS as set out therein.

Determination: Not In Place

Belize's domestic legislative framework is not in place as required as it does not contain several key aspects of the CRS and the Commentary. Significant deficiencies have been identified in relation to the framework to enforce the requirements (SR 1.4). Moreover there are deficiencies in relation to the scope of Reporting Financial Institutions required to report information (SR 1.1) and the scope of Financial Accounts required to be reported (SR 1.2). Most significantly, Belize's domestic legislative framework does not contain rules requiring Reporting Financial Institutions to keep records in accordance with the requirements, does not incorporate a framework for enforcement to address non-compliance, and does not include strong measures to ensure that valid self-certifications are always obtained for New Accounts.

SR 1.1 Jurisdictions should define the scope of Reporting Financial Institutions consistently with the CRS.

Belize has defined the scope of Reporting Financial Institutions in its domestic legislative framework in a manner that is largely consistent with the CRS and its Commentary. However, a deficiency has been identified. More specifically, Belize's legislative framework does not define Investment Entity in accordance with the requirements. The definition of Investment Entity is a key element of the AEOI Standard and is therefore material to its proper functioning.

Recommendations:

Belize should amend its domestic legislative framework to define the term Investment Entity in accordance with the AEOI Standard.

SR 1.2 Jurisdictions should define the scope of Financial Accounts and Reportable Accounts consistently with the CRS and incorporate the due diligence procedures to identify them.

Belize has defined the scope of the Financial Accounts that are required to be reported in its domestic legislative framework and incorporated the due diligence procedures that must be applied to identify them in a manner that is largely consistent with the CRS and its Commentary. However, deficiencies have been identified. More specifically, Belize has provided for two categories of jurisdiction-specific Excluded Accounts that are not in accordance with the requirements. The scope of Financial Accounts, including the provision of Excluded Accounts is material to the proper functioning of the AEOI Standard.

Recommendations:

Belize should amend its domestic legislative framework to remove two entries from its jurisdiction-specific list of Excluded Accounts: i) the Pension Accounts and ii) the Tax Exempt Savings Plans of Cooperative Societies. These do not meet the relevant requirements as i) no restrictions are made in accordance with the AEOI Standard and ii) the contributions into the accounts are not limited and withdrawals are also not restricted to the relevant criteria.

SR 1.3 Jurisdictions should incorporate the reporting requirements contained in Section I of the CRS into their domestic legislative framework.

Belize has incorporated the reporting requirements in its domestic legislative framework in accordance with the CRS and its Commentary.

Recommendations:

No recommendations made.

SR 1.4 Jurisdictions should have a legislative framework in place that allows for the enforcement of the requirements of the CRS in practice.

Belize does not have a legislative framework in place to enforce the requirements in a manner that is consistent with the CRS and its Commentary as significant deficiencies have been identified. More specifically, Belize's domestic legislative framework:

- does not include sanctions on Account Holders and Controlling Persons for the provision of a false self-certification;
- does not incorporate rules requiring Reporting Financial Institutions to keep records in accordance with the requirements;
- does not provide for sanctions on Reporting Financial Institutions for failing to carry out the due diligence procedures; and
- does not incorporate measures to ensure that self-certifications are always obtained and validated for New Accounts as is required.

These are key elements of the required enforcement framework and are therefore material to the proper functioning of the AEOI Standard

Recommendations:

Belize should amend its domestic legislative framework to include sanctions on Account Holders and Controlling Persons for the provision of a false self-certification.

Belize should amend its domestic legislative framework to require Reporting Financials Institutions maintain records for at least five years from the deadline to report the information, rather than six years from when the information relates or during which the due diligence steps were undertaken.

Belize should amend its domestic legislative framework to include sanctions for failure to comply with the due diligence and reporting procedures, rather than being limited to failures leading to incorrect information reporting.

Belize should amend its domestic legislative framework to include strong measures to ensure that valid self-certifications are always obtained for New Accounts in accordance with the requirements.

CR2 International legal framework: Jurisdictions should have exchange relationships in effect with all Interested Appropriate Partners as committed to and that provide for the exchange of information in accordance with the Model CAA.

Determination: In Place

Belize's international legal framework to exchange the information is in place, is consistent with the Model CAA and its Commentary and provides for exchange with all of Belize's Interested Appropriate Partners (i.e. all jurisdictions that are interested in receiving information from Belize and that meet the required standard in relation to confidentiality and data safeguards). (SRs 2.1 – 2.3)

SR 2.1 Jurisdictions should have exchange agreements in effect with all Interested Appropriate Partners that permit the automatic exchange of CRS information.

Belize has exchange agreements that permit the automatic exchange of CRS information in effect with all its Interested Appropriate Partners.

Recommendations:

No recommendations made.

SR 2.2 Such an exchange agreement should be put in place without undue delay, following the receipt of an expression of interest from an Interested Appropriate Partner.

Belize put in place its exchange agreements without undue delay.

Recommendations:

No recommendations made.

SR 2.3 Jurisdictions should ensure that the exchange agreements in effect provide for the exchange of information in accordance with the requirements of the Model CAA.

Belize's exchange agreements provide for the exchange of information in accordance with the requirements of the Model CAA.

Recommendations:

No recommendations made.

Comments by the assessed jurisdiction

Belize has initiated the process to amend its domestic legislative framework to address recommendations made.

Bermuda

Overall findings

Bermuda's legal framework implementing the AEOI Standard is in place and is consistent with the requirements of the AEOI Terms of Reference. This includes Bermuda's domestic legislative framework requiring Reporting Financial Institutions to conduct the due diligence and reporting procedures (CR1) and its international legal framework to exchange the information with all of Bermuda's Interested Appropriate Partners (CR2).

The methodology used for the peer reviews and that therefore underpins this report is outlined in Chapter 2.

Overall determination on the legal framework: In Place

Conclusions on the legal framework

General context

Bermuda commenced exchanges under the AEOI Standard in 2017.

In order to provide for Reporting Financial Institutions to collect and report the information to be exchanged, Bermuda:

- amended its International Cooperation (Tax Information Exchange Agreements) Act 2005;
- introduced International Cooperation (Tax Information Exchange Agreements) Common Reporting Standard Regulations in 2017; and
- introduced further guidance, which is not legally binding.

Under this framework Reporting Financial Institutions were required to commence the due diligence procedures in relation to New Accounts from 1 January 2016. With respect to Preexisting Accounts, Reporting Financial Institutions were required to complete the due diligence procedures on High Value Individual Accounts by 31 December 2016 and on Lower Value Individual Accounts and Entity Accounts by 31 December 2017.

Following the initial Global Forum peer review, Bermuda made various amendments to its legislative framework to address issues identified, the last of which was effective from 18 August 2017.

With respect to the exchange of information under the AEOI Standard, Bermuda:

- has the Convention on Mutual Administrative Assistance in Tax Matters in place[1] and activated the associated CRS Multilateral Competent Authority Agreement in time for exchanges in 2017; and
- put in place three bilateral agreements.[2]

Detailed findings

The detailed findings for Bermuda are below, organised per Core Requirement (CR) and sub-requirement (SR), as extracted from the AEOI Terms of Reference (www.oecd.org/tax/transparency/documents/aeoi-terms-of-reference.pdf).

CR1 Domestic legal framework: Jurisdictions should have a domestic legislative framework in place that requires all Reporting Financial Institutions to conduct the due diligence and reporting procedures in the CRS, and that provides for the effective implementation of the CRS as set out therein.

Determination: In Place

Bermuda's domestic legislative framework is in place and contains all of the key aspects of the CRS and its Commentary requiring Reporting Financial Institutions to conduct the due diligence and reporting procedures (SRs 1.1 – 1.3). It also provides for a framework to enforce the requirements (SR 1.4).

SR 1.1 Jurisdictions should define the scope of Reporting Financial Institutions consistently with the CRS.

Bermuda has defined the scope of Reporting Financial Institutions in its domestic legislative framework in accordance with the CRS and its Commentary.

Recommendations:

No recommendations made.

SR 1.2 Jurisdictions should define the scope of Financial Accounts and Reportable Accounts consistently with the CRS and incorporate the due diligence procedures to identify them.

Bermuda has defined the scope of the Financial Accounts that are required to be reported in its domestic legislative framework and incorporated the due diligence procedures that must be applied to identify them in accordance with the CRS and its Commentary.

Recommendations:

No recommendations made.

SR 1.3 Jurisdictions should incorporate the reporting requirements contained in Section I of the CRS into their domestic legislative framework.

Bermuda has incorporated the reporting requirements in its domestic legislative framework in accordance with the CRS and its Commentary.

Recommendations:

No recommendations made.

SR 1.4 Jurisdictions should have a legislative framework in place that allows for the enforcement of the requirements of the CRS in practice.

Bermuda has a legislative framework in place to enforce the requirements in accordance with the CRS and its Commentary.

Recommendations:

No recommendations made.

CR2 International legal framework: Jurisdictions should have exchange relationships in effect with all Interested Appropriate Partners as committed to and that provide for the exchange of information in accordance with the Model CAA.

Determination: In Place

Bermuda's international legal framework to exchange the information is in place, is consistent with the Model CAA and its Commentary and provides for exchange with all of Bermuda's Interested Appropriate

Partners (i.e. all jurisdictions that are interested in receiving information from Bermuda and that meet the required standard in relation to confidentiality and data safeguards). (SRs 2.1 – 2.3)

SR 2.1 Jurisdictions should have exchange agreements in effect with all Interested Appropriate Partners that permit the automatic exchange of CRS information.

Bermuda has exchange agreements that permit the automatic exchange of CRS information in effect with all its Interested Appropriate Partners.

Recommendations:

No recommendations made.

SR 2.2 Such an exchange agreement should be put in place without undue delay, following the receipt of an expression of interest from an Interested Appropriate Partner.

Bermuda put in place its exchange agreements without undue delay.

Recommendations:

No recommendations made.

SR 2.3 Jurisdictions should ensure that the exchange agreements in effect provide for the exchange of information in accordance with the requirements of the Model CAA.

Bermuda's exchange agreements provide for the exchange of information in accordance with the requirements of the Model CAA.

Recommendations:

No recommendations made.

Comments by the assessed jurisdiction

No comments made.

Notes

[1] Through a territorial extension by the United Kingdom.

[2] With Guernsey, the Isle of Man and the United Kingdom.

Brazil

Overall findings

Brazil's legal framework implementing the AEOI Standard is in place and is consistent with the requirements of the AEOI Terms of Reference. This includes Brazil's domestic legislative framework requiring Reporting Financial Institutions to conduct the due diligence and reporting procedures (CR1) and its international legal framework to exchange the information with all of Brazil's Interested Appropriate Partners (CR2).

The methodology used for the peer reviews and that therefore underpins this report is outlined in Chapter 2.

Overall determination on the legal framework: In Place

Conclusions on the legal framework

General context

Brazil commenced exchanges under the AEOI Standard in 2018.

In order to provide for Reporting Financial Institutions to collect and report the information to be exchanged, Brazil:

- enacted Decree nº 8,842 of 29 August, 2016 (to promulgate the text of the Convention on Mutual Administrative Assistance in Tax Matters as amended by the Protocol of 1 June, 2010 and the CRS Multilateral Competent Authority Agreement);
- introduced the Administrative Act *Instrução Normativa* - IN RFB nº 1.571 of 2 July 2015; the Administrative Act *Instrução Normativa* - IN RFB nº 1.680 of 28 December 2016; the Administrative Act *Instrução Normativa* - IN RFB nº 1.580 of 14 August 2015; the Administrative Act *Instrução Normativa* - IN RFB nº 1.764 of 22 November 2017; and Administrative Act *Instrução Normativa* - IN RFB nº 1905 of 5 August, 2019; and
- issued further guidance, which is legally binding.

Under this framework Reporting Financial Institutions were required to commence the due diligence procedures in relation to New Accounts from 1 January 2017. With respect to Preexisting Accounts, Reporting Financial Institutions were required to complete the due diligence procedures on High Value Individual Accounts by 31 December 2017, and on Lower Value Individual Accounts and Entity Accounts by 31 December 2018.

Following the initial Global Forum peer review, Brazil amended its legislative framework to address issues identified, effective from 5 August 2019.

With respect to the exchange of information under the AEOI Standard, Brazil is a Party to the Convention on Mutual Administrative Assistance in Tax Matters and activated the associated CRS Multilateral Competent Authority Agreement in time for exchanges in 2018.

Detailed findings

The detailed findings for Brazil are below, organised per Core Requirement (CR) and sub-requirement (SR), as extracted from the AEOI Terms of Reference (www.oecd.org/tax/transparency/documents/aeoi-terms-of-reference.pdf).

CR1 Domestic legal framework: Jurisdictions should have a domestic legislative framework in place that requires all Reporting Financial Institutions to conduct the due diligence and reporting procedures in the CRS, and that provides for the effective implementation of the CRS as set out therein.

Determination: In Place

Brazil's domestic legislative framework is in place and contains all of the key aspects of the CRS and its Commentary requiring Reporting Financial Institutions to conduct the due diligence and reporting procedures (SRs 1.1 – 1.3). It also provides for a framework to enforce the requirements (SR 1.4).

SR 1.1 Jurisdictions should define the scope of Reporting Financial Institutions consistently with the CRS.

Brazil has defined the scope of Reporting Financial Institutions in its domestic legislative framework in accordance with the CRS and its Commentary.

Recommendations:

No recommendations made.

SR 1.2 Jurisdictions should define the scope of Financial Accounts and Reportable Accounts consistently with the CRS and incorporate the due diligence procedures to identify them.

Brazil has defined the scope of the Financial Accounts that are required to be reported in its domestic legislative framework and incorporated the due diligence procedures that must be applied to identify them in accordance with the CRS and its Commentary.

Recommendations:

No recommendations made.

SR 1.3 Jurisdictions should incorporate the reporting requirements contained in Section I of the CRS into their domestic legislative framework.

Brazil has incorporated the reporting requirements in its domestic legislative framework in accordance with the CRS and its Commentary.

Recommendations:

No recommendations made.

SR 1.4 Jurisdictions should have a legislative framework in place that allows for the enforcement of the requirements of the CRS in practice.

Brazil has a legislative framework in place to enforce the requirements in accordance with the CRS and its Commentary.

Recommendations:

No recommendations made.

CR2 International legal framework: Jurisdictions should have exchange relationships in effect with all Interested Appropriate Partners as committed to and that provide for the exchange of information in accordance with the Model CAA.

Determination: In Place

Brazil's international legal framework to exchange the information is in place, is consistent with the Model CAA and its Commentary and provides for exchange with all of Brazil's Interested Appropriate Partners (i.e. all jurisdictions that are interested in receiving information from Brazil and that meet the required standard in relation to confidentiality and data safeguards). (SRs 2.1 – 2.3)

SR 2.1 Jurisdictions should have exchange agreements in effect with all Interested Appropriate Partners that permit the automatic exchange of CRS information.

Brazil has exchange agreements that permit the automatic exchange of CRS information in effect with all its Interested Appropriate Partners.

Recommendations:

No recommendations made.

SR 2.2 Such an exchange agreement should be put in place without undue delay, following the receipt of an expression of interest from an Interested Appropriate Partner.

Brazil put in place its exchange agreements without undue delay.

Recommendations:

No recommendations made.

SR 2.3 Jurisdictions should ensure that the exchange agreements in effect provide for the exchange of information in accordance with the requirements of the Model CAA.

Brazil's exchange agreements provide for the exchange of information in accordance with the requirements of the Model CAA.

Recommendations:

No recommendations made.

Comments by the assessed jurisdiction

No comments made.

British Virgin Islands

Overall findings

The British Virgin Islands' legal framework implementing the AEOI Standard is in place but needs improvement in order to be fully consistent with the requirements of the AEOI Terms of Reference. While the British Virgin Islands' international legal framework to exchange the information with all of the British Virgin Islands' Interested Appropriate Partners (CR2) is consistent with the requirements, its domestic legislative framework requiring Reporting Financial Institutions to conduct the due diligence and reporting procedures (CR1) has deficiencies significant to the proper functioning of elements of the AEOI Standard. More specifically, deficiencies have been identified with respect to the British Virgin Islands' enforcement framework.

The methodology used for the peer reviews and that therefore underpins this report is outlined in Chapter 2.

Overall determination on the legal framework: In Place But **Needs Improvement**

Conclusions on the legal framework

General context

The British Virgin Islands commenced exchanges under the AEOI Standard in 2017.

In order to provide for Reporting Financial Institutions to collect and report the information to be exchanged, the British Virgin Islands:

- enacted the Mutual Legal Assistance (Tax Matters) (Amendment) (No.2) Act, 2015, as amended in 2018; and
- issued further guidance, which is not legally binding.

Under this framework Reporting Financial Institutions were required to commence the due diligence procedures in relation to New Accounts from 1 January 2016. With respect to Preexisting Accounts, Reporting Financial Institutions were required to complete the due diligence procedures on High Value Individual Accounts by 31 December 2016 and on Lower Value Individual Accounts and Entity Accounts by 31 December 2017.

Following the initial Global Forum peer review, the British Virgin Islands amended its legislative framework to address issues identified, effective from 17 September 2018.

With respect to the exchange of information under the AEOI Standard, the British Virgin Islands:

- has the Convention on Mutual Administrative Assistance in Tax Matters in place[1] and activated the associated CRS Multilateral Competent Authority Agreement in time for exchanges in 2017; and
- put in place three bilateral agreements.[2]

Detailed findings

The detailed findings for the British Virgin Islands are below, organised per Core Requirement (CR) and sub-requirement (SR), as extracted from the AEOI Terms of Reference (www.oecd.org/tax/transparency/documents/aeoi-terms-of-reference.pdf).

CR1 Domestic legal framework: Jurisdictions should have a domestic legislative framework in place that requires all Reporting Financial Institutions to conduct the due diligence and reporting procedures in the CRS, and that provides for the effective implementation of the CRS as set out therein.

Determination: In Place But **Needs Improvement**

The British Virgin Islands' domestic legislative framework is in place and contains most of the key aspects of the CRS and its Commentary requiring Reporting Financial Institutions to conduct the due diligence and reporting procedures, but it needs improvement in relation to the framework to enforce the requirements (SR 1.4). More specifically, the British Virgin Islands does not impose sanctions on Account Holders and Controlling Persons for the provision of a false self-certification and does not require records to be kept in accordance with the requirements.

SR 1.1 Jurisdictions should define the scope of Reporting Financial Institutions consistently with the CRS.

The British Virgin Islands has defined the scope of Reporting Financial Institutions in its domestic legislative framework in accordance with the CRS and its Commentary.

Recommendations:

No recommendations made.

SR 1.2 Jurisdictions should define the scope of Financial Accounts and Reportable Accounts consistently with the CRS and incorporate the due diligence procedures to identify them.

The British Virgin Islands has defined the scope of the Financial Accounts that are required to be reported in its domestic legislative framework and incorporated the due diligence procedures that must be applied to identify them in accordance with the CRS and its Commentary.

Recommendations:

No recommendations made.

SR 1.3 Jurisdictions should incorporate the reporting requirements contained in Section I of the CRS into their domestic legislative framework.

The British Virgin Islands has incorporated the reporting requirements in its domestic legislative framework in accordance with the CRS and its Commentary.

Recommendations:

No recommendations made.

SR 1.4 Jurisdictions should have a legislative framework in place that allows for the enforcement of the requirements of the CRS in practice.

The British Virgin Islands has a legislative framework in place to enforce the requirements in a manner that is largely consistent with the CRS and its Commentary. However, deficiencies have been identified. More specifically, the British Virgin Islands' legislative framework:

- does not impose sanctions for the provision of a false self-certifications by Account Holders and Controlling Persons; and
- does not include rules requiring Reporting Financial Institutions to keep records in accordance with the requirements.

These are key elements of the required enforcement framework and are therefore material to the proper functioning of the AEOI Standard.

Recommendations:

The British Virgin Islands should amend its domestic legislative framework to include sanctions on Account Holders and Controlling Persons for the provision of a false self-certification.

The British Virgin Islands should amend its domestic legislative framework to require Reporting Financial Institutions to keep records of the steps taken and evidence relied upon for the performance of the procedures, rather than permitting either to be kept.

The British Virgin Islands should amend its domestic legislative framework to require Reporting Financial Institutions to maintain records for at least five years from the deadline to report the information, rather than for six years from the end of the year to which the information relates or during which the due diligence steps were undertaken.

CR2 International legal framework: Jurisdictions should have exchange relationships in effect with all Interested Appropriate Partners as committed to and that provide for the exchange of information in accordance with the Model CAA.

Determination: In Place

The British Virgin Islands' international legal framework to exchange the information is in place, is consistent with the Model CAA and its Commentary and provides for exchanges with all of the British Virgin Islands' Interested Appropriate Partners (i.e. all jurisdictions that are interested in receiving information from the British Virgin Islands and that meet the required standard in relation to confidentiality and data safeguards). (SRs 2.1 – 2.3)

SR 2.1 Jurisdictions should have exchange agreements in effect with all Interested Appropriate Partners that permit the automatic exchange of CRS information.

The British Virgin Islands has exchange agreements that permit the automatic exchange of CRS information in effect with all its Interested Appropriate Partners.

Recommendations:

No recommendations made.

SR 2.2 Such an exchange agreement should be put in place without undue delay, following the receipt of an expression of interest from an Interested Appropriate Partner.

The British Virgin Islands put in place its exchange agreements without undue delay.

Recommendations:

No recommendations made.

SR 2.3 Jurisdictions should ensure that the exchange agreements in effect provide for the exchange of information in accordance with the requirements of the Model CAA.

The British Virgin Islands' exchange agreements provide for the exchange of information in accordance with the requirements of the Model CAA.

Recommendations:

No recommendations made.

Comments by the assessed jurisdiction

No comments made.

Notes

[1] Through a territorial extension by the United Kingdom.

[2] With Guernsey, the Isle of Man and the United Kingdom.

Brunei Darussalam

Overall findings

Brunei Darussalam's legal framework implementing the AEOI Standard is in place and is consistent with the requirements of the AEOI Terms of Reference. This includes Brunei Darussalam's domestic legislative framework requiring Reporting Financial Institutions to conduct the due diligence and reporting procedures (CR1) and its international legal framework to exchange the information with all of Brunei Darussalam's Interested Appropriate Partners (CR2).

The methodology used for the peer reviews and that therefore underpins this report is outlined in Chapter 2.

Overall determination on the legal framework: In Place

Conclusions on the legal framework

General context

Brunei Darussalam commenced exchanges under the AEOI Standard in 2018.

In order to provide for Reporting Financial Institutions to collect and report the information to be exchanged, Brunei Darussalam:

- enacted Income Tax Act (Amendment) No. 3 Order, 2017;
- issued Income Tax (International Tax Compliance Agreements) (Common Reporting Standard) Regulations 2017; and
- published further guidance, which is not legally binding.

Under this framework Reporting Financial Institutions were required to commence the due diligence procedures in relation to New Accounts from 1 January 2017. With respect to Preexisting Accounts, Reporting Financial Institutions were required to complete the due diligence procedures on High Value Individual Accounts by 31 December 2017 and on Lower Value Individual Accounts and Entity Accounts by 31 December 2018.

With respect to the exchange of information under the AEOI Standard, Brunei Darussalam is a Party to the Convention on Mutual Administrative Assistance in Tax Matters and activated the associated CRS Multilateral Competent Authority Agreement in time for exchanges in 2018.

Detailed findings

The detailed findings for Brunei Darussalam are below, organised per Core Requirement (CR) and sub-requirement (SR), as extracted from the AEOI Terms of Reference (www.oecd.org/tax/transparency/documents/aeoi-terms-of-reference.pdf).

CR1 Domestic legal framework: Jurisdictions should have a domestic legislative framework in place that requires all Reporting Financial Institutions to conduct the due diligence and reporting procedures in the CRS, and that provides for the effective implementation of the CRS as set out therein.

Determination: In Place

Brunei Darussalam's domestic legislative framework is in place and contains all of the key aspects of the CRS and its Commentary requiring Reporting Financial Institutions to conduct the due diligence and reporting procedures (SRs 1.1 – 1.3). It also provides for a framework to enforce the requirements (SR 1.4).

SR 1.1 Jurisdictions should define the scope of Reporting Financial Institutions consistently with the CRS.

Brunei Darussalam has defined the scope of Reporting Financial Institutions in its domestic legislative framework in accordance with the CRS and its Commentary.

Recommendations:

No recommendations made.

SR 1.2 Jurisdictions should define the scope of Financial Accounts and Reportable Accounts consistently with the CRS and incorporate the due diligence procedures to identify them.

Brunei Darussalam has defined the scope of the Financial Accounts that are required to be reported in its domestic legislative framework and incorporated the due diligence procedures that must be applied to identify them in accordance with the CRS and its Commentary.

Recommendations:

No recommendations made.

SR 1.3 Jurisdictions should incorporate the reporting requirements contained in Section I of the CRS into their domestic legislative framework.

Brunei Darussalam has incorporated the reporting requirements in its domestic legislative framework in accordance with the CRS and its Commentary.

Recommendations:

No recommendations made.

SR 1.4 Jurisdictions should have a legislative framework in place that allows for the enforcement of the requirements of the CRS in practice.

Brunei Darussalam has a legislative framework in place to enforce the requirements in accordance with the CRS and its Commentary.

Recommendations:

No recommendations made.

CR2 International legal framework: Jurisdictions should have exchange relationships in effect with all Interested Appropriate Partners as committed to and that provide for the exchange of information in accordance with the Model CAA.

Determination: In Place

Brunei Darussalam's international legal framework to exchange the information is in place, is consistent with the Model CAA and its Commentary and provides for exchange with all of Brunei Darussalam's Interested Appropriate Partners (i.e. all jurisdictions that are interested in receiving information from Brunei Darussalam and that meet the required standard in relation to confidentiality and data safeguards). (SRs 2.1 – 2.3)

SR 2.1 Jurisdictions should have exchange agreements in effect with all Interested Appropriate Partners that permit the automatic exchange of CRS information.

Brunei Darussalam has exchange agreements that permit the automatic exchange of CRS information in effect with all its Interested Appropriate Partners.

Recommendations:

No recommendations made.

SR 2.2 Such an exchange agreement should be put in place without undue delay, following the receipt of an expression of interest from an Interested Appropriate Partner.

Brunei Darussalam put in place its exchange agreements without undue delay.

Recommendations:

No recommendations made.

SR 2.3 Jurisdictions should ensure that the exchange agreements in effect provide for the exchange of information in accordance with the requirements of the Model CAA.

Brunei Darussalam's exchange agreements provide for the exchange of information in accordance with the requirements of the Model CAA.

Recommendations:

No recommendations made.

Comments by the assessed jurisdiction

No comments made.

Bulgaria

Overall findings

Bulgaria's legal framework implementing the AEOI Standard is in place and is consistent with the requirements of the AEOI Terms of Reference. This includes Bulgaria's domestic legislative framework requiring Reporting Financial Institutions to conduct the due diligence and reporting procedures (CR1) and its international legal framework to exchange the information with all of Bulgaria's Interested Appropriate Partners (CR2).

The methodology used for the peer reviews and that therefore underpins this report is outlined in Chapter 2.

Overall determination on the legal framework: In Place

Conclusions on the legal framework

General context

Bulgaria commenced exchanges under the AEOI Standard in 2017.

In order to provide for Reporting Financial Institutions to collect and report the information to be exchanged, Bulgaria:

- enacted Art. 142a to Art. 142y of the Tax and Social Security Procedure Code (TSSPC), §1a of the Additional Provisions of the TSSPC;
- enacted Order ZCU-1576/18.12.2015 of the Executive Director of the National Revenue Agency as amended by Order № ZCU-720/22.05.2018 of the Executive Director of the National Revenue Agency;
- introduced § 55 - § 66 of the Transitional and Concluding Provisions; and
- made reference to §2 of the Supplementary Provisions of the Measures Against Money Laundering Act implementing the FATF Recommendations for the purposes of the identification of Controlling Persons under the AEOI Standard.

Under this framework Reporting Financial Institutions were required to commence the due diligence procedures in relation to New Accounts from 1 January 2016. With respect to Preexisting Accounts, Reporting Financial Institutions were required to complete the due diligence procedures on High Value Individual Accounts by 31 December 2016 and on Lower Value Individual Accounts and Entity Accounts by 31 December 2017.

Following the initial Global Forum peer review, Bulgaria amended its legislative framework to address an issue identified, effective from 22 May 2018.

With respect to the exchange of information under the AEOI Standard, Bulgaria:

- is a Party to the Convention on Mutual Administrative Assistance in Tax Matters and activated the associated CRS Multilateral Competent Authority Agreement in time for exchanges in 2017;
- has in place European Directive 2011/16/EU on Administrative Cooperation in the Field of Taxation as amended by Directive 2014/107/EU; and
- has in place European Union agreements with five European third countries.[1]

Detailed findings

The detailed findings for Bulgaria are below, organised per Core Requirement (CR) and sub-requirement (SR), as extracted from the AEOI Terms of Reference (www.oecd.org/tax/transparency/documents/aeoi-terms-of-reference.pdf).

CR1 Domestic legal framework: Jurisdictions should have a domestic legislative framework in place that requires all Reporting Financial Institutions to conduct the due diligence and reporting procedures in the CRS, and that provides for the effective implementation of the CRS as set out therein.

Determination: In Place

Bulgaria's domestic legislative framework is in place and contains all of the key aspects of the CRS and its Commentary requiring Reporting Financial Institutions to conduct the due diligence and reporting procedures (SRs 1.1 – 1.3). It also provides for a framework to enforce the requirements (SR 1.4).

SR 1.1 Jurisdictions should define the scope of Reporting Financial Institutions consistently with the CRS.

Bulgaria has defined the scope of Reporting Financial Institutions in its domestic legislative framework in accordance with the CRS and its Commentary.

Recommendations:

No recommendations made.

SR 1.2 Jurisdictions should define the scope of Financial Accounts and Reportable Accounts consistently with the CRS and incorporate the due diligence procedures to identify them.

Bulgaria has defined the scope of the Financial Accounts that are required to be reported in its domestic legislative framework and incorporated the due diligence procedures that must be applied to identify them in accordance with the CRS and its Commentary.

Recommendations:

No recommendations made.

SR 1.3 Jurisdictions should incorporate the reporting requirements contained in Section I of the CRS into their domestic legislative framework.

Bulgaria has incorporated the reporting requirements in its domestic legislative framework in accordance with the CRS and its Commentary.

Recommendations:

No recommendations made.

SR 1.4 Jurisdictions should have a legislative framework in place that allows for the enforcement of the requirements of the CRS in practice.

Bulgaria has a legislative framework in place to enforce the requirements in accordance with the CRS and its Commentary.

Recommendations:

No recommendations made.

CR2 International legal framework: Jurisdictions should have exchange relationships in effect with all Interested Appropriate Partners as committed to and that provide for the exchange of information in accordance with the Model CAA.

Determination: In Place

Bulgaria's international legal framework to exchange the information is in place, is consistent with the Model CAA and its Commentary and provides for exchange with all of Bulgaria's Interested Appropriate Partners (i.e. all jurisdictions that are interested in receiving information from Bulgaria and that meet the required standard in relation to confidentiality and data safeguards). (SRs 2.1 – 2.3)

SR 2.1 Jurisdictions should have exchange agreements in effect with all Interested Appropriate Partners that permit the automatic exchange of CRS information.

Bulgaria has exchange agreements that permit the automatic exchange of CRS information in effect with all its Interested Appropriate Partners.

Recommendations:

No recommendations made.

SR 2.2 Such an exchange agreement should be put in place without undue delay, following the receipt of an expression of interest from an Interested Appropriate Partner.

Bulgaria put in place its exchange agreements without undue delay.

Recommendations:

No recommendations made.

SR 2.3 Jurisdictions should ensure that the exchange agreements in effect provide for the exchange of information in accordance with the requirements of the Model CAA.

Bulgaria's exchange agreements provide for the exchange of information in accordance with the requirements of the Model CAA.

Recommendations:

No recommendations made.

Comments by the assessed jurisdiction

No comments made.

Note

[1] Andorra, Liechtenstein, Monaco, San Marino and Switzerland.

Canada

Overall findings

Canada's legal framework implementing the AEOI Standard is in place but needs improvement in order to be fully consistent with the requirements of the AEOI Terms of Reference. While Canada's international legal framework to exchange the information with all of Canada's Interested Appropriate Partners (CR2) is consistent with the requirements, its domestic legislative framework requiring Reporting Financial Institutions to conduct the due diligence and reporting procedures (CR1) has deficiencies significant to the proper functioning of elements of the AEOI Standard. More specifically, Canada's legislative framework does not incorporate the definition of Investment Entity in line with the requirements and provides for a jurisdiction-specific Non-Reporting Financial Institution that does not meet the requirements.

The methodology used for the peer reviews and that therefore underpins this report is outlined in Chapter 2.

Overall determination on the legal framework: In Place But **Needs Improvement**

Conclusions on the legal framework

General context

Canada commenced exchanges under the AEOI Standard in 2018.

In order to provide for Reporting Financial Institutions to collect and report the information to be exchanged, Canada:

- enacted Part XIX of the Income Tax Act (ITA);
- Introduced Sections 9005 and 9006 of the Income Tax Regulations; and
- issued further guidance, which is not legally binding.

Under this framework Reporting Financial Institutions were required to commence the due diligence procedures in relation to New Accounts from 1 July 2017. With respect to Preexisting Accounts, Reporting Financial Institutions were required to complete due diligence procedures on High Value Individual Accounts by 31 December 2018 and on Lower Value Individual Accounts and Entity Accounts by 31 December 2019.

Following the initial Global Forum peer review, Canada amended its legislative framework to address issues identified, effective from 10 July 2020.

With respect to the exchange of information under the AEOI Standard, Canada:

- is a Party to the Convention on Mutual Administrative Assistance in Tax Matters and activated the associated CRS Multilateral Competent Authority Agreement in time for exchanges in 2018; and
- put in place two bilateral agreements.[1]

Detailed findings

The detailed findings for Canada are below, organised per Core Requirement (CR) and sub-requirement (SR), as extracted from the AEOI Terms of Reference (www.oecd.org/tax/transparency/documents/aeoi-terms-of-reference.pdf).

CR1 Domestic legal framework: Jurisdictions should have a domestic legislative framework in place that requires all Reporting Financial Institutions to conduct the due diligence and reporting procedures in the CRS, and that provides for the effective implementation of the CRS as set out therein.

Determination: In Place But **Needs Improvement**

Canada's domestic legislative framework is in place and contains most of the key aspects of the CRS and its Commentary requiring Reporting Financial Institutions to conduct the due diligence and reporting procedures, but it needs improvement in relation to the scope of Reporting Financial Institutions required to report information (SR 1.1). More specifically, Canada's legislative framework does not incorporate the definition of Investment Entity in line with the requirements, and provides for a jurisdiction-specific Non-Reporting Financial Institution that does not meet the requirements.

SR 1.1 Jurisdictions should define the scope of Reporting Financial Institutions consistently with the CRS.

Canada has defined the scope of Reporting Financial Institutions in its domestic legislative framework in a manner that is largely consistent with the CRS and its Commentary. However, deficiencies have been identified. More specifically, Canada's legislative framework does not fully incorporate the definition of Investment Entity in line with the requirements. In addition, Canada's legislative framework provides for a jurisdiction-specific Non-Reporting Financial Institution that does not meet the requirements. The definition of Reporting Financial Institutions, including the provision of Non-Reporting Financial Institutions, is material to the proper functioning of the AEOI Standard.

Recommendations:

Canada should amend its domestic legislative framework to ensure that its definition of Investment Entity includes all relevant Entities, not only those promoting or representing themselves to the public as an investment vehicle.

Canada should amend its domestic legislative framework to remove Labour Sponsored Venture Capital Corporations (LSVCCs) from its jurisdiction-specific list of Non-Reporting Financial Institutions as they do not meet the requirements, including not being established to provide benefits upon retirement, disability or death and not having limits on the contributions as required.

SR 1.2 Jurisdictions should define the scope of Financial Accounts and Reportable Accounts consistently with the CRS and incorporate the due diligence procedures to identify them.

Canada has defined the scope of the Financial Accounts that are required to be reported in its domestic legislative framework and incorporated the due diligence procedures that must be applied to identify them in accordance with the CRS and its Commentary.

Recommendations:

No recommendations made.

SR 1.3 Jurisdictions should incorporate the reporting requirements contained in Section I of the CRS into their domestic legislative framework.

Canada has incorporated the reporting requirements in its domestic legislative framework in accordance with the CRS and its Commentary.

Recommendations:

No recommendations made.

SR 1.4 Jurisdictions should have a legislative framework in place that allows for the enforcement of the requirements of the CRS in practice.

Canada has a legislative framework in place to enforce the requirements in accordance with the CRS and its Commentary.

Recommendations:

No recommendations made.

CR2 International legal framework: Jurisdictions should have exchange relationships in effect with all Interested Appropriate Partners as committed to and that provide for the exchange of information in accordance with the Model CAA.

Determination: In Place

Canada's international legal framework to exchange the information is in place, is consistent with the Model CAA and its Commentary and provides for exchange with all of Canada's Interested Appropriate Partners (i.e. all jurisdictions that are interested in receiving information from Canada and that meet the required standard in relation to confidentiality and data safeguards). (SRs 2.1 – 2.3)

SR 2.1 Jurisdictions should have exchange agreements in effect with all Interested Appropriate Partners that permit the automatic exchange of CRS information.

Canada has exchange agreements that permit the automatic exchange of CRS information in effect with all its Interested Appropriate Partners.

Recommendations:

No recommendations made.

SR 2.2 Such an exchange agreement should be put in place without undue delay, following the receipt of an expression of interest from an Interested Appropriate Partner.

Canada put in place its exchange agreements without undue delay.

Recommendations:

No recommendations made.

SR 2.3 Jurisdictions should ensure that the exchange agreements in effect provide for the exchange of information in accordance with the requirements of the Model CAA.

Canada's exchange agreements provide for the exchange of information in accordance with the requirements of the Model CAA.

Recommendations:

No recommendations made.

Comments by the assessed jurisdiction

No comments made.

Note

[1] With Hong Kong (China) and Singapore. Canada has also activated a relationship under the CRS MCAA with Singapore.

Cayman Islands

Overall findings

The Cayman Islands' legal framework implementing the AEOI Standard is in place and is consistent with the requirements of the AEOI Terms of Reference. This includes the Cayman Islands' domestic legislative framework requiring Reporting Financial Institutions to conduct the due diligence and reporting procedures (CR1) and its international legal framework to exchange the information with all of the Cayman Islands' Interested Appropriate Partners (CR2).

The methodology used for the peer reviews and that therefore underpins this report is outlined in Chapter 2.

Overall determination on the legal framework: In Place

Conclusions on the legal framework

General context

The Cayman Islands commenced exchanges under the AEOI Standard in 2017.

In order to provide for Reporting Financial Institutions to collect and report the information to be exchanged, the Cayman Islands:

- enacted the Tax Information Authority Law (2017 Revision);
- introduced the Tax Information Authority (International Tax Compliance) (Common Reporting Standard) Regulations, (2018 Revision), further amended in 2020;
- published further guidance, most recently revised March 2018, which is not legally binding.

Under this framework Reporting Financial Institutions were required to commence the due diligence procedures in relation to New Accounts from 1 January 2016. With respect to Preexisting Accounts, Reporting Financial Institutions were required to complete the due diligence procedures on High Value Individual Accounts by 31 December 2016 and on Lower Value Individual Accounts and Entity Accounts by 31 December 2017.

Following the initial Global Forum peer review, the Cayman Islands amended its legislative framework to address an issue identified, effective from 15 March 2018.

With respect to the exchange of information under the AEOI Standard, the Cayman Islands:

- has the Convention on Mutual Administrative Assistance in Tax Matters in place[1] and activated the associated CRS Multilateral Competent Authority Agreement in time for exchanges in 2017; and
- put in place three bilateral agreements.[2]

Detailed findings

The detailed findings for the Cayman Islands are below, organised per Core Requirement (CR) and sub-requirement (SR), as extracted from the AEOI Terms of Reference (www.oecd.org/tax/transparency/documents/aeoi-terms-of-reference.pdf).

CR1 Domestic legal framework: Jurisdictions should have a domestic legislative framework in place that requires all Reporting Financial Institutions to conduct the due diligence and reporting procedures in the CRS, and that provides for the effective implementation of the CRS as set out therein.

Determination: In Place

The Cayman Islands' domestic legislative framework is in place and contains all of the key aspects of the CRS and its Commentary requiring Reporting Financial Institutions to conduct the due diligence and reporting procedures (SRs 1.1 – 1.3). It also provides for a framework to enforce the requirements (SR 1.4).

SR 1.1 Jurisdictions should define the scope of Reporting Financial Institutions consistently with the CRS.

The Cayman Islands has defined the scope of Reporting Financial Institutions in its domestic legislative framework in accordance with the CRS and its Commentary.

Recommendations:

No recommendations made.

SR 1.2 Jurisdictions should define the scope of Financial Accounts and Reportable Accounts consistently with the CRS and incorporate the due diligence procedures to identify them.

The Cayman Islands has defined the scope of the Financial Accounts that are required to be reported in its domestic legislative framework and incorporated the due diligence procedures that must be applied to identify them in accordance with the CRS and its Commentary.

Recommendations:

No recommendations made.

SR 1.3 Jurisdictions should incorporate the reporting requirements contained in Section I of the CRS into their domestic legislative framework.

The Cayman Islands has incorporated the reporting requirements in its domestic legislative framework in accordance with the CRS and its Commentary.

Recommendations:

No recommendations made.

SR 1.4 Jurisdictions should have a legislative framework in place that allows for the enforcement of the requirements of the CRS in practice.

The Cayman Islands has a legislative framework in place to enforce the requirements in accordance with the CRS and its Commentary.

Recommendations:

No recommendations made.

CR2 International legal framework: Jurisdictions should have exchange relationships in effect with all Interested Appropriate Partners as committed to and that provide for the exchange of information in accordance with the Model CAA.

Determination: In Place

The Cayman Islands' international legal framework to exchange the information is in place, is consistent with the Model CAA and its Commentary and provides for exchange with all of the Cayman Islands' Interested Appropriate Partners (i.e. all jurisdictions that are interested in receiving information from the Cayman Islands and that meet the required standard in relation to confidentiality and data safeguards). (SRs 2.1 – 2.3)

SR 2.1 Jurisdictions should have exchange agreements in effect with all Interested Appropriate Partners that permit the automatic exchange of CRS information.

The Cayman Islands has exchange agreements that permit the automatic exchange of CRS information in effect with all its Interested Appropriate Partners.

Recommendations:

No recommendations made.

SR 2.2 Such an exchange agreement should be put in place without undue delay, following the receipt of an expression of interest from an Interested Appropriate Partner.

The Cayman Islands put in place its exchange agreements without undue delay.

Recommendations:

No recommendations made.

SR 2.3 Jurisdictions should ensure that the exchange agreements in effect provide for the exchange of information in accordance with the requirements of the Model CAA.

The Cayman Islands' exchange agreements provide for the exchange of information in accordance with the requirements of the Model CAA.

Recommendations:

No recommendations made.

Comments by the assessed jurisdiction

No comments made.

Notes

[1] Through a territorial extension by the United Kingdom.

[2] With Guernsey, the Isle of Man and the United Kingdom.

Chile

Overall findings

Chile's legal framework implementing the AEOI Standard is in place but needs improvement in order to be fully consistent with the requirements of the AEOI Terms of Reference. While Chile's international legal framework to exchange the information with all of Chile's Interested Appropriate Partners (CR2) is consistent with the requirements, Chile's domestic legislative framework requiring Reporting Financial Institutions to conduct the due diligence and reporting procedures (CR1) has a deficiency significant to the proper functioning of an element of the AEOI Standard. More specifically, a deficiency has been identified in Chile's enforcement framework.

The methodology used for the peer reviews and that therefore underpins this report is outlined in Chapter 2.

Overall determination on the legal framework: In Place But **Needs Improvement**

Conclusions on the legal framework

General context

Chile commenced exchanges under the AEOI Standard in 2018.

In order to provide for Reporting Financial Institutions to collect and report the information to be exchanged, Chile:

- enacted Decree N°418, 2017, Ministry of Finance, Article 62 ter of the Tax Code which was introduced by Act 21.047; and
- introduced secondary legislation in Resolución Ex. SII N°48 of 31 May 2018 and Resolución Ex. Ministry of Finance N°173 of 27 June 2018.

Under this framework Reporting Financial Institutions were required to commence the due diligence procedures in relation to New Accounts from 1 July 2017. With respect to Preexisting Accounts, Reporting Financial Institutions were required to complete the due diligence procedures on High Value Individual Accounts by 30 June 2018 and on Lower Value Individual Accounts and Entity Accounts by 30 June 2019.

With respect to the exchange of information under the AEOI Standard, Chile is a Party to the Convention on Mutual Administrative Assistance in Tax Matters and activated the associated CRS Multilateral Competent Authority Agreement in time for exchanges in 2018.

Detailed findings

The detailed findings for Chile are below, organised per Core Requirement (CR) and sub-requirement (SR), as extracted from the AEOI Terms of Reference (www.oecd.org/tax/transparency/documents/aeoi-terms-of-reference.pdf).

CR1 Domestic legal framework: Jurisdictions should have a domestic legislative framework in place that requires all Reporting Financial Institutions to conduct the due diligence and reporting procedures in the CRS, and that provides for the effective implementation of the CRS as set out therein.

Determination: In Place But **Needs Improvement**

Chile's domestic legislative framework is in place and contains most of the key aspects of the CRS and its Commentary requiring Reporting Financial Institutions to conduct the due diligence and reporting procedures, but it needs improvement in relation to the framework to enforce the requirements (SR 1.4). More specifically, Chile's legislative framework does not include rules to prevent Financial Institutions, persons or intermediaries from adopting practices intended to circumvent the due diligence and reporting requirements.

SR 1.1 Jurisdictions should define the scope of Reporting Financial Institutions consistently with the CRS.

Chile has defined the scope of Reporting Financial Institutions in its domestic legislative framework in accordance with the CRS and its Commentary. While a deficiency has been identified concerning making explicit how to interpret the term Investment Entity, given there is nothing to suggest the interpretation would otherwise be incorrect, the deficiency is considered to be relatively minor and its impact not to be material.

Recommendations:

Chile should amend its domestic legislative framework to require the term Investment Entity to be interpreted consistently with similar language defining "financial institution" in the Financial Action Task Force Recommendations.

SR 1.2 Jurisdictions should define the scope of Financial Accounts and Reportable Accounts consistently with the CRS and incorporate the due diligence procedures to identify them.

Chile has defined the scope of the Financial Accounts that are required to be reported in its domestic legislative framework and incorporated the due diligence procedures that must be applied to identify them in accordance with the CRS and its Commentary.

Recommendations:

No recommendations made.

SR 1.3 Jurisdictions should incorporate the reporting requirements contained in Section I of the CRS into their domestic legislative framework.

Chile has incorporated the reporting requirements in its domestic legislative framework in accordance with the CRS and its Commentary.

Recommendations:

No recommendations made.

SR 1.4 Jurisdictions should have a legislative framework in place that allows for the enforcement of the requirements of the CRS in practice.

Chile has a legislative framework in place to enforce the requirements in a manner that is largely consistent with the CRS and its Commentary. However, a deficiency has been identified. More specifically, Chile's domestic legislative framework does not contain rules to prevent Financial Institutions, persons or intermediaries from adopting practices intended to circumvent the due diligence and reporting procedures as required. This is a key element of the required enforcement framework and is therefore material to the proper functioning of the AEOI Standard.

Recommendations:

Chile should amend its legislative framework to include rules to prevent Financial Institutions, persons and intermediaries from adopting practices intended to circumvent the due diligence and reporting procedures.

CR2 International legal framework: Jurisdictions should have exchange relationships in effect with all Interested Appropriate Partners as committed to and that provide for the exchange of information in accordance with the Model CAA.

Determination: In Place

Chile's international legal framework to exchange the information is in place, is consistent with the Model CAA and its Commentary and provides for exchange with all of Chile's Interested Appropriate Partners (i.e. all jurisdictions that are interested in receiving information from Chile and that meet the required standard in relation to confidentiality and data safeguards). (SRs 2.1 – 2.3)

SR 2.1 Jurisdictions should have exchange agreements in effect with all Interested Appropriate Partners that permit the automatic exchange of CRS information.

Chile has exchange agreements that permit the automatic exchange of CRS information in effect with all its Interested Appropriate Partners.

Recommendations:

No recommendations made.

SR 2.2 Such an exchange agreement should be put in place without undue delay, following the receipt of an expression of interest from an Interested Appropriate Partner.

Chile put in place its exchange agreements without undue delay.

Recommendations:

No recommendations made.

SR 2.3 Jurisdictions should ensure that the exchange agreements in effect provide for the exchange of information in accordance with the requirements of the Model CAA.

Chile's exchange agreements provide for the exchange of information in accordance with the requirements of the Model CAA.

Recommendations:

No recommendations made.

Comments by the assessed jurisdiction

Chile would like to express its appreciation for the work done by the Global Forum Secretariat, the AEOI Assessment Panel and the AEOI Peer Review Group in evaluating Chile's legal frameworks implementing the AEOI Standard. Chile also thanks the Secretariat of the Global Forum for its valuable assistance throughout this process. Chile supports the work of the Global Forum, remains fully committed to the effective exchange of information and will continue working towards ensuring full compliance with the AEOI Standard.

China (People's Republic of)

Overall findings

China's legal framework implementing the AEOI Standard is in place and is consistent with the requirements of the AEOI Terms of Reference. This includes China's domestic legislative framework requiring Reporting Financial Institutions to conduct the due diligence and reporting procedures (CR1) and its international legal framework to exchange the information with all of China's Interested Appropriate Partners (CR2).

The methodology used for the peer reviews and that therefore underpins this report is outlined in Chapter 2.

Overall determination on the legal framework: In Place

Conclusions on the legal framework

General context

China commenced exchanges under the AEOI Standard in 2018.

In order to provide for Reporting Financial Institutions to collect and report the information to be exchanged, China:

- issued the Regulations of Due Diligence on Financial Accounts of Non-residents for Tax Purposes; and
- published further guidance, which is legally binding.

Under this framework Reporting Financial Institutions were required to commence the due diligence procedures in relation to New Accounts from 1 July 2017. With respect to Preexisting Accounts, Reporting Financial Institutions were required to complete the due diligence procedures on High Value Individual Accounts by 31 December 2017 and on Lower Value Individual Accounts and Entity Accounts by 31 December 2018.

During the initial Global Forum peer review, China made various amendments to its legislative framework, the last of which was effective from 16 September 2020.

With respect to the exchange of information under the AEOI Standard, China:

- is a Party to the Convention on Mutual Administrative Assistance in Tax Matters and activated the associated CRS Multilateral Competent Authority Agreement in time for exchanges in 2018; and
- put in place a bilateral agreement.[1]

Detailed findings

The detailed findings for China are below, organised per Core Requirement (CR) and sub-requirement (SR), as extracted from the AEOI Terms of Reference (www.oecd.org/tax/transparency/documents/aeoi-terms-of-reference.pdf).

CR1 Domestic legal framework: Jurisdictions should have a domestic legislative framework in place that requires all Reporting Financial Institutions to conduct the due diligence and reporting procedures in the CRS, and that provides for the effective implementation of the CRS as set out therein.

Determination: In Place

China's domestic legislative framework is in place and contains all of the key aspects of the CRS and its Commentary requiring Reporting Financial Institutions to conduct the due diligence and reporting procedures (SRs 1.1 – 1.3). It also provides for a framework to enforce the requirements (SR 1.4).

SR 1.1 Jurisdictions should define the scope of Reporting Financial Institutions consistently with the CRS.

China has defined the scope of Reporting Financial Institutions in its domestic legislative framework in accordance with the CRS and its Commentary.

Recommendations:

No recommendations made.

SR 1.2 Jurisdictions should define the scope of Financial Accounts and Reportable Accounts consistently with the CRS and incorporate the due diligence procedures to identify them.

China has defined the scope of the Financial Accounts that are required to be reported in its domestic legislative framework and incorporated the due diligence procedures that must be applied to identify them in accordance with the CRS and its Commentary.

Recommendations:

No recommendations made.

SR 1.3 Jurisdictions should incorporate the reporting requirements contained in Section I of the CRS into their domestic legislative framework.

China has incorporated the reporting requirements in its domestic legislative framework in accordance with the CRS and its Commentary.

Recommendations:

No recommendations made.

SR 1.4 Jurisdictions should have a legislative framework in place that allows for the enforcement of the requirements of the CRS in practice.

China has a legislative framework in place to enforce the requirements in accordance with the CRS and its Commentary.

Recommendations:

No recommendations made.

CR2 International legal framework: Jurisdictions should have exchange relationships in effect with all Interested Appropriate Partners as committed to and that provide for the exchange of information in accordance with the Model CAA.

Determination: In Place

China's international legal framework to exchange the information is in place and consistent with the Model CAA and its Commentary and provides for exchange with all of China's Interested Appropriate Partners (i.e. all jurisdictions that are interested in receiving information from China and that meet the required standard in relation to confidentiality and data safeguards). (SRs 2.1 – 2.3)

SR 2.1 Jurisdictions should have exchange agreements in effect with all Interested Appropriate Partners that permit the automatic exchange of CRS information.

China has exchange agreements that permit the automatic exchange of CRS information in effect with all its Interested Appropriate Partners.

Recommendations:

No recommendations made.

SR 2.2 Such an exchange agreement should be put in place without undue delay, following the receipt of an expression of interest from an Interested Appropriate Partner.

China put in place its exchange agreements without undue delay.

Recommendations:

No recommendations made.

SR 2.3 Jurisdictions should ensure that the exchange agreements in effect provide for the exchange of information in accordance with the requirements of the Model CAA.

China's exchange agreements provide for the exchange of information in accordance with the requirements of the Model CAA.

Recommendations:

No recommendations made.

Comments by the assessed jurisdiction

No comments made.

Note

[1] With Hong Kong (China).

Colombia

Overall findings

Colombia's legal framework implementing the AEOI Standard is in place and is consistent with the requirements of the AEOI Terms of Reference. This includes Colombia's domestic legislative framework requiring Reporting Financial Institutions to conduct the due diligence and reporting procedures (CR1) and its international legal framework to exchange the information with all of Colombia's Interested Appropriate Partners (CR2).

The methodology used for the peer reviews and that therefore underpins this report is outlined in Chapter 2.

Overall determination on the legal framework: In Place

Conclusions on the legal framework

General context

Colombia commenced exchanges under the AEOI Standard in 2017.

In order to provide for Reporting Financial Institutions to collect and report the information to be exchanged, Colombia:

- enacted Law 1661 of 2013 and introduced articles 631-4, , 631-5 and 631-6 of the Colombian Tax Code;
- introduced Resolutions 78 of 2020 and 44 of 2021, as issued by the Colombian Tax and Customs Authority; and
- introduced Resolution 4 of 2020.

Under this framework Reporting Financial Institutions were required to commence the due diligence procedures in relation to New Accounts from 1 January 2016. With respect to Preexisting Accounts, Reporting Financial Institutions were required to complete the due diligence procedures on High Value Individual Accounts by 31 December 2016 and on Lower Value Individual Accounts and Entity Accounts by 31 December 2017.

Following the initial Global Forum peer review, Colombia made various amendments to its legislative framework to address issues identified, the last of which will be effective from 1 January 2021.

With respect to the exchange of information under the AEOI Standard, Colombia is a Party to the Convention on Mutual Administrative Assistance in Tax Matters and activated the associated CRS Multilateral Competent Authority Agreement in time for exchanges in 2017.

Detailed findings

The detailed findings for Colombia are below, organised per Core Requirement (CR) and sub-requirement (SR), as extracted from the AEOI Terms of Reference (www.oecd.org/tax/transparency/documents/aeoi-terms-of-reference.pdf).

CR1 Domestic legal framework: Jurisdictions should have a domestic legislative framework in place that requires all Reporting Financial Institutions to conduct the due diligence and reporting procedures in the CRS, and that provides for the effective implementation of the CRS as set out therein.

Determination: In Place

Colombia's domestic legislative framework is in place and contains all of the key aspects of the CRS and its Commentary requiring Reporting Financial Institutions to conduct the due diligence and reporting procedures (SRs 1.1 – 1.3). It also provides for a framework to enforce the requirements (SR 1.4).

SR 1.1 Jurisdictions should define the scope of Reporting Financial Institutions consistently with the CRS.

Colombia defined the scope of Reporting Financial Institutions in its domestic legislative framework in accordance with the CRS and its Commentary.

Recommendations:

No recommendations made.

SR 1.2 Jurisdictions should define the scope of Financial Accounts and Reportable Accounts consistently with the CRS and incorporate the due diligence procedures to identify them.

Colombia has defined the scope of the Financial Accounts that are required to be reported in its domestic legislative framework and incorporated the due diligence procedures that must be applied to identify them in accordance with the CRS and its Commentary.

Recommendations:

No recommendations made.

SR 1.3 Jurisdictions should incorporate the reporting requirements contained in Section I of the CRS into their domestic legislative framework.

Colombia has incorporated the reporting requirements in its domestic legislative framework in accordance with the CRS and its Commentary.

Recommendations:

No recommendations made.

SR 1.4 Jurisdictions should have a legislative framework in place that allows for the enforcement of the requirements of the CRS in practice.

Colombia has a legislative framework in place to enforce the requirements in accordance with the CRS and its Commentary.

Recommendations:

No recommendations made.

CR2 International legal framework: Jurisdictions should have exchange relationships in effect with all Interested Appropriate Partners as committed to and that provide for the exchange of information in accordance with the Model CAA.

Determination: In Place

Colombia's international legal framework to exchange the information is in place, is consistent with the Model CAA and its Commentary and provides for exchange with all of Colombia's Interested Appropriate

Partners (i.e. all jurisdictions that are interested in receiving information from Colombia and that meet the required standard in relation to confidentiality and data safeguards). (SRs 2.1 – 2.3)

SR 2.1 Jurisdictions should have exchange agreements in effect with all Interested Appropriate Partners that permit the automatic exchange of CRS information.

Colombia has exchange agreements that permit the automatic exchange of CRS information in effect with all its Interested Appropriate Partners.

Recommendations:

No recommendations made.

SR 2.2 Such an exchange agreement should be put in place without undue delay, following the receipt of an expression of interest from an Interested Appropriate Partner.

Colombia put in place its exchange agreements without undue delay.

Recommendations:

No recommendations made.

SR 2.3 Jurisdictions should ensure that the exchange agreements in effect provide for the exchange of information in accordance with the requirements of the Model CAA.

Colombia's exchange agreements provide for the exchange of information in accordance with the requirements of the Model CAA.

Recommendations:

No recommendations made.

Comments by the assessed jurisdiction

No comments made.

Cook Islands

Overall findings

The Cook Islands' legal framework implementing the AEOI Standard is in place and is consistent with the requirements of the AEOI Terms of Reference. This includes the Cook Islands' domestic legislative framework requiring Reporting Financial Institutions to conduct the due diligence and reporting procedures (CR1) and its international legal framework to exchange the information with all of the Cook Islands' Interested Appropriate Partners (CR2).

The methodology used for the peer reviews and that therefore underpins this report is outlined in Chapter 2.

Overall determination on the legal framework: In Place

Conclusions on the legal framework

General context

The Cook Islands commenced exchanges under the AEOI Standard in 2018.

In order to provide for Reporting Financial Institutions to collect and report the information to be exchanged, the Cook Islands:

- enacted amendments to the Income Tax Act 1997;
- issued the Income Tax (Automatic Exchange of Financial Account Information) Regulations 2017; and
- published guidance, which is not legally binding.

Under this framework Reporting Financial Institutions were required to commence the due diligence procedures in relation to New Accounts from 1 January 2017. With respect to Preexisting Accounts, Reporting Financial Institutions were required to complete the due diligence procedures on High Value Individual Accounts by 31 December 2017 and on Lower Value Individual Accounts and Entity Accounts by 31 December 2018.

Following the initial Global Forum peer review, the Cook Islands amended its legislative framework to address an issue identified, effective from 4 December 2019.

With respect to the exchange of information under the AEOI Standard, the Cook Islands is a Party to the Convention on Mutual Administrative Assistance in Tax Matters and activated the associated CRS Multilateral Competent Authority Agreement in time for exchanges in 2018.

Detailed findings

The detailed findings for the Cook Islands are below, organised per Core Requirement (CR) and sub-requirement (SR), as extracted from the AEOI Terms of Reference (www.oecd.org/tax/transparency/documents/aeoi-terms-of-reference.pdf).

CR1 Domestic legal framework: Jurisdictions should have a domestic legislative framework in place that requires all Reporting Financial Institutions to conduct the due diligence and reporting procedures in the CRS, and that provides for the effective implementation of the CRS as set out therein.

Determination: In Place

The Cook Islands' domestic legislative framework is in place and contains all of the key aspects of the CRS and its Commentary requiring Reporting Financial Institutions to conduct the due diligence and reporting procedures (SRs 1.1 – 1.3). It also provides for a framework to enforce the requirements (SR 1.4).

SR 1.1 Jurisdictions should define the scope of Reporting Financial Institutions consistently with the CRS.

The Cook Islands has defined the scope of Reporting Financial Institutions in its domestic legislative framework in accordance with the CRS and its Commentary.

Recommendations:

No recommendations made.

SR 1.2 Jurisdictions should define the scope of Financial Accounts and Reportable Accounts consistently with the CRS and incorporate the due diligence procedures to identify them.

The Cook Islands has defined the scope of the Financial Accounts that are required to be reported in its domestic legislative framework and incorporated the due diligence procedures that must be applied to identify them in accordance with the CRS and its Commentary.

Recommendations:

No recommendations made.

SR 1.3 Jurisdictions should incorporate the reporting requirements contained in Section I of the CRS into their domestic legislative framework.

The Cook Islands has incorporated the reporting requirements in its domestic legislative framework in accordance with the CRS and its Commentary.

Recommendations:

No recommendations made.

SR 1.4 Jurisdictions should have a legislative framework in place that allows for the enforcement of the requirements of the CRS in practice.

The Cook Islands has a legislative framework in place to enforce the requirements in accordance with the CRS and its Commentary.

Recommendations:

No recommendations made.

CR2 International legal framework: Jurisdictions should have exchange relationships in effect with all Interested Appropriate Partners as committed to and that provide for the exchange of information in accordance with the Model CAA.

Determination: In Place

The Cook Islands' international legal framework to exchange the information is in place, is consistent with the Model CAA and its Commentary and provides for exchange with all of the Cook Islands' Interested Appropriate Partners (i.e. all jurisdictions that are interested in receiving information from the Cook Islands and that meet the required standard in relation to confidentiality and data safeguards). (SRs 2.1 – 2.3)

SR 2.1 Jurisdictions should have exchange agreements in effect with all Interested Appropriate Partners that permit the automatic exchange of CRS information.

The Cook Islands has exchange agreements that permit the automatic exchange of CRS information in effect with all its Interested Appropriate Partners.

Recommendations:

No recommendations made.

SR 2.2 Such an exchange agreement should be put in place without undue delay, following the receipt of an expression of interest from an Interested Appropriate Partner.

The Cook Islands put in place its exchange agreements without undue delay.

Recommendations:

No recommendations made.

SR 2.3 Jurisdictions should ensure that the exchange agreements in effect provide for the exchange of information in accordance with the requirements of the Model CAA.

The Cook Islands' exchange agreements provide for the exchange of information in accordance with the requirements of the Model CAA.

Recommendations:

No recommendations made.

Comments by the assessed jurisdiction

No comments made.

Costa Rica

Overall findings

Costa Rica's legal framework implementing the AEOI Standard is not in place in accordance with the requirements of the AEOI Terms of Reference. While Costa Rica's international legal framework to exchange the information with all of Costa Rica's Interested Appropriate Partners (CR2) is consistent with the requirements, its domestic legislative framework requiring Reporting Financial Institutions to conduct the due diligence and reporting procedures (CR1) has significant deficiencies in areas that are fundamental to the proper functioning of the AEOI Standard. More specifically, deficiencies have been identified with respect to Costa Rica's enforcement framework.

The methodology used for the peer reviews and that therefore underpins this report is outlined in Chapter 2.

Overall determination on the legal framework: Not In Place

Conclusions on the legal framework

General context

Costa Rica commenced exchanges under the AEOI Standard in 2018.

In order to provide for Reporting Financial Institutions to collect and report the information to be exchanged, Costa Rica:

- enacted Article 106 quárter of the General Tax Code Law No. 4755; and
- introduced the Resolution No. DGT-R-006-2017, Resolution No. DGT-R-006-2018 and Resolution No. DGT-R-16-2020.

Under this framework Reporting Financial Institutions were required to commence the due diligence procedures in relation to New Accounts from 1 January 2017. With respect to Preexisting Accounts, Reporting Financial Institutions were required to complete the due diligence procedures on High Value Individual Accounts and on Lower Value Individual Accounts and Entity Accounts by 31 December 2017.

Following the initial Global Forum review, Costa Rica amended its legislative framework to address issues identified, effective from 5 August 2020.

With respect to the exchange of information under the AEOI Standard, Costa Rica is a Party to the Convention on Mutual Administrative Assistance in Tax Matters and activated the associated CRS Multilateral Competent Authority Agreement in time for exchanges in 2018.

Detailed findings

The detailed findings for Costa Rica are below, organised per Core Requirement (CR) and sub-requirement (SR), as extracted from the AEOI Terms of Reference (www.oecd.org/tax/transparency/documents/aeoi-terms-of-reference.pdf).

CR1 Domestic legal framework: Jurisdictions should have a domestic legislative framework in place that requires all Reporting Financial Institutions to conduct the due diligence and reporting procedures in the CRS, and that provides for the effective implementation of the CRS as set out therein.

Determination: Not In Place

Costa Rica's domestic legislative framework is not in place as required as it does not contain key aspects of the CRS and its Commentary. Significant deficiencies have been identified relating to the framework to enforce the requirements (SR 1.4). More specifically, Costa Rica's legislative framework does not require records to be kept by Financial Institutions in accordance with the AEOI Standard and it does not apply sanctions for non-compliance in all cases including where self-certifications have not been obtained for New Accounts.

SR 1.1 Jurisdictions should define the scope of Reporting Financial Institutions consistently with the CRS.

Costa Rica has defined the scope of Reporting Financial Institutions in its domestic legislative framework in accordance with the CRS and its Commentary.

Recommendations:

No recommendations made.

SR 1.2 Jurisdictions should define the scope of Financial Accounts and Reportable Accounts consistently with the CRS and incorporate the due diligence procedures to identify them.

Costa Rica has defined the scope of the Financial Accounts that are required to be reported in its domestic legislative framework and incorporated the due diligence procedures that must be applied to identify them in accordance with the CRS and its Commentary.

Recommendations:

No recommendations made.

SR 1.3 Jurisdictions should incorporate the reporting requirements contained in Section I of the CRS into their domestic legislative framework.

Costa Rica has incorporated the reporting requirements in its domestic legislative framework in accordance with the CRS and its Commentary.

Recommendations:

No recommendations made.

SR 1.4 Jurisdictions should have a legislative framework in place that allows for the enforcement of the requirements of the CRS in practice.

Costa Rica does not have a legislative framework in place to enforce the requirements in a manner that is consistent with the CRS and its Commentary, as significant deficiencies have been identified. More specifically, Costa Rica's domestic legislative framework:

- does not include rules requiring Reporting Financial Institutions to keep records in accordance with the requirements;
- does not include rules that ensure that a Reporting Financial Institution is sanctioned for failing to apply due diligence procedures in accordance with the requirements; and
- does not incorporate measures to ensure that self-certifications are always obtained and validated for New Accounts as required.

These are key elements of the required enforcement framework and are therefore material to the proper functioning of the AEOI Standard.

Recommendations:

Costa Rica should amend its domestic legislative framework to require all Reporting Financial Institutions to keep all of the records required to be maintained, rather than relying only on the requirements contained in the AML framework.

Costa Rica should amend its domestic legislative framework to require Reporting Financial Institutions to maintain records for at least five years from the deadline to report the information, in accordance with the AEOI Standard.

Costa Rica should amend its domestic legislative framework to include sanctions for failure to comply with the due diligence and reporting procedures in accordance with the AEOI Standard.

Costa Rica should amend its domestic legislative framework to include strong measures to ensure that valid self-certifications are always obtained for New Accounts and, more specifically, in the limited circumstances where a valid self-certification is permitted to be obtained after the opening of a New Account.

CR2 International legal framework: Jurisdictions should have exchange relationships in effect with all Interested Appropriate Partners as committed to and that provide for the exchange of information in accordance with the Model CAA.

Determination: In Place

Costa Rica's international legal framework to exchange the information is in place, is consistent with the Model CAA and its Commentary and provides for exchange with all of Costa Rica's Interested Appropriate Partners (i.e. all jurisdictions that are interested in receiving information from Costa Rica and that meet the required standard in relation to confidentiality and data safeguards). (SRs 2.1 – 2.3)

SR 2.1 Jurisdictions should have exchange agreements in effect with all Interested Appropriate Partners that permit the automatic exchange of CRS information.

Costa Rica has exchange agreements that permit the automatic exchange of CRS information in effect with all its Interested Appropriate Partners.

Recommendations:

No recommendations made.

SR 2.2 Such an exchange agreement should be put in place without undue delay, following the receipt of an expression of interest from an Interested Appropriate Partner.

Costa Rica put in place its exchange agreements without undue delay.

Recommendations:

No recommendations made.

SR 2.3 Jurisdictions should ensure that the exchange agreements in effect provide for the exchange of information in accordance with the requirements of the Model CAA.

Costa Rica's exchange agreements provide for the exchange of information in accordance with the requirements of the Model CAA.

Recommendations:

No recommendations made.

Comments by the assessed jurisdiction

The Costa Rica Tax Administration appreciates the assistance provided by the Global Forum experts in this assessment in order to amend our secondary legislation (the Resolution) in accordance with the CRS standard.

The recommendations included in this Report are useful and will be part of the specific regulation regarding the implementation of the CRS standard in the Financial Institutions that we are going to draft together with the Superintendence of Financial Entities (GSFE-SUGEF) and the National Council of Financial Supervision in the upcoming months.

Costa Rica has already introduced Resolution DGT-R-27-2021, dated 20 October 2021, intended to address the recommendation on requiring Reporting Financial Institutions to maintain records for at least five years from the deadline to report the information in accordance with the AEOI Standard, and has accordingly requested a reassessment of this aspect of its legal framework.

We renew our commitment with tax transparency in all of its modalities, and in turn, we are always open to receive comments to improve our internal proceedings in order to provide information with the best quality.

Croatia

Overall findings

Croatia's legal framework implementing the AEOI Standard is in place but needs improvement in order to be fully consistent with the requirements of the AEOI Terms of Reference. While Croatia's international legal framework to exchange the information with all of Croatia's Interested Appropriate Partners (CR2) is consistent with the requirements, Croatia's domestic legislative framework requiring Reporting Financial Institutions to conduct the due diligence and reporting procedures (CR1) has a deficiency in an area significant to the proper functioning of an element of the AEOI Standard. More specifically, a deficiency has been identified with respect to Croatia's enforcement framework.

The methodology used for the peer reviews and that therefore underpins this report is outlined in Chapter 2.

Overall determination on the legal framework: In Place But **Needs Improvement**

Conclusions on the legal framework

General context

Croatia commenced exchanges under the AEOI Standard in 2017.

In order to provide for Reporting Financial Institutions to collect and report the information to be exchanged, Croatia:

- amended its Act on Administrative Cooperation in the Field of Taxation (OG 115/2016);
- introduced an Ordinance on the Automatic Exchange of Information in the field of taxation (OG 18/2017, as amended by an Ordinance published in OG 1/2020); and
- issued further guidance, which is not legally binding.

Under this framework Reporting Financial Institutions were required to commence the due diligence procedures in relation to New Accounts from 1 January 2016. With respect to Preexisting Accounts, Reporting Financial Institutions were required to complete the due diligence procedures on High Value Individual Accounts by 31 December 2016 and on Lower Value Individual Accounts and Entity Accounts by 31 December 2017.

Following the initial Global Forum peer review, Croatia made various amendments to its legislative framework to address issues identified, the last of which was effective from 3 January 2020.

With respect to the exchange of information under the AEOI Standard, Croatia:

- is a Party to the Convention on Mutual Administrative Assistance in Tax Matters and activated the associated CRS Multilateral Competent Authority Agreement in time for exchanges in 2017;
- has in place European Directive 2011/16/EU on Administrative Cooperation in the Field of Taxation, as amended by Directive 2014/107/EU; and
- has in place European Union agreements with five European third countries.[1]

Detailed findings

The detailed findings for Croatia are below, organised per Core Requirement (CR) and sub-requirement (SR), as extracted from the AEOI Terms of Reference (www.oecd.org/tax/transparency/documents/aeoi-terms-of-reference.pdf).

CR1 Domestic legal framework: Jurisdictions should have a domestic legislative framework in place that requires all Reporting Financial Institutions to conduct the due diligence and reporting procedures in the CRS, and that provides for the effective implementation of the CRS as set out therein.

Determination: In Place But **Needs Improvement**

Croatia's domestic legislative framework is in place and contains most of the key aspects of the CRS and its Commentary requiring Reporting Financial Institutions to conduct the due diligence and reporting procedures, but it needs improvement in one area relating to the framework to enforce the requirements (SR 1.4). More specifically, Croatia's domestic legislative framework does not impose sanctions on Account Holders and Controlling Persons for providing a false self-certification.

SR 1.1 Jurisdictions should define the scope of Reporting Financial Institutions consistently with the CRS.

Croatia has defined the scope of Reporting Financial Institutions in its domestic legislative framework in accordance with the CRS and its Commentary.

Recommendations:

No recommendations made.

SR 1.2 Jurisdictions should define the scope of Financial Accounts and Reportable Accounts consistently with the CRS and incorporate the due diligence procedures to identify them.

Croatia has defined the scope of the Financial Accounts that are required to be reported in its domestic legislative framework and incorporated the due diligence procedures that must be applied to identify them in accordance with the CRS and its Commentary.

Recommendations:

No recommendations made.

SR 1.3 Jurisdictions should incorporate the reporting requirements contained in Section I of the CRS into their domestic legislative framework.

Croatia has incorporated the reporting requirements in its domestic legislative framework in accordance with the CRS and its Commentary.

Recommendations:

No recommendations made.

SR 1.4 Jurisdictions should have a legislative framework in place that allows for the enforcement of the requirements of the CRS in practice.

Croatia has a legislative framework in place to enforce the requirements in a manner that is largely consistent with the CRS and its Commentary. However, a deficiency has been identified. More specifically, Croatia's domestic legislative framework does not impose sanctions on Account Holders and Controlling Persons for the provision of a false self-certification. This is a key element of the required enforcement framework and is therefore material to the proper functioning of the AEOI Standard.

Recommendations:

Croatia should amend its domestic legislative framework to include sanctions on Account Holders and Controlling Persons for the provision of a false self-certification.

CR2 International legal framework: Jurisdictions should have exchange relationships in effect with all Interested Appropriate Partners as committed to and that provide for the exchange of information in accordance with the Model CAA.

Determination: In Place

Croatia's international legal framework to exchange the information is in place, is consistent with the Model CAA and its Commentary and provides for exchange with all of Croatia's Interested Appropriate Partners (i.e. all jurisdictions that are interested in receiving information from Croatia and that meet the required standard in relation to confidentiality and data safeguards). (SRs 2.1 – 2.3)

SR 2.1 Jurisdictions should have exchange agreements in effect with all Interested Appropriate Partners that permit the automatic exchange of CRS information.

Croatia has exchange agreements that permit the automatic exchange of CRS information in effect with all its Interested Appropriate Partners.

Recommendations:

No recommendations made.

SR 2.2 Such an exchange agreement should be put in place without undue delay, following the receipt of an expression of interest from an Interested Appropriate Partner.

Croatia put in place its exchange agreements without undue delay.

Recommendations:

No recommendations made.

SR 2.3 Jurisdictions should ensure that the exchange agreements in effect provide for the exchange of information in accordance with the requirements of the Model CAA.

Croatia's exchange agreements provide for the exchange of information in accordance with the requirements of the Model CAA.

Recommendations:

No recommendations made.

Comments by the assessed jurisdiction

No comments made.

Note

[1] Andorra, Liechtenstein, Monaco, San Marino and Switzerland.

Curaçao

Overall findings

Curaçao's legal framework implementing the AEOI Standard is not in place in accordance with the requirements of the AEOI Terms of Reference. This is because Curaçao's domestic legislative framework requiring Reporting Financial Institutions to conduct the due diligence and reporting procedures (CR1) has significant deficiencies in areas that are fundamental to the proper functioning of the AEOI Standard. Most significantly, deficiencies have been identified in Curaçao's enforcement framework and in other key areas.

The methodology used for the peer reviews and that therefore underpins this report is outlined in Chapter 2.

Overall determination on the legal framework: Not In Place

Conclusions on the legal framework

General context

Curaçao commenced exchanges under the AEOI Standard in 2018.

In order to provide for Reporting Financial Institutions to collect and report the information to be exchanged, Curaçao:

- enacted National Ordinance International Assistance Taxation;
- introduced National Decree International Assistance Taxation; and
- issued further guidance, which is not legally binding.

Under this framework Reporting Financial Institutions were required to commence the due diligence procedures in relation to New Accounts from 1 January 2017. With respect to Preexisting Accounts, Reporting Financial Institutions were required to complete the due diligence procedures on High Value Individual Accounts by 31 December 2017 and on Lower Value Individual Accounts and Entity Accounts by 31 December 2018.

With respect to the exchange of information under the AEOI Standard, Curaçao has the Convention on Mutual Administrative Assistance in Tax Matters in place[1] and activated the associated CRS Multilateral Competent Authority Agreement in time for exchanges in 2018.

Detailed findings

The detailed findings for Curaçao are below, organised per Core Requirement (CR) and sub-requirement (SR), as extracted from the AEOI Terms of Reference (www.oecd.org/tax/transparency/documents/aeoi-terms-of-reference.pdf).

CR1 Domestic legal framework: Jurisdictions should have a domestic legislative framework in place that requires all Reporting Financial Institutions to conduct the due diligence and reporting procedures in the CRS, and that provides for the effective implementation of the CRS as set out therein.

Determination: Not In Place

Curaçao's domestic legislative framework is not in place as required as it does not contain several key aspects of the CRS and its Commentary. Significant deficiencies have been identified in relation to the framework to enforce the requirements (SR 1.4). Most significantly, Curaçao's domestic legislative framework does not provide for rules to prevent the circumvention of the reporting and due diligence procedures, does not incorporate sanctions for the provision of false self-certifications and does not contain strong measures to ensure valid self-certifications are always obtained for New Accounts. Moreover, there are deficiencies in relation to the scope of Reporting Financial Institutions required to report information (SR 1.1) and the scope of Financial Accounts required to be reported and the due diligence procedures required to identify them (SR 1.2).

SR 1.1 Jurisdictions should define the scope of Reporting Financial Institutions consistently with the CRS.

Curaçao has defined the scope of Reporting Financial Institutions in its domestic legislative framework in a manner that is largely consistent with the CRS and its Commentary. However, deficiencies have been identified. More specifically, Curaçao's legislative framework:

- classifies certain Entities as Non-Financial Entities, which are not in accordance with the requirements set out in the AEOI Standard;
- does not specify the date as of when Qualified Credit Card Issuers need to implement policies for the returning of overpayments, which is required for them to be treated as Non-Reporting Financial Institutions; and
- does not specify the date as of when Exempt Collective Investment Vehicles are prevented from issuing bearer shares nor the date prior to which any existing bearer shares are required to be redeemed or immobilised, which is required for them to be treated as Non-Reporting Financial Institutions.

The scope of Reporting Financial Institutions, including the specification of Non-Reporting Financial Institutions, is material to the proper functioning of the AEOI Standard.

Recommendations:

Curaçao should amend its domestic legislative framework to remove the classifications of entities held by one single family or a very limited group and Trust Office Foundation ("Stichting administratiekantoor" or STAK) as Non-Financial Entities without regard to the requirements to be classified as such.

Curaçao should amend its domestic legislative framework to require Qualified Credit Card Issuers to implement policies with respect to the returning of overpayments from a specified date in order to be treated as Non-Reporting Financial Institutions.

Curaçao should amend its domestic legislative framework to prevent Exempt Collective Investment Vehicles from issuing bearer shares from a specified date and for any existing bearer shares to be redeemed or immobilised prior to that date in order to be treated as Non-Reporting Financial Institutions.

SR 1.2 Jurisdictions should define the scope of Financial Accounts and Reportable Accounts consistently with the CRS and incorporate the due diligence procedures to identify them.

Curaçao has defined the scope of the Financial Accounts that are required to be reported in its domestic legislative framework and has incorporated the due diligence procedures that must be applied to identify them in a manner that is largely consistent with the CRS and its Commentary. However, deficiencies have been identified. More specifically, Curaçao's legislative framework:

- does not specify the date on which a Preexisting Entity Account is first to be identified;
- does not define Controlling Persons in accordance with the requirements;

- does not specify the date as of when Qualified Credit Card Issuers need to implement policies for the returning of overpayments, which is required for Depository Accounts due to not-returned overpayments to be treated as Excluded Accounts; and
- does not follow the conditions set out in the AEOI Standard for when Reporting Financial Institutions can use existing classifications as Documentary Evidence with respect to Preexisting Entity Accounts.

The scope of Financial Accounts and the due diligence procedures to identify them is material to the proper functioning of the AEOI Standard.

Recommendations:

Curaçao should amend its domestic legislative framework to specify the date on which a Preexisting Entity Account is first to be identified using the USD 250 000 balance or value threshold.

Curaçao should amend its domestic legislative framework to require Reporting Financial Institutions to always identify and determine the reportable status of Controlling Persons in accordance with the AEOI Standard.

Curaçao should amend its domestic legislative framework to define Controlling Persons in accordance with the AEOI Standard, by removing the 25% ownership or share of profits threshold for partnerships in order to ensure the identification of all relevant Controlling Persons of partnerships and legal arrangements similar to partnerships.

Curaçao should amend its domestic legislative framework to require Qualified Credit Card Issuers to implement policies with respect to the returning of overpayments from a specified date in order for Depository Accounts due to not-returned overpayments to be treated as Excluded Accounts.

Curaçao should amend its domestic legislative framework to require Reporting Financial Institutions to only use Documentary Evidence in relation to the due diligence procedures for Preexisting Entity Accounts in accordance with the conditions in the AEOI Standard.

SR 1.3 Jurisdictions should incorporate the reporting requirements contained in Section I of the CRS into their domestic legislative framework.

Curaçao has incorporated the reporting requirements in its domestic legislative framework in accordance with the CRS and its Commentary. While a deficiency has been identified with respect to the reporting of the currency denomination, it is considered to be relatively minor as the CRS XML schema will compel the reporting of a currency type.

Recommendations:

Curaçao should amend its domestic legislative framework to require Reporting Financial Institutions to identify the currency in which each account is denominated.

SR 1.4 Jurisdictions should have a legislative framework in place that allows for the enforcement of the requirements of the CRS in practice.

Curaçao does not have a legislative framework in place to enforce the requirements in a manner that is consistent with the CRS and its Commentary as significant deficiencies have been identified. More specifically, Curaçao's legislative framework:

- does not include rules to prevent Financial Institutions, persons or intermediaries from adopting practices intended to circumvent the due diligence and reporting procedures as required;
- does not include sanctions on Account Holders and Controlling Persons for the provision of a false self-certification; and

- allows self-certifications to be obtained after the opening of the account in circumstances beyond those that are permitted.

These are key elements of the required enforcement framework and are therefore material to the proper functioning of the AEOI Standard.

Recommendations:

Curaçao should amend its domestic legislative framework to introduce rules to prevent Financial Institutions, persons and intermediaries from adopting practices intended to circumvent the due diligence and reporting procedures.

Curaçao should amend its domestic legislative framework to include sanctions on Account Holders and Controlling Persons for the provision of a false self-certification.

Curaçao should amend its domestic legislative framework to limit the circumstances when it is permissible to obtain a valid self-certification after the opening of a New Account in accordance with the requirements.

CR2 International legal framework: Jurisdictions should have exchange relationships in effect with all Interested Appropriate Partners as committed to and that provide for the exchange of information in accordance with the Model CAA.

Determination: In Place

Curaçao's international legal framework to exchange the information is in place, is consistent with the Model CAA and its Commentary and provides for exchange with all of Curaçao's Interested Appropriate Partners (i.e. all jurisdictions that are interested in receiving information from Curaçao and that meet the required standard in relation to confidentiality and data safeguards). (SRs 2.1 – 2.3)

SR 2.1 Jurisdictions should have exchange agreements in effect with all Interested Appropriate Partners that permit the automatic exchange of CRS information.

Curaçao has exchange agreements that permit the automatic exchange of CRS information in effect with all its Interested Appropriate Partners.

Recommendations:

No recommendations made.

SR 2.2 Such an exchange agreement should be put in place without undue delay, following the receipt of an expression of interest from an Interested Appropriate Partner.

Curaçao put in place its exchange agreements without undue delay.

Recommendations:

No recommendations made.

SR 2.3 Jurisdictions should ensure that the exchange agreements in effect provide for the exchange of information in accordance with the requirements of the Model CAA.

Curaçao's exchange agreements provide for the exchange of information in accordance with the requirements of the Model CAA.

Recommendations:

No recommendations made.

Comments by the assessed jurisdiction

No comments made.

Note

[1] Through a territorial extension by the Netherlands.

Cyprus

Overall findings

Cyprus' legal framework implementing the AEOI Standard is in place and is consistent with the requirements of the AEOI Terms of Reference. This includes Cyprus' domestic legislative framework requiring Reporting Financial Institutions to conduct the due diligence and reporting procedures (CR1) and its international legal framework to exchange the information with all of Cyprus' Interested Appropriate Partners (CR2).

The methodology used for the peer reviews and that therefore underpins this report is outlined in Chapter 2.

Overall determination on the legal framework: In Place

Conclusions on the legal framework

General context

Cyprus commenced exchanges under the AEOI Standard in 2017.

In order to provide for Reporting Financial Institutions to collect and report the information to be exchanged, Cyprus:

- incorporated Article 6(16) into the Assessment and Collection of Taxes Law (L4/1978), amended on November 2017;
- enacted the National CRS Decree (161/2016); and
- issued further guidance, which is legally binding and which was updated in May 2020.

Under this framework Reporting Financial Institutions were required to commence the due diligence procedures in relation to New Accounts from 1 January 2016. With respect to Preexisting Accounts, Reporting Financial Institutions were required to complete the due diligence procedures on High Value Individual Accounts by 31 December 2016 and on Lower Value Individual Accounts and Entity Accounts by 31 December 2017.

Following the initial Global Forum peer review, Cyprus amended its legislative framework to address issues identified, effective from 10 November 2017.

With respect to the exchange of information under the AEOI Standard, Cyprus:

- is a Party to the Convention on Mutual Administrative Assistance in Tax Matters and activated the associated CRS Multilateral Competent Authority Agreement in time for exchanges in 2017;
- has in place European Directive 2011/16/EU on Administrative Cooperation in the Field of Taxation as amended by Directive 2014/107/EU; and
- has in place European Union agreements with five European third countries.[1]

Detailed findings

The detailed findings for Cyprus are below, organised per Core Requirement (CR) and sub-requirement (SR), as extracted from the AEOI Terms of Reference (www.oecd.org/tax/transparency/documents/aeoi-terms-of-reference.pdf).

CR1 Domestic legal framework: Jurisdictions should have a domestic legislative framework in place that requires all Reporting Financial Institutions to conduct the due diligence and reporting procedures in the CRS, and that provides for the effective implementation of the CRS as set out therein.

Determination: In Place

Cyprus domestic legislative framework is in place and contains all of the key aspects of the CRS and its Commentary requiring Reporting Financial Institutions to conduct the due diligence and reporting procedures (SRs 1.1 – 1.3). It also provides for a framework to enforce the requirements (SR 1.4).

SR 1.1 Jurisdictions should define the scope of Reporting Financial Institutions consistently with the CRS.

Cyprus has defined the scope of Reporting Financial Institutions in its domestic legislative framework in accordance with the CRS and its Commentary.

Recommendations:

No recommendations made.

SR 1.2 Jurisdictions should define the scope of Financial Accounts and Reportable Accounts consistently with the CRS and incorporate the due diligence procedures to identify them.

Cyprus has defined the scope of the Financial Accounts that are required to be reported in its domestic legislative framework and incorporated the due diligence procedures that must be applied to identify them in accordance with the CRS and its Commentary.

Recommendations:

No recommendations made.

SR 1.3 Jurisdictions should incorporate the reporting requirements contained in Section I of the CRS into their domestic legislative framework.

Cyprus has incorporated the reporting requirements in its domestic legislative framework in accordance with the CRS and its Commentary.

Recommendations:

No recommendations made.

SR 1.4 Jurisdictions should have a legislative framework in place that allows for the enforcement of the requirements of the CRS in practice.

Cyprus has a legislative framework in place to enforce the requirements in accordance with the CRS and its Commentary.

Recommendations:

No recommendations made.

CR2 International legal framework: Jurisdictions should have exchange relationships in effect with all Interested Appropriate Partners as committed to and that provide for the exchange of information in accordance with the Model CAA.

Determination: In Place

Cyprus' international legal framework to exchange the information is in place, is consistent with the Model CAA and its Commentary and provides for exchange with all of Cyprus' Interested Appropriate Partners (i.e. all jurisdictions that are interested in receiving information from Cyprus and that meet the required standard in relation to confidentiality and data safeguards). (SRs 2.1 – 2.3)

SR 2.1 Jurisdictions should have exchange agreements in effect with all Interested Appropriate Partners that permit the automatic exchange of CRS information.

Cyprus has exchange agreements that permit the automatic exchange of CRS information in effect with all its Interested Appropriate Partners.

Recommendations:

No recommendations made.

SR 2.2 Such an exchange agreement should be put in place without undue delay, following the receipt of an expression of interest from an Interested Appropriate Partner.

Cyprus put in place its exchange agreements without undue delay.

Recommendations:

No recommendations made.

SR 2.3 Jurisdictions should ensure that the exchange agreements in effect provide for the exchange of information in accordance with the requirements of the Model CAA.

Cyprus' exchange agreements provide for the exchange of information in accordance with the requirements of the Model CAA.

Recommendations:

No recommendations made.

Comments by the assessed jurisdiction

No comments made.

Note

[1] Andorra, Liechtenstein, Monaco, San Marino and Switzerland.

Czech Republic

Overall findings

The Czech Republic's legal framework implementing the AEOI Standard is in place and is consistent with the requirements of the AEOI Terms of Reference. This includes the Czech Republic's domestic legislative framework requiring Reporting Financial Institutions to conduct the due diligence and reporting procedures (CR1) and its international legal framework to exchange the information with all of the Czech Republic's Interested Appropriate Partners (CR2).

The methodology used for the peer reviews and that therefore underpins this report is outlined in Chapter 2.

Overall determination on the legal framework: In Place

Conclusions on the legal framework

General context

The Czech Republic commenced exchanges under the AEOI Standard in 2017.

In order to provide for Reporting Financial Institutions to collect and report the information to be exchanged, the Czech Republic:

- enacted Act No. 164/2013 Coll. as amended by Act No. 105/2016 and Act No. 80/2019;
- introduced Decree No. 108/2016 Coll. repealed and replaced by Decree No. 26/2019 Coll.;
- issued further guidance, which is not legally binding; and
- made reference to Act No 253/2008 Coll. (as amended) and Act No 37/2021 Coll. implementing the FATF Recommendations for the purposes of the identification of Controlling Persons under the AEOI Standard.

Under this framework Reporting Financial Institutions were required to commence the due diligence procedures in relation to New Accounts from 1 January 2016. With respect to Preexisting Accounts, Reporting Financial Institutions were required to complete the due diligence procedures on High Value Individual Accounts by 31 December 2016 and on Lower Value Individual Accounts and Entity Accounts by 31 December 2017.

Following the initial Global Forum peer review, the Czech Republic made various amendments to its legislative framework to address issues identified, the last of which was effective from 1 June 2021.

With respect to the exchange of information under the AEOI Standard, the Czech Republic:

- is a Party to the Convention on Mutual Administrative Assistance in Tax Matters and activated the associated CRS Multilateral Competent Authority Agreement in time for exchanges in 2017;
- has transposed into its domestic law European Directive 2011/16/EU on Administrative Cooperation in the Field of Taxation as amended by Directive 2014/107/EU; and
- has in place EU agreements with five European third countries.[1]

Detailed findings

The detailed findings for the Czech Republic are below, organised per Core Requirement (CR) and sub-requirement (SR), as extracted from the AEOI Terms of Reference (www.oecd.org/tax/transparency/documents/aeoi-terms-of-reference.pdf).

CR1 Domestic legal framework: Jurisdictions should have a domestic legislative framework in place that requires all Reporting Financial Institutions to conduct the due diligence and reporting procedures in the CRS, and that provides for the effective implementation of the CRS as set out therein.

Determination: In Place

The Czech Republic's domestic legislative framework is in place and contains all of the key aspects of the CRS and its Commentary requiring Reporting Financial Institutions to conduct the due diligence and reporting procedures (SRs 1.1 – 1.3). It also provides a framework to enforce the requirements (SR 1.4).

SR 1.1 Jurisdictions should define the scope of Reporting Financial Institutions consistently with the CRS.

The Czech Republic has defined the scope of Reporting Financial Institutions in its domestic legislative framework in accordance with the CRS and its Commentary.

Recommendations:

No recommendations made.

SR 1.2 Jurisdictions should define the scope of Financial Accounts and Reportable Accounts consistently with the CRS and incorporate the due diligence procedures to identify them.

The Czech Republic has defined the scope of the Financial Accounts that are required to be reported in its domestic legislative framework and incorporated the due diligence procedures that must be applied to identify them in accordance with the CRS and its Commentary.

Recommendations:

No recommendations made.

SR 1.3 Jurisdictions should incorporate the reporting requirements contained in Section I of the CRS into their domestic legislative framework.

The Czech Republic has incorporated the reporting requirements in its domestic legislative framework in accordance with the CRS and its Commentary.

Recommendations:

No recommendations made.

SR 1.4 Jurisdictions should have a legislative framework in place that allows for the enforcement of the requirements of the CRS in practice.

The Czech Republic has a legislative framework in place to enforce the requirements in accordance with the CRS and its Commentary.

Recommendations:

No recommendations made.

CR2 International legal framework: Jurisdictions should have exchange relationships in effect with all Interested Appropriate Partners as committed to and that provide for the exchange of information in accordance with the Model CAA.

Determination: In Place

The Czech Republic's international legal framework to exchange the information is in place, is consistent with the Model CAA and its Commentary and provides for exchange with all of the Czech Republic's Interested Appropriate Partners (i.e. all jurisdictions that are interested in receiving information from the Czech Republic and that meet the required standard in relation to confidentiality and data safeguards). (SRs 2.1 – 2.3)

SR 2.1 Jurisdictions should have exchange agreements in effect with all Interested Appropriate Partners that permit the automatic exchange of CRS information.

The Czech Republic has exchange agreements that permit the automatic exchange of CRS information in effect with all its Interested Appropriate Partners.

Recommendations:

No recommendations made.

SR 2.2 Such an exchange agreement should be put in place without undue delay, following the receipt of an expression of interest from an Interested Appropriate Partner.

The Czech Republic put in place its exchange agreements without undue delay.

Recommendations:

No recommendations made.

SR 2.3 Jurisdictions should ensure that the exchange agreements in effect provide for the exchange of information in accordance with the requirements of the Model CAA.

The Czech Republic's exchange agreements provide for the exchange of information in accordance with the requirements of the Model CAA.

Recommendations:

No recommendations made.

Comments by the assessed jurisdiction

No comments made.

Note

[1] Andorra, Liechtenstein, Monaco, San Marino and Switzerland.

Denmark

Overall findings

Denmark's legal framework implementing the AEOI Standard is in place and is consistent with the requirements of the AEOI Terms of Reference. This includes Denmark's domestic legislative framework requiring Reporting Financial Institutions to conduct the due diligence and reporting procedures (CR1) and its international legal framework to exchange the information with all of Denmark's Interested Appropriate Partners (CR2).

The methodology used for the peer reviews and that therefore underpins this report is outlined in Chapter 2.

Overall determination on the legal framework: In Place

Conclusions on the legal framework

General context

Denmark commenced exchanges under the AEOI Standard in 2017.

In order to provide for Reporting Financial Institutions to collect and report the information to be exchanged, Denmark:

- enacted Section 66 of the Tax Control Act and sections 22 and 23 of the Tax Reporting Act (and in connection to sections 22 and 23, paragraphs 2 and 3 of section 48, section 52, paragraphs 5 and 6 of section 54, sections 55-57, and sections 59-63 of the Tax Reporting Act);
- introduced the Regulation on Identification of and Reporting on Foreign Financial Accounts; and
- issued Frequently Asked Questions, which are not legally binding.

Under this framework Reporting Financial Institutions were required to commence the due diligence procedures in relation to New Accounts from 1 January 2016. With respect to Preexisting Accounts, Reporting Financial Institutions were required to complete due diligence procedures on High Value Individual Accounts by 31 December 2016 and on Lower Value Individual Accounts and Entity Accounts by 31 December 2017.

Following the initial Global Forum peer review, Denmark made various amendments to its legislative framework to address issues identified, the last of which was effective from 1 January 2019.

With respect to the exchange of information under the AEOI Standard, Denmark:

- is a Party to the Convention on Mutual Administrative Assistance in Tax Matters and activated the associated CRS Multilateral Competent Authority Agreement in time for exchanges in 2017;
- has in place European Directive 2011/16/EU on Administrative Cooperation in the Field of Taxation as amended by Directive 2014/107/EU;
- has in place European Union agreements with five European third countries[1]; and
- put in place three bilateral agreements.[2]

Detailed findings

The detailed findings for Denmark are below, organised per Core Requirement (CR) and sub-requirement (SR), as extracted from the AEOI Terms of Reference (www.oecd.org/tax/transparency/documents/aeoi-terms-of-reference.pdf).

CR1 Domestic legal framework: Jurisdictions should have a domestic legislative framework in place that requires all Reporting Financial Institutions to conduct the due diligence and reporting procedures in the CRS, and that provides for the effective implementation of the CRS as set out therein.

Determination: In Place

Denmark's domestic legislative framework is in place and contains all of the key aspects of the CRS and its Commentary requiring Reporting Financial Institutions to conduct the due diligence and reporting procedures (SRs 1.1 – 1.3). It also provides for a framework to enforce the requirements (SR 1.4).

SR 1.1 Jurisdictions should define the scope of Reporting Financial Institutions consistently with the CRS.

Denmark has defined the scope of Reporting Financial Institutions in its domestic legislative framework in accordance with the CRS and its Commentary.

Recommendations:

No recommendations made.

SR 1.2 Jurisdictions should define the scope of Financial Accounts and Reportable Accounts consistently with the CRS and incorporate the due diligence procedures to identify them.

Denmark has defined the scope of the Financial Accounts that are required to be reported in its domestic legislative framework and incorporated the due diligence procedures that must be applied to identify them in accordance with the CRS and its Commentary.

Recommendations:

No recommendations made.

SR 1.3 Jurisdictions should incorporate the reporting requirements contained in Section I of the CRS into their domestic legislative framework.

Denmark has incorporated the reporting requirements in its domestic legislative framework in accordance with the CRS and its Commentary.

Recommendations:

No recommendations made.

SR 1.4 Jurisdictions should have a legislative framework in place that allows for the enforcement of the requirements of the CRS in practice.

Denmark has a legislative framework in place to enforce the requirements in accordance with the CRS and its Commentary.

Recommendations:

No recommendations made.

CR2 International legal framework: Jurisdictions should have exchange relationships in effect with all Interested Appropriate Partners as committed to and that provide for the exchange of information in accordance with the Model CAA.

Determination: In Place

Denmark's international legal framework to exchange the information is **in place**, is consistent with the Model CAA and its Commentary and provides for exchange with all of Denmark's Interested Appropriate Partners (i.e. all jurisdictions that are interested in receiving information from Denmark and that meet the required standard in relation to confidentiality and data safeguards). (SRs 2.1 – 2.3)

SR 2.1 Jurisdictions should have exchange agreements in effect with all Interested Appropriate Partners that permit the automatic exchange of CRS information.

Denmark has exchange agreements that permit the automatic exchange of CRS information in effect with all its Interested Appropriate Partners.

Recommendations:

No recommendations made.

SR 2.2 Such an exchange agreement should be put in place without undue delay, following the receipt of an expression of interest from an Interested Appropriate Partner.

Denmark put in place its exchange agreements without undue delay.

Recommendations:

No recommendations made.

SR 2.3 Jurisdictions should ensure that the exchange agreements in effect provide for the exchange of information in accordance with the requirements of the Model CAA.

Denmark's exchange agreements provide for the exchange of information in accordance with the requirements of the Model CAA.

Recommendations:

No recommendations made.

Comments by the assessed jurisdiction

No comments made.

Notes

[1] Andorra, Liechtenstein, Monaco, San Marino and Switzerland.

[2] The Faroe Islands, Greenland and Singapore.

Dominica

Overall findings

Dominica's legal framework implementing the AEOI Standard is in place and is consistent with the requirements of the AEOI Terms of Reference. This includes Dominica's domestic legislative framework requiring Reporting Financial Institutions to conduct the due diligence and reporting procedures (CR1) and its international legal framework to exchange the information with all of Dominica's Interested Appropriate Partners (CR2).

The methodology used for the peer reviews and that therefore underpins this report is outlined in Chapter 2.

Overall determination on the legal framework: In Place

Conclusions on the legal framework

General context

Dominica committed to exchange information by 2018, although due to delays in implementing the legal framework, Dominica does not expect to commence exchanges until the end of 2020.

In order to provide for Reporting Financial Institutions to collect and report the information to be exchanged, Dominica:

- enacted the Automatic Exchange of Financial Account Information (Common Reporting Standard) Act, 2019; and
- made reference to the Money Laundering (Prevention) Statutory Rules and Orders No. 4 of 2013 for the purposes of the identification of Controlling Persons under the AEOI Standard.

Under this framework Reporting Financial Institutions were required to commence the due diligence procedures in relation to New Accounts from 1 January 2019. With respect to Preexisting Accounts, Reporting Financial Institutions were required to complete the due diligence procedures on High Value Individual Accounts by 31 December 2019 and on Lower Value Individual Accounts and Entity Accounts by 31 December 2020.

Following the initial Global Forum peer review, Dominica amended its legislative framework to address issues identified, effective from 14 July 2021.

With respect to the exchange of information under the AEOI Standard, Dominica is a Party to the Convention on Mutual Administrative Assistance in Tax Matters and activated the associated CRS Multilateral Competent Authority Agreement in time for exchanges in 2020.

Detailed findings

The detailed findings for Dominica are below, organised per Core Requirement (CR) and sub-requirement (SR), as extracted from the AEOI Terms of Reference (www.oecd.org/tax/transparency/documents/aeoi-terms-of-reference.pdf).

CR1 Domestic legal framework: Jurisdictions should have a domestic legislative framework in place that requires all Reporting Financial Institutions to conduct the due diligence and reporting procedures in the CRS, and that provides for the effective implementation of the CRS as set out therein.

Determination: In Place

Dominica's domestic legislative framework is in place and contains all of the key aspects of the CRS and its Commentary requiring Reporting Financial Institutions to conduct the due diligence and reporting procedures (SRs 1.1 – 1.3). It also provides for a framework to enforce the requirements (SR 1.4).

SR 1.1 Jurisdictions should define the scope of Reporting Financial Institutions consistently with the CRS.

Dominica has defined the scope of Reporting Financial Institutions in its domestic legislative framework in accordance with the CRS and its Commentary.

Recommendations:

No recommendations made.

SR 1.2 Jurisdictions should define the scope of Financial Accounts and Reportable Accounts consistently with the CRS and incorporate the due diligence procedures to identify them.

Dominica has defined the scope of the Financial Accounts that are required to be reported in its domestic legislative framework and incorporated the due diligence procedures that must be applied to identify them in accordance with the CRS and its Commentary.

Recommendations:

No recommendations made.

SR 1.3 Jurisdictions should incorporate the reporting requirements contained in Section I of the CRS into their domestic legislative framework.

Dominica has incorporated the reporting requirements in its domestic legislative framework in accordance with the CRS and its Commentary.

Recommendations:

No recommendations made.

SR 1.4 Jurisdictions should have a legislative framework in place that allows for the enforcement of the requirements of the CRS in practice.

Dominica has a legislative framework in place to enforce the requirements in accordance with the CRS and its Commentary.

Recommendations:

No recommendations made.

CR2 International legal framework: Jurisdictions should have exchange relationships in effect with all Interested Appropriate Partners as committed to and that provide for the exchange of information in accordance with the Model CAA.

Determination: In Place

Dominica's international legal framework to exchange the information is in place, is consistent with the Model CAA and its Commentary and provides for exchange with all of Dominica's Interested Appropriate

Partners (i.e. all jurisdictions that are interested in receiving information from Dominica and that meet the required standard in relation to confidentiality and data safeguards). (SRs 2.1 – 2.3)

SR 2.1 Jurisdictions should have exchange agreements in effect with all Interested Appropriate Partners that permit the automatic exchange of CRS information.

Dominica has exchange agreements that permit the automatic exchange of CRS information in effect with all its Interested Appropriate Partners.

Recommendations:

No recommendations made.

SR 2.2 Such an exchange agreement should be put in place without undue delay, following the receipt of an expression of interest from an Interested Appropriate Partner.

Dominica put in place its exchange agreements without undue delay.

Recommendations:

No recommendations made.

SR 2.3 Jurisdictions should ensure that the exchange agreements in effect provide for the exchange of information in accordance with the requirements of the Model CAA.

Dominica's exchange agreements provide for the exchange of information in accordance with the requirements of the Model CAA.

Recommendations:

No recommendations made.

Comments by the assessed jurisdiction

No comments made.

Estonia

Overall findings

Estonia's legal framework implementing the AEOI Standard is in place but needs improvement in order to be fully consistent with the requirements of the AEOI Terms of Reference. While Estonia's international legal framework to exchange the information with all of Estonia's Interested Appropriate Partners (CR2) is consistent with the requirements, its domestic legislative framework requiring Reporting Financial Institutions to conduct the due diligence and reporting procedures (CR1) has a deficiency significant to the proper functioning of elements of the AEOI Standard. More specifically, Estonia's legal framework includes a category of jurisdiction-specific Excluded Account that is not in accordance with the AEOI Standard.

The methodology used for the peer reviews and that therefore underpins this report is outlined in Chapter 2.

Overall determination on the legal framework: In Place But **Needs Improvement**

Conclusions on the legal framework

General context

Estonia commenced exchanges under the AEOI Standard in 2017.

In order to provide for Reporting Financial Institutions to collect and report the information to be exchanged, Estonia:

- enacted the Tax Information Exchange Act;
- published further guidance, which is not legally binding; and
- relies on its legal framework implementing the FATF Recommendations for the purposes of the identification of Controlling Persons under the AEOI Standard.

Under this framework Reporting Financial Institutions were required to commence the due diligence procedures in relation to New Accounts from 1 January 2016. With respect to Preexisting Accounts, Reporting Financial Institutions were required to complete the due diligence procedures on High Value Individual Accounts by 31 December 2016 and on Lower Value Individual Accounts and Entity Accounts by 31 December 2017.

Following the initial Global Forum peer review, Estonia amended its legislative framework to address issues identified, effective from 20 July 2020.

With respect to the exchange of information under the AEOI Standard, Estonia:

- is a Party to the Convention on Mutual Administrative Assistance in Tax Matters and activated the associated CRS Multilateral Competent Authority Agreement in time for exchanges in 2017;
- has in place European Directive 2011/16/EU on Administrative Cooperation in the Field of Taxation as amended by Directive 2014/107/EU;
- has in place European Union agreements with five European third countries[1]; and
- put in place a bilateral agreement.[2]

Detailed findings

The detailed findings for Estonia are below, organised per Core Requirement (CR) and sub-requirement (SR), as extracted from the AEOI Terms of Reference (www.oecd.org/tax/transparency/documents/aeoi-terms-of-reference.pdf).

CR1 Domestic legal framework: Jurisdictions should have a domestic legislative framework in place that requires all Reporting Financial Institutions to conduct the due diligence and reporting procedures in the CRS, and that provides for the effective implementation of the CRS as set out therein.

Determination: In Place But **Needs Improvement**

Estonia's domestic legislative framework is in place and contains most of the key aspects of the CRS and its Commentary requiring Reporting Financial Institutions to conduct the due diligence and reporting procedures, but it needs improvement in relation to the scope of Financial Accounts required to be reported (SR 1.2). More specifically, Estonia's legislative framework provides for a category of jurisdiction-specific Excluded Account that does not meet all the requirements.

SR 1.1 Jurisdictions should define the scope of Reporting Financial Institutions consistently with the CRS.

Estonia has defined the scope of Reporting Financial Institutions in its domestic legislative framework in accordance with the CRS and its Commentary.

Recommendations:

No recommendations made.

SR 1.2 Jurisdictions should define the scope of Financial Accounts and Reportable Accounts consistently with the CRS and incorporate the due diligence procedures to identify them.

Estonia has defined the scope of the Financial Accounts that are required to be reported in its domestic legislative framework and incorporated the due diligence procedures that must be applied to identify them in a manner that is largely consistent with the CRS and its Commentary. However, a deficiency has been identified. More specifically, Estonia provides for a jurisdiction-specific Excluded Account that is not in accordance with the requirements. The definition of Financial Accounts, including the provision of Excluded Accounts, is material to the proper functioning of the AEOI Standard.

Recommendations:

Estonia should amend its domestic legislative framework to remove Insurance Contracts for Supplementary Funded Pensions from its jurisdiction-specific list of Excluded Accounts as they do not meet the requirements of the AEOI Standard.

SR 1.3 Jurisdictions should incorporate the reporting requirements contained in Section I of the CRS into their domestic legislative framework.

Estonia has incorporated the reporting requirements in its domestic legislative framework in accordance with the CRS and its Commentary.

Recommendations:

No recommendations made.

SR 1.4 Jurisdictions should have a legislative framework in place that allows for the enforcement of the requirements of the CRS in practice.

Estonia has a legislative framework in place to enforce the requirements in accordance with the CRS and its Commentary.

Recommendations:

No recommendations made.

CR2 International legal framework: Jurisdictions should have exchange relationships in effect with all Interested Appropriate Partners as committed to and that provide for the exchange of information in accordance with the Model CAA.

Determination: In Place

Estonia's international legal framework to exchange the information is in place, is consistent with the Model CAA and its Commentary and provides for exchange with all of Estonia's Interested Appropriate Partners (i.e. all jurisdictions that are interested in receiving information from Estonia and that meet the required standard in relation to confidentiality and data safeguards). (SRs 2.1 – 2.3)

SR 2.1 Jurisdictions should have exchange agreements in effect with all Interested Appropriate Partners that permit the automatic exchange of CRS information.

Estonia has exchange agreements that permit the automatic exchange of CRS information in effect with all its Interested Appropriate Partners.

Recommendations:

No recommendations made.

SR 2.2 Such an exchange agreement should be put in place without undue delay, following the receipt of an expression of interest from an Interested Appropriate Partner.

Estonia put in place its exchange agreements without undue delay.

Recommendations:

No recommendations made.

SR 2.3 Jurisdictions should ensure that the exchange agreements in effect provide for the exchange of information in accordance with the requirements of the Model CAA.

Estonia's exchange agreements provide for the exchange of information in accordance with the requirements of the Model CAA.

Recommendations:

No recommendations made.

Comments by the assessed jurisdiction

No comments made.

Notes

[1] Andorra, Liechtenstein, Monaco, San Marino and Switzerland.

[2] With Singapore. Estonia has also activated a relationship under the CRS MCAA with Singapore.

Faroe Islands

Overall findings

The Faroe Islands' legal framework implementing the AEOI Standard is in place but needs improvement in order to be fully consistent with the requirements of the AEOI Terms of Reference. While the Faroe Islands' international legal framework to exchange the information with all of the Faroe Islands' Interested Appropriate Partners (CR2) is consistent with the requirements, its domestic legislative framework requiring Reporting Financial Institutions to conduct the due diligence and reporting procedures (CR1) has a deficiency significant to the proper functioning of elements of the AEOI Standard. More specifically, the Faroe Islands' legislative framework does not include rules requiring Reporting Financial Institutions to keep records for all Financial Accounts in accordance with the requirements.

The methodology used for the peer reviews and that therefore underpins this report is outlined in Chapter 2.

Overall determination on the legal framework: In Place But **Needs Improvement**

Conclusions on the legal framework

General context

The Faroe Islands commenced exchanges under the AEOI Standard in 2017.

In order to provide for Reporting Financial Institutions to collect and report the information to be exchanged, the Faroe Islands:

- amended the Faroese Tax Act No. 86 of 1 September 1983 (by Act No. 50 of 6 May 2016) and ; and
- introduced the Regulation No. 11 of 19 February 2016, as amended in 2017, 2018, 2019 and 2021.

Under this framework Reporting Financial Institutions were required to commence the due diligence procedures in relation to New Accounts from 1 January 2016. With respect to Preexisting Accounts, Reporting Financial Institutions were required to complete the due diligence procedures on High Value Individual Accounts by 31 December 2016 and on Lower Value Individual Accounts and Entity Accounts by 31 December 2017.

Following the initial Global Forum peer review, the Faroe Islands made various amendments to its legislative framework to address issues identified, the last of which was effective from 26 March 2021.

With respect to the exchange of information under the AEOI Standard, the Faroe Islands:

- has the Convention on Mutual Administrative Assistance in Tax Matters in place,[1] and activated the associated CRS Multilateral Competent Authority Agreement in time for exchanges in 2017; and
- put in place two bilateral agreements.[2]

Detailed findings

The detailed findings for the Faroe Islands are below, organised per Core Requirement (CR) and sub-requirement (SR), as extracted from the AEOI Terms of Reference (www.oecd.org/tax/transparency/documents/aeoi-terms-of-reference.pdf).

CR1 Domestic legal framework: Jurisdictions should have a domestic legislative framework in place that requires all Reporting Financial Institutions to conduct the due diligence and reporting procedures in the CRS, and that provides for the effective implementation of the CRS as set out therein.

Determination: In Place But **Needs Improvement**

The Faroe Islands' domestic legislative framework is in place and contains most of the key aspects of the CRS and its Commentary requiring Reporting Financial Institutions to conduct the due diligence and reporting procedures, but it needs improvement in relation to the framework to enforce the requirements (SR 1.4). More specifically, the Faroe Islands' legislative framework does not include complete rules requiring Reporting Financial Institutions to keep records in accordance with the requirements.

SR 1.1 Jurisdictions should define the scope of Reporting Financial Institutions consistently with the CRS.

The Faroe Islands has defined the scope of Reporting Financial Institutions in its domestic legislative framework in accordance with the CRS and its Commentary.

Recommendations:

No recommendations made.

SR 1.2 Jurisdictions should define the scope of Financial Accounts and Reportable Accounts consistently with the CRS and incorporate the due diligence procedures to identify them.

The Faroe Islands has defined the scope of the Financial Accounts that are required to be reported in its domestic legislative framework and incorporated the due diligence procedures that must be applied to identify them in accordance with the CRS and its Commentary.

Recommendations:

No recommendations made.

SR 1.3 Jurisdictions should incorporate the reporting requirements contained in Section I of the CRS into their domestic legislative framework.

The Faroe Islands has incorporated the reporting requirements in its domestic legislative framework in accordance with the CRS and its Commentary.

Recommendations:

No recommendations made.

SR 1.4 Jurisdictions should have a legislative framework in place that allows for the enforcement of the requirements of the CRS in practice.

The Faroe Islands has a legislative framework in place to enforce the requirements in a manner that is largely consistent with the CRS and its Commentary. However, a deficiency has been identified. More specifically, the Faroe Islands' legislative framework does not include rules requiring Reporting Financial Institutions to keep records in relation to non-Reportable Accounts in accordance with the requirements. This is a key element of the required enforcement framework and is therefore material to the proper functioning of the AEOI Standard.

Recommendations:

The Faroe Islands should amend its domestic legislative framework to require Reporting Financial Institutions to keep records for all Financial Accounts for at least five years after the end of the period within which information is required to be reported, in accordance with the AEOI Standard.

CR2 International legal framework: Jurisdictions should have exchange relationships in effect with all Interested Appropriate Partners as committed to and that provide for the exchange of information in accordance with the Model CAA.

Determination: In Place

The Faroe Islands' international legal framework to exchange the information is in place, is consistent with the Model CAA and its Commentary and provides for exchange with all of the Faroe Islands' Interested Appropriate Partners (i.e. all jurisdictions that are interested in receiving information from The Faroe Islands and that meet the required standard in relation to confidentiality and data safeguards). (SRs 2.1 – 2.3)

SR 2.1 Jurisdictions should have exchange agreements in effect with all Interested Appropriate Partners that permit the automatic exchange of CRS information.

The Faroe Islands has exchange agreements that permit the automatic exchange of CRS information in effect with all its Interested Appropriate Partners.

Recommendations:

No recommendations made.

SR 2.2 Such an exchange agreement should be put in place without undue delay, following the receipt of an expression of interest from an Interested Appropriate Partner.

The Faroe Islands put in place its exchange agreements without undue delay.

Recommendations:

No recommendations made.

SR 2.3 Jurisdictions should ensure that the exchange agreements in effect provide for the exchange of information in accordance with the requirements of the Model CAA.

The Faroe Islands' exchange agreements provide for the exchange of information in accordance with the requirements of the Model CAA.

Recommendations:

No recommendations made.

Comments by the assessed jurisdiction

No comments made.

Notes

[1] Through a territorial extension by Denmark.

[2] With Denmark and Greenland.

Finland

Overall findings

Finland's legal framework implementing the AEOI Standard is in place and is consistent with the requirements of the AEOI Terms of Reference. This includes Finland's domestic legislative framework requiring Reporting Financial Institutions to conduct the due diligence and reporting procedures (CR1) and its international legal framework to exchange the information with all of Finland's Interested Appropriate Partners (CR2).

The methodology used for the peer reviews and that therefore underpins this report is outlined in Chapter 2.

Overall determination on the legal framework: In Place

Conclusions on the legal framework

General context

Finland commenced exchanges under the AEOI Standard in 2017.

In order to provide for Reporting Financial Institutions to collect and report the information to be exchanged, Finland:

- enacted the Act on the amendment of the Act on national implementation of provisions of a legislative nature in Council Directive on administrative cooperation in the field of taxation and repealing Directive 77/799/EEC, and application of the Directive (1703/2015) as amended by the amendment Act (881/2017), and the Act on the amendment of the Tax Assessment Procedure Act (227/2016) as amended by the amendment Act (1560/2019);
- introduced the Decision of the Tax Administration on the requirement to report information on financial accounts (A35/200/2016); and
- issued further guidance, which is legally binding.

Under this framework Reporting Financial Institutions were required to commence the due diligence procedures in relation to New Accounts from 1 January 2016. With respect to Preexisting Accounts, Reporting Financial Institutions were required to complete the due diligence procedures on High Value Individual Accounts by 31 December 2016 and on Lower Value Individual Accounts and Entity Accounts by 31 December 2017.

Following the initial Global Forum peer review, Finland made various amendments to its legislative framework to address issues identified, the last of which was effective from 1 January 2020.

With respect to the exchange of information under the AEOI Standard, Finland:

- is a Party to the Convention on Mutual Administrative Assistance in Tax Matters and activated the associated CRS Multilateral Competent Authority Agreement in time for exchanges in 2017;
- has in place European Directive 2011/16/EU on Administrative Cooperation in the Field of Taxation as amended by Directive 2014/107/EU;
- has in place European Union agreements with five European third countries[1]; and
- put in place a bilateral agreement.[2]

Detailed findings

The detailed findings for Finland are below, organised per Core Requirement (CR) and sub-requirement (SR), as extracted from the AEOI Terms of Reference (www.oecd.org/tax/transparency/documents/aeoi-terms-of-reference.pdf).

CR1 Domestic legal framework: Jurisdictions should have a domestic legislative framework in place that requires all Reporting Financial Institutions to conduct the due diligence and reporting procedures in the CRS, and that provides for the effective implementation of the CRS as set out therein.

Determination: In Place

Finland's domestic legislative framework is in place and contains all of the key aspects of the CRS and its Commentary requiring Reporting Financial Institutions to conduct the due diligence and reporting procedures (SRs 1.1 – 1.3). It also provides for a framework to enforce the requirements (SR 1.4).

SR 1.1 Jurisdictions should define the scope of Reporting Financial Institutions consistently with the CRS.

Finland has defined the scope of Reporting Financial Institutions in its domestic legislative framework in accordance with the CRS and its Commentary.

Recommendations:

No recommendations made.

SR 1.2 Jurisdictions should define the scope of Financial Accounts and Reportable Accounts consistently with the CRS and incorporate the due diligence procedures to identify them.

Finland has defined the scope of the Financial Accounts that are required to be reported in its domestic legislative framework and incorporated the due diligence procedures that must be applied to identify them in accordance with the CRS and its Commentary.

Recommendations:

No recommendations made.

SR 1.3 Jurisdictions should incorporate the reporting requirements contained in Section I of the CRS into their domestic legislative framework.

Finland has incorporated the reporting requirements in its domestic legislative framework in accordance with the CRS and its Commentary.

Recommendations:

No recommendations made.

SR 1.4 Jurisdictions should have a legislative framework in place that allows for the enforcement of the requirements of the CRS in practice.

Finland has a legislative framework in place to enforce the requirements in accordance with the CRS and its Commentary.

Recommendations:

No recommendations made.

CR2 International legal framework: Jurisdictions should have exchange relationships in effect with all Interested Appropriate Partners as committed to and that provide for the exchange of information in accordance with the Model CAA.

Determination: In Place

Finland's international legal framework to exchange the information is in place, is consistent with the Model CAA and its Commentary and provides for exchange with all of Finland's Interested Appropriate Partners (i.e. all jurisdictions that are interested in receiving information from Finland and that meet the required standard in relation to confidentiality and data safeguards). (SRs 2.1 – 2.3)

SR 2.1 Jurisdictions should have exchange agreements in effect with all Interested Appropriate Partners that permit the automatic exchange of CRS information.

Finland has exchange agreements that permit the automatic exchange of CRS information in effect with all its Interested Appropriate Partners.

Recommendations:

No recommendations made.

SR 2.2 Such an exchange agreement should be put in place without undue delay, following the receipt of an expression of interest from an Interested Appropriate Partner.

Finland put in place its exchange agreements without undue delay.

Recommendations:

No recommendations made.

SR 2.3 Jurisdictions should ensure that the exchange agreements in effect provide for the exchange of information in accordance with the requirements of the Model CAA.

Finland's exchange agreements provide for the exchange of information in accordance with the requirements of the Model CAA.

Recommendations:

No recommendations made.

Comments by the assessed jurisdiction

No comments made.

Notes

[1] Andorra, Liechtenstein, Monaco, San Marino and Switzerland.

[2] Singapore.

France

Overall findings

France's legal framework implementing the AEOI Standard is in place and is consistent with the requirements of the AEOI Terms of Reference. This includes France's domestic legislative framework requiring Reporting Financial Institutions to conduct the due diligence and reporting procedures (CR1) and its international legal framework to exchange the information with all of France's Interested Appropriate Partners (CR2).

The methodology used for the peer reviews and that therefore underpins this report is outlined in Chapter 2.

Overall determination on the legal framework: In Place

Conclusions on the legal framework

General context

France commenced exchanges under the AEOI Standard in 2017.

In order to provide for Reporting Financial Institutions to collect and report the information to be exchanged, France:

- enacted *Code général des impôts (CGI), art. 1649AC, and CGI, art. 1736,I 5°, Décret n° 2016-1683 du 5 décembre 2016 fixant les règles et procédures concernant l'échange automatique de renseignements relatifs aux comptes financiers, dites « norme commune de déclaration »*;
- introduced the *Arrêté du 9 décembre 2016 précisant le décret n° 2016-1683 du 5 décembre 2016 fixant les règles et procédures concernant l'échange automatique de renseignements relatifs aux comptes financiers, dites « norme commune de déclaration »*; as amended by the *Arrêté du 10 février 2020*;
- issued further guidance, which is legally binding; and
- made reference to the *Code monétaire et financier* for the purposes of the identification of Controlling Persons under the AEOI Standard.

Under this framework Reporting Financial Institutions were required to commence the due diligence procedures in relation to New Accounts from 1 January 2016. With respect to Preexisting Accounts, Reporting Financial Institutions were required to complete the due diligence procedures on High Value Individual Accounts by 31 December 2016 and on Lower Value Individual Accounts and on Entity Accounts by 31 December 2017.

Following the initial Global Forum peer review, France amended its legislative framework to address issues identified, effective from 16 February 2020.

With respect to the exchange of information under the AEOI Standard, France:

- is a Party to the Convention on Mutual Administrative Assistance in Tax Matters and activated the associated CRS Multilateral Competent Authority Agreement in time for exchanges in 2017;
- has in place European Directive 2011/16/EU on Administrative Cooperation in the Field of Taxation as amended by Directive 2014/107/EU; and
- has in place European Union agreements with five European third countries.[1]

Detailed findings

The detailed findings for France are below, organised per Core Requirement (CR) and sub-requirement (SR), as extracted from the AEOI Terms of Reference (www.oecd.org/tax/transparency/documents/aeoi-terms-of-reference.pdf).

CR1 Domestic legal framework: Jurisdictions should have a domestic legislative framework in place that requires all Reporting Financial Institutions to conduct the due diligence and reporting procedures in the CRS, and that provides for the effective implementation of the CRS as set out therein.

Determination: In Place

France's domestic legislative framework is in place and contains all of the key aspects of the CRS and its Commentary requiring Reporting Financial Institutions to conduct the due diligence and reporting procedures (SRs 1.1 – 1.3). It also provides for a framework to enforce the requirements (SR 1.4).

SR 1.1 Jurisdictions should define the scope of Reporting Financial Institutions consistently with the CRS.

France has defined the scope of Reporting Financial Institutions in its domestic legislative framework in accordance with the CRS and its Commentary.

Recommendations:

No recommendations made.

SR 1.2 Jurisdictions should define the scope of Financial Accounts and Reportable Accounts consistently with the CRS and incorporate the due diligence procedures to identify them.

France has defined the scope of the Financial Accounts that are required to be reported in its domestic legislative framework and incorporated the due diligence procedures that must be applied to identify them in accordance with the CRS and its Commentary.

Recommendations:

No recommendations made.

SR 1.3 Jurisdictions should incorporate the reporting requirements contained in Section I of the CRS into their domestic legislative framework.

France has incorporated the reporting requirements in its domestic legislative framework in accordance with the CRS and its Commentary.

Recommendations:

No recommendations made.

SR 1.4 Jurisdictions should have a legislative framework in place that allows for the enforcement of the requirements of the CRS in practice.

France has a legislative framework in place to enforce the requirements in accordance with the CRS and its Commentary.

Recommendations:

No recommendations made.

CR2 International legal framework: Jurisdictions should have exchange relationships in effect with all Interested Appropriate Partners as committed to and that provide for the exchange of information in accordance with the Model CAA.

Determination: In Place

France's international legal framework to exchange the information is in place, is consistent with the Model CAA and its Commentary and provides for exchange with all of France's Interested Appropriate Partners (i.e. all jurisdictions that are interested in receiving information from France and that meet the required standard in relation to confidentiality and data safeguards). (SRs 2.1 – 2.3)

SR 2.1 Jurisdictions should have exchange agreements in effect with all Interested Appropriate Partners that permit the automatic exchange of CRS information.

France has exchange agreements that permit the automatic exchange of CRS information in effect with all its Interested Appropriate Partners.

Recommendations:

No recommendations made.

SR 2.2 Such an exchange agreement should be put in place without undue delay, following the receipt of an expression of interest from an Interested Appropriate Partner.

France put in place its exchange agreements without undue delay.

Recommendations:

No recommendations made.

SR 2.3 Jurisdictions should ensure that the exchange agreements in effect provide for the exchange of information in accordance with the requirements of the Model CAA.

France's exchange agreements provide for the exchange of information in accordance with the requirements of the Model CAA.

Recommendations:

No recommendations made.

Comments by the assessed jurisdiction

No comments made.

Note

[1] Andorra, Liechtenstein, Monaco, San Marino and Switzerland.

Germany

Overall findings

Germany's legal framework implementing the AEOI Standard is in place but needs improvement in order to be fully consistent with the requirements of the AEOI Terms of Reference. While Germany's international legal framework to exchange the information with all of Germany's Interested Appropriate Partners (CR2) is consistent with the requirements, its domestic legislative framework requiring Reporting Financial Institutions to conduct the due diligence and reporting procedures (CR1) has deficiencies significant to the proper functioning of elements of the AEOI Standard. More specifically, Germany's legislative framework provides for jurisdiction-specific Non-Reporting Financial Institutions and Excluded Accounts that do not meet the requirements, and does not include strong measures to ensure valid self-certifications are obtained in all cases.

The methodology used for the peer reviews and that therefore underpins this report is outlined in Chapter 2.

Overall determination on the legal framework: In Place But **Needs Improvement**

Conclusions on the legal framework

General context

Germany commenced exchanges under the AEOI Standard in 2017.

In order to provide for Reporting Financial Institutions to collect and report the information to be exchanged, Germany:

- enacted the Law of December 21, 2015; announced in the Bundesgesetzblatt Part II, No. 35, December 29, 2015, page 1630 and Law of December 21, 2015; announced in Bundesgesetzblatt Part I, No. 55, December 30, 2015, page 2531; and
- issued further guidance, which is legally binding.

Under this framework Reporting Financial Institutions were required to commence the due diligence procedures in relation to New Accounts from 1 January 2016. With respect to Preexisting Accounts, Reporting Financial Institutions were required to complete the due diligence procedures on High Value Individual Accounts by 31 December 2016 and on Lower Value Individual Accounts and Entity Accounts by 31 December 2017.

With respect to the exchange of information under the AEOI Standard, Germany:

- is a Party to the Convention on Mutual Administrative Assistance in Tax Matters and activated the associated CRS Multilateral Competent Authority Agreement in time for exchanges in 2017;
- has in place European Directive 2011/16/EU on Administrative Cooperation in the Field of Taxation as amended by Directive 2014/107/EU; and
- has in place European Union agreements with five European third countries.[1]

Detailed findings

The detailed findings for Germany are below, organised per Core Requirement (CR) and sub-requirement (SR), as extracted from the AEOI Terms of Reference (www.oecd.org/tax/transparency/documents/aeoi-terms-of-reference.pdf).

CR1 Domestic legal framework: Jurisdictions should have a domestic legislative framework in place that requires all Reporting Financial Institutions to conduct the due diligence and reporting procedures in the CRS, and that provides for the effective implementation of the CRS as set out therein.

Determination: In Place But **Needs Improvement**

Germany's domestic legislative framework is in place and contains many of the key aspects of the CRS and its Commentary requiring Reporting Financial Institutions to conduct the due diligence and reporting procedures, but it needs improvement in relation to the scope of Reporting Financial Institutions required to report information (SR 1.1), the scope of Financial Accounts required to be reported (SR 1.2), and the framework to enforce the requirements (SR 1.4). More specifically, Germany's legislative framework provides for jurisdiction-specific non-Reporting Financial Institutions and Excluded Accounts that do not meet the requirements, and there are insufficient sanctions related to the making and collection of self-certifications.

SR 1.1 Jurisdictions should define the scope of Reporting Financial Institutions consistently with the CRS.

Germany has defined the scope of Reporting Financial Institutions in its domestic legislative framework in a manner that is largely consistent with the CRS and its Commentary. However, deficiencies have been identified. More specifically, Germany provides for seven jurisdiction-specific Non-Reporting Financial Institutions that are not in accordance with the requirements. The definition of Reporting Financial Institutions, including the provision of Non-Reporting Financial Institutions, is material to the proper functioning of the AEOI Standard, although it should be noted that several of the incorrect entries are likely to have a very limited impact.

Recommendations:

Germany should amend its domestic legislative framework to remove four entries from its jurisdiction-specific list of categories of Non-Reporting Financial Institutions as they are Non-Financial Entities and should therefore be treated as such under the AEOI Standard. The entries are: i) "bad banks"; ii) leasing entities; iii) factoring entities; and iv) Chambers of Commerce.

Germany should amend its domestic legislative framework to remove a further three entries from its jurisdiction-specific list of categories of Non-Reporting Financial Institutions as they do not meet the requirements. The entries are: i) foundations; ii) closed ended funds; and iii) Building and Loan Associations.

SR 1.2 Jurisdictions should define the scope of Financial Accounts and Reportable Accounts consistently with the CRS and incorporate the due diligence procedures to identify them.

Germany has defined scope of the Financial Accounts that are required to be reported in its domestic legislative framework and incorporated the due diligence procedures that must be applied to identify them in a manner that is largely consistent with the CRS and its Commentary. However, deficiencies have been identified. More specifically, Germany provides for 19 jurisdiction-specific Excluded Accounts that are not in accordance with the requirements. The definition of Financial Accounts, including the provision of Excluded Accounts, is material to the proper functioning of the AEOI Standard, although it should be noted that several of the incorrect entries are likely to have a very limited impact.

Recommendations:

Germany should amend its domestic legislative framework to remove 19 entries from its jurisdiction-specific list of categories of Excluded Accounts as they are either not Financial Accounts or do not meet the requirements for exclusion from being Financial Accounts. The entries are: i) (OTC Derivatives and similarly derived non-depository instruments; ii) letters of credit; iii) deposits without financial instruments; iv) customer cards; v) personal credit; vi) liens; vii) corporate mortgages; viii) credit lines; ix) factoring products; x) leasing products; xi) receivables in cash management; xii) passive loans, in particular promissory note (bond) loans; xiii) Riester accounts; xiv) collateral orders; xv) financing arrangements; xvi) credit line accounts; xvii) time-limited overdraft facilities; xviii) pocket-money accounts; and xix) escrow/securities accounts managed by lawyers, auditors, chartered accountants (tax advisers) and insolvency administrators.

SR 1.3 Jurisdictions should incorporate the reporting requirements contained in Section I of the CRS into their domestic legislative framework.

Germany has incorporated the reporting requirements in its domestic legislative framework in accordance with the CRS and its Commentary.

Recommendations:

No recommendations made.

SR 1.4 Jurisdictions should have a legislative framework in place that allows for the enforcement of the requirements of the CRS in practice.

Germany has a legislative framework in place to enforce the requirements in a manner that is largely consistent with the CRS and its Commentary. However, deficiencies have been identified. More specifically, Germany's legislative framework:

- does not impose sanctions on Account Holders and Controlling Persons for the provision of a false self-certification; and
- does not incorporate measures to ensure that self-certifications are always obtained and validated by Reporting Financial Institutions and in particular in the limited circumstances where valid self-certifications may be obtained after the opening of the account as required,

These are key elements of the required enforcement framework and are therefore material to the proper functioning of the AEOI Standard.

Recommendations:

Germany should amend its domestic legislative framework to include sanctions on Account Holders and Controlling Persons for the provision of a false self-certification.

Germany should amend its domestic legislative framework to include strong measures to ensure that valid self-certifications are always obtained for New Accounts and, more specifically, in the limited circumstances where a valid self-certification is permitted to be obtained after the opening of a New Account.

CR2 International legal framework: Jurisdictions should have exchange relationships in effect with all Interested Appropriate Partners as committed to and that provide for the exchange of information in accordance with the Model CAA.

Determination: In Place

Germany's international legal framework to exchange the information is in place, is consistent with the Model CAA and its Commentary and provides for exchange with all of Germany's Interested Appropriate Partners (i.e. all jurisdictions that are interested in receiving information from Germany and that meet the required standard in relation to confidentiality and data safeguards). (SRs 2.1 – 2.3)

SR 2.1 Jurisdictions should have exchange agreements in effect with all Interested Appropriate Partners that permit the automatic exchange of CRS information.

Germany has exchange agreements that permit the automatic exchange of CRS information in effect with all its Interested Appropriate Partners.

Recommendations:

No recommendations made.

SR 2.2 Such an exchange agreement should be put in place without undue delay, following the receipt of an expression of interest from an Interested Appropriate Partner.

Germany put in place its exchange agreements without undue delay.

Recommendations:

No recommendations made.

SR 2.3 Jurisdictions should ensure that the exchange agreements in effect provide for the exchange of information in accordance with the requirements of the Model CAA.

Germany's exchange agreements provide for the exchange of information in accordance with the requirements of the Model CAA.

Recommendations:

No recommendations made.

Comments by the assessed jurisdiction

With regard to the recommendations for SR 1.1, 1.2 and 1.4, Germany will promptly make changes to its regulations and will then apply for a reassessment.

Note

[1] Andorra, Liechtenstein, Monaco, San Marino and Switzerland.

Ghana

Overall findings

Ghana's legal framework implementing the AEOI Standard is in place but needs improvement in order to be fully consistent with the requirements of the AEOI Terms of Reference. While Ghana's international legal framework to exchange the information with all of Ghana's Interested Appropriate Partners (CR2) is consistent with the requirements, its domestic legislative framework requiring Reporting Financial Institutions to conduct the due diligence and reporting procedures (CR1) has deficiencies significant to the proper functioning of elements of the AEOI Standard. Most significantly, deficiencies have been identified in Ghana's enforcement framework.

The methodology used for the peer reviews and that therefore underpins this report is outlined in Chapter 2.

Overall determination on the legal framework: In Place But **Needs Improvement**

Conclusions on the legal framework

General context

Ghana commenced exchanges under the AEOI Standard in 2019.

In order to provide for Reporting Financial Institutions to collect and report the information to be exchanged, Ghana:

- enacted the Standard for Automatic Exchange of Financial Account Information Act, 2018; and
- issued further guidance, which is not legally binding.

Under this framework Reporting Financial Institutions were required to commence the due diligence procedures in relation to New Accounts from 1 January 2018. With respect to Preexisting Accounts, Reporting Financial Institutions were required to complete the due diligence procedures on High Value Individual Accounts by 31 December 2018 and on Lower Value Individual Accounts and Entity Accounts by 31 December 2019.

With respect to the exchange of information under the AEOI Standard, Ghana has the Convention on Mutual Administrative Assistance in Tax Matters in place, and activated the associated CRS Multilateral Competent Authority Agreement in time for exchanges in 2019.

Detailed findings

The detailed findings for Ghana are below, organised per Core Requirement (CR) and sub-requirement (SR), as extracted from the AEOI Terms of Reference (www.oecd.org/tax/transparency/documents/aeoi-terms-of-reference.pdf).

CR1 Domestic legal framework: Jurisdictions should have a domestic legislative framework in place that requires all Reporting Financial Institutions to conduct the due diligence and reporting procedures in the CRS, and that provides for the effective implementation of the CRS as set out therein.

Determination: In Place But **Needs Improvement**

Ghana's domestic legislative framework is in place and contains most of the key aspects of the CRS and its Commentary requiring Reporting Financial Institutions to conduct the due diligence and reporting procedures, but it needs improvement in relation to the scope of Financial Accounts required to be reported (SR 1.2), and the framework to enforce the requirements (SR 1.4). Most significantly, Ghana's legislative framework does not include rules to prevent circumvention of due diligence and reporting obligations and there are no sanctions on Account Holders and Controlling Persons for the provision of false self-certifications.

SR 1.1 Jurisdictions should define the scope of Reporting Financial Institutions consistently with the CRS.

Ghana has defined the scope of Reporting Financial Institutions in its domestic legislative framework in accordance with the CRS and its Commentary.

Recommendations:

No recommendations made.

SR 1.2 Jurisdictions should define the scope of Financial Accounts and Reportable Accounts consistently with the CRS and incorporate the due diligence procedures to identify them.

Ghana has defined the scope of the Financial Accounts that are required to be reported in its domestic legislative framework and incorporated the due diligence procedures that must be applied to identify them in a manner that is largely consistent with the CRS and its Commentary. However, a deficiency has been identified. More specifically, Ghana does not specify the date as of when a Financial Institution needs to implement policies for the returning of overpayments, which is required in order for Depository Accounts due to not-returned overpayments to be treated as Excluded Accounts.

Recommendations:

Ghana should amend its domestic legislative framework to require that Financial Institutions to implement policies and procedures with respect to limiting or returning overpayments from a specified date in order for Depository Accounts due to not-returned overpayments to be treated as Excluded Accounts.

SR 1.3 Jurisdictions should incorporate the reporting requirements contained in Section I of the CRS into their domestic legislative framework.

Ghana has incorporated the reporting requirements in its domestic legislative framework in accordance with the CRS and its Commentary.

Recommendations:

No recommendations made.

SR 1.4 Jurisdictions should have a legislative framework in place that allows for the enforcement of the requirements of the CRS in practice.

Ghana has a legislative framework in place to enforce the requirements in a manner that is largely consistent with the CRS and its Commentary. However, deficiencies have been identified. More specifically, Ghana's legislative framework:

- does not include rules to prevent all Financial Institutions, persons or intermediaries from adopting practices intended to circumvent the due diligence and reporting procedures as required;
- does not impose sanctions for the provision of a false self-certifications by Account Holders and Controlling Persons; and
- does not include rules requiring Reporting Financial Institutions to keep records of self-certifications in accordance with the requirements.

These are key elements of the required enforcement framework and are therefore material to the proper functioning of the AEOI Standard.

Recommendations:

Ghana should amend its domestic legislative framework to include rules to prevent all Financial Institutions, persons and intermediaries from adopting practices intended to circumvent the reporting and due diligence procedures, rather than just those on whom the AEOI Standard imposes an obligation.

Ghana should amend its domestic legislative framework to include sanctions on Account Holders and Controlling Persons for the provision of a false self-certification.

Ghana should amend its domestic legislative framework to require Reporting Financial Institutions to maintain records of self-certifications for at least five years from the deadline to report the information, rather than six years from the date when an account is closed.

CR2 International legal framework: Jurisdictions should have exchange relationships in effect with all Interested Appropriate Partners as committed to and that provide for the exchange of information in accordance with the Model CAA.

Determination: In Place

Ghana's international legal framework to exchange the information is in place, is consistent with the Model CAA and its Commentary and provides for exchange with all of Ghana's Interested Appropriate Partners (i.e. all jurisdictions that are interested in receiving information from Ghana and that meet the required standard in relation to confidentiality and data safeguards). (SRs 2.1 – 2.3)

SR 2.1 Jurisdictions should have exchange agreements in effect with all Interested Appropriate Partners that permit the automatic exchange of CRS information.

Ghana has exchange agreements that permit the automatic exchange of CRS information in effect with all its Interested Appropriate Partners.

Recommendations:

No recommendations made.

SR 2.2 Such an exchange agreement should be put in place without undue delay, following the receipt of an expression of interest from an Interested Appropriate Partner.

Ghana put in place its exchange agreements without undue delay.

Recommendations:

No recommendations made.

SR 2.3 Jurisdictions should ensure that the exchange agreements in effect provide for the exchange of information in accordance with the requirements of the Model CAA.

Ghana's exchange agreements provide for the exchange of information in accordance with the requirements of the Model CAA.

Recommendations:

No recommendations made.

Comments by the assessed jurisdiction

No comments made.

Gibraltar

Overall findings

Gibraltar's legal framework implementing the AEOI Standard is in place and is consistent with the requirements of the AEOI Terms of Reference. This includes Gibraltar's domestic legislative framework requiring Reporting Financial Institutions to conduct the due diligence and reporting procedures (CR1) and its international legal framework to exchange the information with all of Gibraltar's Interested Appropriate Partners (CR2).

The methodology used for the peer reviews and that therefore underpins this report is outlined in Chapter 2.

Overall determination on the legal framework: In Place

Conclusions on the legal framework

General context

Gibraltar commenced exchanges under the AEOI Standard in 2017.

In order to provide for Reporting Financial Institutions to collect and report the information to be exchanged, Gibraltar:

- enacted the Taxation (Mutual Administrative Assistance) Act 2014;
- introduced the International Co-operation (Improvement of International Tax Compliance) (Amendment No. 2) Regulations 2017; and
- issued further guidance, which not legally binding.

Under this framework Reporting Financial Institutions were required to commence the due diligence procedures in relation to New Accounts from 1 January 2016. With respect to Preexisting Accounts, Reporting Financial Institutions were required to complete due diligence procedures on High Value Individual Accounts by 31 December 2016 and on Lower Value Individual Accounts and Entity Accounts by 31 December 2017.

With respect to the exchange of information under the AEOI Standard, Gibraltar:

- has the Convention on Mutual Administrative Assistance in Tax Matters in place[1] and activated the associated CRS Multilateral Competent Authority Agreement in time for exchanges in 2017; and
- put in place two bilateral agreements.[2]

Detailed findings

The detailed findings for Gibraltar are below, organised per Core Requirement (CR) and sub-requirement (SR), as extracted from the AEOI Terms of Reference (www.oecd.org/tax/transparency/documents/aeoi-terms-of-reference.pdf).

CR1 Domestic legal framework: Jurisdictions should have a domestic legislative framework in place that requires all Reporting Financial Institutions to conduct the due diligence and reporting procedures in the CRS, and that provides for the effective implementation of the CRS as set out therein.

Determination: In Place

Gibraltar's domestic legislative framework is in place and contains all of the key aspects of the CRS and its Commentary requiring Reporting Financial Institutions to conduct the due diligence and reporting procedures (SRs 1.1 – 1.3). It also provides for a framework to enforce the requirements (SR 1.4).

SR 1.1 Jurisdictions should define the scope of Reporting Financial Institutions consistently with the CRS.

Gibraltar has defined the scope of Reporting Financial Institutions in its domestic legislative framework in accordance with the CRS and its Commentary.

Recommendations:

No recommendations made.

SR 1.2 Jurisdictions should define the scope of Financial Accounts and Reportable Accounts consistently with the CRS and incorporate the due diligence procedures to identify them.

Gibraltar has defined the scope of the Financial Accounts that are required to be reported in its domestic legislative framework and incorporated the due diligence procedures that must be applied to identify them in accordance with the CRS and its Commentary.

Recommendations:

No recommendations made.

SR 1.3 Jurisdictions should incorporate the reporting requirements contained in Section I of the CRS into their domestic legislative framework.

Gibraltar has incorporated the reporting requirements in its domestic legislative framework in accordance with the CRS and its Commentary.

Recommendations:

No recommendations made.

SR 1.4 Jurisdictions should have a legislative framework in place that allows for the enforcement of the requirements of the CRS in practice.

Gibraltar has a legislative framework in place to enforce the requirements in accordance with the CRS and its Commentary.

Recommendations:

No recommendations made.

CR2 International legal framework: Jurisdictions should have exchange relationships in effect with all Interested Appropriate Partners as committed to and that provide for the exchange of information in accordance with the Model CAA.

Determination: In Place

Gibraltar's international legal framework to exchange the information is in place, is consistent with the Model CAA and its Commentary and provides for exchange with all of Gibraltar's Interested Appropriate

Partners (i.e. all jurisdictions that are interested in receiving information from Gibraltar and that meet the required standard in relation to confidentiality and data safeguards). (SRs 2.1 – 2.3)

SR 2.1 Jurisdictions should have exchange agreements in effect with all Interested Appropriate Partners that permit the automatic exchange of CRS information.

Gibraltar has exchange agreements that permit the automatic exchange of CRS information in effect with all its Interested Appropriate Partners.

Recommendations:

No recommendations made.

SR 2.2 Such an exchange agreement should be put in place without undue delay, following the receipt of an expression of interest from an Interested Appropriate Partner.

Gibraltar put in place its exchange agreements without undue delay.

Recommendations:

No recommendations made.

SR 2.3 Jurisdictions should ensure that the exchange agreements in effect provide for the exchange of information in accordance with the requirements of the Model CAA.

Gibraltar's exchange agreements provide for the exchange of information in accordance with the requirements of the Model CAA.

Recommendations:

No recommendations made.

Comments by the assessed jurisdiction

Gibraltar would like to take this opportunity to thank the Global Forum Secretariat and in particular the AEOI Assessment Panel involved in the review of Gibraltar's AEOI legal framework, namely Mr. Colin Yan, Mr. Antti Kurikka and Mr. Safarali Cavadov.

The result of this review demonstrates Gibraltar's continuing commitment to maintaining the AEOI Standard consistently in-line with the requirements of the AEOI Terms of Reference.

Notes

[1] Through a territorial extension by the United Kingdom.

[2] Guernsey and the Isle of Man.

Greece

Overall findings

Greece's legal framework implementing the AEOI Standard is in place and is consistent with the requirements of the AEOI Terms of Reference. This includes Greece's domestic legislative framework requiring Reporting Financial Institutions to conduct the due diligence and reporting procedures (CR1) and its international legal framework to exchange the information with all of Greece's Interested Appropriate Partners (CR2).

The methodology used for the peer reviews and that therefore underpins this report is outlined in Chapter 2.

Overall determination on the legal framework: In Place

Conclusions on the legal framework

General context

Greece commenced exchanges under the AEOI Standard in 2017.

In order to provide for Reporting Financial Institutions to collect and report the information to be exchanged Greece:

- enacted Law 4428/2016, "Ratification of Multilateral Competent Authority Agreement on Automatic Exchange of Financial Account Information and implementing provisions";
- made reference to Law 4174/2013 "Tax Procedure Code and other provisions";
- issued the following Decisions from the Governor of the Independent Authority for Public Revenue: No. 1130/2017 as amended, No. 1133/2017 as amended and No. 1137/2017 as amended;
- issued the Joint Decision No. 1157/2018 of the Governor of the Independent Authority for Public Revenue and the Minister of Finance; and
- made reference to Law 4557/2018, "Prevention and suppression of money laundering and terrorist financing (transposition of Directive 2015/849/EU) and other provisions" for the purposes of the identification of Controlling Persons under the AEOI Standard.

Under this framework Reporting Financial Institutions were required to commence the due diligence procedures in relation to New Accounts from 1 January 2016. With respect to Preexisting Accounts, Reporting Financial Institutions were required to complete the due diligence procedures on High Value Individual Accounts by 31 December 2016 and on Lower Value Individual Accounts and Entity Accounts by 31 December 2017.

Following the initial Global Forum peer review, Greece made several amendments to its legislative framework to address issues identified, the last of which was effective from 9 July 2018.

With respect to the exchange of information under the AEOI Standard, Greece:

- Is a Party to the Convention on Mutual Administrative Assistance in Tax Matters and activated the associated CRS Multilateral Competent Authority Agreement in time for exchanges in 2017;
- has in place European Directive 2011/16/EU on Administrative Cooperation in the Field of Taxation, as amended by Directive 2014/107/EU; and
- has in place European Union agreements with five European third countries.[1]

Detailed findings

The detailed findings for Greece are below, organised per Core Requirement (CR) and sub-requirement (SR), as extracted from the AEOI Terms of Reference (www.oecd.org/tax/transparency/documents/aeoi-terms-of-reference.pdf).

CR1 Domestic legal framework: Jurisdictions should have a domestic legislative framework in place that requires all Reporting Financial Institutions to conduct the due diligence and reporting procedures in the CRS, and that provides for the effective implementation of the CRS as set out therein.

Determination: In Place

Greece's domestic legislative framework is in place and contains all of the key aspects of the CRS and its Commentary requiring Reporting Financial Institutions to conduct the due diligence and reporting procedures (SRs 1.1 – 1.3). It also provides for a framework to enforce the requirements (SR 1.4).

SR 1.1 Jurisdictions should define the scope of Reporting Financial Institutions consistently with the CRS.

Greece has defined the scope of Reporting Financial Institutions in its domestic legislative framework in accordance with the CRS and its Commentary.

Recommendations:

No recommendations made.

SR 1.2 Jurisdictions should define the scope of Financial Accounts and Reportable Accounts consistently with the CRS and incorporate the due diligence procedures to identify them.

Greece has defined the scope of the Financial Accounts that are required to be reported in its domestic legislative framework and incorporated the due diligence procedures that must be applied to identify them in accordance with the CRS and its Commentary.

Recommendations:

No recommendations made.

SR 1.3 Jurisdictions should incorporate the reporting requirements contained in Section I of the CRS into their domestic legislative framework.

Greece has incorporated the reporting requirements in its domestic legislative framework in accordance with the CRS and its Commentary.

Recommendations:

No recommendations made.

SR 1.4 Jurisdictions should have a legislative framework in place that allows for the enforcement of the requirements of the CRS in practice.

Greece has a legislative framework in place to enforce the requirements in accordance with the CRS and its Commentary.

Recommendations:

No recommendations made.

CR2 International legal framework: Jurisdictions should have exchange relationships in effect with all Interested Appropriate Partners as committed to and that provide for the exchange of information in accordance with the Model CAA.

Determination: In Place

Greece's international legal framework to exchange the information is in place, is consistent with the Model CAA and its Commentary and provides for exchange with all of Greece's Interested Appropriate Partners (i.e. all jurisdictions that are interested in receiving information from Greece and that meet the required standard in relation to confidentiality and data safeguards). (SRs 2.1 – 2.3)

SR 2.1 Jurisdictions should have exchange agreements in effect with all Interested Appropriate Partners that permit the automatic exchange of CRS information.

Greece has exchange agreements that permit the automatic exchange of CRS information in effect with all its Interested Appropriate Partners.

Recommendations:

No recommendations made.

SR 2.2 Such an exchange agreement should be put in place without undue delay, following the receipt of an expression of interest from an Interested Appropriate Partner.

Greece put in place its exchange agreements without undue delay.

Recommendations:

No recommendations made.

SR 2.3 Jurisdictions should ensure that the exchange agreements in effect provide for the exchange of information in accordance with the requirements of the Model CAA.

Greece's exchange agreements provide for the exchange of information in accordance with the requirements of the Model CAA.

Recommendations:

No recommendations made.

Comments by the assessed jurisdiction

Greece is satisfied with the overall determination of the legal framework by which the Common Reporting Standard is applied as in place. It is our strong commitment to implement the global standard in compliance with the AEOI Terms of Reference and to follow-up with any necessary improvements with a view to enhancing the outcomes of administrative cooperation.

Note

[1] Andorra, Liechtenstein, Monaco, San Marino and Switzerland.

Greenland

Overall findings

Greenland's legal framework implementing the AEOI Standard is in place and is consistent with the requirements of the AEOI Terms of Reference. This includes Greenland's domestic legislative framework requiring Reporting Financial Institutions to conduct the due diligence and reporting procedures (CR1) and its international legal framework to exchange the information with all of Greenland's Interested Appropriate Partners (CR2).

The methodology used for the peer reviews and that therefore underpins this report is outlined in Chapter 2.

Overall determination on the legal framework: In Place

Conclusions on the legal framework

General context

Greenland commenced exchanges under the AEOI Standard in 2018.

In order to provide for Reporting Financial Institutions to collect and report the information to be exchanged, Greenland enacted the Government of Greenland Executive Order No. 13 of 30 August 2017 on Identification of and Reporting on Foreign Financial Accounts, pursuant to Section 35 of Greenland Landsting's Act No. 11 of 2 November of 2016 on administration of taxes. The Government of Greenland Executive Order No. 13 was later amended through the Government of Greenland Executive Order No. 15 of 24 October 2019.

Under this framework Reporting Financial Institutions were required to commence the due diligence procedures in relation to New Accounts from 1 January 2016. With respect to Preexisting Accounts, Reporting Financial Institutions were required to complete the due diligence procedures on High Value Individual Accounts by 1 August 2017 and on Lower Value Individual Accounts and Entity Accounts by 31 December 2017.

Following the initial Global Forum peer review, Greenland amended its legislative framework to address issues identified, effective from 1 January 2020.

With respect to the exchange of information under the AEOI Standard, Greenland:

- has the Convention on Mutual Administrative Assistance in Tax Matters in place[1] and activated the associated CRS Multilateral Competent Authority Agreement in time for exchanges in 2018; and
- put in place two bilateral agreements.[2]

Detailed findings

The detailed findings for Greenland are below, organised per Core Requirement (CR) and sub-requirement (SR), as extracted from the AEOI Terms of Reference (www.oecd.org/tax/transparency/documents/aeoi-terms-of-reference.pdf).

CR1 Domestic legal framework: Jurisdictions should have a domestic legislative framework in place that requires all Reporting Financial Institutions to conduct the due diligence and reporting procedures in the CRS, and that provides for the effective implementation of the CRS as set out therein.

Determination: In Place

Greenland's domestic legislative framework is in place and contains all of the key aspects of the CRS and its Commentary requiring Reporting Financial Institutions to conduct the due diligence and reporting procedures (SRs 1.1 – 1.3). It also provides for a framework to enforce the requirements (SR 1.4).

SR 1.1 Jurisdictions should define the scope of Reporting Financial Institutions consistently with the CRS.

Greenland has defined the scope of Reporting Financial Institutions in its domestic legislative framework in accordance with the CRS and its Commentary.

Recommendations:

No recommendations made.

SR 1.2 Jurisdictions should define the scope of Financial Accounts and Reportable Accounts consistently with the CRS and incorporate the due diligence procedures to identify them.

Greenland has defined the scope of the Financial Accounts that are required to be reported in its domestic legislative framework and incorporated the due diligence procedures that must be applied to identify them in accordance with the CRS and its Commentary.

Recommendations:

No recommendations made.

SR 1.3 Jurisdictions should incorporate the reporting requirements contained in Section I of the CRS into their domestic legislative framework.

Greenland has incorporated the reporting requirements in its domestic legislative framework in accordance with the CRS and its Commentary.

Recommendations:

No recommendations made.

SR 1.4 Jurisdictions should have a legislative framework in place that allows for the enforcement of the requirements of the CRS in practice.

Greenland has a legislative framework in place to enforce the requirements in accordance with the CRS and its Commentary.

Recommendations:

No recommendations made.

CR2 International legal framework: Jurisdictions should have exchange relationships in effect with all Interested Appropriate Partners as committed to and that provide for the exchange of information in accordance with the Model CAA.

Determination: In Place

Greenland's international legal framework to exchange the information is in place, is consistent with the Model CAA and its Commentary and provides for exchange with all of Greenland's Interested Appropriate

Partners (i.e. all jurisdictions that are interested in receiving information from Greenland and that meet the required standard in relation to confidentiality and data safeguards). (SRs 2.1 – 2.3)

SR 2.1 Jurisdictions should have exchange agreements in effect with all Interested Appropriate Partners that permit the automatic exchange of CRS information.

Greenland has exchange agreements that permit the automatic exchange of CRS information in effect with all its Interested Appropriate Partners.

Recommendations:

No recommendations made.

SR 2.2 Such an exchange agreement should be put in place without undue delay, following the receipt of an expression of interest from an Interested Appropriate Partner.

Greenland put in place its exchange agreements without undue delay.

Recommendations:

No recommendations made.

SR 2.3 Jurisdictions should ensure that the exchange agreements in effect provide for the exchange of information in accordance with the requirements of the Model CAA.

Greenland's exchange agreements provide for the exchange of information in accordance with the requirements of the Model CAA.

Recommendations:

No recommendations made.

Comments by the assessed jurisdiction

No comments made.

Notes

[1] Through a territorial extension by Denmark.

[2] With Denmark and the Faroe Islands.

Grenada

Overall findings

Grenada's legal framework implementing the AEOI Standard is not in place in accordance with the requirements of the AEOI Terms of Reference. While Grenada's international legal framework to exchange the information with all of Grenada's Interested Appropriate Partners (CR2) is consistent with the requirements, Grenada's domestic legislative framework requiring Reporting Financial Institutions to conduct the due diligence and reporting procedures (CR1) has significant deficiencies in areas that are fundamental to the proper functioning of the AEOI Standard. More specifically, deficiencies have been identified in Grenada's enforcement framework and in other key areas.

The methodology used for the peer reviews and that therefore underpins this report is outlined in Chapter 2.

Overall determination on the legal framework: Not In Place

Conclusions on the legal framework

General context

Grenada commenced exchanges under the AEOI Standard in 2018.

In order to provide for Reporting Financial Institutions to collect and report the information to be exchanged, Grenada:

- enacted the Mutual Exchange of Information on Taxation Matters Act 24 as amended by Act no.14 of 2017 and the Tax Administration Act; and
- introduced the Mutual Exchange of Information on Tax Matters (Common Reporting Standard) Regulations.

Under this framework Reporting Financial Institutions were required to commence the due diligence procedures in relation to New Accounts from 1 January 2017. With respect to Preexisting Accounts, Reporting Financial Institutions were required to complete the due diligence procedures on High Value Individual Accounts by 31 December 2017 and on Lower Value Individual Accounts and Entity Accounts by 31 December 2018.

With respect to the exchange of information under the AEOI Standard, Grenada is a Party to the Convention on Mutual Administrative Assistance in Tax Matters and activated the associated CRS Multilateral Competent Authority Agreement in time for exchanges in 2018.

Detailed findings

The detailed findings for Grenada are below, organised per Core Requirement (CR) and sub-requirement (SR), as extracted from the AEOI Terms of Reference (www.oecd.org/tax/transparency/documents/aeoi-terms-of-reference.pdf).

CR1 Domestic legal framework: Jurisdictions should have a domestic legislative framework in place that requires all Reporting Financial Institutions to conduct the due diligence and reporting procedures in the CRS, and that provides for the effective implementation of the CRS as set out therein.

Determination: Not In Place

Grenada's domestic legislative framework is not in place as required as it does not contain several key aspects of the CRS and the Commentary. Most significantly, deficiencies have been identified in relation to the framework to enforce the requirements (SR 1.4), such as the lack of rules to prevent the circumvention of the reporting and due diligence procedures and to impose record keeping requirements, of a framework for enforcement to address non-compliance, and of strong measures to obtain a valid self-certification for New Accounts. Moreover Grenada's domestic legislative framework needs improvement in relation to the scope of Reporting Financial Institutions required to report information (SR 1.1), the due diligence procedures to be applied (SR 1.2) and the information required to be reported (SR 1.3).

SR 1.1 Jurisdictions should define the scope of Reporting Financial Institutions consistently with the CRS.

Grenada has defined the scope of Reporting Financial Institutions in its domestic legislative framework in a manner that is largely consistent with the CRS and its Commentary. However, a deficiency has been identified. More specifically, Grenada's domestic legislative framework does not provide for the interpretation of "managed by" in accordance with the requirements. The scope of Reporting Financial Institution is material to the proper functioning of the AEOI Standard.

Recommendations:

Grenada should amend its domestic legislative framework to incorporate the definition of "managed by" in relation to the definition of Investment Entity.

SR 1.2 Jurisdictions should define the scope of Financial Accounts and Reportable Accounts consistently with the CRS and incorporate the due diligence procedures to identify them.

Grenada has defined the scope of the Financial Accounts that are required to be reported in its domestic legislative framework and incorporated the due diligence procedures that must be applied to identify them in a manner that is largely consistent with the CRS and its Commentary. However, deficiencies have been identified. Most significantly, Grenada's legislative framework does not require Reporting Financial Institutions to always obtain a self-certification from the Account Holder or Controlling Person of a Passive NFE to establish whether the Controlling Person is a Reportable Person. The due diligence procedures are material to the proper functioning of the AEOI Standard.

Recommendations:

Grenada should amend its domestic legislative framework to specify that, for New Entity Accounts, Reporting Financial Institutions may only rely on a self-certification provided by a Passive NFE Account Holder or its Controlling Person to determine whether the Controlling Person is a Reportable Person.

Grenada should amend its domestic legislative framework to require Reportable Accounts to be treated as such from the date they are identified as such.

Grenada should amend its domestic legislative framework to ensure that the responsibility to fulfil the due diligence and reporting obligations remains with Reporting Financial Institutions, even if service providers are used.

Grenada should amend its domestic legislative framework to remove the permission for Financial Institutions to not apply certain procedures with respect to Preexisting Individual Accounts if it is not "reasonably possible".

SR 1.3 Jurisdictions should incorporate the reporting requirements contained in Section I of the CRS into their domestic legislative framework.

Grenada has incorporated the reporting requirements in its domestic legislative framework in a manner that is largely consistent with the CRS and its Commentary. However, deficiencies have been identified. Most significantly, Grenada's legislative framework does not require Reporting Financial Institutions to report the jurisdiction of residence or to use reasonable efforts to obtain the TIN(s) or date of birth of the Account Holder with respect to Preexisting Accounts. The reporting requirements are material to the proper functioning of the AEOI Standard.

Recommendations:

Grenada should amend its domestic legislative framework to require Reporting Financial Institutions to report the jurisdiction of residence for each Reportable Account.

Grenada should amend its domestic legislative framework to require Reporting Financial Institutions to use reasonable efforts, where they are needed to obtain a TIN or date of birth of a Preexisting Account Holder by the end of the second calendar year following the year in which a Preexisting Account is identified as a Reportable Account.

Grenada should amend its domestic legislative framework to require Reporting Financial Institutions to identify the currency in which each account is denominated.

Grenada should amend its domestic legislative framework to require Reporting Financial Institutions to report the account balance or value if an appropriate period other than a calendar year is used.

SR 1.4 Jurisdictions should have a legislative framework in place that allows for the enforcement of the requirements of the CRS in practice.

Grenada does not have a legislative framework in place to enforce the requirements in a manner that is consistent with the CRS and its Commentary as significant deficiencies have been identified. More specifically, Grenada's legislative framework:

- does not include rules to prevent Financial Institutions, persons or intermediaries from adopting practices intended to circumvent the reporting and due diligence procedures as required;
- does not incorporate rules requiring Reporting Financial Institutions to keep records in accordance with the requirements;
- does not provide for an enforcement framework to address non-compliance in relation to the due diligence procedures; or
- does not incorporate measures to ensure that self-certifications are always obtained and validated for New Accounts as is required, including in the limited circumstances where they may be obtained after account opening.

These are key elements of the required enforcement framework and are therefore material to the proper functioning of the AEOI Standard.

Recommendations:

Grenada should amend its domestic legislative framework to include rules to prevent Financial Institutions, persons and intermediaries from adopting practices intended to circumvent the reporting and due diligence procedures.

Grenada should amend its domestic legislative framework to require Reporting Financial Institutions to keep records of the steps undertaken and evidence relied on for the performance of the due diligence procedures in accordance with the AEOI Standard.

Grenada should amend its domestic legislative framework to require Reporting Financial Institutions to maintain records for at least five years from the deadline to report the information, in accordance with the AEOI Standard.

Grenada should amend its domestic legislative framework to include sanctions for failure to comply with the due diligence and reporting procedures, rather than being limited to failures leading to incorrect information reporting.

Grenada should amend its domestic legislative framework to include strong measures to ensure that valid self-certifications are always obtained for New Accounts in accordance with the requirements.

CR2 International legal framework: Jurisdictions should have exchange relationships in effect with all Interested Appropriate Partners as committed to and that provide for the exchange of information in accordance with the Model CAA.

Determination: In Place

Grenada's international legal framework to exchange the information is in place, is consistent with the Model CAA and its Commentary and provides for exchange with all of Grenada's Interested Appropriate Partners (i.e. all jurisdictions that are interested in receiving information from Grenada and that meet the required standard in relation to confidentiality and data safeguards). (SRs 2.1 – 2.3)

SR 2.1 Jurisdictions should have exchange agreements in effect with all Interested Appropriate Partners that permit the automatic exchange of CRS information.

Grenada has exchange agreements that permit the automatic exchange of CRS information in effect with all its Interested Appropriate Partners.

Recommendations:

No recommendations made.

SR 2.2 Such an exchange agreement should be put in place without undue delay, following the receipt of an expression of interest from an Interested Appropriate Partner.

Grenada put in place its exchange agreements without undue delay.

Recommendations:

No recommendations made.

SR 2.3 Jurisdictions should ensure that the exchange agreements in effect provide for the exchange of information in accordance with the requirements of the Model CAA.

Grenada's exchange agreements provide for the exchange of information in accordance with the requirements of the Model CAA.

Recommendations:

No recommendations made.

Comments by the assessed jurisdiction

No comments made.

Guernsey

Overall findings

Guernsey's legal framework implementing the AEOI Standard is in place and is consistent with the requirements of the AEOI Terms of Reference. This includes Guernsey's domestic legislative framework requiring Reporting Financial Institutions to conduct the due diligence and reporting procedures (CR1) and its international legal framework to exchange the information with all of Guernsey's Interested Appropriate Partners (CR2).

The methodology used for the peer reviews and that therefore underpins this report is outlined in Chapter 2.

Overall determination on the legal framework: In Place

Conclusions on the legal framework

General context

Guernsey commenced exchanges under the AEOI Standard in 2017.

In order to provide for Reporting Financial Institutions to collect and report the information to be exchanged, Guernsey:

- relies on Section 75C(4) and Section 75CC of the Income Tax Law, 1975;
- enacted The Income Tax (Approved International Agreements) (Implementation) (Common Reporting Standard) Regulations, 2015 (known as "the 2015 Regulations"), that was later amended in 2020 (known as "the 2020 amending Regulations"); and
- issued further guidance, which is not legally binding.

Under this framework Reporting Financial Institutions were required to commence the due diligence procedures in relation to New Accounts from 1 January 2016. With respect to Preexisting Accounts, Reporting Financial Institutions were required to complete the due diligence procedures on High Value Individual Accounts by 31 December 2016 and Lower Value Individual Accounts and on Entity Accounts by 31 December 2017.

Following the initial Global Forum peer review, Guernsey amended its legislative framework to address issues identified, effective from 12 May 2020.

With respect to the exchange of information under the AEOI Standard, Guernsey:

- has the Convention on Mutual Administrative Assistance in Tax Matters in place[1] and activated the associated CRS Multilateral Competent Authority Agreement in time for exchanges in 2017; and
- put in place nine bilateral agreements.[2]

Detailed findings

The detailed findings for Guernsey are below, organised per Core Requirement (CR) and sub-requirement (SR), as extracted from the AEOI Terms of Reference (www.oecd.org/tax/transparency/documents/aeoi-terms-of-reference.pdf).

CR1 Domestic legal framework: Jurisdictions should have a domestic legislative framework in place that requires all Reporting Financial Institutions to conduct the due diligence and reporting procedures in the CRS, and that provides for the effective implementation of the CRS as set out therein.

Determination: In Place

Guernsey's domestic legislative framework is in place and contains all of the key aspects of the CRS and its Commentary requiring Reporting Financial Institutions to conduct the due diligence and reporting procedures (SRs 1.1 – 1.3). It also provides for a framework to enforce the requirements (SR 1.4).

SR 1.1 Jurisdictions should define the scope of Reporting Financial Institutions consistently with the CRS.

Guernsey has defined the scope of Reporting Financial Institutions in its domestic legislative framework in accordance with the CRS and its Commentary.

Recommendations:

No recommendations made.

SR 1.2 Jurisdictions should define the scope of Financial Accounts and Reportable Accounts consistently with the CRS and incorporate the due diligence procedures to identify them.

Guernsey has defined the scope of the Financial Accounts that are required to be reported in its domestic legislative framework and incorporated the due diligence procedures that must be applied to identify them in accordance with the CRS and its Commentary.

Recommendations:

No recommendations made.

SR 1.3 Jurisdictions should incorporate the reporting requirements contained in Section I of the CRS into their domestic legislative framework.

Guernsey has incorporated the reporting requirements in its domestic legislative framework in accordance with the CRS and its Commentary.

Recommendations:

No recommendations made.

SR 1.4 Jurisdictions should have a legislative framework in place that allows for the enforcement of the requirements of the CRS in practice.

Guernsey has a legislative framework in place to enforce the requirements in accordance with the CRS and its Commentary.

Recommendations:

No recommendations made.

CR2 International legal framework: Jurisdictions should have exchange relationships in effect with all Interested Appropriate Partners as committed to and that provide for the exchange of information in accordance with the Model CAA.

Determination: In Place

Guernsey's international legal framework to exchange the information is in place, is consistent with the Model CAA and its Commentary and provides for exchange with all of Guernsey's Interested Appropriate

Partners (i.e. all jurisdictions that are interested in receiving information from Guernsey and that meet the required standard in relation to confidentiality and data safeguards). (SRs 2.1 – 2.3)

SR 2.1 Jurisdictions should have exchange agreements in effect with all Interested Appropriate Partners that permit the automatic exchange of CRS information.

Guernsey has exchange agreements that permit the automatic exchange of CRS information in effect with all its Interested Appropriate Partners.

Recommendations:

No recommendations made.

SR 2.2 Such an exchange agreement should be put in place without undue delay, following the receipt of an expression of interest from an Interested Appropriate Partner.

Guernsey put in place its exchange agreements without undue delay.

Recommendations:

No recommendations made.

SR 2.3 Jurisdictions should ensure that the exchange agreements in effect provide for the exchange of information in accordance with the requirements of the Model CAA.

Guernsey's exchange agreements provide for the exchange of information in accordance with the requirements of the Model CAA.

Recommendations:

No recommendations made.

Comments by the assessed jurisdiction

No comments made.

Notes

[1] Through a territorial extension by the United Kingdom.

[2] With Anguilla, Bermuda, the British Virgin Islands, the Cayman Islands, Gibraltar, Hong Kong (China), the Isle of Man, Jersey and the United Kingdom.

Hong Kong (China)

Overall findings

Hong Kong's legal framework implementing the AEOI Standard is in place and is consistent with the requirements of the AEOI Terms of Reference. This includes Hong Kong's domestic legislative framework requiring Reporting Financial Institutions to conduct the due diligence and reporting procedures (CR1) and its international legal framework to exchange the information with all of Hong Kong's Interested Appropriate Partners (CR2).

The methodology used for the peer reviews and that therefore underpins this report is outlined in Chapter 2.

Overall determination on the legal framework: In Place

Conclusions on the legal framework

General context

Hong Kong commenced exchanges under the AEOI Standard in 2018.

In order to provide for Reporting Financial Institutions to collect and report the information to be exchanged, Hong Kong:

- amended the Inland Revenue Ordinance (Cap. 112) by inserting new provisions implementing the CRS and its Commentary; and
- issued further guidance, which is admissible in evidence before a court though is not legally binding.

Under this framework Reporting Financial Institutions were required to commence the due diligence procedures in relation to New Accounts from 1 January 2017. With respect to Preexisting Accounts, Reporting Financial Institutions were required to complete the due diligence procedures on High Value Individual Accounts by 31 December 2017 and on Lower Value Individual Accounts and Entity Accounts by 31 December 2018.

Following the initial Global Forum peer review, Hong Kong made various amendments to its legislative framework to address issues identified, the last of which will be effective from 1 January 2021.

With respect to the exchange of information under the AEOI Standard, Hong Kong:

- has the Convention on Mutual Administrative Assistance in Tax Matters in place[1] and activated the associated CRS Multilateral Competent Authority Agreement in time for exchanges in 2018; and
- put in place 15 bilateral agreements under which exchanges started in 2018[2] and 2019[3].

Detailed findings

The detailed findings for Hong Kong are below, organised per Core Requirement (CR) and sub-requirement (SR), as extracted from the AEOI Terms of Reference (www.oecd.org/tax/transparency/documents/aeoi-terms-of-reference.pdf).

CR1 Domestic legal framework: Jurisdictions should have a domestic legislative framework in place that requires all Reporting Financial Institutions to conduct the due diligence and reporting procedures in the CRS, and that provides for the effective implementation of the CRS as set out therein.

Determination: In Place

Hong Kong's domestic legislative framework is in place and contains all of the key aspects of the CRS and its Commentary requiring Reporting Financial Institutions to conduct the due diligence and reporting procedures (SRs 1.1 – 1.3). It also provides for a framework to enforce the requirements (SR 1.4).

SR 1.1 Jurisdictions should define the scope of Reporting Financial Institutions consistently with the CRS.

Hong Kong has defined the scope of Reporting Financial Institutions in its domestic legislative framework in accordance with the CRS and its Commentary.

Recommendations:

No recommendations made.

SR 1.2 Jurisdictions should define the scope of Financial Accounts and Reportable Accounts consistently with the CRS and incorporate the due diligence procedures to identify them.

Hong Kong has defined the scope of the Financial Accounts that are required to be reported in its domestic legislative framework and incorporated the due diligence procedures that must be applied to identify them in accordance with the CRS and its Commentary.

Recommendations:

No recommendations made.

SR 1.3 Jurisdictions should incorporate the reporting requirements contained in Section I of the CRS into their domestic legislative framework.

Hong Kong has incorporated the reporting requirements in its domestic legislative framework in accordance with the CRS and its Commentary.

Recommendations:

No recommendations made.

SR 1.4 Jurisdictions should have a legislative framework in place that allows for the enforcement of the requirements of the CRS in practice.

Hong Kong has a legislative framework in place to enforce the requirements in accordance with the CRS and its Commentary.

Recommendations:

No recommendations made.

CR2 International legal framework: Jurisdictions should have exchange relationships in effect with all Interested Appropriate Partners as committed to and that provide for the exchange of information in accordance with the Model CAA.

Determination: In Place

Hong Kong's international legal framework to exchange the information is in place, is consistent with the Model CAA and its Commentary and provides for exchange with all of Hong Kong's Interested Appropriate

Partners (i.e. all jurisdictions that are interested in receiving information from Hong Kong and that meet the required standard in relation to confidentiality and data safeguards). (SRs 2.1 – 2.3)

SR 2.1 Jurisdictions should have exchange agreements in effect with all Interested Appropriate Partners that permit the automatic exchange of CRS information.

Hong Kong has exchange agreements that permit the automatic exchange of CRS information in effect with all its Interested Appropriate Partners.

Recommendations:

No recommendations made.

SR 2.2 Such an exchange agreement should be put in place without undue delay, following the receipt of an expression of interest from an Interested Appropriate Partner.

Hong Kong put in place its exchange agreements without undue delay.

Recommendations:

No recommendations made.

SR 2.3 Jurisdictions should ensure that the exchange agreements in effect provide for the exchange of information in accordance with the requirements of the Model CAA.

Hong Kong's exchange agreements provide for the exchange of information in accordance with the requirements of the Model CAA.

Recommendations:

No recommendations made.

Comments by the assessed jurisdiction

Hong Kong, China ("Hong Kong") would like to thank the Secretariat, members of the AEOI Assessment Panel and the AEOI Peer Review Group for their efforts and contributions in finalising the report on Hong Kong.

Notes

[1] Through a territorial extension by China.

[2] With Canada, China, Guernsey, Indonesia, Ireland, Italy, Japan, Mexico, the Netherlands, New Zealand, Portugal, South Africa and the United Kingdom.

[3] With Korea and Switzerland.

Hungary

Overall findings

Hungary's legal framework implementing the AEOI Standard is in place but needs improvement in order to be fully consistent with the requirements of the AEOI Terms of Reference. While Hungary's international legal framework to exchange the information with all of Hungary's Interested Appropriate Partners (CR2) is consistent with the requirements, its domestic legislative framework requiring Reporting Financial Institutions to conduct the due diligence and reporting procedures has deficiencies significant to the proper functioning of elements of the AEOI Standard. More specifically, deficiencies have been identified in relation to the scope of Financial Accounts and the due diligence procedures to identify them and the enforcement framework.

The methodology used for the peer reviews and that therefore underpins this report is outlined in Chapter 2.

Overall determination on the legal framework: In Place But **Needs Improvement**

Conclusions on the legal framework

General context

Hungary commenced exchanges under the AEOI Standard in 2017.

In order to provide for Reporting Financial Institutions to collect and report the information to be exchanged, Hungary:

- enacted Act CXC of 2015 on the publication of the Multilateral Competent Authority Agreement on Automatic Exchange of Financial Account Information and Annexes 1 and 2, and Section V/B of the Act XXXVII of 2013 on the international administrative cooperation in tax matters;
- issued further guidance, which is not legally binding; and
- made reference to Act LIII of 2017 Preventing and Combating Money Laundering and Terrorist Financing implementing the FATF Recommendations for the purposes of the identification of Controlling Persons under the AEOI Standard.

Under this framework Reporting Financial Institutions were required to commence the due diligence procedures in relation to New Accounts from 1 January 2016. With respect to Preexisting Accounts, Reporting Financial Institutions were required to complete the due diligence procedures on High Value Individual Accounts by 31 December 2016 and on Lower Value Individual Accounts and Entity Accounts by 31 December 2017.

With respect to the exchange of information under the AEOI Standard, Hungary:

- is a Party to the Convention on Mutual Administrative Assistance in Tax Matters and activated the associated CRS Multilateral Competent Authority Agreement in time for exchanges in 2017;
- has in place European Directive 2011/16/EU on Administrative Cooperation in the Field of Taxation as amended by Directive 2014/107/EU; and
- has in place European Union agreements with five European third countries.[1]

Detailed findings

The detailed findings for Hungary are below, organised per Core Requirement (CR) and sub-requirement (SR), as extracted from the AEOI Terms of Reference (www.oecd.org/tax/transparency/documents/aeoi-terms-of-reference.pdf).

CR1 Domestic legal framework: Jurisdictions should have a domestic legislative framework in place that requires all Reporting Financial Institutions to conduct the due diligence and reporting procedures in the CRS, and that provides for the effective implementation of the CRS as set out therein.

Determination: In Place But **Needs Improvement**

Hungary's domestic legislative framework is in place and contains many of the key aspects of the CRS and its Commentary requiring Reporting Financial Institutions to conduct the due diligence and reporting procedures, but it needs improvement in several areas relating to the scope of Financial Accounts required to be reported and the due diligence procedures to identity them (SR 1.2) and the framework to enforce the requirements (SR 1.4).

SR 1.1 Jurisdictions should define the scope of Reporting Financial Institutions consistently with the CRS.

Hungary has defined the scope of Reporting Financial Institutions in its domestic legislative framework in accordance with the CRS and its Commentary.

Recommendations:

No recommendations made.

SR 1.2 Jurisdictions should define the scope of Financial Accounts and Reportable Accounts consistently with the CRS and incorporate the due diligence procedures to identify them.

Hungary has defined the scope of the Financial Accounts that are required to be reported in its domestic legislative framework and incorporated the due diligence procedures that must be applied to identify them in a manner that is largely consistent with the CRS and its Commentary. However, deficiencies have been identified. More specifically, Hungary's domestic legislative framework:

- provides for four jurisdiction-specific Excluded Accounts that are not in accordance with the requirements.
- does not explicitly require Reporting Financial Institutions to use a "current" residence address for the purposes of the residence address test; and
- does not provide for the full required procedures when there is a change of circumstances with respect to New Entity Accounts.

The deficiencies relate to key elements of the AEOI Standard and are therefore material to its proper functioning.

Recommendations:

Hungary should amend its domestic legislative framework to remove four entries from its jurisdiction-specific list of Excluded Accounts as they do not meet the requirements. They are: i) Stability Saving Accounts; ii) Pension savings accounts; iii) Deposit accounts held by public notaries and advocates; and iv) Treasury Start Security Accounts (Start Accounts).

Hungary should amend its domestic legislative framework to require Reporting Financial Institutions to use only a "current" residence address when applying the residence address test.

Hungary should amend its domestic legislative framework to require Reporting Financial Institutions to apply all of the specific procedures if there is a change of circumstance in relation to a New Entity Account.

Hungary should amend its domestic legislative framework to require Reporting Financial Institution to apply all of the specified procedures if there is a change of circumstance in relation to a Preexisting Entity Account.

SR 1.3 Jurisdictions should incorporate the reporting requirements contained in Section I of the CRS into their domestic legislative framework.

Hungary has incorporated the reporting requirements in its domestic legislative framework in accordance with the CRS and its Commentary.

Recommendations:

No recommendations made.

SR 1.4 Jurisdictions should have a legislative framework in place that allows for the enforcement of the requirements of the CRS in practice.

Hungary has a legislative framework in place to enforce the requirements in a manner that is largely consistent with the CRS and its Commentary. However, a deficiency has been identified. More specifically, Hungary's legislative framework does not require Reporting Financial Institutions to keep records for the duration of time required. This is a key element of the required enforcement framework and is therefore material to the proper functioning of the AEOI Standard.

Recommendations:

Hungary should amend its domestic legislative framework to require Reporting Financial Institutions to maintain records for at least five years from the deadline to report the information, in accordance with the AEOI Standard.

CR2 International legal framework: Jurisdictions should have exchange relationships in effect with all Interested Appropriate Partners as committed to and that provide for the exchange of information in accordance with the Model CAA.

Determination: In Place

Hungary's international legal framework to exchange the information is in place, is consistent with the Model CAA and its Commentary and provides for exchange with all of Hungary's Interested Appropriate Partners (i.e. all jurisdictions that are interested in receiving information from Hungary and that meet the required standard in relation to confidentiality and data safeguards). (SRs 2.1 – 2.3)

SR 2.1 Jurisdictions should have exchange agreements in effect with all Interested Appropriate Partners that permit the automatic exchange of CRS information.

Hungary has exchange agreements that permit the automatic exchange of CRS information in effect with all its Interested Appropriate Partners.

Recommendations:

No recommendations made.

SR 2.2 Such an exchange agreement should be put in place without undue delay, following the receipt of an expression of interest from an Interested Appropriate Partner.

Hungary put in place its exchange agreements without undue delay.

Recommendations:

No recommendations made.

SR 2.3 Jurisdictions should ensure that the exchange agreements in effect provide for the exchange of information in accordance with the requirements of the Model CAA.

Hungary's exchange agreements provide for the exchange of information in accordance with the requirements of the Model CAA.

Recommendations:

No recommendations made.

Comments by the assessed jurisdiction

Hungary expresses its thanks and gratitude to the assessment team and to the Secretariat for the preparation of this report, for their availability and for the constructive collaboration throughout this review. Hungary takes due note of the findings of the report and the recommendations made and will examine them carefully, with the aim of further improving its legal framework in the area of automatic exchange of information.

Note

[1] Andorra, Liechtenstein, Monaco, San Marino and Switzerland.

Iceland

Overall findings

Iceland's legal framework implementing the AEOI Standard is in place and is consistent with the requirements of the AEOI Terms of Reference. This includes Iceland's domestic legislative framework requiring Reporting Financial Institutions to conduct the due diligence and reporting procedures (CR1) and its international legal framework to exchange the information with all of Iceland's Interested Appropriate Partners (CR2).

The methodology used for the peer reviews and that therefore underpins this report is outlined in Chapter 2.

Overall determination on the legal framework: In Place

Conclusions on the legal framework

General context

Iceland commenced exchanges under the AEOI Standard in 2017.

In order to provide for Reporting Financial Institutions to collect and report the information to be exchanged, Iceland:

- enacted Paragraphs 6 and 8 of Art. 92 in the Income Tax Law no. 90/2003;
- introduced Regulation No. 1240/2015 as amended by Regulations No. 206/2016, No. 1231/2016, No. 940/2017 and No. 557/2019;
- issued further guidance, which is legally binding; and
- made reference to the Act on Measures Against Money Laundering and Terrorist Financing No. 140/2018 implementing the FATF Recommendations for the purposes of the identification of Controlling Persons under the AEOI Standard.

Under this framework Reporting Financial Institutions were required to commence the due diligence procedures in relation to New Accounts from 1 January 2016. With respect to Preexisting Accounts, Reporting Financial Institutions were required to complete the due diligence procedures on High Value Individual Accounts by 31 December 2016 and on Lower Value Individual Accounts and Entity Accounts by 31 December 2017.

Following the initial Global Forum peer review, Iceland made various amendments to its legislative framework to address issues identified, the last of which was effective from 28 May 2019.

With respect to the exchange of information under the AEOI Standard, Iceland:

- is a Party to the Convention on Mutual Administrative Assistance in Tax Matters and activated the associated CRS Multilateral Competent Authority Agreement in time for exchanges in 2017; and
- put in place a bilateral agreement.[1]

Detailed findings

The detailed findings for Iceland are below, organised per Core Requirement (CR) and sub-requirement (SR), as extracted from the AEOI Terms of Reference (www.oecd.org/tax/transparency/documents/aeoi-terms-of-reference.pdf).

CR1 Domestic legal framework: Jurisdictions should have a domestic legislative framework in place that requires all Reporting Financial Institutions to conduct the due diligence and reporting procedures in the CRS, and that provides for the effective implementation of the CRS as set out therein.

Determination: In Place

Iceland's domestic legislative framework is in place and contains all of the key aspects of the CRS and its Commentary requiring Reporting Financial Institutions to conduct the due diligence and reporting procedures (SRs 1.1 – 1.3). It also provides for a framework to enforce the requirements (SR 1.4).

SR 1.1 Jurisdictions should define the scope of Reporting Financial Institutions consistently with the CRS.

Iceland has defined the scope of Reporting Financial Institutions in its domestic legislative framework in accordance with the CRS and its Commentary.

Recommendations:

No recommendations made.

SR 1.2 Jurisdictions should define the scope of Financial Accounts and Reportable Accounts consistently with the CRS and incorporate the due diligence procedures to identify them.

Iceland has defined the scope of the Financial Accounts that are required to be reported in its domestic legislative framework and incorporated the due diligence procedures that must be applied to identify them in accordance with the CRS and its Commentary.

Recommendations:

No recommendations made.

SR 1.3 Jurisdictions should incorporate the reporting requirements contained in Section I of the CRS into their domestic legislative framework.

Iceland has incorporated the reporting requirements in its domestic legislative framework in accordance with the CRS and its Commentary.

Recommendations:

No recommendations made.

SR 1.4 Jurisdictions should have a legislative framework in place that allows for the enforcement of the requirements of the CRS in practice.

Iceland has a legislative framework in place to enforce the requirements in accordance with the CRS and its Commentary.

Recommendations:

No recommendations made.

CR2 International legal framework: Jurisdictions should have exchange relationships in effect with all Interested Appropriate Partners as committed to and that provide for the exchange of information in accordance with the Model CAA.

Determination: In Place

Iceland's international legal framework to exchange the information is in place, is consistent with the Model CAA and its Commentary and provides for exchange with all of Iceland's Interested Appropriate Partners (i.e. all jurisdictions that are interested in receiving information from Iceland and that meet the required standard in relation to confidentiality and data safeguards). (SRs 2.1 – 2.3)

SR 2.1 Jurisdictions should have exchange agreements in effect with all Interested Appropriate Partners that permit the automatic exchange of CRS information.

Iceland has exchange agreements that permit the automatic exchange of CRS information in effect with all its Interested Appropriate Partners.

Recommendations:

No recommendations made.

SR 2.2 Such an exchange agreement should be put in place without undue delay, following the receipt of an expression of interest from an Interested Appropriate Partner.

Iceland put in place its exchange agreements without undue delay.

Recommendations:

No recommendations made.

SR 2.3 Jurisdictions should ensure that the exchange agreements in effect provide for the exchange of information in accordance with the requirements of the Model CAA.

Iceland's exchange agreements provide for the exchange of information in accordance with the requirements of the Model CAA.

Recommendations:

No recommendations made.

Comments by the assessed jurisdiction

No comments made.

Note

[1] Singapore.

India

Overall findings

India's legal framework implementing the AEOI Standard is in place but needs improvement in order to be fully consistent with the requirements of the AEOI Terms of Reference. While India's international legal framework to exchange the information with all of India's Interested Appropriate Partners (CR2) is consistent with the requirements, its domestic legislative framework requiring Reporting Financial Institutions to conduct the due diligence and reporting procedures (CR1) has deficiencies in areas significant to the proper functioning of the AEOI Standard. More specifically, India's legislative framework provides for several categories of jurisdiction-specific Non-Reporting Financial Institutions that do not meet the requirements of the AEOI Standard.

The methodology used for the peer reviews and that therefore underpins this report is outlined in Chapter 2.

Overall determination on the legal framework: In Place But **Needs Improvement**

Conclusions on the legal framework

General context

India commenced exchanges under the AEOI Standard in 2017.

In order to provide for Reporting Financial Institutions to collect and report the information to be exchanged, India:

- enacted Section 285BA of the Income-tax Act 1961 and Rules 114F to 114H of the Income-tax Rules, 1962;
- issued further guidance, which was amended on 30 July 2020 and is legally binding; and
- made reference to the Prevention of Money-laundering (Maintenance of Records) Rules, 2005 for the purposes of the identification of Controlling Persons under the AEOI Standard.

Under this framework Reporting Financial Institutions were required to commence the due diligence procedures in relation to New Accounts from 1 January 2016. With respect to Preexisting Accounts, Reporting Financial Institutions were required to complete the due diligence procedures on High Value Individual Accounts by 31 December 2016 and on Lower Value Individual Accounts and Entity Accounts by 30 June 2017.

Following the initial Global Forum peer review, India amended its legislative framework to address issues identified, effective from 30 July 2020.

With respect to the exchange of information under the AEOI Standard, India is a Party to the Convention on Mutual Administrative Assistance in Tax Matters and activated the associated CRS Multilateral Competent Authority Agreement in time for exchanges in 2017.

Detailed findings

The detailed findings for India are below, organised per Core Requirement (CR) and sub-requirement (SR), as extracted from the AEOI Terms of Reference (www.oecd.org/tax/transparency/documents/aeoi-terms-of-reference.pdf).

CR1 Domestic legal framework: Jurisdictions should have a domestic legislative framework in place that requires all Reporting Financial Institutions to conduct the due diligence and reporting procedures in the CRS, and that provides for the effective implementation of the CRS as set out therein.

Determination: In Place But **Needs Improvement**

India's domestic legislative framework is in place and contains many of the key aspects of the CRS and its Commentary requiring Reporting Financial Institutions to conduct the due diligence and reporting procedures but it needs improvement in relation to the scope of Reporting Financial Institutions required to report information (SR 1.1). More specifically, India provides for six categories of jurisdiction-specific Non-Reporting Financial Institutions that are not in line with the requirements.

SR 1.1 Jurisdictions should define the scope of Reporting Financial Institutions consistently with the CRS.

India has defined the scope of Reporting Financial Institutions in its domestic legislative framework in a manner that is largely consistent with the CRS and its Commentary. However, deficiencies have been identified. Most significantly, India has provided for four categories of jurisdiction-specific Non-Reporting Financial Institution that do not correspond to any of the categories of Non-Reporting Financial Institutions foreseen in the AEOI Standard. The definition of Reporting Financial Institutions, including the provision of Non-Reporting Financial Institutions, is material to the proper functioning of the AEOI Standard.

Recommendations:

India should amend its domestic legislative framework to remove four categories from its jurisdiction-specific list of Non-Reporting Financial Institutions as they do not correspond to any of the categories of Non-Reporting Financial Institution foreseen in the AEOI Standard. The entries are: i) Financial Institutions with Low Value Accounts; ii) Local Banks; iii) Treaty Qualified Retirement Funds and iv) Financial Institutions with a local client base.

India should amend its domestic legislative framework to remove two further categories from its jurisdiction-specific list of Non-Reporting Financial Institutions as they are Non-Financial Entities and should therefore be treated as such under the AEOI Standard. The categories are: (i) the Gratuity Fund and (ii) the Non-Public Fund of the Armed Forces.

SR 1.2 Jurisdictions should define the scope of Financial Accounts and Reportable Accounts consistently with the CRS and incorporate the due diligence procedures to identify them.

India has defined the scope of the Financial Accounts that are required to be reported in its domestic legislative framework and incorporated the due diligence procedures that must be applied to identify them in accordance with the CRS and its Commentary.

Recommendations:

No recommendations made.

SR 1.3 Jurisdictions should incorporate the reporting requirements contained in Section I of the CRS into their domestic legislative framework.

India has incorporated the reporting requirements in its domestic legislative framework in accordance with the CRS and its Commentary.

Recommendations:

No recommendations made.

SR 1.4 Jurisdictions should have a legislative framework in place that allows for the enforcement of the requirements of the CRS in practice.

India has a legislative framework in place to enforce the requirements in accordance with the CRS and its Commentary.

Recommendations:

No recommendations made.

CR2 International legal framework: Jurisdictions should have exchange relationships in effect with all Interested Appropriate Partners as committed to and that provide for the exchange of information in accordance with the Model CAA.

Determination: In Place

India's international legal framework to exchange the information is in place, is consistent with the Model CAA and its Commentary and provides for exchange with all of India's Interested Appropriate Partners (i.e. all jurisdictions that are interested in receiving information from India and that meet the required standard in relation to confidentiality and data safeguards). (SRs 2.1 – 2.3)

SR 2.1 Jurisdictions should have exchange agreements in effect with all Interested Appropriate Partners that permit the automatic exchange of CRS information.

India has exchange agreements that permit the automatic exchange of CRS information in effect with all its Interested Appropriate Partners.

Recommendations:

No recommendations made.

SR 2.2 Such an exchange agreement should be put in place without undue delay, following the receipt of an expression of interest from an Interested Appropriate Partner.

India put in place its exchange agreements without undue delay.

Recommendations:

No recommendations made.

SR 2.3 Jurisdictions should ensure that the exchange agreements in effect provide for the exchange of information in accordance with the requirements of the Model CAA.

India's exchange agreements provide for the exchange of information in accordance with the requirements of the Model CAA.

Recommendations:

No recommendations made.

Comments by the assessed jurisdiction

No comments made.

Indonesia

Overall findings

Indonesia's legal framework implementing the AEOI Standard is in place and is consistent with the requirements of the AEOI Terms of Reference. This includes Indonesia's domestic legislative framework requiring Reporting Financial Institutions to conduct the due diligence and reporting procedures (CR1) and its international legal framework to exchange the information with all of Indonesia's Interested Appropriate Partners (CR2).

The methodology used for the peer reviews and that therefore underpins this report is outlined in Chapter 2.

Overall determination on the legal framework: In Place

Conclusions on the legal framework

General context

Indonesia commenced exchanges under the AEOI Standard in 2018.

In order to provide for Reporting Financial Institutions to collect and report the information to be exchanged, Indonesia:

- enacted Law Number 9 of 2017 on Enactment of Government Regulation in Lieu of Law of The Republic of Indonesia, Number 1 of 2017 on Access to Financial Information for Tax Purposes to Become Law; and
- Introduced the Regulation of the Minister of Finance Number 70/PMK.03/2017 as most recently amended by Regulation of the Minister of Finance Number 19/PMK.03/2018 on Technical Guidance on Access to Financial Information for Tax Purposes.

Under this framework Reporting Financial Institutions were required to commence the due diligence procedures in relation to New Accounts from 1 July 2017. With respect to Preexisting Accounts, Reporting Financial Institutions were required to complete the due diligence procedures on High Value Individual Accounts by 31 December 2017 and on Lower Value Individual Accounts and Entity Accounts by 31 December 2018.

Following the initial Global Forum peer review, Indonesia amended its legislative framework to address issues identified, effective from 19 February 2019.

With respect to the exchange of information under the AEOI Standard, Indonesia:

- is a Party to the Convention on Mutual Administrative Assistance in Tax Matters and activated the associated CRS Multilateral Competent Authority Agreement in time for exchanges in 2018; and
- put in place a bilateral agreement.[1]

Detailed findings

The detailed findings for Indonesia are below, organised per Core Requirement (CR) and sub-requirement (SR), as extracted from the AEOI Terms of Reference (www.oecd.org/tax/transparency/documents/aeoi-terms-of-reference.pdf).

CR1 Domestic legal framework: Jurisdictions should have a domestic legislative framework in place that requires all Reporting Financial Institutions to conduct the due diligence and reporting procedures in the CRS, and that provides for the effective implementation of the CRS as set out therein.

Determination: In Place

Indonesia's domestic legislative framework is in place and contains all of the key aspects of the CRS and its Commentary requiring Reporting Financial Institutions to conduct the due diligence and reporting procedures (SRs 1.1 – 1.3). It also provides for a framework to enforce the requirements (SR 1.4).

SR 1.1 Jurisdictions should define the scope of Reporting Financial Institutions consistently with the CRS.

Indonesia has defined the scope of Reporting Financial Institutions in its domestic legislative framework in accordance with the CRS and its Commentary.

Recommendations:

No recommendations made.

SR 1.2 Jurisdictions should define the scope of Financial Accounts and Reportable Accounts consistently with the CRS and incorporate the due diligence procedures to identify them.

Indonesia has defined the scope of the Financial Accounts that are required to be reported in its domestic legislative framework and incorporated the due diligence procedures that must be applied to identify them in accordance with the CRS and its Commentary.

Recommendations:

No recommendations made.

SR 1.3 Jurisdictions should incorporate the reporting requirements contained in Section I of the CRS into their domestic legislative framework.

Indonesia has incorporated the reporting requirements in its domestic legislative framework in accordance with the CRS and its Commentary.

Recommendations:

No recommendations made.

SR 1.4 Jurisdictions should have a legislative framework in place that allows for the enforcement of the requirements of the CRS in practice.

Indonesia has a legislative framework in place to enforce the requirements in accordance with the CRS and its Commentary.

Recommendations:

No recommendations made.

CR2 International legal framework: Jurisdictions should have exchange relationships in effect with all Interested Appropriate Partners as committed to and that provide for the exchange of information in accordance with the Model CAA.

Determination: In Place

Indonesia's international legal framework to exchange the information is in place, is consistent with the Model CAA and its Commentary and provides for exchange with all of Indonesia's Interested Appropriate

Partners (i.e. all jurisdictions that are interested in receiving information from Indonesia and that meet the required standard in relation to confidentiality and data safeguards). (SRs 2.1 – 2.3)

SR 2.1 Jurisdictions should have exchange agreements in effect with all Interested Appropriate Partners that permit the automatic exchange of CRS information.

Indonesia has exchange agreements that permit the automatic exchange of CRS information in effect with all its Interested Appropriate Partners.

Recommendations:

No recommendations made.

SR 2.2 Such an exchange agreement should be put in place without undue delay, following the receipt of an expression of interest from an Interested Appropriate Partner.

Indonesia put in place its exchange agreements without undue delay.

Recommendations:

No recommendations made.

SR 2.3 Jurisdictions should ensure that the exchange agreements in effect provide for the exchange of information in accordance with the requirements of the Model CAA.

Indonesia's exchange agreements provide for the exchange of information in accordance with the requirements of the Model CAA.

Recommendations:

No recommendations made.

Comments by the assessed jurisdiction

No comments made.

Note

[1] With Hong Kong (China).

Ireland

Overall findings

Ireland's legal framework implementing the AEOI Standard is in place and is consistent with the requirements of the AEOI Terms of Reference. This includes Ireland's domestic legislative framework requiring Reporting Financial Institutions to conduct the due diligence and reporting procedures (CR1) and its international legal framework to exchange the information with all of Ireland's Interested Appropriate Partners (CR2).

The methodology used for the peer reviews and that therefore underpins this report is outlined in Chapter 2.

Overall determination on the legal framework: In Place

Conclusions on the legal framework

General context

Ireland commenced exchanges under the AEOI Standard in 2017.

In order to provide for Reporting Financial Institutions to collect and report the information to be exchanged, Ireland:

- amended Chapter 3 of Part 38 of the Taxes Consolidation Act, 1997 through Section 28 of the Finance Act 2014, to insert a new section 891F into the Taxes Consolidation Act, 1997;
- enacted Statutory Instrument No. 583 of 2015 and Statutory Instrument No. 560 of 2016 (European Union (Anti-Money Laundering: Beneficial Ownership of Corporate Entities) Regulations 2016);
- issued further guidance, which is not legally binding; and
- made reference to the Criminal Justice (Money Laundering and Terrorist Financing)(Amendment) Act, 2018 implementing the FATF Recommendations for the purposes of the identification of Controlling Persons under the AEOI Standard.

Under this framework Reporting Financial Institutions were required to commence the due diligence procedures in relation to New Accounts from 1 January 2016. With respect to Preexisting Accounts, Reporting Financial Institutions were required to complete the due diligence procedures on High Value Individual Accounts by 31 December 2016 and on Lower Value Individual Accounts and Entity Accounts by 31 December 2017.

With respect to the exchange of information under the AEOI Standard, Ireland:

- is a Party to the Convention on Mutual Administrative Assistance in Tax Matters and activated the associated CRS Multilateral Competent Authority Agreement in time for exchanges in 2017;
- has in place European Directive 2011/16/EU on Administrative Cooperation in the Field of Taxation as amended by Directive 2014/107/EU;
- has in place European Union agreements with five European third countries[1]; and
- put in place three bilateral agreements.[2]

Detailed findings

The detailed findings for Ireland are below, organised per Core Requirement (CR) and sub-requirement (SR), as extracted from the AEOI Terms of Reference (www.oecd.org/tax/transparency/documents/aeoi-terms-of-reference.pdf).

CR1 Domestic legal framework: Jurisdictions should have a domestic legislative framework in place that requires all Reporting Financial Institutions to conduct the due diligence and reporting procedures in the CRS, and that provides for the effective implementation of the CRS as set out therein.

Determination: In Place

Ireland's domestic legislative framework is in place and contains all of the key aspects of the CRS and its Commentary requiring Reporting Financial Institutions to conduct the due diligence and reporting procedures (SRs 1.1 – 1.3). It also provides for a framework to enforce the requirements (SR 1.4).

SR 1.1 Jurisdictions should define the scope of Reporting Financial Institutions consistently with the CRS.

Ireland has defined the scope of Reporting Financial Institutions in its domestic legislative framework in accordance with the CRS and its Commentary.

Recommendations:

No recommendations made.

SR 1.2 Jurisdictions should define the scope of Financial Accounts and Reportable Accounts consistently with the CRS and incorporate the due diligence procedures to identify them.

Ireland has defined the scope of the Financial Accounts that are required to be reported in its domestic legislative framework and incorporated the due diligence procedures that must be applied to identify them in accordance with the CRS and its Commentary.

Recommendations:

No recommendations made.

SR 1.3 Jurisdictions should incorporate the reporting requirements contained in Section I of the CRS into their domestic legislative framework.

Ireland has incorporated the reporting requirements in its domestic legislative framework in accordance with the CRS and its Commentary.

Recommendations:

No recommendations made.

SR 1.4 Jurisdictions should have a legislative framework in place that allows for the enforcement of the requirements of the CRS in practice.

Ireland has a legislative framework in place to enforce the requirements in accordance with the CRS and its Commentary.

Recommendations:

No recommendations made.

CR2 International legal framework: Jurisdictions should have exchange relationships in effect with all Interested Appropriate Partners as committed to and that provide for the exchange of information in accordance with the Model CAA.

Determination: In Place

Ireland's international legal framework to exchange the information is in place, is consistent with the Model CAA and its Commentary and provides for exchange with all of Ireland's Interested Appropriate Partners (i.e. all jurisdictions that are interested in receiving information from Ireland and that meet the required standard in relation to confidentiality and data safeguards). (SRs 2.1 – 2.3)

SR 2.1 Jurisdictions should have exchange agreements in effect with all Interested Appropriate Partners that permit the automatic exchange of CRS information.

Ireland has exchange agreements that permit the automatic exchange of CRS information in effect with all its Interested Appropriate Partners.

Recommendations:

No recommendations made.

SR 2.2 Such an exchange agreement should be put in place without undue delay, following the receipt of an expression of interest from an Interested Appropriate Partner.

Ireland put in place its exchange agreements without undue delay.

Recommendations:

No recommendations made.

SR 2.3 Jurisdictions should ensure that the exchange agreements in effect provide for the exchange of information in accordance with the requirements of the Model CAA.

Ireland's exchange agreements provide for the exchange of information in accordance with the requirements of the Model CAA.

Recommendations:

No recommendations made.

Comments by the assessed jurisdiction

No comments made.

Notes

[1] Andorra, Liechtenstein, Monaco, San Marino and Switzerland.

[2] With Hong Kong (China), Qatar and Singapore. Ireland has also activated a relationship under the CRS MCAA with Qatar.

Isle of Man

Overall findings

The Isle of Man's legal framework implementing the AEOI Standard is in place and is consistent with the requirements of the AEOI Terms of Reference. This includes the Isle of Man's domestic legislative framework requiring Reporting Financial Institutions to conduct the due diligence and reporting procedures (CR1) and its international legal framework to exchange the information with all of the Isle of Man's Interested Appropriate Partners (CR2).

The methodology used for the peer reviews and that therefore underpins this report is outlined in Chapter 2.

Overall determination on the legal framework: In Place

Conclusions on the legal framework

General context

The Isle of Man commenced exchanges under the AEOI Standard in 2017.

In order to provide for Reporting Financial Institutions to collect and report the information to be exchanged, the Isle of Man:

- issued Income Tax (Common Reporting Standard) Regulations in 2015, amended in 2017 and 2019; and
- introduced further guidance, last updated in December 2017, which is not legally binding.

Under this framework Reporting Financial Institutions were required to commence the due diligence procedures in relation to New Accounts from 1 January 2016. With respect to Preexisting Accounts, Reporting Financial Institutions were required to complete the due diligence procedures on High Value Individual Accounts by 31 December 2016 and on Lower Value Individual Accounts and Entity Accounts by 31 December 2017.

Following the initial Global Forum peer review, the Isle of Man made various amendments to its legislative framework to address issues identified, the last of which was effective from 21 March 2019.

With respect to the exchange of information under the AEOI Standard, the Isle of Man:

- has the Convention on Mutual Administrative Assistance in Tax Matters in place[1] and activated the associated CRS Multilateral Competent Authority Agreement in time for exchanges in 2017; and
- put in place nine bilateral agreements.[2]

Detailed findings

The detailed findings for the Isle of Man are below, organised per Core Requirement (CR) and sub-requirement (SR), as extracted from the AEOI Terms of Reference (www.oecd.org/tax/transparency/documents/aeoi-terms-of-reference.pdf).

CR1 Domestic legal framework: Jurisdictions should have a domestic legislative framework in place that requires all Reporting Financial Institutions to conduct the due diligence and reporting procedures in the CRS, and that provides for the effective implementation of the CRS as set out therein.

Determination: In Place

The Isle of Man's domestic legislative framework is in place and contains all of the key aspects of the CRS and its Commentary requiring Reporting Financial Institutions to conduct the due diligence and reporting procedures (SRs 1.1 – 1.3). It also provides for a framework to enforce the requirements (SR 1.4).

SR 1.1 Jurisdictions should define the scope of Reporting Financial Institutions consistently with the CRS.

The Isle of Man has defined the scope of Reporting Financial Institutions in its domestic legislative framework in accordance with the CRS and its Commentary.

Recommendations:

No recommendations made.

SR 1.2 Jurisdictions should define the scope of Financial Accounts and Reportable Accounts consistently with the CRS and incorporate the due diligence procedures to identify them.

The Isle of Man has defined the scope of the Financial Accounts that are required to be reported in its domestic legislative framework and incorporated the due diligence procedures that must be applied to identify them in accordance with the CRS and its Commentary.

Recommendations:

No recommendations made.

SR 1.3 Jurisdictions should incorporate the reporting requirements contained in Section I of the CRS into their domestic legislative framework.

The Isle of Man has incorporated the reporting requirements in its domestic legislative framework in accordance with the CRS and its Commentary.

Recommendations:

No recommendations made.

SR 1.4 Jurisdictions should have a legislative framework in place that allows for the enforcement of the requirements of the CRS in practice.

The Isle of Man has a legislative framework in place to enforce the requirements in accordance with the CRS and its Commentary.

Recommendations:

No recommendations made.

CR2 International legal framework: Jurisdictions should have exchange relationships in effect with all Interested Appropriate Partners as committed to and that provide for the exchange of information in accordance with the Model CAA.

Determination: In Place

The Isle of Man's international legal framework to exchange the information is in place, is consistent with the Model CAA and its Commentary and provides for exchange with all of the Isle of Man's Interested

Appropriate Partners (i.e. all jurisdictions that are interested in receiving information from the Isle of Man and that meet the required standard in relation to confidentiality and data safeguards). (SRs 2.1 – 2.3)

SR 2.1 Jurisdictions should have exchange agreements in effect with all Interested Appropriate Partners that permit the automatic exchange of CRS information.

The Isle of Man has exchange agreements that permit the automatic exchange of CRS information in effect with all its Interested Appropriate Partners.

Recommendations:

No recommendations made.

SR 2.2 Such an exchange agreement should be put in place without undue delay, following the receipt of an expression of interest from an Interested Appropriate Partner.

The Isle of Man put in place its exchange agreements without undue delay.

Recommendations:

No recommendations made.

SR 2.3 Jurisdictions should ensure that the exchange agreements in effect provide for the exchange of information in accordance with the requirements of the Model CAA.

The Isle of Man's exchange agreements provide for the exchange of information in accordance with the requirements of the Model CAA.

Recommendations:

No recommendations made.

Comments by the assessed jurisdiction

No comments made.

Notes

[1] Through a territorial extension by the United Kingdom.

[2] With Anguilla, Bermuda, the British Virgin Islands, the Cayman Islands, Gibraltar, Guernsey, Jersey, the Turks and Caicos Islands and the United Kingdom.

Israel

Overall findings

Israel's legal framework implementing the AEOI Standard is not in place in accordance with the requirements of the AEOI Terms of Reference. While Israel's international legal framework to exchange the information with all of Israel's Interested Appropriate Partners (CR2) is consistent with the requirements, the domestic legislative framework requiring Reporting Financial Institutions to conduct the due diligence and reporting procedures (CR1) has significant deficiencies in areas that are fundamental to the proper functioning of the AEOI Standard. More specifically, the deficiencies relate to the scope of Reporting Financial Institutions, the scope of Financial Accounts, the due diligence procedures to identify Reportable Accounts, and to the enforcement framework.

The methodology used for the peer reviews and that therefore underpins this report is outlined in Chapter 2.

Overall determination on the legal framework: Not In Place

Conclusions on the legal framework

General context

Israel committed to commence exchanges under the AEOI Standard in 2018. Due to delays in putting in place the necessary domestic legal framework, Israel commenced exchanges in 2019 and, where possible, also exchanged the information that was due to be exchanged in 2018.

In order to provide for Reporting Financial Institutions to collect and report the information to be exchanged, Israel:

- amended the Tax Ordinance; and
- issued the Income Tax Regulations (Implementation of the Common Standard on Reporting and Due Diligence for Financial Account information) in 2019.

Under this framework Reporting Financial Institutions were required to commence the due diligence procedures in relation to New Accounts from 1 April 2019. With respect to Preexisting Accounts, Reporting Financial Institutions were required to complete the due diligence procedures on High Value Individual Accounts by 31 December 2019 and on Lower Value Individual Accounts and Entity Accounts by 31 December 2020.

With respect to the exchange of information under the AEOI Standard, Israel is a Party to the Convention on Mutual Administrative Assistance in Tax Matters and activated the associated CRS Multilateral Competent Authority Agreement in time for exchanges in 2019.

Detailed findings

The detailed findings for Israel are below, organised per Core Requirement (CR) and sub-requirement (SR), as extracted from the AEOI Terms of Reference (www.oecd.org/tax/transparency/documents/aeoi-terms-of-reference.pdf).

CR1 Domestic legal framework: Jurisdictions should have a domestic legislative framework in place that requires all Reporting Financial Institutions to conduct the due diligence and reporting procedures in the CRS, and that provides for the effective implementation of the CRS as set out therein.

Determination: Not In Place

Israel's domestic legislative framework is not in place as required as it does not contain several key aspects of the CRS and the Commentary. Significant deficiencies have been identified relating to the scope of Financial Accounts and the due diligence procedures to identify Reportable Accounts (SR 1.2) and the framework to enforce the requirements (SR 1.4). Furthermore, Israel provides for several jurisdiction-specific Non-Reporting Financial Institutions (SR 1.1) that do not meet the requirements of the AEOI Standard.

SR 1.1 Jurisdictions should define the scope of Reporting Financial Institutions consistently with the CRS.

Israel has defined the scope of Reporting Financial Institutions in its domestic legislative framework in a manner that is largely consistent with the CRS and its Commentary. However, deficiencies have been identified. More specifically, Israel provides for two jurisdiction-specific Non-Reporting Financial Institutions that are not in accordance with the requirements. The definition of Reporting Financial Institutions, including the provision of Non-Reporting Financial Institutions, is material to the proper functioning of the AEOI Standard.

Recommendations:

Israel should amend its domestic legislative framework to remove two entries from its jurisdiction-specific list of categories of Non-Reporting Financial Institutions as they do not meet the requirements. The entries are: i) provident funds; and ii) small financial institutions.

SR 1.2 Jurisdictions should define the scope of Financial Accounts and Reportable Accounts consistently with the CRS and incorporate the due diligence procedures to identify them.

Israel has not defined the scope of the Financial Accounts that are required to be reported in its domestic legislative framework in a manner that is consistent with the CRS and its Commentary and has not incorporated the due diligence procedures that must be applied to identify them correctly as significant deficiencies have been identified. More specifically, the exclusion of certain equity and debt interests from the definition of Financial Account is not in accordance with the AEOI Standard. Furthermore, Israel provides for several jurisdiction-specific Excluded Accounts that are not in accordance with the requirements. The scope of Financial Accounts and the due diligence procedures to identify them are material to the proper functioning of the AEOI Standard.

Recommendations:

Israel should amend its domestic legislative framework to include all of the required categories of Equity or debt interest in the definition of Financial Account in accordance with the AEOI Standard.

Israel should amend its domestic legislative framework to define the term Active NFE in accordance with the AEOI Standard.

Israel should amend its domestic legislative framework to remove three entries from its jurisdiction-specific list of categories of Excluded Accounts as they do not meet the requirements. The entries are: i) undefined group of beneficiary accounts; ii) escrow accounts maintained by lawyers, rabbinical pleaders or accountants; and iii) dormant accounts.

SR 1.3 Jurisdictions should incorporate the reporting requirements contained in Section I of the CRS into their domestic legislative framework.

Israel has incorporated the reporting requirements in its domestic legislative framework in accordance with the CRS and its Commentary.

Recommendations:

No recommendations made.

SR 1.4 Jurisdictions should have a legislative framework in place that allows for the enforcement of the requirements of the CRS in practice.

Israel does not have a legislative framework in place to enforce the requirements in a manner that is consistent with the CRS and its Commentary as significant deficiencies have been identified. More specifically, Israel's legislative framework:

- does not contain rules to prevent Financial Institutions, persons or intermediaries from adopting practices intended to circumvent the reporting and due diligence procedures as required; and
- does not include rules requiring Reporting Financial Institutions to keep records in accordance with the requirements.

These are key elements of the required enforcement framework and are therefore material to the proper functioning of the AEOI Standard.

Recommendations:

Israel should amend its domestic legislative framework to include rules to prevent Financial Institutions, persons and intermediaries from adopting practices intended to circumvent the due diligence and reporting procedures.

Israel should amend its domestic legislative framework to require all Reporting Financial Institutions to keep all of the records required to be maintained, rather than relying only on the requirements contained in the AML framework.

Israel should amend its domestic legislative framework to require Reporting Financial Institutions to maintain records for at least five years from the deadline to report the information, in accordance with the AEOI Standard.

CR2 International legal framework: Jurisdictions should have exchange relationships in effect with all Interested Appropriate Partners as committed to and that provide for the exchange of information in accordance with the Model CAA.

Determination: In Place

Israel's international legal framework to exchange the information is in place, is consistent with the Model CAA and its Commentary and provides for exchange with all of Israel's Interested Appropriate Partners (i.e. all jurisdictions that are interested in receiving information from Israel and that meet the required standard in relation to confidentiality and data safeguards). (SRs 2.1 – 2.3)

SR 2.1 Jurisdictions should have exchange agreements in effect with all Interested Appropriate Partners that permit the automatic exchange of CRS information.

Israel has exchange agreements that permit the automatic exchange of CRS information in effect with all its Interested Appropriate Partners.

Recommendations:

No recommendations made.

SR 2.2 Such an exchange agreement should be put in place without undue delay, following the receipt of an expression of interest from an Interested Appropriate Partner.

Israel put in place its exchange agreements without undue delay.

Recommendations:

No recommendations made.

SR 2.3 Jurisdictions should ensure that the exchange agreements in effect provide for the exchange of information in accordance with the requirements of the Model CAA.

Israel's exchange agreements provide for the exchange of information in accordance with the requirements of the Model CAA.

Recommendations:

No recommendations made.

Comments by the assessed jurisdiction

No comments made.

Italy

Overall findings

Italy's legal framework implementing the AEOI Standard is in place and is consistent with the requirements of the AEOI Terms of Reference. This includes Italy's domestic legislative framework requiring Reporting Financial Institutions to conduct the due diligence and reporting procedures (CR1) and its international legal framework to exchange the information with all of Italy's Interested Appropriate Partners (CR2).

The methodology used for the peer reviews and that therefore underpins this report is outlined in Chapter 2.

Overall determination on the legal framework: In Place

Conclusions on the legal framework

General context

Italy commenced exchanges under the AEOI Standard in 2017.

In order to provide for Reporting Financial Institutions to collect and report the information to be exchanged, Italy:

- enacted the Law of 18 June 2015, n. 95 (*Legge 18 giugno 2015*, n. 95);
- introduced the Ministerial Decree of 28 December 2015 (DM 28-12-2015); and
- issued guidance, which is not legally binding.

Under this framework Reporting Financial Institutions were required to commence the due diligence procedures in relation to New Accounts from 1 January 2016. With respect to Preexisting Accounts, Reporting Financial Institutions were required to complete the due diligence procedures on High Value Individual Accounts by 31 December 2016 and on Lower Value Individual Accounts and Entity Accounts by 31 December 2017.

With respect to the exchange of information under the AEOI Standard, Italy:

- is a Party to the Convention on Mutual Administrative Assistance in Tax Matters and activated the associated CRS Multilateral Competent Authority Agreement in time for exchanges in 2017;
- has in place European Directive 2011/16/EU on Administrative Cooperation in the Field of Taxation as amended by Directive 2014/107/EU;
- has in place European Union agreements with five European third countries[1]; and
- has in place two bilateral agreements.[2]

Detailed findings

The detailed findings for Italy are below, organised per Core Requirement (CR) and sub-requirement (SR), as extracted from the AEOI Terms of Reference (www.oecd.org/tax/transparency/documents/aeoi-terms-of-reference.pdf).

CR1 Domestic legal framework: Jurisdictions should have a domestic legislative framework in place that requires all Reporting Financial Institutions to conduct the due diligence and reporting procedures in the CRS, and that provides for the effective implementation of the CRS as set out therein.

Determination: In Place

Italy's domestic legislative framework is in place and contains all of the key aspects of the CRS and its Commentary requiring Reporting Financial Institutions to conduct the due diligence and reporting procedures (SRs 1.1 – 1.3). It also provides for a framework to enforce the requirements (SR 1.4).

SR 1.1 Jurisdictions should define the scope of Reporting Financial Institutions consistently with the CRS.

Italy has defined the scope of Reporting Financial Institutions in its domestic legislative framework in accordance with the CRS and its Commentary.

Recommendations:

No recommendations made.

SR 1.2 Jurisdictions should define the scope of Financial Accounts and Reportable Accounts consistently with the CRS and incorporate the due diligence procedures to identify them.

Italy has defined the scope of the Financial Accounts that are required to be reported in its domestic legislative framework and incorporated the due diligence procedures that must be applied to identify them in accordance with the CRS and its Commentary.

Recommendations:

No recommendations made.

SR 1.3 Jurisdictions should incorporate the reporting requirements contained in Section I of the CRS into their domestic legislative framework.

Italy has incorporated the reporting requirements in its domestic legislative framework in accordance with the CRS and its Commentary.

Recommendations:

No recommendations made.

SR 1.4 Jurisdictions should have a legislative framework in place that allows for the enforcement of the requirements of the CRS in practice.

Italy has a legislative framework in place to enforce the requirements in accordance with the CRS and its Commentary.

Recommendations:

No recommendations made.

CR2 International legal framework: Jurisdictions should have exchange relationships in effect with all Interested Appropriate Partners as committed to and that provide for the exchange of information in accordance with the Model CAA.

Determination: In Place

Italy's international legal framework to exchange the information is in place, is consistent with the Model CAA and its Commentary and provides for exchange with all of Italy's Interested Appropriate Partners (i.e.

all jurisdictions that are interested in receiving information from Italy and that meet the required standard in relation to confidentiality and data safeguards). (SRs 2.1 – 2.3)

SR 2.1 Jurisdictions should have exchange agreements in effect with all Interested Appropriate Partners that permit the automatic exchange of CRS information.

Italy has exchange agreements that permit the automatic exchange of CRS information in effect with all its Interested Appropriate Partners.

Recommendations:

No recommendations made.

SR 2.2 Such an exchange agreement should be put in place without undue delay, following the receipt of an expression of interest from an Interested Appropriate Partner.

Italy put in place its exchange agreements without undue delay.

Recommendations:

No recommendations made.

SR 2.3 Jurisdictions should ensure that the exchange agreements in effect provide for the exchange of information in accordance with the requirements of the Model CAA.

Italy's exchange agreements provide for the exchange of information in accordance with the requirements of the Model CAA.

Recommendations:

No recommendations made.

Comments by the assessed jurisdiction

No comments made.

Notes

[1] Andorra, Liechtenstein, Monaco, San Marino and Switzerland.

[2] Hong Kong (China) and Singapore. Italy has also activated a relationship under the CRS MCAA with Singapore.

Japan

Overall findings

Japan's legal framework implementing the AEOI Standard is in place but needs improvement in order to be fully consistent with the requirements of the AEOI Terms of Reference. While Japan's international legal framework to exchange the information with all of Japan's Interested Appropriate Partners (CR2) is consistent with the requirements, its domestic legislative framework requiring Reporting Financial Institutions to conduct the due diligence and reporting procedures (CR1) has deficiencies significant to the proper functioning of elements of the AEOI Standard. More specifically, Japan's legislative framework is deficient as far as the definition and identification process for Controlling Persons is concerned.

The methodology used for the peer reviews and that therefore underpins this report is outlined in Chapter 2.

Overall determination on the legal framework: In Place But **Needs Improvement**

Conclusions on the legal framework

General context

Japan commenced exchanges under the AEOI Standard in 2018.

In order to provide for Reporting Financial Institutions to collect and report the information to be exchanged, Japan:

- enacted the Act on Special Provisions of the Income Tax Act, the Corporation Tax Act and the Local Tax Act Incidental to Enforcement of Tax Treaties (CRS Act), as amended;
- introduced the Order for the Enforcement of the Act on Special Provisions of the Income Tax Act, the Corporation Tax Act and the Local Tax Act Incidental to Enforcement of Tax Treaties (CRS Order), as amended;
- introduced the Ordinance for the Enforcement of the Act on Special Provisions of the Income Tax Act, the Corporation Tax Act and the Local Tax Act Incidental to Enforcement of Tax Treaties (CRS Ordinance), as amended; and
- made reference to the Order for Enforcement of the Act on Prevention of Transfer of Criminal Proceeds as well as the Ordinance for Enforcement of the Act on Prevention of Transfer of Criminal Proceeds for the purposes of implementing the FATF Recommendations for the purposes of the identification of Controlling Persons under the AEOI Standard.

Under this framework Reporting Financial Institutions were required to commence the due diligence procedures in relation to New Accounts from 1 January 2017. With respect to Preexisting Accounts, Reporting Financial Institutions were required to complete the due diligence procedures on High Value Individual Accounts by 31 December 2017 and on Lower Value Individual Accounts and Entity Accounts by 31 December 2018.

Following the initial Global Forum peer review, Japan amended its legislative framework to address issues identified, effective from 1 April 2020.

With respect to the exchange of information under the AEOI Standard, Japan:

- is a Party to the Convention on Mutual Administrative Assistance in Tax Matters and activated the associated CRS Multilateral Competent Authority Agreement in time for exchanges in 2018; and

- put in place two bilateral agreements.[1]

Detailed findings

The detailed findings for Japan are below, organised per Core Requirement (CR) and sub-requirement (SR), as extracted from the AEOI Terms of Reference (www.oecd.org/tax/transparency/documents/aeoi-terms-of-reference.pdf).

CR1 Domestic legal framework: Jurisdictions should have a domestic legislative framework in place that requires all Reporting Financial Institutions to conduct the due diligence and reporting procedures in the CRS, and that provides for the effective implementation of the CRS as set out therein.

Determination: In Place But **Needs Improvement**

Japan's domestic legislative framework is in place and contains most of the key aspects of the CRS and its Commentary requiring Reporting Financial Institutions to conduct the due diligence and reporting procedures, but it needs improvement in relation to the scope of Financial Accounts required to be reported (SR 1.2). More specifically, Japan's legislative framework does not fully incorporate the definitions and processes related to the identification of Controlling Persons of trusts and similar legal arrangements.

SR 1.1 Jurisdictions should define the scope of Reporting Financial Institutions consistently with the CRS.

Japan has defined the scope of Reporting Financial Institutions in its domestic legislative framework in accordance with the CRS and its Commentary.

Recommendations:

No recommendations made.

SR 1.2 Jurisdictions should define the scope of Financial Accounts and Reportable Accounts consistently with the CRS and incorporate the due diligence procedures to identify them.

Japan has defined the scope of the Financial Accounts that are required to be reported in its domestic legislative framework and incorporated the due diligence procedures that must be applied to identify them in a manner that is largely consistent with the CRS and its Commentary. However, deficiencies have been identified. More specifically, Japan's legislative framework does not fully incorporate the definition of Controlling Persons as required and does not fully incorporate the due diligence procedures to identify Controlling Persons. The definition and identification of Controlling Persons is material to the proper functioning of the AEOI Standard.

Recommendations:

Japan should amend its domestic legislative framework to require Reporting Financial Institutions to always identify and determine the reportable status of the Controlling Persons of trusts and similar legal arrangements in accordance with the AEOI Standard.

Japan should amend its domestic legislative framework to fully incorporate the definition of Controlling Persons in accordance with the AEOI Standard by including all natural persons required to be identified with respect to trusts and similar legal arrangements.

SR 1.3 Jurisdictions should incorporate the reporting requirements contained in Section I of the CRS into their domestic legislative framework.

Japan has incorporated the reporting requirements in its domestic legislative framework in accordance with the CRS and its Commentary.

Recommendations:

No recommendations made.

SR 1.4 Jurisdictions should have a legislative framework in place that allows for the enforcement of the requirements of the CRS in practice.

Japan has a legislative framework in place to enforce the requirements in accordance with the CRS and its Commentary.

Recommendations:

No recommendations made.

CR2 International legal framework: Jurisdictions should have exchange relationships in effect with all Interested Appropriate Partners as committed to and that provide for the exchange of information in accordance with the Model CAA.

Determination: In Place

Japan's international legal framework to exchange the information is in place, is consistent with the Model CAA and its Commentary and provides for exchange with all of Japan's Interested Appropriate Partners (i.e. all jurisdictions that are interested in receiving information from Japan and that meet the required standard in relation to confidentiality and data safeguards). (SRs 2.1 – 2.3)

SR 2.1 Jurisdictions should have exchange agreements in effect with all Interested Appropriate Partners that permit the automatic exchange of CRS information.

Japan has exchange agreements that permit the automatic exchange of CRS information in effect with all its Interested Appropriate Partners.

Recommendations:

No recommendations made.

SR 2.2 Such an exchange agreement should be put in place without undue delay, following the receipt of an expression of interest from an Interested Appropriate Partner.

Japan put in place its exchange agreements without undue delay.

Recommendations:

No recommendations made.

SR 2.3 Jurisdictions should ensure that the exchange agreements in effect provide for the exchange of information in accordance with the requirements of the Model CAA.

Japan's exchange agreements provide for the exchange of information in accordance with the requirements of the Model CAA.

Recommendations:

No recommendations made.

Comments by the assessed jurisdiction

Japan would like to extend its sincere appreciation to the assessment team for their dedicated work and professionalism throughout the peer review process. Japan will work on the implementation of the recommendations indicated in the report taking account of further contributions toward enhancing international tax transparency.

Note

[1] With Hong Kong (China) and Singapore. Japan has also activated a relationship under the CRS MCAA with Singapore.

Jersey

Overall findings

Jersey's legal framework implementing the AEOI Standard is in place and is consistent with the requirements of the AEOI Terms of Reference. This includes Jersey's domestic legislative framework requiring Reporting Financial Institutions to conduct the due diligence and reporting procedures (CR1) and its international legal framework to exchange the information with all of Jersey's Interested Appropriate Partners (CR2).

The methodology used for the peer reviews and that therefore underpins this report is outlined in Chapter 2.

Overall determination on the legal framework: In Place

Conclusions on the legal framework

General context

Jersey commenced exchanges under the AEOI Standard in 2017.

In order to provide for Reporting Financial Institutions to collect and report the information to be exchanged, Jersey:

- relies on the Taxation (Implementation) (Jersey) Law 2004;
- introduced the Taxation (Implementation) (International Tax Compliance) (Common Reporting Standard) (Jersey) Regulations in 2015; and
- issued further guidance, which is not legally binding.

Under this framework Reporting Financial Institutions were required to commence the due diligence procedures in relation to New Accounts from 1 January 2016. With respect to Preexisting Accounts, Reporting Financial Institutions were required to complete the due diligence procedures on High Value Individual Accounts by 31 December 2016 and on Lower Value Individual Accounts and Entity Accounts by 31 December 2017.

Following the initial Global Forum peer review, Jersey made various amendments to its legislative framework to address issues identified, the last of which was effective from 17 October 2017.

With respect to the exchange of information under the AEOI Standard, Jersey:

- has the Convention on Mutual Administrative Assistance in Tax Matters in place[1] and activated the associated CRS Multilateral Competent Authority Agreement in time for exchanges in 2017; and
- put in place three bilateral agreements.[2]

Detailed findings

The detailed findings for Jersey are below, organised per Core Requirement (CR) and sub-requirement (SR), as extracted from the AEOI Terms of Reference (www.oecd.org/tax/transparency/documents/aeoi-terms-of-reference.pdf).

CR1 Domestic legal framework: Jurisdictions should have a domestic legislative framework in place that requires all Reporting Financial Institutions to conduct the due diligence and reporting procedures in the CRS, and that provides for the effective implementation of the CRS as set out therein.

Determination: In Place

Jersey's domestic legislative framework is in place and contains all of the key aspects of the CRS and its Commentary requiring Reporting Financial Institutions to conduct the due diligence and reporting procedures (SRs 1.1 – 1.3). It also provides for a framework to enforce the requirements (SR 1.4).

SR 1.1 Jurisdictions should define the scope of Reporting Financial Institutions consistently with the CRS.

Jersey has defined the scope of Reporting Financial Institutions in its domestic legislative framework in accordance with the CRS and its Commentary.

Recommendations:

No recommendations made.

SR 1.2 Jurisdictions should define the scope of Financial Accounts and Reportable Accounts consistently with the CRS and incorporate the due diligence procedures to identify them.

Jersey has defined the scope of the Financial Accounts that are required to be reported in its domestic legislative framework and incorporated the due diligence procedures that must be applied to identify them in accordance with the CRS and its Commentary.

Recommendations:

No recommendations made.

SR 1.3 Jurisdictions should incorporate the reporting requirements contained in Section I of the CRS into their domestic legislative framework.

Jersey has incorporated the reporting requirements in its domestic legislative framework in accordance with the CRS and its Commentary.

Recommendations:

No recommendations made.

SR 1.4 Jurisdictions should have a legislative framework in place that allows for the enforcement of the requirements of the CRS in practice.

Jersey has a legislative framework in place to enforce the requirements in accordance with the CRS and its Commentary.

Recommendations:

No recommendations made.

CR2 International legal framework: Jurisdictions should have exchange relationships in effect with all Interested Appropriate Partners as committed to and that provide for the exchange of information in accordance with the Model CAA.

Determination: In Place

Jersey's international legal framework to exchange the information is in place, is consistent with the Model CAA and its Commentary and provides for exchange with all of Jersey's Interested Appropriate Partners (i.e. all jurisdictions that are interested in receiving information from Jersey and that meet the required standard in relation to confidentiality and data safeguards). (SRs 2.1 – 2.3)

SR 2.1 Jurisdictions should have exchange agreements in effect with all Interested Appropriate Partners that permit the automatic exchange of CRS information.

Jersey has exchange agreements that permit the automatic exchange of CRS information in effect with all its Interested Appropriate Partners.

Recommendations:

No recommendations made.

SR 2.2 Such an exchange agreement should be put in place without undue delay, following the receipt of an expression of interest from an Interested Appropriate Partner.

Jersey put in place its exchange agreements without undue delay.

Recommendations:

No recommendations made.

SR 2.3 Jurisdictions should ensure that the exchange agreements in effect provide for the exchange of information in accordance with the requirements of the Model CAA.

Jersey's exchange agreements provide for the exchange of information in accordance with the requirements of the Model CAA.

Recommendations:

No recommendations made.

Comments by the assessed jurisdiction

No comments made.

Notes

[1] Through a territorial extension by the United Kingdom.

[2] With Guernsey, the Isle of Man and the United Kingdom.

Korea

Overall findings

Korea's legal framework implementing the AEOI Standard is in place and is consistent with the requirements of the AEOI Terms of Reference. This includes Korea's domestic legislative framework requiring Reporting Financial Institutions to conduct the due diligence and reporting procedures (CR1) and its international legal framework to exchange the information with all of Korea's Interested Appropriate Partners (CR2).

The methodology used for the peer reviews and that therefore underpins this report is outlined in Chapter 2.

Overall determination on the legal framework: In Place

Conclusions on the legal framework

General context

Korea commenced exchanges under the AEOI Standard in 2017.

In order to provide for Reporting Financial Institutions to collect and report the information to be exchanged, Korea:

- enacted Paragraphs 3~11 of Art. 31 of the Law for the Coordination of International Tax Affairs;
- introduced regulation number 47 "Enforcement degree of the Act on reporting and Using Specified Financial Transaction Information"; and
- issued further guidance, which is legally binding.

Under this framework Reporting Financial Institutions were required to commence the due diligence procedures in relation to New Accounts from 1 January 2016. With respect to Preexisting Accounts, Reporting Financial Institutions were required to complete the due diligence procedures on High Value Individual Accounts by 31 December 2016 and on Lower Value Individual Accounts and on Entity Accounts by 31 December 2017.

Following the initial Global Forum peer review, Korea amended its legislative framework to address issues identified, effective from 31 May 2019.

With respect to the exchange of information under the AEOI Standard, Korea:

- is a Party to the Convention on Mutual Administrative Assistance in Tax Matters and activated the associated CRS Multilateral Competent Authority Agreement in time for exchanges in 2017; and
- put in place three bilateral agreements.[1]

Detailed findings

The detailed findings for Korea are below, organised per Core Requirement (CR) and sub-requirement (SR), as extracted from the AEOI Terms of Reference (www.oecd.org/tax/transparency/documents/aeoi-terms-of-reference.pdf).

CR1 Domestic legal framework: Jurisdictions should have a domestic legislative framework in place that requires all Reporting Financial Institutions to conduct the due diligence and reporting procedures in the CRS, and that provides for the effective implementation of the CRS as set out therein.

Determination: In Place

Korea's domestic legislative framework is in place and contains all of the key aspects of the CRS and its Commentary requiring Reporting Financial Institutions to conduct the due diligence and reporting procedures (SRs 1.1 – 1.3). It also provides for a framework to enforce the requirements (SR 1.4).

SR 1.1 Jurisdictions should define the scope of Reporting Financial Institutions consistently with the CRS.

Korea has defined the scope of Reporting Financial Institutions in its domestic legislative framework in accordance with the CRS and its Commentary.

Recommendations:

No recommendations made.

SR 1.2 Jurisdictions should define the scope of Financial Accounts and Reportable Accounts consistently with the CRS and incorporate the due diligence procedures to identify them.

Korea has defined the scope of the Financial Accounts that are required to be reported in its domestic legislative framework and incorporated the due diligence procedures that must be applied to identify them in accordance with the CRS and its Commentary.

Recommendations:

No recommendations made.

SR 1.3 Jurisdictions should incorporate the reporting requirements contained in Section I of the CRS into their domestic legislative framework.

Korea has incorporated the reporting requirements in its domestic legislative framework in accordance with the CRS and its Commentary.

Recommendations:

No recommendations made.

SR 1.4 Jurisdictions should have a legislative framework in place that allows for the enforcement of the requirements of the CRS in practice.

Korea has a legislative framework in place to enforce the requirements in accordance with the CRS and its Commentary.

Recommendations:

No recommendations made.

CR2 International legal framework: Jurisdictions should have exchange relationships in effect with all Interested Appropriate Partners as committed to and that provide for the exchange of information in accordance with the Model CAA.

Determination: In Place

Korea's international legal framework to exchange the information is in place, is consistent with the Model CAA and its Commentary and provides for exchange with all of Korea's Interested Appropriate Partners (i.e. all jurisdictions that are interested in receiving information from Korea and that meet the required standard in relation to confidentiality and data safeguards). (SRs 2.1 – 2.3)

SR 2.1 Jurisdictions should have exchange agreements in effect with all Interested Appropriate Partners that permit the automatic exchange of CRS information.

Korea has exchange agreements that permit the automatic exchange of CRS information in effect with all its Interested Appropriate Partners.

Recommendations:

No recommendations made.

SR 2.2 Such an exchange agreement should be put in place without undue delay, following the receipt of an expression of interest from an Interested Appropriate Partner.

Korea put in place its exchange agreements without undue delay.

Recommendations:

No recommendations made.

SR 2.3 Jurisdictions should ensure that the exchange agreements in effect provide for the exchange of information in accordance with the requirements of the Model CAA.

Korea's exchange agreements provide for the exchange of information in accordance with the requirements of the Model CAA.

Recommendations:

No recommendations made.

Comments by the assessed jurisdiction

No comments made.

Note

[1] With Hong Kong (China), Qatar and Singapore. Korea has also activated relationships under the CRS MCAA with Qatar and Singapore.

Kuwait

Overall findings

Kuwait's legal framework implementing the AEOI Standard is not in place in accordance with the requirements of the AEOI Terms of Reference. While Kuwait's international legal framework to exchange the information with all of Kuwait's Interested Appropriate Partners (CR2) is consistent with the requirements, the domestic legislative framework requiring Reporting Financial Institutions to conduct the due diligence and reporting procedures (CR1) has significant deficiencies in areas that are fundamental to the proper functioning of the AEOI Standard. More specifically, deficiencies have been identified in Kuwait's enforcement framework.

The methodology used for the peer reviews and that therefore underpins this report is outlined in Chapter 2.

Overall determination on the legal framework: Not In Place

Conclusions on the legal framework

General context

Kuwait commenced exchanges under the AEOI Standard in 2019, when it exchanged information relating to both 2017 and 2018.

In order to provide for Reporting Financial Institutions to collect and report the information to be exchanged, Kuwait issued Ministerial Decision No. (36) for the year 2017.

Under this framework Reporting Financial Institutions were required to commence the due diligence procedures in relation to New Accounts from 1 April 2017. With respect to Preexisting Accounts, Reporting Financial Institutions were required to complete the due diligence procedures on High Value Individual Accounts by 31 December 2017 and on Lower Value Individual Accounts and Entity Accounts by 31 December 2018.

With respect to the exchange of information under the AEOI Standard, Kuwait is a Party to the Convention on Mutual Administrative Assistance in Tax Matters and activated the associated CRS Multilateral Competent Authority Agreement in time for exchanges in 2019.

Detailed findings

The detailed findings for Kuwait are below, organised per Core Requirement (CR) and sub-requirement (SR), as extracted from the AEOI Terms of Reference (www.oecd.org/tax/transparency/documents/aeoi-terms-of-reference.pdf).

CR1 Domestic legal framework: Jurisdictions should have a domestic legislative framework in place that requires all Reporting Financial Institutions to conduct the due diligence and reporting procedures in the CRS, and that provides for the effective implementation of the CRS as set out therein.

Determination: Not In Place

Kuwait's domestic legislative framework is not in place as required as it does not contain several key aspects of the CRS and the Commentary. Significant deficiencies have been identified in relation to the framework to enforce the requirements (SR 1.4). Most significantly, Kuwait's domestic legislative framework does not provide relevant authorities access to records kept by Financial Institutions, does not incorporate a framework for enforcement to address non-compliance, and does not include strong measures to ensure that valid self-certifications are always obtained for New Accounts.

SR 1.1 Jurisdictions should define the scope of Reporting Financial Institutions consistently with the CRS.

Kuwait has defined the scope of Reporting Financial Institutions in its domestic legislative framework in accordance with the CRS and its Commentary.

Recommendations:

No recommendations made.

SR 1.2 Jurisdictions should define the scope of Financial Accounts and Reportable Accounts consistently with the CRS and incorporate the due diligence procedures to identify them.

Kuwait has defined the scope of the Financial Accounts that are required to be reported in its domestic legislative framework and incorporated the due diligence procedures that must be applied to identify them in accordance with the CRS and its Commentary.

Recommendations:

No recommendations made.

SR 1.3 Jurisdictions should incorporate the reporting requirements contained in Section I of the CRS into their domestic legislative framework.

Kuwait has incorporated the reporting requirements in its domestic legislative framework in accordance with the CRS and its Commentary.

Recommendations:

No recommendations made.

SR 1.4 Jurisdictions should have a legislative framework in place that allows for the enforcement of the requirements of the CRS in practice.

Kuwait does not have a legislative framework in place to enforce the requirements in a manner that is consistent with the CRS and its Commentary as significant deficiencies have been identified. More specifically, Kuwait's legislative framework:

- does not include sanctions on Account Holders and Controlling Persons for the provision of a false self-certification;
- does not provide the relevant authorities with the power to access the records held by Reporting Financial Institutions in relation to the due diligence procedures applied;
- does not provide for sanctions on Reporting Financial Institutions for failing to carry out the due diligence procedures; and
- does not incorporate measures to ensure that self-certifications are always obtained and validated for New Accounts as is required.

These are key elements of the required enforcement framework and are therefore material to the proper functioning of the AEOI Standard.

Recommendations:

Kuwait should amend its domestic legislative framework to include sanctions on Account Holders and Controlling Persons for the provision of a false self-certification.

Kuwait should amend its domestic legislative framework to provide the appropriate authorities with access to the records required to be kept by Reporting Financial Institutions.

Kuwait should amend its domestic legislative framework to include sanctions for failure to comply with the due diligence and reporting procedures.

Kuwait should amend its domestic legislative framework to include strong measures to ensure that valid self-certifications are always obtained for New Accounts in accordance with the requirements.

CR2 International legal framework: Jurisdictions should have exchange relationships in effect with all Interested Appropriate Partners as committed to and that provide for the exchange of information in accordance with the Model CAA.

Determination: In Place

Kuwait's international legal framework to exchange the information is in place, is consistent with the Model CAA and its Commentary and provides for exchange with all of Kuwait's Interested Appropriate Partners (i.e. all jurisdictions that are interested in receiving information from Kuwait and that meet the required standard in relation to confidentiality and data safeguards). (SRs 2.1 – 2.3)

SR 2.1 Jurisdictions should have exchange agreements in effect with all Interested Appropriate Partners that permit the automatic exchange of CRS information.

Kuwait has exchange agreements that permit the automatic exchange of CRS information in effect with all its Interested Appropriate Partners.

Recommendations:

No recommendations made.

SR 2.2 Such an exchange agreement should be put in place without undue delay, following the receipt of an expression of interest from an Interested Appropriate Partner.

Kuwait put in place its exchange agreements without undue delay.

Recommendations:

No recommendations made.

SR 2.3 Jurisdictions should ensure that the exchange agreements in effect provide for the exchange of information in accordance with the requirements of the Model CAA.

Kuwait's exchange agreements provide for the exchange of information in accordance with the requirements of the Model CAA.

Recommendations:

No recommendations made.

Comments by the assessed jurisdiction

No comments made.

Latvia

Overall findings

Latvia's legal framework implementing the AEOI Standard is in place but needs improvement in order to be fully consistent with the requirements of the AEOI Terms of Reference. While Latvia's international legal framework to exchange the information with all of Latvia's Interested Appropriate Partners (CR2) is consistent with the requirements, its domestic legislative framework requiring Reporting Financial Institutions to conduct the due diligence and reporting procedures (CR1) has deficiencies significant to the proper functioning of elements of the AEOI Standard. More specifically, deficiencies have been identified in Latvia's enforcement framework.

The methodology used for the peer reviews and that therefore underpins this report is outlined in Chapter 2.

Overall determination on the legal framework: In Place But **Needs Improvement**

Conclusions on the legal framework

General context

Latvia commenced exchanges under the AEOI Standard in 2017.

In order to provide for Reporting Financial Institutions to collect and report the information to be exchanged, Latvia:

- amended the Law "On Taxes and Duties"; and
- introduced Regulation No. 20 "Procedures by which a Financial Institution Implements the Due Diligence Procedures for Financial Accounts and Provides Financial Accounts Information to the State Revenue Service".

Under this framework Reporting Financial Institutions were required to commence the due diligence procedures in relation to New Accounts from 1 January 2016. With respect to Preexisting Accounts, Reporting Financial Institutions were required to complete due diligence procedures on High Value Individual Accounts by 31 December 2016 and on Lower Value Individual Accounts and Entity Accounts by 31 December 2017.

Following the initial Global Forum peer review, Latvia made amendments to its legislative framework to address issues identified, the last of which was effective from 19 March 2020.

With respect to the exchange of information under the AEOI Standard, Latvia:

- is a Party to the Convention on Mutual Administrative Assistance in Tax Matters and activated the associated CRS Multilateral Competent Authority Agreement in time for exchanges in 2017;
- has in place European Union Directive 2011/16/EU on Administrative Cooperation in the Field of Taxation, as amended by Directive 2014/107/EU;
- has in place agreements with five European third countries[1]; and
- put in place three bilateral agreements.[2].

Detailed findings

The detailed findings for Latvia are below, organised per Core Requirement (CR) and sub-requirement (SR), as extracted from the AEOI Terms of Reference (www.oecd.org/tax/transparency/documents/aeoi-terms-of-reference.pdf).

CR1 Domestic legal framework: Jurisdictions should have a domestic legislative framework in place that requires all Reporting Financial Institutions to conduct the due diligence and reporting procedures in the CRS, and that provides for the effective implementation of the CRS as set out therein.

Determination: In Place But **Needs Improvement**

Latvia's domestic legislative framework is in place and contains most of the key aspects of the CRS and its Commentary requiring Reporting Financial Institutions to conduct the due diligence and reporting procedures, but it needs improvement in relation to the scope of Reporting Financial Institutions (SR 1.1) and the framework to enforce the requirements (SR 1.4). Most significantly, Latvia's domestic legislative framework does not incorporate sanctions on Account Holders and Controlling Persons for the provision of false self-certifications and does not include strong measures to ensure that valid self-certifications are obtained for New Accounts.

SR 1.1 Jurisdictions should define the scope of Reporting Financial Institutions consistently with the CRS.

Latvia has defined the scope of Reporting Financial Institutions in its domestic legislative framework in a manner that is largely consistent with the CRS and its Commentary. However, deficiencies have been identified. More specifically, the definition of Investment Entity and the definition of the term "managed by" are not in accordance with the requirements. The scope of Reporting Financial Institutions is material to the proper functioning of the AEOI Standard.

Recommendations:

Latvia should amend its domestic legislative framework to include the definition of "managed by" in relation to the definition of Investment Entity.

Latvia should amend its domestic legislative framework to require the term Investment Entity to be interpreted consistently with similar language defining "financial institution" in the Financial Action Task Force Recommendations.

SR 1.2 Jurisdictions should define the scope of Financial Accounts and Reportable Accounts consistently with the CRS and incorporate the due diligence procedures to identify them.

Latvia has defined the scope of the Financial Accounts that are required to be reported in its domestic legislative framework and incorporated the due diligence procedures that must be applied to identify them in accordance with the CRS and its Commentary.

Recommendations:

No recommendations made.

SR 1.3 Jurisdictions should incorporate the reporting requirements contained in Section I of the CRS into their domestic legislative framework.

Latvia has incorporated the reporting requirements in its domestic legislative framework in accordance with the CRS and its Commentary.

Recommendations:

No recommendations made.

SR 1.4 Jurisdictions should have a legislative framework in place that allows for the enforcement of the requirements of the CRS in practice.

Latvia has a legislative framework in place to enforce the requirements in a manner that is largely consistent with the CRS and its Commentary. However, deficiencies have been identified. More specifically, Latvia's legislative framework:

- does not impose sanctions on Account Holders and Controlling Persons for the provision of a false self-certification; and
- does not incorporate measures to ensure that self-certifications are always obtained and validated for New Accounts as is required.

The deficiencies relate to key elements of the AEOI Standard and are therefore material to its proper functioning.

Recommendations:

Latvia should amend its domestic legislative framework to include sanctions on Account Holders and Controlling Persons for the provision of a false self-certification.

Latvia should amend its domestic legislative framework to include strong measures to ensure that valid self-certifications are always obtained for New Accounts in accordance with the requirements.

CR2 International legal framework: Jurisdictions should have exchange relationships in effect with all Interested Appropriate Partners as committed to and that provide for the exchange of information in accordance with the Model CAA.

Determination: In Place

Latvia's international legal framework to exchange the information is in place, is consistent with the Model CAA and its Commentary and provides for exchange with all of Latvia's Interested Appropriate Partners (i.e. all jurisdictions that are interested in receiving information from Latvia and that meet the required standard in relation to confidentiality and data safeguards). (SRs 2.1 – 2.3)

SR 2.1 Jurisdictions should have exchange agreements in effect with all Interested Appropriate Partners that permit the automatic exchange of CRS information.

Latvia has exchange agreements that permit the automatic exchange of CRS information in effect with all its Interested Appropriate Partners.

Recommendations:

No recommendations made.

SR 2.2 Such an exchange agreement should be put in place without undue delay, following the receipt of an expression of interest from an Interested Appropriate Partner.

Latvia put in place its exchange agreements without undue delay.

Recommendations:

No recommendations made.

SR 2.3 Jurisdictions should ensure that the exchange agreements in effect provide for the exchange of information in accordance with the requirements of the Model CAA.

Latvia's exchange agreements provide for the exchange of information in accordance with the requirements of the Model CAA.

Recommendations:

No recommendations made.

Comments by the assessed jurisdiction

In general, Latvia agrees with the findings of this report as they comply with the findings of the Checklist "Assessment of the domestic legislative framework implementing the AEOI Standard". However, we are in a position that our legislation provides the sanctions on Account Holders and Controlling Persons for the provision of false self-certification. These sanctions are a part of the Latvian anti-money laundering legislation, and we believe they are also applicable for the AEOI Standard. When addressing the recommendation put in the Checklist and this report, we will carry out consultations with the responsible institutions, providing a more detailed analysis on this issue and finding the optimal solution compatible with our legal system.

Notes

[1] Andorra, Liechtenstein, Monaco, San Marino and Switzerland.

[2] With Qatar, Singapore and Turkey. Latvia has also activated relationships under the CRS MCAA with Qatar and Turkey.

Lebanon

Overall findings

Lebanon's legal framework implementing the AEOI Standard is in place and is consistent with the requirements of the AEOI Terms of Reference. This includes Lebanon's domestic legislative framework requiring Reporting Financial Institutions to conduct the due diligence and reporting procedures (CR1) and its international legal framework to exchange the information with all of Lebanon's Interested Appropriate Partners (CR2).

The methodology used for the peer reviews and that therefore underpins this report is outlined in Chapter 2.

Overall determination on the legal framework: In Place

Conclusions on the legal framework

General context

Lebanon commenced exchanges under the AEOI Standard in 2018.

In order to provide for Reporting Financial Institutions to collect and report the information to be exchanged, Lebanon:

- enacted Law 55 of 27 October 2016; and
- introduced Decree 1022 of 7 July 2017, Central Bank Decision 12625 of 21 July 2017 and the Decision of the Minister of Finance 1248 of 6 December 2017.

Under this framework Reporting Financial Institutions were required to commence the due diligence procedures in relation to New Accounts from 1 July 2017. With respect to Preexisting Accounts, Reporting Financial Institutions were required to complete the due diligence procedures on High Value Individual Accounts by 31 December 2017 and on Lower Value Individual Accounts and Entity Accounts by 31 December 2018.

With respect to the exchange of information under the AEOI Standard, Lebanon is a Party to the Convention on Mutual Administrative Assistance in Tax Matters and activated the associated CRS Multilateral Competent Authority Agreement in time for exchanges in 2018.

Detailed findings

The detailed findings for Lebanon are below, organised per Core Requirement (CR) and sub-requirement (SR), as extracted from the AEOI Terms of Reference (www.oecd.org/tax/transparency/documents/aeoi-terms-of-reference.pdf).

CR1 Domestic legal framework: Jurisdictions should have a domestic legislative framework in place that requires all Reporting Financial Institutions to conduct the due diligence and reporting procedures in the CRS, and that provides for the effective implementation of the CRS as set out therein.

Determination: In Place

Lebanon's domestic legislative framework is in place and contains all of the key aspects of the CRS and its Commentary requiring Reporting Financial Institutions to conduct the due diligence and reporting procedures (SRs 1.1 – 1.3). It also provides for a framework to enforce the requirements (SR 1.4).

SR 1.1 Jurisdictions should define the scope of Reporting Financial Institutions consistently with the CRS.

Lebanon has defined the scope of Reporting Financial Institutions in its domestic legislative framework in accordance with the CRS and its Commentary.

Recommendations:

No recommendations made.

SR 1.2 Jurisdictions should define the scope of Financial Accounts and Reportable Accounts consistently with the CRS and incorporate the due diligence procedures to identify them.

Lebanon has defined the scope of the Financial Accounts that are required to be reported in its domestic legislative framework and incorporated the due diligence procedures that must be applied to identify them in accordance with the CRS and its Commentary.

Recommendations:

No recommendations made.

SR 1.3 Jurisdictions should incorporate the reporting requirements contained in Section I of the CRS into their domestic legislative framework.

Lebanon has incorporated the reporting requirements in its domestic legislative framework in accordance with the CRS and its Commentary.

Recommendations:

No recommendations made.

SR 1.4 Jurisdictions should have a legislative framework in place that allows for the enforcement of the requirements of the CRS in practice.

Lebanon has a legislative framework in place to enforce the requirements in accordance with the CRS and its Commentary.

Recommendations:

No recommendations made.

CR2 International legal framework: Jurisdictions should have exchange relationships in effect with all Interested Appropriate Partners as committed to and that provide for the exchange of information in accordance with the Model CAA.

Determination: In Place

Lebanon's international legal framework to exchange the information is in place, is consistent with the Model CAA and its Commentary and provides for exchange with all of Lebanon's Interested Appropriate Partners (i.e. all jurisdictions that are interested in receiving information from Lebanon and that meet the required standard in relation to confidentiality and data safeguards). (SRs 2.1 – 2.3)

SR 2.1 Jurisdictions should have exchange agreements in effect with all Interested Appropriate Partners that permit the automatic exchange of CRS information.

Lebanon has exchange agreements that permit the automatic exchange of CRS information in effect with all its Interested Appropriate Partners.

Recommendations:

No recommendations made.

SR 2.2 Such an exchange agreement should be put in place without undue delay, following the receipt of an expression of interest from an Interested Appropriate Partner.

Lebanon put in place its exchange agreements without undue delay.

Recommendations:

No recommendations made.

SR 2.3 Jurisdictions should ensure that the exchange agreements in effect provide for the exchange of information in accordance with the requirements of the Model CAA.

Lebanon's exchange agreements provide for the exchange of information in accordance with the requirements of the Model CAA.

Recommendations:

No recommendations made.

Comments by the assessed jurisdiction

No comments made.

Liechtenstein

Overall findings

Liechtenstein's legal framework implementing the AEOI Standard is in place and is consistent with the requirements of the AEOI Terms of Reference. This includes Liechtenstein's domestic legislative framework requiring Reporting Financial Institutions to conduct the due diligence and reporting procedures (CR1) and its international legal framework to exchange the information with all of Liechtenstein's Interested Appropriate Partners (CR2).

The methodology used for the peer reviews and that therefore underpins this report is outlined in Chapter 2.

Overall determination on the legal framework: In Place

Conclusions on the legal framework

General context

Liechtenstein commenced exchanges under the AEOI Standard in 2017.

In order to provide for Reporting Financial Institutions to collect and report the information to be exchanged, Liechtenstein:

- enacted the Act on international automatic exchange of information in tax matters (AEOI Act), National Gazette 2015, No. 355, as amended in 2017, 2018 and 2020;
- introduced the Ordinance on international automatic exchange of information in tax matters (AEOI Ordinance), National Gazette 2015, No. 358, as amended in 2016, 2017, 2018, 2019 and 2020; and
- issued further guidance, which is legally binding.

Under this framework Reporting Financial Institutions were required to commence the due diligence procedures in relation to New Accounts from 1 January 2016. With respect to Preexisting Accounts, Reporting Financial Institutions were required to complete the due diligence procedures on High Value Individual Accounts by 31 December 2016 and on Lower Value Individual Accounts and Entity Accounts by 31 December 2017.

Following the initial Global Forum peer review, Liechtenstein made various amendments to its legislative framework to address issues identified, the last of which was effective from 1 January 2021.

With respect to the exchange of information under the AEOI Standard, Liechtenstein:

- is a Party to the Convention on Mutual Administrative Assistance in Tax Matters and activated the associated CRS Multilateral Competent Authority Agreement in time for exchanges in 2017; and
- has in place an agreement with the European Union.

Detailed findings

The detailed findings for Liechtenstein are below, organised per Core Requirement (CR) and sub-requirement (SR), as extracted from the AEOI Terms of Reference (www.oecd.org/tax/transparency/documents/aeoi-terms-of-reference.pdf).

CR1 Domestic legal framework: Jurisdictions should have a domestic legislative framework in place that requires all Reporting Financial Institutions to conduct the due diligence and reporting procedures in the CRS, and that provides for the effective implementation of the CRS as set out therein.

Determination: In Place

Liechtenstein's domestic legislative framework is in place and contains all of the key aspects of the CRS and its Commentary requiring Reporting Financial Institutions to conduct the due diligence and reporting procedures (SRs 1.1 – 1.3). It also provides a framework to enforce the requirements (SR 1.4).

SR 1.1 Jurisdictions should define the scope of Reporting Financial Institutions consistently with the CRS.

Liechtenstein has defined the scope of Reporting Financial Institutions in its domestic legislative framework in accordance with the CRS and its Commentary.

Recommendations:

No recommendations made.

SR 1.2 Jurisdictions should define the scope of Financial Accounts and Reportable Accounts consistently with the CRS and incorporate the due diligence procedures to identify them.

Liechtenstein has defined the scope of the Financial Accounts that are required to be reported in its domestic legislative framework and incorporated the due diligence procedures that must be applied to identify them in accordance with the CRS and its Commentary.

Recommendations:

No recommendations made.

SR 1.3 Jurisdictions should incorporate the reporting requirements contained in Section I of the CRS into their domestic legislative framework.

Liechtenstein has incorporated the reporting requirements in its domestic legislative framework in accordance with the CRS and its Commentary.

Recommendations:

No recommendations made.

SR 1.4 Jurisdictions should have a legislative framework in place that allows for the enforcement of the requirements of the CRS in practice.

Liechtenstein has a legislative framework in place to enforce the requirements in accordance with the CRS and its Commentary.

Recommendations:

No recommendations made.

CR2 International legal framework: Jurisdictions should have exchange relationships in effect with all Interested Appropriate Partners as committed to and that provide for the exchange of information in accordance with the Model CAA.

Determination: In Place

Liechtenstein's international legal framework to exchange the information is in place, is consistent with the Model CAA and its Commentary and provides for exchange with all of Liechtenstein's Interested

Appropriate Partners (i.e. all jurisdictions that are interested in receiving information from Liechtenstein and that meet the required standard in relation to confidentiality and data safeguards). (SRs 2.1 – 2.3)

SR 2.1 Jurisdictions should have exchange agreements in effect with all Interested Appropriate Partners that permit the automatic exchange of CRS information.

Liechtenstein has exchange agreements that permit the automatic exchange of CRS information in effect with all its Interested Appropriate Partners.

Recommendations:

No recommendations made.

SR 2.2 Such an exchange agreement should be put in place without undue delay, following the receipt of an expression of interest from an Interested Appropriate Partner.

Liechtenstein put in place its exchange agreements without undue delay.

Recommendations:

No recommendations made.

SR 2.3 Jurisdictions should ensure that the exchange agreements in effect provide for the exchange of information in accordance with the requirements of the Model CAA.

Liechtenstein's exchange agreements provide for the exchange of information in accordance with the requirements of the Model CAA.

Recommendations:

No recommendations made.

Comments by the assessed jurisdiction

No comments made.

Lithuania

Overall findings

Lithuania's legal framework implementing the AEOI Standard is in place and is consistent with the requirements of the AEOI Terms of Reference. This includes Lithuania's domestic legislative framework requiring Reporting Financial Institutions to conduct the due diligence and reporting procedures (CR1) and its international legal framework to exchange the information with all of Lithuania's Interested Appropriate Partners (CR2).

The methodology used for the peer reviews and that therefore underpins this report is outlined in Chapter 2.

Overall determination on the legal framework: In Place

Conclusions on the legal framework

General context

Lithuania commenced exchanges under the AEOI Standard in 2017.

In order to provide for Reporting Financial Institutions to collect and report the information to be exchanged, Lithuania:

- enacted Article 61-[1] of the Law on Tax Administration, Resolution No. 1017 of 23 September 2015 and Article 198-[1] of the Code of Administrative Offences;
- introduced the Rules for the Provision of Information Necessary for Implementation of the International Cooperation Obligations Concerning Automatic Exchange of Financial Account Information;
- introduced Article 198-[1] of the Code of Administrative Offences of 3 December 2019; and
- issued further guidance, which is legally binding.

Under this framework Reporting Financial Institutions were required to commence the due diligence procedures in relation to New Accounts from 1 January 2016. With respect to Preexisting Accounts, Reporting Financial Institutions were required to complete the due diligence procedures on High Value Individual Accounts by 31 December 2016 and on Lower Value Individual Accounts and Entity Accounts by 31 December 2017.

Following the initial Global Forum peer review, Lithuania amended its legislative framework to address issues identified, effective from 10 September 2020.

With respect to the exchange of information under the AEOI Standard, Lithuania:

- is a Party to the Convention on Mutual Administrative Assistance in Tax Matters and activated the associated CRS Multilateral Competent Authority Agreement in time for exchanges in 2017;
- has in place the European Directive 2011/16/EU on Administrative Cooperation in the Field of Taxation as amended by Directive 2014/107/EU;
- has in place European Union agreements with five European third countries;[1] and
- put in place a bilateral agreement.[2]

Detailed findings

The detailed findings for Lithuania are below, organised per Core Requirement (CR) and sub-requirement (SR), as extracted from the AEOI Terms of Reference (www.oecd.org/tax/transparency/documents/aeoi-terms-of-reference.pdf).

CR1 Domestic legal framework: Jurisdictions should have a domestic legislative framework in place that requires all Reporting Financial Institutions to conduct the due diligence and reporting procedures in the CRS, and that provides for the effective implementation of the CRS as set out therein.

Determination: In Place

Lithuania's domestic legislative framework is in place and contains all of the key aspects of the CRS and its Commentary requiring Reporting Financial Institutions to conduct the due diligence and reporting procedures (SRs 1.1 – 1.3). It also provides for a framework to enforce the requirements (SR 1.4).

SR 1.1 Jurisdictions should define the scope of Reporting Financial Institutions consistently with the CRS.

Lithuania has defined the scope of Reporting Financial Institutions in its domestic legislative framework in accordance with the CRS and its Commentary.

Recommendations:

No recommendations made.

SR 1.2 Jurisdictions should define the scope of Financial Accounts and Reportable Accounts consistently with the CRS and incorporate the due diligence procedures to identify them.

Lithuania has defined the scope of the Financial Accounts that are required to be reported in its domestic legislative framework and incorporated the due diligence procedures that must be applied to identify them in accordance with the CRS and its Commentary.

Recommendations:

No recommendations made.

SR 1.3 Jurisdictions should incorporate the reporting requirements contained in Section I of the CRS into their domestic legislative framework.

Lithuania has incorporated the reporting requirements in its domestic legislative framework in accordance with the CRS and its Commentary.

Recommendations:

No recommendations made.

SR 1.4 Jurisdictions should have a legislative framework in place that allows for the enforcement of the requirements of the CRS in practice.

Lithuania has a legislative framework in place to enforce the requirements in accordance with the CRS and its Commentary.

Recommendations:

No recommendations made.

CR2 International legal framework: Jurisdictions should have exchange relationships in effect with all Interested Appropriate Partners as committed to and that provide for the exchange of information in accordance with the Model CAA.

Determination: In Place

Lithuania's international legal framework to exchange the information is in place, is consistent with the Model CAA and its Commentary and provides for exchange with all of Lithuania's Interested Appropriate Partners (i.e. all jurisdictions that are interested in receiving information from Lithuania and that meet the required standard in relation to confidentiality and data safeguards). (SRs 2.1 – 2.3)

SR 2.1 Jurisdictions should have exchange agreements in effect with all Interested Appropriate Partners that permit the automatic exchange of CRS information.

Lithuania has exchange agreements that permit the automatic exchange of CRS information in effect with all its Interested Appropriate Partners.

Recommendations:

No recommendations made.

SR 2.2 Such an exchange agreement should be put in place without undue delay, following the receipt of an expression of interest from an Interested Appropriate Partner.

Lithuania put in place its exchange agreements without undue delay.

Recommendations:

No recommendations made.

SR 2.3 Jurisdictions should ensure that the exchange agreements in effect provide for the exchange of information in accordance with the requirements of the Model CAA.

Lithuania's exchange agreements provide for the exchange of information in accordance with the requirements of the Model CAA.

Recommendations:

No recommendations made.

Comments by the assessed jurisdiction

No comments made.

Notes

[1] Andorra, Liechtenstein, Monaco, San Marino and Switzerland.

[2] With Singapore.

Luxembourg

Overall findings

Luxembourg's legal framework implementing the AEOI Standard is in place and is consistent with the requirements of the AEOI Terms of Reference. This includes Luxembourg's domestic legislative framework requiring Reporting Financial Institutions to conduct the due diligence and reporting procedures (CR1) and its international legal framework to exchange the information with all of Luxembourg's Interested Appropriate Partners (CR2).

The methodology used for the peer reviews and that therefore underpins this report is outlined in Chapter 2.

Overall determination on the legal framework: In Place

Conclusions on the legal framework

General context

Luxembourg commenced exchanges under the AEOI Standard in 2017.

In order to provide for Reporting Financial Institutions to collect and report the information to be exchanged, Luxembourg:

- enacted the law of 18 December 2015 related to the Common Reporting Standard, which has been amended several times and most recently by a law of 18 June 2020;
- enacted the grand-ducal regulation of 15 March 2016 executing article 2 paragraph 4 of the modified law of 18 December 2015, which has been amended several times and most recently by a grand-ducal regulation of 24 January 2020; and
- issued Frequently Asked Questions, which are not legally binding

Under this framework Reporting Financial Institutions were required to commence the due diligence procedures in relation to New Accounts from 1 January 2016. With respect to Preexisting Accounts, Reporting Financial Institutions were required to complete the due diligence procedures on High Value Individual Accounts by 31 December 2016 and on Lower Value Individual Accounts and Entity Accounts by 31 December 2017.

Following the initial Global Forum peer review, Luxembourg made various amendments to its legislative framework to address issues identified, the last of which will be effective from 1 January 2021.

With respect to the exchange of information under the AEOI Standard, Luxembourg:

- is a Party to the Convention on Mutual Administrative Assistance in Tax Matters and activated the associated CRS Multilateral Competent Authority Agreement in time for exchanges in 2017;
- has in place European Directive 2011/16/EU on Administrative Cooperation in the Field of Taxation as amended by Directive 2014/107/EU; and
- has in place agreements with five European third countries.[1]

Detailed findings

The detailed findings for Luxembourg are below, organised per Core Requirement (CR) and sub-requirement (SR), as extracted from the AEOI Terms of Reference (www.oecd.org/tax/transparency/documents/aeoi-terms-of-reference.pdf).

CR1 Domestic legal framework: Jurisdictions should have a domestic legislative framework in place that requires all Reporting Financial Institutions to conduct the due diligence and reporting procedures in the CRS, and that provides for the effective implementation of the CRS as set out therein.

Determination: In Place

Luxembourg's domestic legislative framework is in place and contains all of the key aspects of the CRS and its Commentary requiring Reporting Financial Institutions to conduct the due diligence and reporting procedures (SRs 1.1 – 1.3). It also provides for a framework to enforce the requirements (SR 1.4).

SR 1.1 Jurisdictions should define the scope of Reporting Financial Institutions consistently with the CRS.

Luxembourg has defined the scope of Reporting Financial Institutions in its domestic legislative framework in accordance with the CRS and its Commentary.

Recommendations:

No recommendations made.

SR 1.2 Jurisdictions should define the scope of Financial Accounts and Reportable Accounts consistently with the CRS and incorporate the due diligence procedures to identify them.

Luxembourg has defined the scope of the Financial Accounts that are required to be reported in its domestic legislative framework and incorporated the due diligence procedures that must be applied to identify them in accordance with the CRS and its Commentary.

Recommendations:

No recommendations made.

SR 1.3 Jurisdictions should incorporate the reporting requirements contained in Section I of the CRS into their domestic legislative framework.

Luxembourg has incorporated the reporting requirements in its domestic legislative framework in accordance with the CRS and its Commentary.

Recommendations:

No recommendations made.

SR 1.4 Jurisdictions should have a legislative framework in place that allows for the enforcement of the requirements of the CRS in practice.

Luxembourg has a legislative framework in place to enforce the requirements in accordance with the CRS and its Commentary.

Recommendations:

No recommendations made.

CR2 International legal framework: Jurisdictions should have exchange relationships in effect with all Interested Appropriate Partners as committed to and that provide for the exchange of information in accordance with the Model CAA.

Determination: In Place

Luxembourg's international legal framework to exchange the information is in place, is consistent with the Model CAA and its Commentary and provides for exchange with all of Luxembourg's Interested Appropriate Partners (i.e. all jurisdictions that are interested in receiving information from Luxembourg and that meet the required standard in relation to confidentiality and data safeguards). (SRs 2.1 – 2.3)

SR 2.1 Jurisdictions should have exchange agreements in effect with all Interested Appropriate Partners that permit the automatic exchange of CRS information.

Luxembourg has exchange agreements that permit the automatic exchange of CRS information in effect with all its Interested Appropriate Partners.

Recommendations:

No recommendations made.

SR 2.2 Such an exchange agreement should be put in place without undue delay, following the receipt of an expression of interest from an Interested Appropriate Partner.

Luxembourg put in place its exchange agreements without undue delay.

Recommendations:

No recommendations made.

SR 2.3 Jurisdictions should ensure that the exchange agreements in effect provide for the exchange of information in accordance with the requirements of the Model CAA.

Luxembourg's exchange agreements provide for the exchange of information in accordance with the requirements of the Model CAA.

Recommendations:

No recommendations made.

Comments by the assessed jurisdiction

No comments made.

Note

[1] Andorra, Liechtenstein, Monaco, San Marino and Switzerland.

Macau (China)

Overall findings

Macau's legal framework implementing the AEOI Standard is not in place in accordance with the requirements of the AEOI Terms of Reference. While Macau's international legal framework to exchange the information with all of Macau's Interested Appropriate Partners (CR2) is consistent with the requirements, its domestic legislative framework requiring Reporting Financial Institutions to conduct the due diligence and reporting procedures (CR1) has significant deficiencies in areas that are fundamental to the proper functioning of the AEOI Standard. More specifically, deficiencies have been identified in Macau's enforcement framework.

The methodology used for the peer reviews and that therefore underpins this report is outlined in Chapter 2.

Overall determination on the legal framework: Not In Place

Conclusions on the legal framework

General context

Macau commenced exchanges under the AEOI Standard in 2018.

In order to provide for Reporting Financial Institutions to collect and report the information to be exchanged, Macau:

- enacted Law No. 5/2017 (Legal System of Tax Information Exchange);
- issued Chief Executive Resolution No. 211/2017; and
- enacted Law No. 21/2019 (Revision of Complementary Tax Regulation) which revises Articles 4, 5, 10 and 11 of Law No. 5/2017.

Under this framework Reporting Financial Institutions were required to commence the due diligence procedures in relation to New Accounts from 1 July 2017. With respect to Preexisting Accounts, Reporting Financial Institutions were required to complete the due diligence procedures on High Value Individual Accounts by 30 June 2018 and on Lower Value Individual Accounts and Entity Accounts by 30 June 2019.

Following the initial Global Forum peer review, Macau amended its legislative framework to address issues identified, effective from 1 January 2021.

With respect to the exchange of information under the AEOI Standard, Macau has the Convention on Mutual Administrative Assistance in Tax Matters in place[1] and Macau activated the associated CRS Multilateral Competent Authority Agreement in time for exchanges in 2018.

Detailed findings

The detailed findings for Macau are below, organised per Core Requirement (CR) and sub-requirement (SR), as extracted from the AEOI Terms of Reference (www.oecd.org/tax/transparency/documents/aeoi-terms-of-reference.pdf).

CR1 Domestic legal framework: Jurisdictions should have a domestic legislative framework in place that requires all Reporting Financial Institutions to conduct the due diligence and reporting procedures in the CRS, and that provides for the effective implementation of the CRS as set out therein.

Determination: Not In Place

Macau's domestic legislative framework is not in place as required as it does not contain key aspects of the CRS and its Commentary. Significant deficiencies have been identified in relation to the framework to enforce the requirements (SR 1.4). More specifically, Macau's legislative framework does not require records to be kept by Financial Institutions in accordance with the AEOI Standard and it does not have rules to prevent the circumvention of the due diligence and reporting procedures.

SR 1.1 Jurisdictions should define the scope of Reporting Financial Institutions consistently with the CRS.

Macau has defined the scope of Reporting Financial Institutions in its domestic legislative framework in accordance with the CRS and its Commentary.

Recommendations:

No recommendations made.

SR 1.2 Jurisdictions should define the scope of Financial Accounts and Reportable Accounts consistently with the CRS and incorporate the due diligence procedures to identify them.

Macau has defined the scope of the Financial Accounts that are required to be reported in its domestic legislative framework and incorporated the due diligence procedures that must be applied to identify them in accordance with the CRS and its Commentary.

Recommendations:

No recommendations made.

SR 1.3 Jurisdictions should incorporate the reporting requirements contained in Section I of the CRS into their domestic legislative framework.

Macau has incorporated the reporting requirements in its domestic legislative framework in accordance with the CRS and its Commentary.

Recommendations:

No recommendations made.

SR 1.4 Jurisdictions should have a legislative framework in place that allows for the enforcement of the requirements of the CRS in practice.

Macau does not have a legislative framework in place to enforce the requirements in a manner that is consistent with the CRS and its Commentary as significant deficiencies have been identified. More specifically, Macau's legislative framework:

- does not contain rules to prevent Financial Institutions, persons or intermediaries from adopting practices intended to circumvent the reporting and due diligence procedures as required;
- does not provide for sanctions on Reporting Financial Institutions for failing to apply the due diligence procedures; and
- does not incorporate measures to ensure that self-certifications are always obtained and validated for New Accounts as is required.

These are key areas of the required enforcement framework are therefore material to the proper functioning of the AEOI Standard.

Recommendations:

Macau should amend its domestic legislative framework to include rules to prevent Financial Institutions, persons and intermediaries from adopting practices intended to circumvent the due diligence and reporting procedures.

Macau should amend its domestic legislative framework to include sanctions for failure to apply the due diligence and reporting procedures in accordance with the AEOI Standard.

Macau should amend its domestic legislative framework to include strong measures to ensure that valid self-certifications are always obtained for New Accounts in accordance with the requirements.

CR2 International legal framework: Jurisdictions should have exchange relationships in effect with all Interested Appropriate Partners as committed to and that provide for the exchange of information in accordance with the Model CAA.

Determination: In Place

Macau's international legal framework to exchange the information is in place, is consistent with the Model CAA and its Commentary and provides for exchange with all of Macau's Interested Appropriate Partners (i.e. all jurisdictions that are interested in receiving information from Macau and that meet the required standard in relation to confidentiality and data safeguards). (SRs 2.1 – 2.3)

SR 2.1 Jurisdictions should have exchange agreements in effect with all Interested Appropriate Partners that permit the automatic exchange of CRS information.

Macau has exchange agreements that permit the automatic exchange of CRS information in effect with all its Interested Appropriate Partners.

Recommendations:

No recommendations made.

SR 2.2 Such an exchange agreement should be put in place without undue delay, following the receipt of an expression of interest from an Interested Appropriate Partner.

Macau put in place its exchange agreements without undue delay.

Recommendations:

No recommendations made.

SR 2.3 Jurisdictions should ensure that the exchange agreements in effect provide for the exchange of information in accordance with the requirements of the Model CAA.

Macau's exchange agreements provide for the exchange of information in accordance with the requirements of the Model CAA.

Recommendations:

No recommendations made.

Comments by the assessed jurisdiction

To ensure Macau's domestic legislative framework is fully consistent with the requirements of the AEOI Standard, Macau is amending the domestic legislative framework to include rules to prevent circumvention, sanctions for failure to apply the due diligence and reporting procedures, as well as strong measures to ensure that valid self-certifications are always obtained for New Accounts. The administrative procedure for such an amendment to the law is in progress.

Note

[1] Through a territorial extension by China.

Malaysia

Overall findings

Malaysia's legal framework implementing the AEOI Standard is in place and is consistent with the requirements of the AEOI Terms of Reference. This includes Malaysia's domestic legislative framework requiring Reporting Financial Institutions to conduct the due diligence and reporting procedures (CR1) and its international legal framework to exchange the information with all of Malaysia's Interested Appropriate Partners (CR2).

The methodology used for the peer reviews and that therefore underpins this report is outlined in Chapter 2.

Overall determination on the legal framework: In Place

Conclusions on the legal framework

General context

Malaysia commenced exchanges under the AEOI Standard in 2018.

In order to provide for Reporting Financial Institutions to collect and report the information to be exchanged, Malaysia:

- enacted Sections 113A, 119B, 132B and 154(1)(c) of the Income Tax Act 1967;
- introduced the Income Tax (Automatic Exchange of Financial Account Information) Rules 2016 - P.U.(A) 355/2016 as amended in 2017 and 2020;
- introduced the Labuan Business Activity Tax (Automatic Exchange of Financial Account Information) Regulations 2018 – P.U.(A) 20/2018 (with effect from 1 July 2017) as amended in 2020; and
- issued further guidance, which is not legally binding.

Under this framework Reporting Financial Institutions were required to commence the due diligence procedures in relation to New Accounts from 1 July 2017. With respect to Preexisting Accounts, Reporting Financial Institutions were required to complete the due diligence procedures on High Value Individual Accounts by 30 June 2018 and on Lower Value Individual Accounts and Entity Accounts by 30 June 2019.

Following the initial Global Forum peer review, Malaysia amended its legislative framework to address an issue identified, which was effective from 28 August 2020.

With respect to the exchange of information under the AEOI Standard, Malaysia is a Party to the Convention on Mutual Administrative Assistance in Tax Matters and activated the associated CRS Multilateral Competent Authority Agreement in time for exchanges in 2018.

Detailed findings

The detailed findings for Malaysia are below, organised per Core Requirement (CR) and sub-requirement (SR), as extracted from the AEOI Terms of Reference (www.oecd.org/tax/transparency/documents/aeoi-terms-of-reference.pdf).

CR1 Domestic legal framework: Jurisdictions should have a domestic legislative framework in place that requires all Reporting Financial Institutions to conduct the due diligence and reporting procedures in the CRS, and that provides for the effective implementation of the CRS as set out therein.

Determination: In Place

Malaysia's domestic legislative framework is in place and contains all of the key aspects of the CRS and its Commentary requiring Reporting Financial Institutions to conduct the due diligence and reporting procedures (SRs 1.1 – 1.3). It also provides for a framework to enforce the requirements (SR 1.4).

SR 1.1 Jurisdictions should define the scope of Reporting Financial Institutions consistently with the CRS.

Malaysia has defined the scope of Reporting Financial Institutions in its domestic legislative framework in accordance with the CRS and its Commentary.

Recommendations:

No recommendations made.

SR 1.2 Jurisdictions should define the scope of Financial Accounts and Reportable Accounts consistently with the CRS and incorporate the due diligence procedures to identify them.

Malaysia has defined the scope of the Financial Accounts that are required to be reported in its domestic legislative framework and incorporated the due diligence procedures that must be applied to identify them in accordance with the CRS and its Commentary.

Recommendations:

No recommendations made.

SR 1.3 Jurisdictions should incorporate the reporting requirements contained in Section I of the CRS into their domestic legislative framework.

Malaysia has incorporated the reporting requirements in its domestic legislative framework in accordance with the CRS and its Commentary.

Recommendations:

No recommendations made.

SR 1.4 Jurisdictions should have a legislative framework in place that allows for the enforcement of the requirements of the CRS in practice.

Malaysia has a legislative framework in place to enforce the requirements in accordance with the CRS and its Commentary.

Recommendations:

No recommendations made.

CR2 International legal framework: Jurisdictions should have exchange relationships in effect with all Interested Appropriate Partners as committed to and that provide for the exchange of information in accordance with the Model CAA.

Determination: In Place

Malaysia's international legal framework to exchange the information is in place, is consistent with the Model CAA and its Commentary and provides for exchange with all of Malaysia's Interested Appropriate

Partners (i.e. all jurisdictions that are interested in receiving information from Malaysia and that meet the required standard in relation to confidentiality and data safeguards). (SRs 2.1 – 2.3)

SR 2.1 Jurisdictions should have exchange agreements in effect with all Interested Appropriate Partners that permit the automatic exchange of CRS information.

Malaysia has exchange agreements that permit the automatic exchange of CRS information in effect with all its Interested Appropriate Partners.

Recommendations:

No recommendations made.

SR 2.2 Such an exchange agreement should be put in place without undue delay, following the receipt of an expression of interest from an Interested Appropriate Partner.

Malaysia put in place its exchange agreements without undue delay.

Recommendations:

No recommendations made.

SR 2.3 Jurisdictions should ensure that the exchange agreements in effect provide for the exchange of information in accordance with the requirements of the Model CAA.

Malaysia's exchange agreements provide for the exchange of information in accordance with the requirements of the Model CAA.

Recommendations:

No recommendations made.

Comments by the assessed jurisdiction

No comments made.

Malta

Overall findings

Malta's legal framework implementing the AEOI Standard is in place and is consistent with the requirements of the AEOI Terms of Reference. This includes Malta's domestic legislative framework requiring Reporting Financial Institutions to conduct the due diligence and reporting procedures (CR1) and its international legal framework to exchange the information with all of Malta's Interested Appropriate Partners (CR2).

The methodology used for the peer reviews and that therefore underpins this report is outlined in Chapter 2.

Overall determination on the legal framework: In Place

Conclusions on the legal framework

General context

Malta commenced exchanges under the AEOI Standard in 2017.

In order to provide for Reporting Financial Institutions to collect and report the information to be exchanged, Malta:

- amended its Income Tax Act and Income Tax Management Act;
- introduced the Cooperation with Other Jurisdiction on Tax Matters (Amendment) Regulations, 2015; and
- issued further guidance, which is legally binding.

Under this framework Reporting Financial Institutions were required to commence the due diligence procedures in relation to New Accounts from 1 January 2016. With respect to Preexisting Accounts, Reporting Financial Institutions were required to complete the due diligence procedures on High Value Individual Accounts by 31 December 2016 and on Lower Value Individual Accounts and Entity Accounts by 31 December 2017.

Following the initial Global Forum peer review, Malta issued amended its legislative framework to address issues identified, effective from 1 January 2016.

With respect to the exchange of information under the AEOI Standard, Malta:

- is a Party to the Convention on Mutual Administrative Assistance in Tax Matters and activated the associated CRS Multilateral Competent Authority Agreement in time for exchanges in 2017;
- has in place European Directive 2011/16/EU on Administrative Cooperation in the Field of Taxation as amended by Directive 2014/107/EU; and
- has in place European Union agreements with five European third countries.[1]
- put in place two bilateral agreements.[2]

Detailed findings

The detailed findings for Malta are below, organised per Core Requirement (CR) and sub-requirement (SR), as extracted from the AEOI Terms of Reference (www.oecd.org/tax/transparency/documents/aeoi-terms-of-reference.pdf).

CR1 Domestic legal framework: Jurisdictions should have a domestic legislative framework in place that requires all Reporting Financial Institutions to conduct the due diligence and reporting procedures in the CRS, and that provides for the effective implementation of the CRS as set out therein.

Determination: In Place

Malta's domestic legislative framework is in place and contains all of the key aspects of the CRS and its Commentary requiring Reporting Financial Institutions to conduct the due diligence and reporting procedures (SRs 1.1 – 1.3). It also provides for a framework to enforce the requirements (SR 1.4).

SR 1.1 Jurisdictions should define the scope of Reporting Financial Institutions consistently with the CRS.

Malta has defined the scope of Reporting Financial Institutions in its domestic legislative framework in accordance with the CRS and its Commentary.

Recommendations:

No recommendations made.

SR 1.2 Jurisdictions should define the scope of Financial Accounts and Reportable Accounts consistently with the CRS and incorporate the due diligence procedures to identify them.

Malta has defined the scope of the Financial Accounts that are required to be reported in its domestic legislative framework and incorporated the due diligence procedures that must be applied to identify them in accordance with the CRS and its Commentary.

Recommendations:

No recommendations made.

SR 1.3 Jurisdictions should incorporate the reporting requirements contained in Section I of the CRS into their domestic legislative framework.

Malta has incorporated the reporting requirements in its domestic legislative framework in accordance with the CRS and its Commentary.

Recommendations:

No recommendations made.

SR 1.4 Jurisdictions should have a legislative framework in place that allows for the enforcement of the requirements of the CRS in practice.

Malta has a legislative framework in place to enforce the requirements in accordance with the CRS and its Commentary.

Recommendations:

No recommendations made.

CR2 International legal framework: Jurisdictions should have exchange relationships in effect with all Interested Appropriate Partners as committed to and that provide for the exchange of information in accordance with the Model CAA.

Determination: In Place

Malta's international legal framework to exchange the information is in place, is consistent with the Model CAA and its Commentary and provides for exchange with all of Malta's Interested Appropriate Partners (i.e. all jurisdictions that are interested in receiving information from Malta and that meet the required standard in relation to confidentiality and data safeguards). (SRs 2.1 – 2.3)

SR 2.1 Jurisdictions should have exchange agreements in effect with all Interested Appropriate Partners that permit the automatic exchange of CRS information.

Malta has exchange agreements that permit the automatic exchange of CRS information in effect with all its Interested Appropriate Partners.

Recommendations:

No recommendations made.

SR 2.2 Such an exchange agreement should be put in place without undue delay, following the receipt of an expression of interest from an Interested Appropriate Partner.

Malta put in place its exchange agreements without undue delay.

Recommendations:

No recommendations made.

SR 2.3 Jurisdictions should ensure that the exchange agreements in effect provide for the exchange of information in accordance with the requirements of the Model CAA.

Malta's exchange agreements provide for the exchange of information in accordance with the requirements of the Model CAA.

Recommendations:

No recommendations made.

Comments by the assessed jurisdiction

No comments made.

Notes

[1] Andorra, Liechtenstein, Monaco, San Marino and Switzerland.

[2] With Qatar and Singapore. Malta has also activated a relationship under the CRS MCAA with Qatar.

Marshall Islands

Overall findings

The Marshall Islands' legal framework implementing the AEOI Standard is in place and is consistent with the requirements of the AEOI Terms of Reference. This includes the Marshall Islands' domestic legislative framework requiring Reporting Financial Institutions to conduct the due diligence and reporting procedures (CR1) and its international legal framework to exchange the information with all of the Marshall Islands' Interested Appropriate Partners (CR2).

The methodology used for the peer reviews and that therefore underpins this report is outlined in Chapter 2.

Overall determination on the legal framework: In Place

Conclusions on the legal framework

General context

The Marshall Islands commenced exchanges under the AEOI Standard in 2018.

In order to provide for Reporting Financial Institutions to collect and report the information to be exchanged, the Marshall Islands:

- enacted the Automatic Exchange of Financial Account Information Act, 2016;
- relies on Chapter 5 of Title 48 of the Marshall Islands Revised Code; and
- introduced the AEOI Regulation 2016.

Under this framework Reporting Financial Institutions were required to commence the due diligence procedures in relation to New Accounts from 1 January 2017. With respect to Preexisting Accounts, Reporting Financial Institutions were required to complete the due diligence procedures on High Value Individual Accounts by 31 December 2017 and on Lower Value Individual Accounts and Entity Accounts by 31 December 2018.

With respect to the exchange of information under the AEOI Standard, the Marshall Islands is a Party to the Convention on Mutual Administrative Assistance in Tax Matters and activated the associated CRS Multilateral Competent Authority Agreement in time for exchanges in 2018.

Detailed findings

The detailed findings for the Marshall Islands are below, organised per Core Requirement (CR) and sub-requirement (SR), as extracted from the AEOI Terms of Reference (www.oecd.org/tax/transparency/documents/aeoi-terms-of-reference.pdf).

CR1 Domestic legal framework: Jurisdictions should have a domestic legislative framework in place that requires all Reporting Financial Institutions to conduct the due diligence and reporting procedures in the CRS, and that provides for the effective implementation of the CRS as set out therein.

Determination: In Place

The Marshall Islands' domestic legislative framework is in place and contains all of the key aspects of the CRS and its Commentary requiring Reporting Financial Institutions to conduct the due diligence and reporting procedures (SRs 1.1 – 1.3). It also provides for a framework to enforce the requirements (SR 1.4).

SR 1.1 Jurisdictions should define the scope of Reporting Financial Institutions consistently with the CRS.

The Marshall Islands has defined the scope of Reporting Financial Institutions in its domestic legislative framework in accordance with the CRS and its Commentary.

Recommendations:

No recommendations made.

SR 1.2 Jurisdictions should define the scope of Financial Accounts and Reportable Accounts consistently with the CRS and incorporate the due diligence procedures to identify them.

The Marshall Islands has defined the scope of the Financial Accounts that are required to be reported in its domestic legislative framework and incorporated the due diligence procedures that must be applied to identify them in accordance with the CRS and its Commentary.

Recommendations:

No recommendations made.

SR 1.3 Jurisdictions should incorporate the reporting requirements contained in Section I of the CRS into their domestic legislative framework.

The Marshall Islands has incorporated the reporting requirements in its domestic legislative framework in accordance with the CRS and its Commentary.

Recommendations:

No recommendations made.

SR 1.4 Jurisdictions should have a legislative framework in place that allows for the enforcement of the requirements of the CRS in practice.

The Marshall Islands has a legislative framework in place to enforce the requirements in accordance with the CRS and its Commentary.

Recommendations:

No recommendations made.

CR2 International legal framework: Jurisdictions should have exchange relationships in effect with all Interested Appropriate Partners as committed to and that provide for the exchange of information in accordance with the Model CAA.

Determination: In Place

The Marshall Islands' international legal framework to exchange the information is in place, is consistent with the Model CAA and its Commentary and provides for exchange with all of the Marshall Islands' Interested Appropriate Partners (i.e. all jurisdictions that are interested in receiving information from the Marshall Islands and that meet the required standard in relation to confidentiality and data safeguards). (SRs 2.1 – 2.3)

SR 2.1 Jurisdictions should have exchange agreements in effect with all Interested Appropriate Partners that permit the automatic exchange of CRS information.

The Marshall Islands has exchange agreements that permit the automatic exchange of CRS information in effect with all its Interested Appropriate Partners.

Recommendations:

No recommendations made.

SR 2.2 Such an exchange agreement should be put in place without undue delay, following the receipt of an expression of interest from an Interested Appropriate Partner.

The Marshall Islands put in place its exchange agreements without undue delay.

Recommendations:

No recommendations made.

SR 2.3 Jurisdictions should ensure that the exchange agreements in effect provide for the exchange of information in accordance with the requirements of the Model CAA.

The Marshall Islands' exchange agreements provide for the exchange of information in accordance with the requirements of the Model CAA.

Recommendations:

No recommendations made.

Comments by the assessed jurisdiction

No comments made.

Mauritius

Overall findings

Mauritius' legal framework implementing the AEOI Standard is in place and is consistent with the requirements of the AEOI Terms of Reference. This includes Mauritius' domestic legislative framework requiring Reporting Financial Institutions to conduct the due diligence and reporting procedures (CR1) and its international legal framework to exchange the information with all of Mauritius' Interested Appropriate Partners (CR2).

The methodology used for the peer reviews and that therefore underpins this report is outlined in Chapter 2.

Overall determination on the legal framework: In Place

Conclusions on the legal framework

General context

Mauritius commenced exchanges under the AEOI Standard in 2018.

In order to provide for Reporting Financial Institutions to collect and report the information to be exchanged, Mauritius:

- enacted Section 76 (5A) and (5B) of the Income Tax Act;
- introduced the Income Tax (Common Reporting Standard) Regulations 2016, as amended by the Income Tax (Common Reporting Standard) Regulations 2019 and GN 87/2019; and
- issued further guidance, which is legally binding.

Under this framework Reporting Financial Institutions were required to commence the due diligence procedures in relation to New Accounts from 1 January 2017. With respect to Preexisting Accounts, Reporting Financial Institutions were required to complete the due diligence procedures on High Value Individual Accounts by 31 December 2017 and on Lower Value Individual Accounts and Entity Accounts by 31 December 2018.

Following the initial Global Forum peer review, Mauritius amended its legislative framework to address issues identified, effective from 23 April 2019.

With respect to the exchange of information under the AEOI Standard, Mauritius is a Party to the Convention on Mutual Administrative Assistance in Tax Matters and activated the associated CRS Multilateral Competent Authority Agreement in time for exchanges in 2018.

Detailed findings

The detailed findings for Mauritius are below, organised per Core Requirement (CR) and sub-requirement (SR), as extracted from the AEOI Terms of Reference (www.oecd.org/tax/transparency/documents/aeoi-terms-of-reference.pdf).

CR1 Domestic legal framework: Jurisdictions should have a domestic legislative framework in place that requires all Reporting Financial Institutions to conduct the due diligence and reporting procedures in the CRS, and that provides for the effective implementation of the CRS as set out therein.

Determination: In Place

Mauritius' domestic legislative framework is in place and contains all of the key aspects of the CRS and its Commentary requiring Reporting Financial Institutions to conduct the due diligence and reporting procedures (SRs 1.1 – 1.3). It also provides for a framework to enforce the requirements (SR 1.4).

SR 1.1 Jurisdictions should define the scope of Reporting Financial Institutions consistently with the CRS.

Mauritius has defined the scope of Reporting Financial Institutions in its domestic legislative framework in accordance with the CRS and its Commentary.

Recommendations:

No recommendations made.

SR 1.2 Jurisdictions should define the scope of Financial Accounts and Reportable Accounts consistently with the CRS and incorporate the due diligence procedures to identify them.

Mauritius has defined the scope of the Financial Accounts that are required to be reported in its domestic legislative framework and incorporated the due diligence procedures that must be applied to identify them in accordance with the CRS and its Commentary.

Recommendations:

No recommendations made.

SR 1.3 Jurisdictions should incorporate the reporting requirements contained in Section I of the CRS into their domestic legislative framework.

Mauritius has incorporated the reporting requirements in its domestic legislative framework in accordance with the CRS and its Commentary.

Recommendations:

No recommendations made.

SR 1.4 Jurisdictions should have a legislative framework in place that allows for the enforcement of the requirements of the CRS in practice.

Mauritius has a legislative framework in place to enforce the requirements in accordance with the CRS and its Commentary.

Recommendations:

No recommendations made.

CR2 International legal framework: Jurisdictions should have exchange relationships in effect with all Interested Appropriate Partners as committed to and that provide for the exchange of information in accordance with the Model CAA.

Determination: In Place

Mauritius' international legal framework to exchange the information is in place, is consistent with the Model CAA and its Commentary and provides for exchange with all of Mauritius' Interested Appropriate Partners (i.e. all jurisdictions that are interested in receiving information from Mauritius and that meet the required standard in relation to confidentiality and data safeguards). (SRs 2.1 – 2.3)

SR 2.1 Jurisdictions should have exchange agreements in effect with all Interested Appropriate Partners that permit the automatic exchange of CRS information.

Mauritius has exchange agreements that permit the automatic exchange of CRS information in effect with all its Interested Appropriate Partners.

Recommendations:

No recommendations made.

SR 2.2 Such an exchange agreement should be put in place without undue delay, following the receipt of an expression of interest from an Interested Appropriate Partner.

Mauritius put in place its exchange agreements without undue delay.

Recommendations:

No recommendations made.

SR 2.3 Jurisdictions should ensure that the exchange agreements in effect provide for the exchange of information in accordance with the requirements of the Model CAA.

Mauritius' exchange agreements provide for the exchange of information in accordance with the requirements of the Model CAA.

Recommendations:

No recommendations made.

Comments by the assessed jurisdiction

No comments made.

Mexico

Overall findings

Mexico's legal framework implementing the AEOI Standard is in place but needs improvement in order to be fully consistent with the requirements of the AEOI Terms of Reference. While Mexico's international legal framework to exchange the information with all of Mexico's Interested Appropriate Partners (CR2) is consistent with the requirements, its domestic legislative framework requiring Reporting Financial Institutions to conduct the due diligence and reporting procedures (CR1) has deficiencies in an area relevant to the proper functioning of the AEOI Standard. More specifically, Mexico provides for three jurisdiction-specific Excluded Accounts that do not meet the requirements.

The methodology used for the peer reviews and that therefore underpins this report is outlined in Chapter 2.

Overall determination on the legal framework: In Place But **Needs Improvement**

Conclusions on the legal framework

General context

Mexico commenced exchanges under the AEOI Standard in 2017.

In order to provide for Reporting Financial Institutions to collect and report the information to be exchanged, Mexico:

- relies on Article 32-B Bis of the Mexican Tax Code; and
- enacted Annex 25-Bis of the Mexican Administrative Tax Regulations.

Under this framework Reporting Financial Institutions were required to commence the due diligence procedures in relation to New Accounts from 1 January 2016. With respect to Preexisting Accounts, Reporting Financial Institutions were required to complete the due diligence procedures on High Value Individual Accounts by 31 December 2016 and on Lower Value Individual Accounts and Entity Accounts by 31 December 2017.

Following the initial Global Forum peer review, Mexico made various amendments to its legislative framework to address issues identified, the last of which was effective from 8 May 2019.

With respect to the exchange of information under the AEOI Standard, Mexico:

- is a Party to the Convention on Mutual Administrative Assistance in Tax Matters and activated the associated CRS Multilateral Competent Authority Agreement in time for exchanges in 2017; and
- put in place a bilateral agreement.[1]

Detailed findings

The detailed findings for Mexico are below, organised per Core Requirement (CR) and sub-requirement (SR), as extracted from the AEOI Terms of Reference (www.oecd.org/tax/transparency/documents/aeoi-terms-of-reference.pdf).

CR1 Domestic legal framework: Jurisdictions should have a domestic legislative framework in place that requires all Reporting Financial Institutions to conduct the due diligence and reporting procedures in the CRS, and that provides for the effective implementation of the CRS as set out therein.

Determination: In Place But **Needs Improvement**

Mexico's domestic legislative framework is in place and contains most of the key aspects of the CRS and its Commentary requiring Reporting Financial Institutions to conduct the due diligence and reporting procedures, but it needs improvement in one area relating to the scope of Financial Accounts required to be reported (SR 1.2). More specifically, Mexico's legal framework provides for three jurisdiction-specific Excluded Accounts that do not meet the requirements.

SR 1.1 Jurisdictions should define the scope of Reporting Financial Institutions consistently with the CRS.

Mexico has defined the scope of Reporting Financial Institutions in its domestic legislative framework in accordance with the CRS and its Commentary.

Recommendations:

No recommendations made.

SR 1.2 Jurisdictions should define the scope of Financial Accounts and Reportable Accounts consistently with the CRS and incorporate the due diligence procedures to identify them.

Mexico has defined the scope of the Financial Accounts that are required to be reported in its domestic legislative framework and incorporated the due diligence procedures that must be applied to identify them in a manner that is largely consistent with the CRS and its Commentary. However, deficiencies have been identified. More specifically, Mexico provides for three jurisdiction-specific Excluded Accounts that are not in accordance with the requirements. The definition of Financial Accounts, including the provision of Excluded Accounts, is material to the proper functioning of the AEOI Standard, although it should be noted that the incorrect entries are likely to currently have a very limited impact.

Recommendations:

Mexico should amend its domestic legal framework to remove three entries from its jurisdiction-specific list of Excluded Accounts as they do not meet the requirements because withdrawals are permitted before reaching a specified retirement age, disability or death with the only penalty being a different treatment for the purposes of calculating the annual income tax. The entities are: i) Voluntary contributions for retirement funds; ii) Accounts for individual retirement programme and iii) Retirement insurance contracts.

SR 1.3 Jurisdictions should incorporate the reporting requirements contained in Section I of the CRS into their domestic legislative framework.

Mexico has incorporated the reporting requirements in its domestic legislative framework in accordance with the CRS and its Commentary.

Recommendations:

No recommendations made.

SR 1.4 Jurisdictions should have a legislative framework in place that allows for the enforcement of the requirements of the CRS in practice.

Mexico has a legislative framework in place to enforce the requirements in accordance with the CRS and its Commentary.

Recommendations:

No recommendations made.

CR2 International legal framework: Jurisdictions should have exchange relationships in effect with all Interested Appropriate Partners as committed to and that provide for the exchange of information in accordance with the Model CAA.

Determination: In Place

Mexico's international legal framework to exchange the information is in place, is consistent with the Model CAA and its Commentary and provides for exchange with all of Mexico's Interested Appropriate Partners (i.e. all jurisdictions that are interested in receiving information from Mexico and that meet the required standard in relation to confidentiality and data safeguards). (SRs 2.1 – 2.3)

SR 2.1 Jurisdictions should have exchange agreements in effect with all Interested Appropriate Partners that permit the automatic exchange of CRS information.

Mexico has exchange agreements that permit the automatic exchange of CRS information in effect with all its Interested Appropriate Partners.

Recommendations:

No recommendations made.

SR 2.2 Such an exchange agreement should be put in place without undue delay, following the receipt of an expression of interest from an Interested Appropriate Partner.

Mexico put in place its exchange agreements without undue delay.

Recommendations:

No recommendations made.

SR 2.3 Jurisdictions should ensure that the exchange agreements in effect provide for the exchange of information in accordance with the requirements of the Model CAA.

Mexico's exchange agreements provide for the exchange of information in accordance with the requirements of the Model CAA.

Recommendations:

No recommendations made.

Comments by the assessed jurisdiction

No comments made.

Note

[1] With Hong Kong (China).

Monaco

Overall findings

Monaco's legal framework implementing the AEOI Standard is in place but needs improvement in order to be fully consistent with the requirements of the AEOI Terms of Reference. While Monaco's international legal framework to exchange the information with all of Monaco's Interested Appropriate Partners (CR2) is consistent with the requirements, its domestic legislative framework requiring Reporting Financial Institutions to conduct the due diligence and reporting procedures (CR1) has a deficiency significant to the proper functioning of an element of the AEOI Standard. More specifically, the rules in Monaco's legislative framework to prevent persons or intermediaries from adopting practices intended to circumvent the reporting and due diligence procedures are insufficient in scope.

The methodology used for the peer reviews and that therefore underpins this report is outlined in Chapter 2.

Overall determination on the legal framework: In Place But **Needs Improvement**

Conclusions on the legal framework

General context

Monaco commenced exchanges under the AEOI Standard in 2018.

In order to provide for Reporting Financial Institutions to collect and report the information to be exchanged, Monaco:

- enacted *Ordonnance souveraine n°6.208, Loi n°1.444 portant diverses mesures en matière de protection des informations nominatives et de confidentialité dans le cadre de l'échange automatique de renseignements en matière fiscale*;
- introduced *Loi n°1.445 portant diverses mesures relatives à la prescription et aux sanctions pénales applicables en matière d'échange automatique de renseignements en matière fiscale*; and
- issued further guidance, which is not legally binding.

Under this framework Reporting Financial Institutions were required to commence the due diligence procedures in relation to New Accounts from 1 January 2017. With respect to Preexisting Accounts, Reporting Financial Institutions were required to complete the due diligence procedures on High Value Individual Accounts by 31 December 2017 and on Lower Value Individual Accounts and Entity Accounts by 31 December 2018.

With respect to the exchange of information under the AEOI Standard, Monaco:

- is a Party to the Convention on Mutual Administrative Assistance in Tax Matters and activated the associated CRS Multilateral Competent Authority Agreement in time for exchanges in 2018; and
- has in place an agreement with the European Union.

Detailed findings

The detailed findings for Monaco are below, organised per Core Requirement (CR) and sub-requirement (SR), as extracted from the AEOI Terms of Reference (www.oecd.org/tax/transparency/documents/aeoi-terms-of-reference.pdf).

CR1 Domestic legal framework: Jurisdictions should have a domestic legislative framework in place that requires all Reporting Financial Institutions to conduct the due diligence and reporting procedures in the CRS, and that provides for the effective implementation of the CRS as set out therein.

Determination: In Place But **Needs Improvement**

Monaco's domestic legislative framework is in place and contains most of the key aspects of the CRS and its Commentary requiring Reporting Financial Institutions to conduct the due diligence and reporting procedures, but it needs improvement in one area relating to the framework to enforce the requirements (SR 1.4). More specifically, the rules in Monaco's legislative framework to prevent persons or intermediaries from adopting practices intended to circumvent the reporting and due diligence procedures are insufficient in scope as they do not cover all relevant persons and circumstances.

SR 1.1 Jurisdictions should define the scope of Reporting Financial Institutions consistently with the CRS.

Monaco has defined the scope of Reporting Financial Institutions in its domestic legislative framework in accordance with the CRS and its Commentary.

Recommendations:

No recommendations made.

SR 1.2 Jurisdictions should define the scope of Financial Accounts and Reportable Accounts consistently with the CRS and incorporate the due diligence procedures to identify them.

Monaco has defined the scope of the Financial Accounts that are required to be reported in its domestic legislative framework and incorporated the due diligence procedures that must be applied to identify them in accordance with the CRS and its Commentary.

Recommendations:

No recommendations made.

SR 1.3 Jurisdictions should incorporate the reporting requirements contained in Section I of the CRS into their domestic legislative framework.

Monaco has incorporated the reporting requirements in its domestic legislative framework in accordance with the CRS and its Commentary.

Recommendations:

No recommendations made.

SR 1.4 Jurisdictions should have a legislative framework in place that allows for the enforcement of the requirements of the CRS in practice.

Monaco has a legislative framework in place to enforce the requirements in a manner that is largely consistent with the CRS and its Commentary. However, a deficiency has been identified. More specifically, Monaco's legislative framework does not include rules to prevent all relevant persons (including Reporting Financial Institutions, other persons and intermediaries) from adopting any practices intended to circumvent the reporting and due diligence procedures as required. This is a key element of the required enforcement framework and is therefore material to the proper functioning of the AEOI Standard.

Recommendations:

Monaco should amend its domestic legislative framework to include rules to prevent all Financial Institutions, persons and intermediaries from adopting practices intended to circumvent the due diligence and reporting procedures, rather than just Reporting Financial Institutions involved in a transaction or arrangement with the purpose of causing an account not to be a Reportable Account.

CR2 International legal framework: Jurisdictions should have exchange relationships in effect with all Interested Appropriate Partners as committed to and that provide for the exchange of information in accordance with the Model CAA.

Determination: In Place

Monaco's international legal framework to exchange the information is in place, is consistent with the Model CAA and its Commentary and provides for exchange with all of Monaco's Interested Appropriate Partners (i.e. all jurisdictions that are interested in receiving information from Monaco and that meet the required standard in relation to confidentiality and data safeguards). (SRs 2.1 – 2.3)

SR 2.1 Jurisdictions should have exchange agreements in effect with all Interested Appropriate Partners that permit the automatic exchange of CRS information.

Monaco has exchange agreements that permit the automatic exchange of CRS information in effect with all its Interested Appropriate Partners.

Recommendations:

No recommendations made.

SR 2.2 Such an exchange agreement should be put in place without undue delay, following the receipt of an expression of interest from an Interested Appropriate Partner.

Monaco put in place its exchange agreements without undue delay.

Recommendations:

No recommendations made.

SR 2.3 Jurisdictions should ensure that the exchange agreements in effect provide for the exchange of information in accordance with the requirements of the Model CAA.

Monaco's exchange agreements provide for the exchange of information in accordance with the requirements of the Model CAA.

Recommendations:

No recommendations made.

Comments by the assessed jurisdiction

No comments made.

Montserrat

Overall findings

Montserrat's legal framework implementing the AEOI Standard is in place and is consistent with the requirements of the AEOI Terms of Reference. This includes Montserrat's domestic legislative framework requiring Reporting Financial Institutions to conduct the due diligence and reporting procedures (CR1) and its international legal framework to exchange the information with all of Montserrat's Interested Appropriate Partners (CR2).

The methodology used for the peer reviews and that therefore underpins this report is outlined in Chapter 2.

Overall determination on the legal framework: In Place

Conclusions on the legal framework

General context

Montserrat commenced exchanges under the AEOI Standard in 2017.

In order to provide for Reporting Financial Institutions to collect and report the information to be exchanged, Montserrat:

- enacted the Tax Information Exchange Act; and
- introduced the Tax Information Exchange (FATCA Agreement) (UK IGA) (CRS) (Montserrat) (Implementation) Regulations 2016, as amended in 2019.

Under this framework Reporting Financial Institutions were required to commence the due diligence procedures in relation to New Accounts from 1 January 2016. With respect to Preexisting Accounts, Reporting Financial Institutions were required to complete the due diligence procedures on High Value Individual Accounts by 31 December 2016 and on Lower Value Individual Accounts and Entity Accounts by 31 December 2017.

Following the initial Global Forum peer review, Montserrat amended its legislative framework to address issues identified, effective from 5 July 2019.

With respect to the exchange of information under the AEOI Standard, Montserrat:

- has the Convention on Mutual Administrative Assistance in Tax Matters in place[1] and activated the associated CRS Multilateral Competent Authority Agreement in time for exchanges in 2017; and
- put in place a bilateral agreement.[2]

Detailed findings

The detailed findings for Montserrat are below, organised per Core Requirement (CR) and sub-requirement (SR), as extracted from the AEOI Terms of Reference (www.oecd.org/tax/transparency/documents/aeoi-terms-of-reference.pdf).

CR1 Domestic legal framework: Jurisdictions should have a domestic legislative framework in place that requires all Reporting Financial Institutions to conduct the due diligence and reporting procedures in the CRS, and that provides for the effective implementation of the CRS as set out therein.

Determination: In Place

Montserrat's domestic legislative framework is in place and contains all of the key aspects of the CRS and its Commentary requiring Reporting Financial Institutions to conduct the due diligence and reporting procedures (SRs 1.1 – 1.3). It also provides for a framework to enforce the requirements (SR 1.4).

SR 1.1 Jurisdictions should define the scope of Reporting Financial Institutions consistently with the CRS.

Montserrat has defined the scope of Reporting Financial Institutions in its domestic legislative framework in accordance with the CRS and its Commentary.

Recommendations:

No recommendations made.

SR 1.2 Jurisdictions should define the scope of Financial Accounts and Reportable Accounts consistently with the CRS and incorporate the due diligence procedures to identify them.

Montserrat has defined the scope of the Financial Accounts that are required to be reported in its domestic legislative framework and incorporated the due diligence procedures that must be applied to identify them in accordance with the CRS and its Commentary.

Recommendations:

No recommendations made.

SR 1.3 Jurisdictions should incorporate the reporting requirements contained in Section I of the CRS into their domestic legislative framework.

Montserrat has incorporated the reporting requirements in its domestic legislative framework in accordance with the CRS and its Commentary.

Recommendations:

No recommendations made.

SR 1.4 Jurisdictions should have a legislative framework in place that allows for the enforcement of the requirements of the CRS in practice.

Montserrat has a legislative framework in place to enforce the requirements in accordance with the CRS and its Commentary.

Recommendations:

No recommendations made.

CR2 International legal framework: Jurisdictions should have exchange relationships in effect with all Interested Appropriate Partners as committed to and that provide for the exchange of information in accordance with the Model CAA.

Determination: In Place

Montserrat's international legal framework to exchange the information is in place, is consistent with the Model CAA and its Commentary and provides for exchange with all of Montserrat's Interested Appropriate

Partners (i.e. all jurisdictions that are interested in receiving information from Montserrat and that meet the required standard in relation to confidentiality and data safeguards). (SRs 2.1 – 2.3)

SR 2.1 Jurisdictions should have exchange agreements in effect with all Interested Appropriate Partners that permit the automatic exchange of CRS information.

Montserrat has exchange agreements that permit the automatic exchange of CRS information in effect with all its Interested Appropriate Partners.

Recommendations:

No recommendations made.

SR 2.2 Such an exchange agreement should be put in place without undue delay, following the receipt of an expression of interest from an Interested Appropriate Partner.

Montserrat put in place its exchange agreements without undue delay.

Recommendations:

No recommendations made.

SR 2.3 Jurisdictions should ensure that the exchange agreements in effect provide for the exchange of information in accordance with the requirements of the Model CAA.

Montserrat's exchange agreements provide for the exchange of information in accordance with the requirements of the Model CAA.

Recommendations:

No recommendations made.

Comments by the assessed jurisdiction

The assessment presented in this report is accepted. However, notwithstanding the Confidentiality and Data Security assessment, Montserrat continues to be committed to ensuring that there is transparency in the tax systems and to exchange information with other partners where required. We continue to work with the United Kingdom to complete the required review and corresponding action plan. This will enable Montserrat to meet all of the international Confidentiality and Data Safeguard standards.

Notes

[1] Through a territorial extension by the United Kingdom.

[2] With the United Kingdom.

Nauru

Overall findings

Nauru's legal framework implementing the AEOI Standard is in place and is consistent with the requirements of the AEOI Terms of Reference. This includes Nauru's domestic legislative framework requiring Reporting Financial Institutions to conduct the due diligence and reporting procedures (CR1) and its international legal framework to exchange the information with all of Nauru's Interested Appropriate Partners (CR2).

The methodology used for the peer reviews and that therefore underpins this report is outlined in Chapter 2.

Overall determination on the legal framework: In Place

Conclusions on the legal framework

General context

Nauru commenced exchanges under the AEOI Standard in 2018.

In order to provide for Reporting Financial Institutions to collect and report the information to be exchanged, Nauru:

- enacted the Automatic Exchange of Financial Account Information Act 2016; and
- introduced the Automatic Exchange of Financial Account Information Regulations 2017.

Under this framework Reporting Financial Institutions were required to commence the due diligence procedures in relation to New Accounts from 1 January 2017. With respect to Preexisting Accounts, Reporting Financial Institutions were required to complete the due diligence procedures on High Value Individual Accounts by 31 December 2017 and on Lower Value Individual Accounts and Entity Accounts by 31 December 2018.

With respect to the exchange of information under the AEOI Standard, Nauru is a Party to the Convention on Mutual Administrative Assistance in Tax Matters and activated the associated CRS Multilateral Competent Authority Agreement in time for exchanges in 2017.

Detailed findings

The detailed findings for Nauru are below, organised per Core Requirement (CR) and sub-requirement (SR), as extracted from the AEOI Terms of Reference (www.oecd.org/tax/transparency/documents/aeoi-terms-of-reference.pdf).

CR1 Domestic legal framework: Jurisdictions should have a domestic legislative framework in place that requires all Reporting Financial Institutions to conduct the due diligence and reporting procedures in the CRS, and that provides for the effective implementation of the CRS as set out therein.

Determination: In Place

Nauru's domestic legislative framework is in place and contains all of the key aspects of the CRS and its Commentary requiring Reporting Financial Institutions to conduct the due diligence and reporting procedures (SRs 1.1 – 1.3). It also provides for a framework to enforce the requirements (SR 1.4).

SR 1.1 Jurisdictions should define the scope of Reporting Financial Institutions consistently with the CRS.

Nauru has defined the scope of Reporting Financial Institutions in its domestic legislative framework in accordance with the CRS and its Commentary.

Recommendations:

No recommendations made.

SR 1.2 Jurisdictions should define the scope of Financial Accounts and Reportable Accounts consistently with the CRS and incorporate the due diligence procedures to identify them.

Nauru has defined the scope of the Financial Accounts that are required to be reported in its domestic legislative framework and incorporated the due diligence procedures that must be applied to identify them in accordance with the CRS and its Commentary.

Recommendations:

No recommendations made.

SR 1.3 Jurisdictions should incorporate the reporting requirements contained in Section I of the CRS into their domestic legislative framework.

Nauru has incorporated the reporting requirements in its domestic legislative framework in accordance with the CRS and its Commentary.

Recommendations:

No recommendations made.

SR 1.4 Jurisdictions should have a legislative framework in place that allows for the enforcement of the requirements of the CRS in practice.

Nauru has a legislative framework in place to enforce the requirements in accordance with the CRS and its Commentary.

Recommendations:

No recommendations made.

CR2 International legal framework: Jurisdictions should have exchange relationships in effect with all Interested Appropriate Partners as committed to and that provide for the exchange of information in accordance with the Model CAA.

Determination: In Place

Nauru's international legal framework to exchange the information is in place, is consistent with the Model CAA and its Commentary and provides for exchange with all of Nauru's Interested Appropriate Partners (i.e. all jurisdictions that are interested in receiving information from Nauru and that meet the required standard in relation to confidentiality and data safeguards). (SRs 2.1 – 2.3)

SR 2.1 Jurisdictions should have exchange agreements in effect with all Interested Appropriate Partners that permit the automatic exchange of CRS information.

Nauru has exchange agreements that permit the automatic exchange of CRS information in effect with all its Interested Appropriate Partners.

Recommendations:

No recommendations made.

SR 2.2 Such an exchange agreement should be put in place without undue delay, following the receipt of an expression of interest from an Interested Appropriate Partner.

Nauru put in place its exchange agreements without undue delay.

Recommendations:

No recommendations made.

SR 2.3 Jurisdictions should ensure that the exchange agreements in effect provide for the exchange of information in accordance with the requirements of the Model CAA.

Nauru's exchange agreements provide for the exchange of information in accordance with the requirements of the Model CAA.

Recommendations:

No recommendations made.

Comments by the assessed jurisdiction

No comments made.

Netherlands

Overall findings

The Netherlands' legal framework implementing the AEOI Standard is in place but needs improvement in order to be fully consistent with the requirements of the AEOI Terms of Reference. While the Netherlands' international legal framework to exchange the information with all of the Netherlands' Interested Appropriate Partners (CR2) is consistent with the requirements, the Netherlands' domestic legislative framework requiring Reporting Financial Institutions to conduct the due diligence and reporting procedures (CR1) has a deficiency significant to the proper functioning of an element of the AEOI Standard. More specifically, a deficiency has been identified in the Netherlands' enforcement framework.

The methodology used for the peer reviews and that therefore underpins this report is outlined in Chapter 2.

Overall determination on the legal framework: In Place But **Needs Improvement**

Conclusions on the legal framework

General context

The Netherlands commenced exchanges under the AEOI Standard in 2017.

In order to provide for Reporting Financial Institutions to collect and report the information to be exchanged, the Netherlands:

- introduced the Decree of 23 December 2015 (Common Reporting Standard Identification and Reporting Requirements (Implementation) Decree);
- introduced the Ministerial Order on the Common Reporting Standard made on 30 December 2015;
- amended the International Assistance (Levying of Taxes) Act and Money Laundering and Terrorist Financing (Prevention) Act (Implementation) Decree 2018; and
- issued further guidance, which is not legally binding.

Under this framework Reporting Financial Institutions were required to commence the due diligence procedures in relation to New Accounts from 1 January 2016. With respect to Preexisting Accounts, Reporting Financial Institutions were required to complete due diligence procedures on High Value Individual Accounts by 31 December 2016 and on Lower Value Individual Accounts and Entity Accounts by 31 December 2017.

With respect to the exchange of information under the AEOI Standard, the Netherlands:

- is a Party to the Convention on Mutual Administrative Assistance in Tax Matters and activated the associated CRS Multilateral Competent Authority Agreement in time for exchanges in 2017;
- has in place European Union Directive 2011/16/EU on Administrative Cooperation in the Field of Taxation, as amended by Directive 2014/107/EU;
- has in place European Union agreements with five European third countries[1]; and
- put in place three bilateral agreements.[2]

Detailed findings

The detailed findings for the Netherlands are below, organised per Core Requirement (CR) and sub-requirement (SR), as extracted from the AEOI Terms of Reference (www.oecd.org/tax/transparency/documents/aeoi-terms-of-reference.pdf).

CR1 Domestic legal framework: Jurisdictions should have a domestic legislative framework in place that requires all Reporting Financial Institutions to conduct the due diligence and reporting procedures in the CRS, and that provides for the effective implementation of the CRS as set out therein.

Determination: In Place But **Needs Improvement**

The Netherlands' domestic legislative framework is in place and contains most of the key aspects of the CRS and its Commentary requiring Reporting Financial Institutions to conduct the due diligence and reporting procedures, but it needs improvement in one area relating to the framework to enforce the requirements (SR 1.4). More specifically, the Netherlands does not have rules to prevent the circumvention of the due diligence and reporting procedures.

SR 1.1 Jurisdictions should define the scope of Reporting Financial Institutions consistently with the CRS.

The Netherlands has defined the scope of Reporting Financial Institutions in its domestic legislative framework in accordance with the CRS and its Commentary.

Recommendations:

No recommendations made.

SR 1.2 Jurisdictions should define the scope of Financial Accounts and Reportable Accounts consistently with the CRS and incorporate the due diligence procedures to identify them.

The Netherlands has defined the scope of the Financial Accounts that are required to be reported in its domestic legislative framework and incorporated the due diligence procedures that must be applied to identify them in accordance with the CRS and its Commentary.

Recommendations:

No recommendations made.

SR 1.3 Jurisdictions should incorporate the reporting requirements contained in Section I of the CRS into their domestic legislative framework.

The Netherlands has incorporated the reporting requirements in its domestic legislative framework in accordance with the CRS and its Commentary.

Recommendations:

No recommendations made.

SR 1.4 Jurisdictions should have a legislative framework in place that allows for the enforcement of the requirements of the CRS in practice.

The Netherlands has a legislative framework in place to enforce the requirements in a manner that is largely consistent with the CRS and its Commentary. However, a deficiency has been identified. More specifically, the Netherlands' legislative framework does not include rules to prevent Financial Institutions, persons or intermediaries from adopting practices intended to circumvent the due diligence and reporting procedures. This is a key element of the required enforcement framework and is therefore material to the proper functioning of the AEOI Standard.

It is noted that the Netherlands has EU Directive 2018/22 (DAC 6) (the implementation of the Mandatory Disclosure Rules in the European Union) in place, which facilitates tax authorities becoming aware of practices intended to circumvent the reporting and due diligence procedures. The AEOI Standard, however, requires rules to be in place to prevent or ensure the effective implementation of the AEOI Standard once such practices are discovered.

Recommendations:

The Netherlands should amend its domestic legislative framework to include rules to prevent Financial Institutions, persons and intermediaries adopting practices intended to circumvent the due diligence and reporting procedures. While it is acknowledged that the mandatory reporting requirements in place will facilitate the identification of such practices, additional rules are needed to prevent such practices.

CR2 International legal framework: Jurisdictions should have exchange relationships in effect with all Interested Appropriate Partners as committed to and that provide for the exchange of information in accordance with the Model CAA.

Determination: In Place

The Netherlands' international legal framework to exchange the information is in place, is consistent with the Model CAA and its Commentary and provides for exchange with all of the Netherlands' Interested Appropriate Partners (i.e. all jurisdictions that are interested in receiving information from the Netherlands and that meet the required standard in relation to confidentiality and data safeguards). (SRs 2.1 – 2.3)

SR 2.1 Jurisdictions should have exchange agreements in effect with all Interested Appropriate Partners that permit the automatic exchange of CRS information.

The Netherlands has exchange agreements that permit the automatic exchange of CRS information in effect with all its Interested Appropriate Partners.

Recommendations:

No recommendations made.

SR 2.2 Such an exchange agreement should be put in place without undue delay, following the receipt of an expression of interest from an Interested Appropriate Partner.

The Netherlands put in place its exchange agreements without undue delay.

Recommendations:

No recommendations made.

SR 2.3 Jurisdictions should ensure that the exchange agreements in effect provide for the exchange of information in accordance with the requirements of the Model CAA.

The Netherlands' exchange agreements provide for the exchange of information in accordance with the requirements of the Model CAA.

Recommendations:

No recommendations made.

Comments by the assessed jurisdiction

We took note of the recommendation and initiated legislation to implement adequate rules to prevent or ensure the effective implementation of the AEOI Standard once anti-avoidance practices are discovered.

These rules will be comparable to the provisions of the UK and/or Canada. However, the implementation of new legislation takes time and the new rules will be in place as of 1 January 2022.

Notes

[1] Andorra, Liechtenstein, Monaco, San Marino and Switzerland.

[2] With Hong Kong (China), Qatar and Singapore. The Netherlands has also activated relationships under the CRS MCAA with Qatar and Singapore.

New Zealand

Overall findings

New Zealand's legal framework implementing the AEOI Standard is in place and is consistent with the requirements of the AEOI Terms of Reference. This includes New Zealand's domestic legislative framework requiring Reporting Financial Institutions to conduct the due diligence and reporting procedures (CR1) and its international legal framework to exchange the information with all of New Zealand's Interested Appropriate Partners (CR2).

The methodology used for the peer reviews and that therefore underpins this report is outlined in Chapter 2.

Overall determination on the legal framework: In Place

Conclusions on the legal framework

General context

New Zealand commenced exchanges under the AEOI Standard in 2018.

In order to provide for Reporting Financial Institutions to collect and report the information to be exchanged, New Zealand:

- enacted legislation, primarily located in Part 11B of the Tax Administration Act 1994; and
- issued further guidance, which is not legally binding.

Under this framework Reporting Financial Institutions were required to commence the due diligence procedures in relation to New Accounts from 1 July 2017. With respect to Preexisting Accounts, Reporting Financial Institutions were required to complete the due diligence procedures on High Value Individual Accounts by 30 June 2018 and on Lower Value Individual Accounts and Entity Accounts by 30 June 2019.

With respect to the exchange of information under the AEOI Standard, New Zealand:

- is a Party to the Convention on Mutual Administrative Assistance in Tax Matters and activated the associated CRS Multilateral Competent Authority Agreement in time for exchanges in 2018; and
- put in place two bilateral agreements.[1]

Detailed findings

The detailed findings for New Zealand are below, organised per Core Requirement (CR) and sub-requirement (SR), as extracted from the AEOI Terms of Reference (www.oecd.org/tax/transparency/documents/aeoi-terms-of-reference.pdf).

CR1 Domestic legal framework: Jurisdictions should have a domestic legislative framework in place that requires all Reporting Financial Institutions to conduct the due diligence and reporting procedures in the CRS, and that provides for the effective implementation of the CRS as set out therein.

Determination: In Place

New Zealand's domestic legislative framework is in place and contains all of the key aspects of the CRS and its Commentary requiring Reporting Financial Institutions to conduct the due diligence and reporting procedures (SRs 1.1 – 1.3). It also provides for a framework to enforce the requirements (SR 1.4).

SR 1.1 Jurisdictions should define the scope of Reporting Financial Institutions consistently with the CRS.

New Zealand has defined the scope of Reporting Financial Institutions in its domestic legislative framework in accordance with the CRS and its Commentary.

Recommendations:

No recommendations made.

SR 1.2 Jurisdictions should define the scope of Financial Accounts and Reportable Accounts consistently with the CRS and incorporate the due diligence procedures to identify them.

New Zealand has defined the scope of the Financial Accounts that are required to be reported in its domestic legislative framework and incorporated the due diligence procedures that must be applied to identify them in accordance with the CRS and its Commentary.

Recommendations:

No recommendations made.

SR 1.3 Jurisdictions should incorporate the reporting requirements contained in Section I of the CRS into their domestic legislative framework.

New Zealand has incorporated the reporting requirements in its domestic legislative framework in accordance with the CRS and its Commentary.

Recommendations:

No recommendations made.

SR 1.4 Jurisdictions should have a legislative framework in place that allows for the enforcement of the requirements of the CRS in practice.

New Zealand has a legislative framework in place to enforce the requirements in accordance with the CRS and its Commentary.

Recommendations:

No recommendations made.

CR2 International legal framework: Jurisdictions should have exchange relationships in effect with all Interested Appropriate Partners as committed to and that provide for the exchange of information in accordance with the Model CAA.

Determination: In Place

New Zealand's international legal framework to exchange the information is in place, is consistent with the Model CAA and its Commentary and provides for exchange with all of New Zealand's Interested Appropriate Partners (i.e. all jurisdictions that are interested in receiving information from New Zealand and that meet the required standard in relation to confidentiality and data safeguards). (SRs 2.1 – 2.3)

SR 2.1 Jurisdictions should have exchange agreements in effect with all Interested Appropriate Partners that permit the automatic exchange of CRS information.

New Zealand has exchange agreements that permit the automatic exchange of CRS information in effect with all its Interested Appropriate Partners.

Recommendations:

No recommendations made.

SR 2.2 Such an exchange agreement should be put in place without undue delay, following the receipt of an expression of interest from an Interested Appropriate Partner.

New Zealand put in place its exchange agreements without undue delay.

Recommendations:

No recommendations made.

SR 2.3 Jurisdictions should ensure that the exchange agreements in effect provide for the exchange of information in accordance with the requirements of the Model CAA.

New Zealand's exchange agreements provide for the exchange of information in accordance with the requirements of the Model CAA.

Recommendations:

No recommendations made.

Comments by the assessed jurisdiction

New Zealand agrees with the assessment.

Note

[1] With Hong Kong (China) and Singapore. New Zealand has also activated a relationship under the CRS MCAA with Singapore.

Niue

Overall findings

Niue's legal framework implementing the AEOI Standard is in place and is consistent with the requirements of the AEOI Terms of Reference. This includes Niue's domestic legislative framework requiring Reporting Financial Institutions to conduct the due diligence and reporting procedures (CR1) and its international legal framework to exchange the information with all of Niue's Interested Appropriate Partners (CR2).

The methodology used for the peer reviews and that therefore underpins this report is outlined in Chapter 2.

Overall determination on the legal framework: In Place

Conclusions on the legal framework

General context

Niue committed to commence exchanges under the AEOI Standard by 2018 although was delayed in activating the CRS Multilateral Competent Authority Agreement (CRS MCAA) and while it has now activated the CRS MCAA Niue has still not commenced exchanges.

In order to provide for Reporting Financial Institutions to collect and report the information to be exchanged, Niue:

- enacted the Niue Tax Amendment Act 2016 and Niue Income Tax Act 1961; and
- introduced the Income Tax (Automatic Exchange of Information) Regulations 2017.

Under this framework Reporting Financial Institutions were required to commence the due diligence procedures in relation to New Accounts from 1 July 2017. With respect to Preexisting Accounts, Reporting Financial Institutions were required to complete the due diligence procedures on High Value Individual Accounts by 31 December 2017 and on Lower Value Individual Accounts and Entity Accounts by 31 December 2018.

With respect to the exchange of information under the AEOI Standard, Niue is a Party to the Convention on Mutual Administrative Assistance in Tax Matters and activated the associated CRS Multilateral Competent Authority Agreement in time for exchanges in 2019.

Detailed findings

The detailed findings for Niue are below, organised per Core Requirement (CR) and sub-requirement (SR), as extracted from the AEOI Terms of Reference (www.oecd.org/tax/transparency/documents/aeoi-terms-of-reference.pdf).

CR1 Domestic legal framework: Jurisdictions should have a domestic legislative framework in place that requires all Reporting Financial Institutions to conduct the due diligence and reporting procedures in the CRS, and that provides for the effective implementation of the CRS as set out therein.

Determination: In Place

Niue's domestic legislative framework is in place and contains all of the key aspects of the CRS and its Commentary requiring Reporting Financial Institutions to conduct the due diligence and reporting procedures (SRs 1.1 – 1.3). It also provides for a framework to enforce the requirements (SR 1.4).

SR 1.1 Jurisdictions should define the scope of Reporting Financial Institutions consistently with the CRS.

Niue has defined the scope of Reporting Financial Institutions in its domestic legislative framework in accordance with the CRS and its Commentary.

Recommendations:

No recommendations made.

SR 1.2 Jurisdictions should define the scope of Financial Accounts and Reportable Accounts consistently with the CRS and incorporate the due diligence procedures to identify them.

Niue has defined the scope of the Financial Accounts that are required to be reported in its domestic legislative framework and incorporated the due diligence procedures that must be applied to identify them in accordance with the CRS and its Commentary.

Recommendations:

No recommendations made.

SR 1.3 Jurisdictions should incorporate the reporting requirements contained in Section I of the CRS into their domestic legislative framework.

Niue has incorporated the reporting requirements in its domestic legislative framework in accordance with the CRS and its Commentary.

Recommendations:

No recommendations made.

SR 1.4 Jurisdictions should have a legislative framework in place that allows for the enforcement of the requirements of the CRS in practice.

Niue has a legislative framework in place to enforce the requirements in accordance with the CRS and its Commentary.

Recommendations:

No recommendations made.

CR2 International legal framework: Jurisdictions should have exchange relationships in effect with all Interested Appropriate Partners as committed to and that provide for the exchange of information in accordance with the Model CAA.

Determination: In Place

Niue's international legal framework to exchange the information is in place, is consistent with the Model CAA and its Commentary and provides for exchange with all of Niue's Interested Appropriate Partners (i.e. all jurisdictions that are interested in receiving information from Niue and that meet the required standard in relation to confidentiality and data safeguards). (SRs 2.1 – 2.3)

SR 2.1 Jurisdictions should have exchange agreements in effect with all Interested Appropriate Partners that permit the automatic exchange of CRS information.

Niue has exchange agreements that permit the automatic exchange of CRS information in effect with all its Interested Appropriate Partners.

Recommendations:

No recommendations made.

SR 2.2 Such an exchange agreement should be put in place without undue delay, following the receipt of an expression of interest from an Interested Appropriate Partner.

Niue put in place its exchange agreements without undue delay.

Recommendations:

No recommendations made.

SR 2.3 Jurisdictions should ensure that the exchange agreements in effect provide for the exchange of information in accordance with the requirements of the Model CAA.

Niue's exchange agreements provide for the exchange of information in accordance with the requirements of the Model CAA.

Recommendations:

No recommendations made.

Comments by the assessed jurisdiction

Niue appreciates the opportunity to comment on this report.

Niue notes the assessment.

Niue also looks forward to continuing dialogue within the Global Forum regarding participation and compliance challenges for Small Island Developing States.

Norway

Overall findings

Norway's legal framework implementing the AEOI Standard is in place and is consistent with the requirements of the AEOI Terms of Reference. This includes Norway's domestic legislative framework requiring Reporting Financial Institutions to conduct the due diligence and reporting procedures (CR1) and its international legal framework to exchange the information with all of Norway's Interested Appropriate Partners (CR2).

The methodology used for the peer reviews and that therefore underpins this report is outlined in Chapter 2.

Overall determination on the legal framework: In Place

Conclusions on the legal framework

General context

Norway commenced exchanges under the AEOI Standard in 2017.

In order to provide for Reporting Financial Institutions to collect and report the information to be exchanged, Norway:

- enacted the Tax Administration Act of 27 May 2016 no. 14 (skatteforvaltningsloven);
- introduced the Tax Administration Regulation of 23 November 2016 no. 1360 (skatteforvaltningsforskriften);
- issued further guidance, which is not legally binding; and
- made reference to the Act relating to Measures to Combat Money Laundering and Terrorist Financing implementing the FATF Recommendations for the purposes of the identification of Controlling Persons under the AEOI Standard.

Under this framework Reporting Financial Institutions were required to commence the due diligence procedures in relation to New Accounts from 1 January 2016. With respect to Preexisting Accounts, Reporting Financial Institutions were required to complete the due diligence procedures on High Value Individual Accounts by 31 December 2016 and on Lower Value Individual Accounts and Entity Accounts by 31 December 2017.

With respect to the exchange of information under the AEOI Standard, Norway:

- is a Party to the Convention on Mutual Administrative Assistance in Tax Matters and activated the associated CRS Multilateral Competent Authority Agreement in time for exchanges in 2017; and
- put in place two bilateral agreements.[1]

Detailed findings

The detailed findings for Norway are below, organised per Core Requirement (CR) and sub-requirement (SR), as extracted from the AEOI Terms of Reference (www.oecd.org/tax/transparency/documents/aeoi-terms-of-reference.pdf).

CR1 Domestic legal framework: Jurisdictions should have a domestic legislative framework in place that requires all Reporting Financial Institutions to conduct the due diligence and reporting procedures in the CRS, and that provides for the effective implementation of the CRS as set out therein.

Determination: In Place

Norway's domestic legislative framework is in place and contains all of the key aspects of the CRS and its Commentary requiring Reporting Financial Institutions to conduct the due diligence and reporting procedures (SRs 1.1 – 1.3). It also provides for a framework to enforce the requirements (SR 1.4).

SR 1.1 Jurisdictions should define the scope of Reporting Financial Institutions consistently with the CRS.

Norway has defined the scope of Reporting Financial Institutions in its domestic legislative framework in accordance with the CRS and its Commentary.

Recommendations:

No recommendations made.

SR 1.2 Jurisdictions should define the scope of Financial Accounts and Reportable Accounts consistently with the CRS and incorporate the due diligence procedures to identify them.

Norway has defined the scope of the Financial Accounts that are required to be reported in its domestic legislative framework and incorporated the due diligence procedures that must be applied to identify them in accordance with the CRS and its Commentary.

Recommendations:

No recommendations made.

SR 1.3 Jurisdictions should incorporate the reporting requirements contained in Section I of the CRS into their domestic legislative framework.

Norway has incorporated the reporting requirements in its domestic legislative framework in accordance with the CRS and its Commentary.

Recommendations:

No recommendations made.

SR 1.4 Jurisdictions should have a legislative framework in place that allows for the enforcement of the requirements of the CRS in practice.

Norway has a legislative framework in place to enforce the requirements in accordance with the CRS and its Commentary.

Recommendations:

No recommendations made.

CR2 International legal framework: Jurisdictions should have exchange relationships in effect with all Interested Appropriate Partners as committed to and that provide for the exchange of information in accordance with the Model CAA.

Determination: In Place

Norway's international legal framework to exchange the information is in place, is consistent with the Model CAA and its Commentary and provides for exchange with all of Norway's Interested Appropriate Partners (i.e. all jurisdictions that are interested in receiving information from Norway and that meet the required standard in relation to confidentiality and data safeguards) (SRs 2.1 – 2.3)

SR 2.1 Jurisdictions should have exchange agreements in effect with all Interested Appropriate Partners that permit the automatic exchange of CRS information.

Norway has exchange agreements that permit the automatic exchange of CRS information in effect with all its Interested Appropriate Partners.

Recommendations:

No recommendations made.

SR 2.2 Such an exchange agreement should be put in place without undue delay, following the receipt of an expression of interest from an Interested Appropriate Partner.

Norway put in place its exchange agreements without undue delay.

Recommendations:

No recommendations made.

SR 2.3 Jurisdictions should ensure that the exchange agreements in effect provide for the exchange of information in accordance with the requirements of the Model CAA.

Norway's exchange agreements provide for the exchange of information in accordance with the requirements of the Model CAA.

Recommendations:

No recommendations made.

Comments by the assessed jurisdiction

No comments made.

Note

[1] With Singapore and Turkey. Norway has also activated a relationship under the CRS MCAA with Turkey.

Pakistan

Overall findings

Pakistan's legal framework implementing the AEOI Standard is in place and is consistent with the requirements of the AEOI Terms of Reference. This includes Pakistan's domestic legislative framework requiring Reporting Financial Institutions to conduct the due diligence and reporting procedures (CR1) and its international legal framework to exchange the information with all of Pakistan's Interested Appropriate Partners (CR2).

The methodology used for the peer reviews and that therefore underpins this report is outlined in Chapter 2.

Overall determination on the legal framework: In Place

Conclusions on the legal framework

General context

Pakistan commenced exchanges under the AEOI Standard in 2018.

In order to provide for Reporting Financial Institutions to collect and report the information to be exchanged, Pakistan:

- enacted section 107, section 165B and section 182 of the Income Tax Ordinance, 2001;
- issued the Common Standard Rules (CRS Rules) vide SRO 166(I)/2017; and
- published a Guidance Note, which is not legally binding.

Under this framework Reporting Financial Institutions were required to commence the due diligence procedures in relation to New Accounts from 1 July 2017. With respect to Preexisting Accounts, Reporting Financial Institutions were required to complete the due diligence procedures on High Value Individual Accounts by 31 December 2017 and on Lower Value Individual Accounts and Entity Accounts by 31 December 2018.

Following the initial Global Forum peer review, Pakistan amended its legislative framework to address issues identified, effective from 24 August 2020.

With respect to the exchange of information under the AEOI Standard, Pakistan is a Party to the Convention on Mutual Administrative Assistance in Tax Matters and activated the associated CRS Multilateral Competent Authority Agreement in time for exchanges in 2018.

Detailed findings

The detailed findings for Pakistan are below, organised per Core Requirement (CR) and sub-requirement (SR), as extracted from the AEOI Terms of Reference (www.oecd.org/tax/transparency/documents/aeoi-terms-of-reference.pdf).

CR1 Domestic legal framework: Jurisdictions should have a domestic legislative framework in place that requires all Reporting Financial Institutions to conduct the due diligence and reporting procedures in the CRS, and that provides for the effective implementation of the CRS as set out therein.

Determination: In Place

Pakistan's domestic legislative framework is in place and contains all of the key aspects of the CRS and its Commentary requiring Reporting Financial Institutions to conduct the due diligence and reporting procedures (SRs 1.1 – 1.3). It also provides for a framework to enforce the requirements (SR 1.4).

SR 1.1 Jurisdictions should define the scope of Reporting Financial Institutions consistently with the CRS.

Pakistan has defined the scope of Reporting Financial Institutions in its domestic legislative framework in accordance with the CRS and its Commentary.

Recommendations:

No recommendations made.

SR 1.2 Jurisdictions should define the scope of Financial Accounts and Reportable Accounts consistently with the CRS and incorporate the due diligence procedures to identify them.

Pakistan has defined the scope of the Financial Accounts that are required to be reported in its domestic legislative framework and incorporated the due diligence procedures that must be applied to identify them in accordance with the CRS and its Commentary.

Recommendations:

No recommendations made.

SR 1.3 Jurisdictions should incorporate the reporting requirements contained in Section I of the CRS into their domestic legislative framework.

Pakistan has incorporated the reporting requirements in its domestic legislative framework in accordance with the CRS and its Commentary.

Recommendations:

No recommendations made.

SR 1.4 Jurisdictions should have a legislative framework in place that allows for the enforcement of the requirements of the CRS in practice.

Pakistan has a legislative framework in place to enforce the requirements in accordance with the CRS and its Commentary.

Recommendations:

No recommendations made.

CR2 International legal framework: Jurisdictions should have exchange relationships in effect with all Interested Appropriate Partners as committed to and that provide for the exchange of information in accordance with the Model CAA.

Determination: In Place

Pakistan's international legal framework to exchange the information is in place and consistent with the Model CAA and its Commentary and provides for exchange with all of Pakistan's Interested Appropriate

Partners (i.e. all jurisdictions that are interested in receiving information from Pakistan and that meet the required standard in relation to confidentiality and data safeguards). (SRs 2.1 – 2.3)

SR 2.1 Jurisdictions should have exchange agreements in effect with all Interested Appropriate Partners that permit the automatic exchange of CRS information.

Pakistan has exchange agreements that permit the automatic exchange of CRS information in effect with all its Interested Appropriate Partners.

Recommendations:

No recommendations made.

SR 2.2 Such an exchange agreement should be put in place without undue delay, following the receipt of an expression of interest from an Interested Appropriate Partner.

Pakistan put in place its exchange agreements without undue delay.

Recommendations:

No recommendations made.

SR 2.3 Jurisdictions should ensure that the exchange agreements in effect provide for the exchange of information in accordance with the requirements of the Model CAA.

Pakistan's exchange agreements provide for the exchange of information in accordance with the requirements of the Model CAA.

Recommendations:

No recommendations made.

Comments by the assessed jurisdiction

No comments made.

Panama

Overall findings

Panama's legal framework implementing the AEOI Standard is in place but needs improvement in order to be fully consistent with the requirements of the AEOI Terms of Reference. While Panama's international legal framework to exchange the information with all of Panama's Interested Appropriate Partners (CR2) is consistent with the requirements, its domestic legislative framework requiring Reporting Financial Institutions to conduct the due diligence and reporting procedures (CR1) has deficiencies significant to the proper functioning of elements of the AEOI Standard. More specifically, Panama does not fully incorporate some of the due diligence procedures and does not incorporate the categories of Non-Reporting Financial Institutions in accordance with the requirements. Moreover, there is a deficiency in Panama's legal framework for the enforcement of the requirements.

The methodology used for the peer reviews and that therefore underpins this report is outlined in Chapter 2.

Overall determination on the legal framework: In Place But **Needs Improvement**

Conclusions on the legal framework

General context

Panama commenced exchanges under the AEOI Standard in 2018.

In order to provide for Reporting Financial Institutions to collect and report the information to be exchanged, Panama:

- enacted the Law 51 of 27 October 2016;
- promulgated the Executive Decree 124 of 12 May 2017;
- promulgated the Executive Decree 461 of 26 December 2017; and
- issued Resolution No 201-3931 of 29 June 2017.

Under this framework Reporting Financial Institutions were required to commence the due diligence procedures in relation to New Accounts from 1 July 2017. With respect to Preexisting Accounts, Reporting Financial Institutions were required to complete due diligence procedures on High Value Individual Accounts by 30 June 2018 and on Lower Value Individual Accounts and Entity Accounts by 30 June 2019.

With respect to the exchange of information under the AEOI Standard, Panama is a Party to the Convention on Mutual Administrative Assistance in Tax Matters and activated the associated CRS Multilateral Competent Authority Agreement in time for exchanges in 2018.

Detailed findings

The detailed findings for Panama are below, organised per Core Requirement (CR) and sub-requirement (SR), as extracted from the AEOI Terms of Reference (www.oecd.org/tax/transparency/documents/aeoi-terms-of-reference.pdf).

CR1 Domestic legal framework: Jurisdictions should have a domestic legislative framework in place that requires all Reporting Financial Institutions to conduct the due diligence and reporting procedures in the CRS, and that provides for the effective implementation of the CRS as set out therein.

Determination: In Place But **Needs Improvement**

Panama's domestic legislative framework is in place and contains many of the key aspects of the CRS and its Commentary requiring Reporting Financial Institutions to conduct the due diligence and reporting procedures, but it needs improvement in relation to the scope of Reporting Financial Institutions required to report information (SR 1.1), the due diligence procedures that must be applied to Financial Accounts (SR 1.2) and the framework to enforce the requirements (SR 1.4). Most significantly, Panama provides for two Non-Reporting Financial Institutions that do not meet the requirements. Furthermore, Panama does not fully incorporate some of the due diligence procedures, and there is a deficiency in Panama's enforcement framework.

SR 1.1 Jurisdictions should define the scope of Reporting Financial Institutions consistently with the CRS.

Panama has defined the scope of Reporting Financial Institutions in its domestic legislative framework in a manner that is largely consistent with the CRS and its Commentary. However, deficiencies have been identified. Most significantly, Panama does not fully incorporate the category of Exempt Collective Investment Vehicle as a Non-Reporting Financial Institution and provides for a jurisdiction-specific Non-Reporting Financial Institution that is not in accordance with the requirements. The scope of Reporting Financial Institutions, including the provision of Non-Reporting Financial Institutions, is material to the proper functioning of the AEOI Standard.

Recommendations:

Panama should amend its domestic legislative framework to prevent Exempt Collective Investment Vehicles from issuing bearer shares from a specified date in order to be treated as Non-Reporting Financial Institutions.

Panama should amend its domestic legislative framework to remove *Fideicomisos* (trusts) that serve solely as escrow for a debt or purchase obligation of a settlor from its jurisdiction-specific list of Non-Reporting Financial Institutions as this type of Entity is a Non-Financial Entity so should be treated as such under the AEOI Standard.

Panama should amend its domestic legislative framework to fully incorporate the term "managed by" in relation to the definition of Investment Entity.

SR 1.2 Jurisdictions should define the scope of Financial Accounts and Reportable Accounts consistently with the CRS and incorporate the due diligence procedures to identify them.

Panama has defined the scope of the Financial Accounts that are required to be reported in its domestic legislative framework and incorporated the due diligence procedures that must be applied to identify them in a manner that is largely consistent with the CRS and its Commentary. However, deficiencies have been identified. More specifically, Panama's legal framework:

- does not specify that Reporting Financial Institutions may only rely on a self-certification for the purposes of determining whether a Controlling Person of a Passive NFE is a Reportable Person;
- does not incorporate all the elements related to the residence address test for the purposes of identifying Reportable Accounts among Preexisting Individual Lower Value Accounts; and
- sets a threshold for the identification of Controlling Persons that differs from the one defined in its AML law.

These elements of the due diligence procedures are material to the proper functioning of the AEOI Standard.

Recommendations:

Panama should amend its domestic legislative framework to specify that, for New Entity Accounts, Reporting Financial Institutions may only rely on a self-certification provided by a Passive NFE Account Holder or its Controlling Person to determine whether the Controlling Person is a Reportable Person.

Panama should amend its domestic legislative framework to require Reporting Financial Institutions to use only a "current" residence address when applying the residence address test, in particular by specifying that if mail has been returned as undeliverable, then the address cannot be considered as "current".

Panama's should amend its domestic legislative framework to require Reporting Financial Institutions to apply the specified procedures if there is a change of circumstance relating to the cases where the residence address test was used.

Panama should amend its domestic legislative framework to ensure that the approach to determine Controlling Persons under the AEOI Standard is aligned to its approach to determine beneficial owners under its domestic AML/KYC procedures, by including a 10% threshold with respect to financial entities and a 25% threshold in relation to non-financial entities.

SR 1.3 Jurisdictions should incorporate the reporting requirements contained in Section I of the CRS into their domestic legislative framework.

Panama has incorporated the reporting requirements in its domestic legislative framework in accordance with the CRS and its Commentary.

Recommendations:

No recommendations made.

SR 1.4 Jurisdictions should have a legislative framework in place that allows for the enforcement of the requirements of the CRS in practice.

Panama has a legislative framework in place to enforce the requirements in a manner that is largely consistent with the CRS and its Commentary. However, a deficiency has been identified. More specifically, Panama's domestic legal framework does not include sufficient rules to prevent Financial Institutions, persons or intermediaries from adopting practices intended to circumvent the reporting and due diligence procedures as required. This is a key element of the required enforcement framework and is therefore material to the proper functioning of the AEOI Standard.

Recommendations:

Panama should amend its domestic legislative framework to include rules to prevent all Financial Institutions, persons and intermediaries from adopting practices intended to circumvent the due diligence and reporting procedures, rather than only Financial Institutions, persons and intermediaries located within the territory of Panama.

CR2 International legal framework: Jurisdictions should have exchange relationships in effect with all Interested Appropriate Partners as committed to and that provide for the exchange of information in accordance with the Model CAA.

Determination: In Place

Panama's international legal framework to exchange the information is in place, is consistent with the Model CAA and its Commentary and provides for exchange with all of Panama's Interested Appropriate

Partners (i.e. all jurisdictions that are interested in receiving information from Panama and that meet the required standard in relation to confidentiality and data safeguards). (SRs 2.1 – 2.3)

SR 2.1 Jurisdictions should have exchange agreements in effect with all Interested Appropriate Partners that permit the automatic exchange of CRS information.

Panama has exchange agreements that permit the automatic exchange of CRS information in effect with all its Interested Appropriate Partners.

Recommendations:

No recommendations made.

SR 2.2 Such an exchange agreement should be put in place without undue delay, following the receipt of an expression of interest from an Interested Appropriate Partner.

Panama put in place its exchange agreements without undue delay.

Recommendations:

No recommendations made.

SR 2.3 Jurisdictions should ensure that the exchange agreements in effect provide for the exchange of information in accordance with the requirements of the Model CAA.

Panama's exchange agreements provide for the exchange of information in accordance with the requirements of the Model CAA.

Recommendations:

No recommendations made.

Comments by the assessed jurisdiction

No comments made.

Poland

Overall findings

Poland's legal framework implementing the AEOI Standard is in place but needs improvement in order to be fully consistent with the requirements of the AEOI Terms of Reference. While Poland's international legal framework to exchange the information with all of Poland's Interested Appropriate Partners (CR2) is consistent with the requirements, its domestic legislative framework requiring Reporting Financial Institutions to conduct the due diligence and reporting procedures (CR1) has deficiencies significant to the proper functioning of elements of the AEOI Standard. Most significantly, Poland's legislative framework does not define the scope of Reporting Financial Institutions in line with the requirements nor does it have rules to prevent practices intended to circumvent the due diligence and reporting procedures.

The methodology used for the peer reviews and that therefore underpins this report is outlined in Chapter 2.

Overall determination on the legal framework: In Place But **Needs Improvement**

Conclusions on the legal framework

General context

Poland commenced exchanges under the AEOI Standard in 2017.

In order to provide for Reporting Financial Institutions to collect and report the information to be exchanged, Poland:

- enacted the Act of March 9, 2017 on exchange of tax information with other countries; and
- made reference to the Act of November 16, 2000 on countering money laundering and terrorism financing for the purposes of the identification of Controlling Persons under the AEOI Standard.

Under this framework Reporting Financial Institutions were required to commence the due diligence procedures in relation to New Accounts from 1 January 2016. With respect to Preexisting Accounts, Reporting Financial Institutions were required to complete the due diligence procedures on High Value Individual Accounts by 31 December 2017 and on Lower Value Individual Accounts and Entity Accounts by 31 December 2018.

With respect to the exchange of information under the AEOI Standard, Poland:

- is a Party to the Convention on Mutual Administrative Assistance in Tax Matters and activated the associated CRS Multilateral Competent Authority Agreement in time for exchanges in 2017;
- has in place European Directive 2011/16/EU on Administrative Cooperation in the Field of Taxation as amended by Directive 2014/107/EU; and
- has in place European Union agreements with five European third countries.[1]

Detailed findings

The detailed findings for Poland are below, organised per Core Requirement (CR) and sub-requirement (SR), as extracted from the AEOI Terms of Reference (www.oecd.org/tax/transparency/documents/aeoi-terms-of-reference.pdf).

CR1 Domestic legal framework: Jurisdictions should have a domestic legislative framework in place that requires all Reporting Financial Institutions to conduct the due diligence and reporting procedures in the CRS, and that provides for the effective implementation of the CRS as set out therein.

Determination: In Place But **Needs Improvement**

Poland's domestic legislative framework is in place and contains most of the key aspects of the CRS and its Commentary requiring Reporting Financial Institutions to conduct the due diligence and reporting procedures, but it needs improvement in relation to the scope of Reporting Financial Institutions required to report information (SR 1.1) and the framework to enforce the requirements (SR1.4). Most significantly, Poland's legislative framework does not define Financial Assets in accordance with the requirements nor does it contain rules to prevent practices intended to circumvent the reporting and due diligence procedures.

SR 1.1 Jurisdictions should define the scope of Reporting Financial Institutions consistently with the CRS.

Poland has defined the scope of Reporting Financial Institutions in its domestic legislative framework in a manner that is largely consistent with the CRS and its Commentary. However, deficiencies have been identified. Most significantly, Poland's legislative framework defines Financial Assets through an exhaustive list, which is not in accordance with the requirements. This is a key element to the definition of Reporting Financial Institution and is therefore material to the proper functioning of the AEOI Standard.

Recommendations:

Poland should amend its domestic legislative framework to define Financial Asset using an inclusive approach as contained in the AEOI Standard, rather than using an exhaustive list.

Poland should amend its domestic legislative framework to require the term Investment Entity to be interpreted consistently with the language defining "financial institution" in the Financial Action Task Force Recommendation, although it is noted that the non-binding Explanatory Memorandum instructs that the interpretation of the Act be commensurate with the Commentary.

SR 1.2 Jurisdictions should define the scope of Financial Accounts and Reportable Accounts consistently with the CRS and incorporate the due diligence procedures to identify them.

Poland has defined the scope of the Financial Accounts that are required to be reported in its domestic legislative framework and incorporated the due diligence procedures that must be applied to identify them in accordance with the CRS and its Commentary. While a deficiency has been identified concerning New Accounts opened during a transitory period, as alternative procedures were required and as the transitional period ended in on 30 April 2017, this is considered to be relatively minor and its impact not to be material.

Recommendations:

Poland should ensure that New Accounts opened during the transitory period of 1 January 2016 to 30 April 2017 are subjected to due diligence procedures that are in accordance with the AEOI Standard.

SR 1.3 Jurisdictions should incorporate the reporting requirements contained in Section I of the CRS into their domestic legislative framework.

Poland has incorporated the reporting requirements in its domestic legislative framework in accordance with the CRS and its Commentary.

Recommendations:

No recommendations made.

SR 1.4 Jurisdictions should have a legislative framework in place that allows for the enforcement of the requirements of the CRS in practice.

Poland has a legislative framework in place to enforce the requirements in a manner that is largely consistent with the CRS and its Commentary. However, a deficiency has been identified. More specifically, Poland's legislative framework does not include rules to prevent Financial Institutions, persons and intermediaries from adopting practices intended to circumvent the reporting and due diligence procedures as required. This is a key element of the required enforcement framework and is therefore material to the proper functioning of the AEOI Standard.

Recommendations:

Poland should amend its domestic legislative framework to include rules to prevent Financial Institutions, persons and intermediaries from adopting practices intended to circumvent the due diligence and reporting procedures. While it is acknowledged that the mandatory reporting requirements in place will facilitate the identification of such practices, additional rules are needed to prevent such practices.

CR2 International legal framework: Jurisdictions should have exchange relationships in effect with all Interested Appropriate Partners as committed to and that provide for the exchange of information in accordance with the Model CAA.

Determination: In Place

Poland's international legal framework to exchange the information is in place, is consistent with the Model CAA and its Commentary and provides for exchange with all of Poland's Interested Appropriate Partners (i.e. all jurisdictions that are interested in receiving information from Poland and that meet the required standard in relation to confidentiality and data safeguards). (SRs 2.1 – 2.3)

SR 2.1 Jurisdictions should have exchange agreements in effect with all Interested Appropriate Partners that permit the automatic exchange of CRS information.

Poland has exchange agreements that permit the automatic exchange of CRS information in effect with all its Interested Appropriate Partners.

Recommendations:

No recommendations made.

SR 2.2 Such an exchange agreement should be put in place without undue delay, following the receipt of an expression of interest from an Interested Appropriate Partner.

Poland put in place its exchange agreements without undue delay.

Recommendations:

No recommendations made.

SR 2.3 Jurisdictions should ensure that the exchange agreements in effect provide for the exchange of information in accordance with the requirements of the Model CAA.

Poland's exchange agreements provide for the exchange of information in accordance with the requirements of the Model CAA.

Recommendations:

No recommendations made.

Comments by the assessed jurisdiction

As for the recommendation regarding SR 1.2, we would like to clarify that within our internal legal framework Financial Institutions are obliged to contact the account holders and request self-certification (with information on the residence as at the date of account opening) in order to document all accounts opened between 1 January 2016 and 30 April 2017 (apart from application of due diligence procedures for pre-existing accounts which they also have to apply). Based on current reporting status, financial institutions carried out most of required due diligence activities, with updated information subsequently transferred by the Polish tax administration to other countries participating in the CRS exchange.

We would like to underline that the Polish definition of Financial Asset includes all of the examples of assets listed within the paragraph 7 of the Section VIII of the Model Rules. At the same time, we want to emphasize that, although the list itself is exhaustive, the items listed in it (e.g. "security") are not strictly defined in the Polish internal legal framework. Therefore, due to the broad and not strictly limited scope of the items included within the list, the definition allows a wide range of various assets to be covered.

As per the recommendation in respect of the definition of Investment Entity, we would like to add that we have published an official explanation (on the official website of the Ministry of Finance: https://www.gov.pl/web/finanse/informacja-w-sprawie-interpretacji-pojecia-podmiot-inwestujacy) in which we clearly state that the interpretation of term must be consistent with the Directive as well as the CRS standard (by extension, AML framework). We believe that our communication in this matter (although it is non-binding) leaves no doubt as to market practice in the interpretation of the term of Investment Entity.

Nevertheless, Polish Ministry of Finance is reconsidering the further recommendations related to the enforcement framework and to introducing adjusting amendments in the legal definitions of financial assets and investment entity.

Note

[1] Andorra, Liechtenstein, Monaco, San Marino and Switzerland.

Portugal

Overall findings

Portugal's legal framework implementing the AEOI Standard is in place and is consistent with the requirements of the AEOI Terms of Reference. This includes Portugal's domestic legislative framework requiring Reporting Financial Institutions to conduct the due diligence and reporting procedures (CR1) and its international legal framework to exchange the information with all of Portugal's Interested Appropriate Partners (CR2).

The methodology used for the peer reviews and that therefore underpins this report is outlined in Chapter 2.

Overall determination on the legal framework: In Place

Conclusions on the legal framework

General context

Portugal commenced exchanges under the AEOI Standard in 2017.

In order to provide for Reporting Financial Institutions to collect and report the information to be exchanged, Portugal:

- enacted Decree-Law No. 64/2016, of 11 October (as amended by Decree-Law No. 83/2017); and
- introduced several Ministerial Orders.

Under this framework Reporting Financial Institutions were required to commence the due diligence procedures in relation to New Accounts from 1 January 2016. With respect to Preexisting Accounts, Reporting Financial Institutions were required to complete the due diligence procedures on High Value Individual Accounts by 31 December 2016 and on Lower Value Individual Accounts and Entity Accounts by 31 December 2017.

With respect to the exchange of information under the AEOI Standard, Portugal:

- is a Party to the Convention on Mutual Administrative Assistance in Tax Matters and activated the associated CRS Multilateral Competent Authority Agreement in time for exchanges in 2017;
- has in place European Directive 2011/16/EU on Administrative Cooperation in the Field of Taxation as amended by Directive 2014/107/EU;
- has in place European Union agreements with five European third countries;[1] and
- put in place a bilateral agreement.[2]

Detailed findings

The detailed findings for Portugal are below, organised per Core Requirement (CR) and sub-requirement (SR), as extracted from the AEOI Terms of Reference (www.oecd.org/tax/transparency/documents/aeoi-terms-of-reference.pdf).

CR1 Domestic legal framework: Jurisdictions should have a domestic legislative framework in place that requires all Reporting Financial Institutions to conduct the due diligence and reporting procedures in the CRS, and that provides for the effective implementation of the CRS as set out therein.

Determination: In Place

Portugal's domestic legislative framework is in place and contains all of the key aspects of the CRS and its Commentary requiring Reporting Financial Institutions to conduct the due diligence and reporting procedures (SRs 1.1 – 1.3). It also provides for a framework to enforce the requirements (SR 1.4).

SR 1.1 Jurisdictions should define the scope of Reporting Financial Institutions consistently with the CRS.

Portugal has defined the scope of Reporting Financial Institutions in its domestic legislative framework in accordance with the CRS and its Commentary.

Recommendations:

No recommendations made.

SR 1.2 Jurisdictions should define the scope of Financial Accounts and Reportable Accounts consistently with the CRS and incorporate the due diligence procedures to identify them.

Portugal has defined the scope of the Financial Accounts that are required to be reported in its domestic legislative framework and incorporated the due diligence procedures that must be applied to identify them in accordance with the CRS and its Commentary.

Recommendations:

No recommendations made.

SR 1.3 Jurisdictions should incorporate the reporting requirements contained in Section I of the CRS into their domestic legislative framework.

Portugal has incorporated the reporting requirements in its domestic legislative framework in accordance with the CRS and its Commentary.

Recommendations:

No recommendations made.

SR 1.4 Jurisdictions should have a legislative framework in place that allows for the enforcement of the requirements of the CRS in practice.

Portugal has a legislative framework in place to enforce the requirements in accordance with the CRS and its Commentary.

Recommendations:

No recommendations made.

CR2 International legal framework: Jurisdictions should have exchange relationships in effect with all Interested Appropriate Partners as committed to and that provide for the exchange of information in accordance with the Model CAA.

Determination: In Place

Portugal's international legal framework to exchange the information is in place, is consistent with the Model CAA and its Commentary and provides for exchange with all of Portugal's Interested Appropriate

Partners (i.e. all jurisdictions that are interested in receiving information from Portugal and that meet the required standard in relation to confidentiality and data safeguards). (SRs 2.1 – 2.3)

SR 2.1 Jurisdictions should have exchange agreements in effect with all Interested Appropriate Partners that permit the automatic exchange of CRS information.

Portugal has exchange agreements that permit the automatic exchange of CRS information in effect with all its Interested Appropriate Partners.

Recommendations:

No recommendations made.

SR 2.2 Such an exchange agreement should be put in place without undue delay, following the receipt of an expression of interest from an Interested Appropriate Partner.

Portugal put in place its exchange agreements without undue delay.

Recommendations:

No recommendations made.

SR 2.3 Jurisdictions should ensure that the exchange agreements in effect provide for the exchange of information in accordance with the requirements of the Model CAA.

Portugal's exchange agreements provide for the exchange of information in accordance with the requirements of the Model CAA.

Recommendations:

No recommendations made.

Comments by the assessed jurisdiction

No comments made.

Notes

[1] Andorra, Liechtenstein, Monaco, San Marino and Switzerland.

[2] With Hong Kong (China).

Qatar

Overall findings

Qatar's legal framework implementing the AEOI Standard is in place and is consistent with the requirements of the AEOI Terms of Reference. This includes Qatar's domestic legislative framework requiring Reporting Financial Institutions to conduct the due diligence and reporting procedures (CR1) and its international legal framework to exchange the information with all of Qatar's Interested Appropriate Partners (CR2).

The methodology used for the peer reviews and that therefore underpins this report is outlined in Chapter 2.

Overall determination on the legal framework: In Place

Conclusions on the legal framework

General context

Qatar commenced exchanges under the AEOI Standard in 2018.

In order to provide for Reporting Financial Institutions to collect and report the information to be exchanged, Qatar:

- enacted Article 34 of the Income Tax Law promulgated by Law No. 24 of the year 2019;
- introduced MOF Decisions No.1 of 2018, and No.17 of 2019; and
- introduced GTA Decisions No.8 of 2019, and No. 6 of 2020.

Under this framework Reporting Financial Institutions were required to commence the due diligence procedures in relation to New Accounts from 1 July 2017. With respect to Preexisting Accounts, Reporting Financial Institutions were required to complete the due diligence procedures on High Value Individual Accounts by 30 June 2018 and on Lower Value Individual Accounts and Entity Accounts by 30 June 2019.

Following the initial Global Forum peer review, Qatar amended its legislative framework to address issues identified, effective from 23 August 2020.

With respect to the exchange of information under the AEOI Standard, Qatar:

- put in place seven bilateral agreements in time for exchanges in 2018[1]; and
- is a Party to the Convention on Mutual Administrative Assistance in Tax Matters and activated the associated CRS Multilateral Competent Authority Agreement in time for exchanges in 2019.

Detailed findings

The detailed findings for Qatar are below, organised per Core Requirement (CR) and sub-requirement (SR), as extracted from the AEOI Terms of Reference (www.oecd.org/tax/transparency/documents/aeoi-terms-of-reference.pdf).

CR1 Domestic legal framework: Jurisdictions should have a domestic legislative framework in place that requires all Reporting Financial Institutions to conduct the due diligence and reporting procedures in the CRS, and that provides for the effective implementation of the CRS as set out therein.

Determination: In Place

Qatar's domestic legislative framework is in place and contains all of the key aspects of the CRS and its Commentary requiring Reporting Financial Institutions to conduct the due diligence and reporting procedures (SRs 1.1 – 1.3). It also provides for a framework to enforce the requirements (SR 1.4).

SR 1.1 Jurisdictions should define the scope of Reporting Financial Institutions consistently with the CRS.

Qatar has defined the scope of Reporting Financial Institutions in its domestic legislative framework in accordance with the CRS and its Commentary.

Recommendations:

No recommendations made.

SR 1.2 Jurisdictions should define the scope of Financial Accounts and Reportable Accounts consistently with the CRS and incorporate the due diligence procedures to identify them.

Qatar has defined the scope of the Financial Accounts that are required to be reported in its domestic legislative framework and incorporated the due diligence procedures that must be applied to identify them in accordance with the CRS and its Commentary.

Recommendations:

No recommendations made.

SR 1.3 Jurisdictions should incorporate the reporting requirements contained in Section I of the CRS into their domestic legislative framework.

Qatar has incorporated the reporting requirements in its domestic legislative framework in accordance with the CRS and its Commentary.

Recommendations:

No recommendations made.

SR 1.4 Jurisdictions should have a legislative framework in place that allows for the enforcement of the requirements of the CRS in practice.

Qatar has a legislative framework in place to enforce the requirements in accordance with the CRS and its Commentary.

Recommendations:

No recommendations made.

CR2 International legal framework: Jurisdictions should have exchange relationships in effect with all Interested Appropriate Partners as committed to and that provide for the exchange of information in accordance with the Model CAA.

Determination: In Place

Qatar's international legal framework to exchange the information is in place, is consistent with the Model CAA and its Commentary and provides for exchange with all of Qatar's Interested Appropriate Partners (i.e. all jurisdictions that are interested in receiving information from Qatar and that meet the required standard in relation to confidentiality and data safeguards). (SRs 2.1 – 2.3)

SR 2.1 Jurisdictions should have exchange agreements in effect with all Interested Appropriate Partners that permit the automatic exchange of CRS information.

Qatar has exchange agreements that permit the automatic exchange of CRS information in effect with all its Interested Appropriate Partners.

Recommendations:

No recommendations made.

SR 2.2 Such an exchange agreement should be put in place without undue delay, following the receipt of an expression of interest from an Interested Appropriate Partner.

Qatar put in place its exchange agreements without undue delay.

Recommendations:

No recommendations made.

SR 2.3 Jurisdictions should ensure that the exchange agreements in effect provide for the exchange of information in accordance with the requirements of the Model CAA.

Qatar's exchange agreements provide for the exchange of information in accordance with the requirements of the Model CAA.

Recommendations:

No recommendations made.

Comments by the assessed jurisdiction

No comments made.

Note

[1] With Ireland, Korea, Latvia, Malta, the Netherlands, South Africa and the United Kingdom. Qatar has also activated relationships under the CRS MCAA with all of these jurisdictions.

Romania

Overall findings

Romania's legal framework implementing the AEOI Standard is not in place in accordance with the requirements of the AEOI Terms of Reference. While Romania's international legal framework to exchange the information with all of Romania's Interested Appropriate Partners (CR2) is consistent with the requirements, its domestic legislative framework requiring Reporting Financial Institutions to conduct the due diligence and reporting procedures (CR1) has significant deficiencies in areas that are fundamental to the proper functioning of the AEOI Standard. Most significantly, there are deficiencies in relation to the due diligence procedures to identify Reportable Accounts and the enforcement framework.

The methodology used for the peer reviews and that therefore underpins this report is outlined in Chapter 2.

Overall determination on the legal framework: Not In Place

Conclusions on the legal framework

General context

Romania commenced exchanges under the AEOI Standard in 2017.

In order to provide for Reporting Financial Institutions to collect and report the information to be exchanged, Romania:

- enacted Law No. 70/2016;
- introduced Order No. 1939/2016 and Order No. 4142/2017;
- amended Law No. 207/2015 on the Fiscal Procedure Code; and
- enacted Law No. 129/2019 for preventing and combating money laundering and terrorist financing as amended by Emergency Government Ordinance No. 111/2020, which came into effect on 15 July 2020.

Under this framework Reporting Financial Institutions were required to commence the due diligence procedures in relation to New Accounts from 1 January 2016. With respect to Preexisting Accounts, Reporting Financial Institutions were required to complete the due diligence procedures on High Value Individual Accounts by 31 December 2016 and on Lower Value Individual Accounts and Entity Accounts by 31 December 2017.

Following the initial Global Forum peer review, Romania amended its legislative framework to address issues identified, effective from 15 July 2020.

With respect to the exchange of information under the AEOI Standard, Romania:

- is a Party to the Convention on Mutual Administrative Assistance in Tax Matters and activated the associated CRS Multilateral Competent Authority Agreement in time for exchanges in 2017;
- has in place European Directive 2011/16/EU on Administrative Cooperation in the Field of Taxation as amended by Directive 2014/107/EU; and
- has in place European Union agreements with five European third countries.[1]

Detailed findings

The detailed findings for Romania are below, organised per Core Requirement (CR) and sub-requirement (SR), as extracted from the AEOI Terms of Reference (www.oecd.org/tax/transparency/documents/aeoi-terms-of-reference.pdf).

CR1 Domestic legal framework: Jurisdictions should have a domestic legislative framework in place that requires all Reporting Financial Institutions to conduct the due diligence and reporting procedures in the CRS, and that provides for the effective implementation of the CRS as set out therein.

Determination: Not In Place

Romania's domestic legislative framework is not in place as required as it does not contain several key aspects of the CRS and its Commentary. Significant deficiencies have been identified in relation to the due diligence procedures to identify Reportable Accounts (SR 1.2) and the framework to enforce the requirements (SR 1.4). Most significantly, Romania's legislative framework does not require records to be kept by Financial Institutions in accordance with the AEOI Standard and it does not provide for sanctions for failing to apply due diligence procedures in accordance with the requirements.

SR 1.1 Jurisdictions should define the scope of Reporting Financial Institutions consistently with the CRS.

Romania has defined the scope of Reporting Financial Institutions in its domestic legislative framework in accordance with the CRS and its Commentary. While two deficiencies have been identified with respect to the definition of Financial Institutions, as there is nothing to suggest they will lead to an incorrect interpretation, they are considered to be relatively minor and their impact to not to be material.

Recommendations:

Romania should amend its domestic legislative framework to require the term Investment Entity to be interpreted consistently with the similar language defining "financial institution" in the Financial Action Task Force Recommendations.

Romania should amend its legislative framework to fully incorporate the term "managed by" in in relation to the definition of Investment Entity.

SR 1.2 Jurisdictions should define the scope of Financial Accounts and Reportable Accounts consistently with the CRS and incorporate the due diligence procedures to identify them

Romania has not incorporated the due diligence procedures that must be applied to identify Reportable Accounts in a manner that is consistent with the CRS and its Commentary as significant deficiencies have been identified. Most significantly, Romania's legislative framework:

- does not fully incorporate the provisions regarding the requirement that the residence address shall be "current";
- does not set out the definition of the term "passive income" as required; and
- does not include the requirement to re-determine the status of a Preexisting Entity Account where there is a change of circumstances that causes the Reporting Financial Institution to have reason to know that the self-certification or other documentation associated with the account is incorrect or unreliable.

The due diligence rules are material to the proper functioning of the AEOI Standard.

Recommendations:

Romania should amend its domestic legislative framework to require Reporting Financial Institutions to use only a "current" residence address when applying the residence address test, in particular by specifying that if mail has been returned as undeliverable, then the address cannot be considered "current".

Romania should amend its domestic legislative framework to fully incorporate the definition of Documentary Evidence for the purposes of the residence address test.

Romania should amend its domestic legislative framework to define "passive income" in accordance with the AEOI Standard.

Romania should amend its domestic legislative framework to require Reporting Financial Institutions apply the specified procedures where they have reason to know that the original self-certification obtained is incorrect or unreliable.

Romania should amend its domestic legislative framework to require Reporting Financial Institutions to apply the change of circumstance procedures in relation to Preexisting Entity Accounts in accordance with the AEOI Standard.

SR 1.3 Jurisdictions should incorporate the reporting requirements contained in Section I of the CRS into their domestic legislative framework.

Romania has incorporated the reporting requirements in its domestic legislative framework in accordance with the CRS and its Commentary. While a deficiency has been identified with respect to the reporting of the currency denomination, it is considered to be relatively minor as the CRS XML Schema will compel the reporting of a currency type.

Recommendations:

Romania should amend its domestic legislative framework to require Reporting Financial Institutions to identify the currency in which each account is denominated.

SR 1.4 Jurisdictions should have a legislative framework in place that allows for the enforcement of the requirements of the CRS in practice.

Romania does not have a legislative framework in place to enforce the requirements in a manner that is consistent with the CRS and its Commentary as significant deficiencies have been identified. More specifically, Romania's legislative framework:

- does not include rules to prevent Financial Institutions, persons or intermediaries from adopting practices intended to circumvent the due diligence and reporting procedures as required;
- does not include rules requiring Reporting Financial Institutions to keep records in accordance with the requirements;
- does not include sanctions for failing to apply the due diligence procedures; and
- does not include measures to ensure that valid self-certifications are always obtained in accordance with the requirements.

These are key elements of the required enforcement framework and are therefore material to the proper functioning of the AEOI Standard.

Recommendations:

Romania should amend its domestic legislative framework to include rules to prevent Financial Institutions, persons and intermediaries from adopting practices intended to circumvent the due diligence and reporting procedures. While it is acknowledged that the mandatory reporting requirements in place will facilitate the identification of such practices, additional rules are needed to prevent such practices.

Romania should amend its domestic legislative framework to require Reporting Financial Institutions to keep records of the steps undertaken and any evidence relied upon for the performance of the due diligence procedures in accordance with the AEOI Standard.

Romania should amend its domestic legislative framework to include sanctions for failure to apply the due diligence and reporting procedures, rather than being limited to failures leading to incorrect reporting.

Romania should amend its domestic legislative framework to include strong measures to ensure that valid self-certifications are always obtained for New Accounts in accordance with the requirements.

CR2 International legal framework: Jurisdictions should have exchange relationships in effect with all Interested Appropriate Partners as committed to and that provide for the exchange of information in accordance with the Model CAA.

Determination: In Place

Romania's international legal framework to exchange the information is in place, is consistent with the Model CAA and its Commentary and provides for exchange with all of Romania's Interested Appropriate Partners (i.e. all jurisdictions that are interested in receiving information from Romania and that meet the required standard in relation to confidentiality and data safeguards). (SRs 2.1 – 2.3)

SR 2.1 Jurisdictions should have exchange agreements in effect with all Interested Appropriate Partners that permit the automatic exchange of CRS information.

Romania has exchange agreements that permit the automatic exchange of CRS information in effect with all its Interested Appropriate Partners.

Recommendations:

No recommendations made.

SR 2.2 Such an exchange agreement should be put in place without undue delay, following the receipt of an expression of interest from an Interested Appropriate Partner.

Romania put in place its exchange agreements without undue delay.

Recommendations:

No recommendations made.

SR 2.3 Jurisdictions should ensure that the exchange agreements in effect provide for the exchange of information in accordance with the requirements of the Model CAA.

Romania's exchange agreements provide for the exchange of information in accordance with the requirements of the Model CAA.

Recommendations:

No recommendations made.

Comments by the assessed jurisdiction

First of all, we would like to express our gratitude for the support provided throughout the assessment process. We acknowledge the proposed recommendations. At the same time, we would like to note that Law No. 129/2019 and Emergency Government Ordinance No. 111/2020 that came into effect on 15 July 2020, as referred to above, has in our view already addressed the recommendations made under Sub-Requirement 1.2 relating to the definition and the due diligence procedures to identify Controlling

Persons. While we understand that this has been brought to the attention of AEOI Peers too late to have it reflected in this year's report, we look forward to seeing these recommendations removed in accordance with the peer review process in the next year's report.

In relation to the other recommendations, eight months ago we started the process of re-evaluation of the legal framework currently in place. Alongside this measure, we have established an inter-institutional working party with the main objective to rethink the way the AEOI Standard is implemented.

However, the current pandemic has changed not only the way we live, but also how we work. On this note, maintaining a regular schedule for the working party meetings has been very troublesome, to the point that for extended periods of time we had to suspend the activity of the group.

On top of this, the pandemic called for immediate reactions at a policy level, therefore we were forced to prioritise imminent and urgent matters in order to help the economy maintain a relatively stable evolution.

We intend to keep the technical experts of the Secretariat up to date on the evolution of the national legislation implementing the CRS.

We re-affirm our commitment to continue our work to address the outstanding recommendations and have this reflected in the next year's report.

Note

[1] Andorra, Liechtenstein, Monaco, San Marino and Switzerland.

Russia

Overall findings

Russia's legal framework implementing the AEOI Standard is in place but needs improvement in order to be fully consistent with the requirements of the AEOI Terms of Reference. While Russia's international legal framework to exchange the information with all of Russia's Interested Appropriate Partners (CR2) is consistent with the requirements, its domestic legislative framework requiring Reporting Financial Institutions to conduct the due diligence and reporting procedures (CR1) has deficiencies significant to the proper functioning of elements of AEOI Standard. Most significantly, the scope of Reporting Financial Institutions and Reportable Accounts are not fully in accordance with the AEOI Standard and there are deficiencies in relation to the framework to enforce of the requirements.

The methodology used for the peer reviews and that therefore underpins this report is outlined in Chapter 2.

Overall determination on the legal framework: In Place But **Needs Improvement**

Conclusions on the legal framework

General context

Russia commenced exchanges under the AEOI Standard in 2018.

In order to provide for Reporting Financial Institutions to collect and report the information to be exchanged, Russia:

- enacted Federal Law No. 340-FZ;
- introduced Decree of June 16, 2018 No. 693; and
- issued further guidance, which is not legally binding.

Under this framework Reporting Financial Institutions were required to commence the due diligence procedures in relation to New Accounts from 20 July 2018. With respect to Preexisting Accounts, Reporting Financial Institutions were required to complete the due diligence procedures on High Value Individual Accounts by 31 July 2018 and on Lower Value Individual Accounts and Entity Accounts by 31 December 2018.

With respect to the exchange of information under the AEOI Standard, Russia is a Party to the Convention on Mutual Administrative Assistance in Tax Matters and activated the associated CRS Multilateral Competent Authority Agreement in time for exchanges in 2018.

Detailed findings

The detailed findings for Russia are below, organised per Core Requirement (CR) and sub-requirement (SR), as extracted from the AEOI Terms of Reference (www.oecd.org/tax/transparency/documents/aeoi-terms-of-reference.pdf).

CR1 Domestic legal framework: Jurisdictions should have a domestic legislative framework in place that requires all Reporting Financial Institutions to conduct the due diligence and reporting procedures in the CRS, and that provides for the effective implementation of the CRS as set out therein.

Determination: In Place But **Needs Improvement**

Russia's domestic legislative framework is in place and contains many of the key aspects of the CRS and its Commentary requiring Reporting Financial Institutions to conduct the due diligence and reporting procedures, but it needs improvement in relation to the scope of Reporting Financial Institutions required to report information (SR 1.1), the due diligence procedures to be applied (SR 1.2), and the framework to enforce the requirements (SR 1.4). Most significantly, key definitions significant to the scope of Reporting Financial Institutions, including Participating Jurisdiction Financial Institution and Financial Assets, are not in accordance with the requirements.

SR 1.1 Jurisdictions should define the scope of Reporting Financial Institutions consistently with the CRS.

Russia has defined the scope of Reporting Financial Institutions in its domestic legislative framework in a manner that is largely consistent with the CRS and its Commentary. However, deficiencies have been identified. Most significantly, Russia's legislative framework does not explicitly incorporate the definition of Participating Jurisdiction Financial Institution, and the definition of Financial Assets is not in accordance with the requirements. The scope of Reporting Financial Institutions is material to the proper functioning of the AEOI Standard.

Recommendations:

Russia should amend its domestic legislative framework to define Financial Asset using an inclusive approach as contained in the AEOI Standard, rather than using an exhaustive list.

Russia should amend its domestic legislative framework to explicitly incorporate the relevant definitions defining the scope of Reporting Financial Institutions, such as the definition of Participating Jurisdiction Financial Institution.

Russia should amend its legislative framework to incorporate the definition of "managed by" in relation to the definition of Investment Entity.

Russia should amend its domestic legislative framework to require the interpretation of Investment Entity to be consistent with similar language defining "financial institution" in the Financial Action Task Force Recommendations.

SR 1.2 Jurisdictions should define the scope of Financial Accounts and Reportable Accounts consistently with the CRS and incorporate the due diligence procedures to identify them.

Russia has defined the scope of the Financial Accounts that are required to be reported in its domestic legislative framework and has incorporated the due diligence procedures that must be applied to identify them in a manner that is largely consistent with the CRS and its Commentary. However, deficiencies have been identified. More specifically, Russia's legislative framework:

- does not provide for the interpretation of "change of circumstances" in accordance with the requirements; and
- does not define Reportable Jurisdiction Person or Account Holder in accordance with the requirements.

The deficiencies relate to key elements of the AEOI Standard and are therefore material to its proper functioning.

Recommendations:

Russia should amend its domestic legislative framework to ensure that "change of circumstances" is defined in accordance with the AEOI Standard, rather than being restricted to circumstances that lead or may lead to the change of residence for tax purposes.

Russia should amend its domestic legislative framework to define Account Holder in accordance with the AEOI Standard.

Russia should amend its domestic legislative framework to explicitly include the estate of a decedent that was a resident of a Reportable Jurisdiction as a Reportable Jurisdiction Person.

SR 1.3 Jurisdictions should incorporate the reporting requirements contained in Section I of the CRS into their domestic legislative framework.

Russia has incorporated the reporting requirements in its domestic legislative framework in accordance with the CRS and its Commentary.

Recommendations:

No recommendations made.

SR 1.4 Jurisdictions should have a legislative framework in place that allows for the enforcement of the requirements of the CRS in practice.

Russia has a legislative framework in place to enforce the requirements in a manner that is largely consistent with the CRS and its Commentary. However, deficiencies have been identified. More specifically, Russia's legislative framework:

- does not include rules to prevent Financial Institutions, persons or intermediaries from adopting practices intended to circumvent the due diligence and reporting procedures as required; and
- does not impose sanctions on Accounts Holders and Controlling Persons for the provision of a false self-certification.

These are key elements of the required enforcement framework and are therefore material to the proper functioning of the AEOI Standard.

Recommendations:

Russia should amend its domestic legislative framework to include rules to prevent Financial Institutions, persons and intermediaries from adopting practices intended to circumvent the due diligence and reporting procedures.

Russia should amend its domestic legislative framework to include sanctions on Account Holders and Controlling Persons for the provision of a false self-certification.

CR2 International legal framework: Jurisdictions should have exchange relationships in effect with all Interested Appropriate Partners as committed to and that provide for the exchange of information in accordance with the Model CAA.

Determination: In Place

Russia's international legal framework to exchange the information is in place, is consistent with the Model CAA and its Commentary and provides for exchange with all of Russia's Interested Appropriate Partners (i.e. all jurisdictions that are interested in receiving information from Russia and that meet the required standard in relation to confidentiality and data safeguards). (SRs 2.1 – 2.3)

SR 2.1 Jurisdictions should have exchange agreements in effect with all Interested Appropriate Partners that permit the automatic exchange of CRS information.

Russia has exchange agreements that permit the automatic exchange of CRS information in effect with all its Interested Appropriate Partners.

Recommendations:

No recommendations made.

SR 2.2 Such an exchange agreement should be put in place without undue delay, following the receipt of an expression of interest from an Interested Appropriate Partner.

Russia put in place its exchange agreements without undue delay.

Recommendations:

No recommendations made.

SR 2.3 Jurisdictions should ensure that the exchange agreements in effect provide for the exchange of information in accordance with the requirements of the Model CAA.

Russia's exchange agreements provide for the exchange of information in accordance with the requirements of the Model CAA.

Recommendations:

No recommendations made.

Comments by the assessed jurisdiction

No comments made.

Saint Kitts and Nevis

Overall findings

Saint Kitts and Nevis' legal framework implementing the AEOI Standard is in place and is consistent with the requirements of the AEOI Terms of Reference. This includes Saint Kitts and Nevis' domestic legislative framework requiring Reporting Financial Institutions to conduct the due diligence and reporting procedures (CR1) and its international legal framework to exchange the information with all of Saint Kitts and Nevis' Interested Appropriate Partners (CR2).

The methodology used for the peer reviews and that therefore underpins this report is outlined in Chapter 2.

Overall determination on the legal framework: In Place

Conclusions on the legal framework

General context

Saint Kitts and Nevis commenced exchanges under the AEOI Standard in 2018.

In order to provide for Reporting Financial Institutions to collect and report the information to be exchanged, Saint Kitts and Nevis:

- enacted the Common Reporting Standard (Automatic Exchange of Financial Account Information) Act 2016, as amended in 2018; and
- introduced the Common Reporting Standard (Automatic Exchange of Financial Account Information) Regulations 2016, as amended in 2018.

Under this framework Reporting Financial Institutions were required to commence the due diligence procedures in relation to New Accounts from 1 January 2017. With respect to Preexisting Accounts, Reporting Financial Institutions were required to complete the due diligence procedures on High Value Individual Accounts by 31 December 2017 and on Lower Value Individual Accounts and Entity Accounts by 31 December 2018.

Following the initial Global Forum peer review, Saint Kitts and Nevis made various amendments to its legislative framework to address issues identified, the last of which was effective from 16 August 2018.

With respect to the exchange of information under the AEOI Standard, Saint Kitts and Nevis is a Party to the Convention on Mutual Administrative Assistance in Tax Matters and activated the associated CRS Multilateral Competent Authority Agreement in time for exchanges in 2018.

Detailed findings

The detailed findings for Saint Kitts and Nevis are below, organised per Core Requirement (CR) and sub-requirement (SR), as extracted from the AEOI Terms of Reference (www.oecd.org/tax/transparency/documents/aeoi-terms-of-reference.pdf).

CR1 Domestic legal framework: Jurisdictions should have a domestic legislative framework in place that requires all Reporting Financial Institutions to conduct the due diligence and reporting procedures in the CRS, and that provides for the effective implementation of the CRS as set out therein.

Determination: In Place

Saint Kitts and Nevis' domestic legislative framework is in place and contains all of the key aspects of the CRS and its Commentary requiring Reporting Financial Institutions to conduct the due diligence and reporting procedures (SRs 1.1 – 1.3). It also provides for a framework to enforce the requirements (SR 1.4).

SR 1.1 Jurisdictions should define the scope of Reporting Financial Institutions consistently with the CRS.

Saint Kitts and Nevis has defined the scope of Reporting Financial Institutions in its domestic legislative framework in accordance with the CRS and its Commentary.

Recommendations:

No recommendations made.

SR 1.2 Jurisdictions should define the scope of Financial Accounts and Reportable Accounts consistently with the CRS and incorporate the due diligence procedures to identify them.

Saint Kitts and Nevis has defined the scope of the Financial Accounts that are required to be reported in its domestic legislative framework and incorporated the due diligence procedures that must be applied to identify them in accordance with the CRS and its Commentary.

Recommendations:

No recommendations made.

SR 1.3 Jurisdictions should incorporate the reporting requirements contained in Section I of the CRS into their domestic legislative framework.

Saint Kitts and Nevis has incorporated the reporting requirements in its domestic legislative framework in accordance with the CRS and its Commentary.

Recommendations:

No recommendations made.

SR 1.4 Jurisdictions should have a legislative framework in place that allows for the enforcement of the requirements of the CRS in practice.

Saint Kitts and Nevis has a legislative framework in place to enforce the requirements in accordance with the CRS and its Commentary.

Recommendations:

No recommendations made.

CR2 International legal framework: Jurisdictions should have exchange relationships in effect with all Interested Appropriate Partners as committed to and that provide for the exchange of information in accordance with the Model CAA.

Determination: In Place

Saint Kitts and Nevis' international legal framework to exchange the information in place, is consistent with the Model CAA and its Commentary and provides for exchange with all of Saint Kitts and Nevis' Interested

Appropriate Partners (i.e. all jurisdictions that are interested in receiving information from Saint Kitts and Nevis and that meet the required standard in relation to confidentiality and data safeguards). (SRs 2.1 – 2.3)

SR 2.1 Jurisdictions should have exchange agreements in effect with all Interested Appropriate Partners that permit the automatic exchange of CRS information.

Saint Kitts and Nevis has exchange agreements that permit the automatic exchange of CRS information in effect with all its Interested Appropriate Partners.

Recommendations:

No recommendations made.

SR 2.2 Such an exchange agreement should be put in place without undue delay, following the receipt of an expression of interest from an Interested Appropriate Partner.

Saint Kitts and Nevis put in place its exchange agreements without undue delay.

Recommendations:

No recommendations made.

SR 2.3 Jurisdictions should ensure that the exchange agreements in effect provide for the exchange of information in accordance with the requirements of the Model CAA.

Saint Kitts and Nevis' exchange agreements provide for the exchange of information in accordance with the requirements of the Model CAA.

Recommendations:

No recommendations made.

Comments by the assessed jurisdiction

Saint Kitts and Nevis is in agreement with the findings and determinations that are reflected in the report and would like to thank the assessors for their dedication and collaboration during the process.

Saint Lucia

Overall findings

Saint Lucia's legal framework implementing the AEOI Standard is in place but needs improvement in order to be fully consistent with the requirements of the AEOI Terms of Reference. While Saint Lucia's international legal framework to exchange the information with all of Saint Lucia's Interested Appropriate Partners (CR2) is consistent with the requirements, its domestic legislative framework requiring Reporting Financial Institutions to conduct the due diligence and reporting procedures (CR1) has deficiencies significant to the proper functioning of elements of the AEOI Standard. Most significantly, Saint Lucia's legislative framework provides for a category of jurisdiction-specific Excluded Account that is not in accordance with the requirements and does not impose sanctions for the provision of a false self-certification.

The methodology used for the peer reviews and that therefore underpins this report is outlined in Chapter 2.

Overall determination on the legal framework: In Place But **Needs Improvement**

Conclusions on the legal framework

General context

Saint Lucia commenced exchanges under the AEOI Standard in 2018.

In order to provide for Reporting Financial Institutions to collect and report the information to be exchanged, Saint Lucia:

- enacted the Automatic Exchange of Financial Account Information Act No. 22 of 2016, which was subsequently amended by the Automatic Exchange of Financial Account Information (Amendment) Act No. 10 of 2017, the Automatic Exchange of Financial Account Information (Amendment Schedule 2) Order S.I. 105 of 2017 and the Automatic Exchange of Financial Account Information (Amendment) Act No. 7 of 2018;
- introduced the Automatic Exchange of Financial Account Information (Designation of Excluded Accounts) Order No. 106 of 2017 and the Automatic Exchange of Financial Account Information (Designation of Non-Reporting Financial Institution) Order No. 107 of 2017, which were subsequently amended by the Automatic Exchange of Financial Account Information (Designation of Excluded Accounts) Order No. 119 of 2017, the Automatic Exchange of Financial Account Information (Designation of Non-Reporting Financial Institution) Order No. 7 of 2019 and the Automatic Exchange of Financial Account Information (Designation of Excluded Accounts) Order No. 8 of 2019; and
- issued further guidance, which is not legally binding.

Under this framework Reporting Financial Institutions were required to commence the due diligence procedures in relation to New Accounts from 1 January 2017. With respect to Preexisting Accounts, Reporting Financial Institutions were required to complete the due diligence procedures on High Value Individual Accounts by 31 December 2017 and on Lower Value Individual Accounts and Entity Accounts by 31 December 2018.

Following the initial Global Forum peer review, Saint Lucia made various amendments to its legislative framework to address issues identified, the last of which was effective from 11 February 2019.

With respect to the exchange of information under the AEOI Standard, Saint Lucia is a Party to the Convention on Mutual Administrative Assistance in Tax Matters and activated the associated CRS Multilateral Competent Authority Agreement in time for exchanges in 2018.

Detailed findings

The detailed findings for Saint Lucia are below, organised per Core Requirement (CR) and sub-requirement (SR), as extracted from the AEOI Terms of Reference (www.oecd.org/tax/transparency/documents/aeoi-terms-of-reference.pdf).

CR1 Domestic legal framework: Jurisdictions should have a domestic legislative framework in place that requires all Reporting Financial Institutions to conduct the due diligence and reporting procedures in the CRS, and that provides for the effective implementation of the CRS as set out therein.

Determination: In Place But **Needs Improvement**

Saint Lucia's domestic legislative framework is in place and contains most of the key aspects of the CRS and its Commentary requiring Reporting Financial Institutions to conduct the due diligence and reporting procedures, but it needs improvement in relation to the scope of Financial Accounts required to be reported (SR 1.2) and the enforcement framework (SR 1.4). Most significantly, Saint Lucia provides for a category of jurisdiction-specific Excluded Account that is not in accordance with the requirements and does not impose sanctions on Accounts Holders and Controlling Persons for providing a false self-certification.

SR 1.1 Jurisdictions should define the scope of Reporting Financial Institutions consistently with the CRS.

Saint Lucia has defined the scope of Reporting Financial Institutions in its domestic legislative framework in accordance with the CRS and its Commentary.

Recommendations:

No recommendations made.

SR 1.2 Jurisdictions should define the scope of Financial Accounts and Reportable Accounts consistently with the CRS and incorporate the due diligence procedures to identify them.

Saint Lucia has defined the scope of the Financial Accounts that are required to be reported in its domestic legislative framework and incorporated the due diligence procedures that must be applied to identify them largely in accordance with the CRS and its Commentary. However, a deficiency has been identified. More specifically, Saint Lucia has provided for a jurisdiction-specific Excluded Account that is not in accordance with the requirements. The scope of Financial Accounts, including the provision of Excluded Accounts, is material to the proper functioning of the AEOI Standard.

Recommendations:

Saint Lucia should amend its domestic legislative framework to remove the Pension Fund Accounts from its jurisdiction-specific list of Excluded Accounts as they do not meet the requirements in the AEOI Standard, such as full reporting to the authorities with respect to the Account Holders and penalties on early withdrawals.

SR 1.3 Jurisdictions should incorporate the reporting requirements contained in Section I of the CRS into their domestic legislative framework.

Saint Lucia has incorporated the reporting requirements in its domestic legislative framework in accordance with the CRS and its Commentary.

Recommendations:

No recommendations made.

SR 1.4 Jurisdictions should have a legislative framework in place that allows for the enforcement of the requirements of the CRS in practice.

Saint Lucia has a legislative framework in place to enforce the requirements in a manner that is largely consistent with the CRS and its Commentary. However, deficiencies have been identified. Most significantly, Saint Lucia's legislative framework does not impose sanctions on Account Holders and Controlling Persons for the provision of a false self-certification. This is a key element of the required enforcement framework and is therefore material to the proper functioning of the AEOI Standard.

Recommendations:

Saint Lucia should amend its domestic legislative framework to include sanctions on Account Holders and Controlling Persons for the provision of a false self-certification.

Saint Lucia should amend its domestic legislative framework to require Reporting Financial Institutions to maintain records of self-certifications for at least five years from the deadline to report the information, rather than six years from the date when an account is closed.

CR2 International legal framework: Jurisdictions should have exchange relationships in effect with all Interested Appropriate Partners as committed to and that provide for the exchange of information in accordance with the Model CAA.

Determination: In Place

Saint Lucia's international legal framework to exchange the information is in place, is consistent with the Model CAA and its Commentary and provides for exchange with all of Saint Lucia's Interested Appropriate Partners (i.e. all jurisdictions that are interested in receiving information from Saint Lucia and that meet the required standard in relation to confidentiality and data safeguards). (SRs 2.1 – 2.3)

SR 2.1 Jurisdictions should have exchange agreements in effect with all Interested Appropriate Partners that permit the automatic exchange of CRS information.

Saint Lucia has exchange agreements that permit the automatic exchange of CRS information in effect with all its Interested Appropriate Partners.

Recommendations:

No recommendations made.

SR 2.2 Such an exchange agreement should be put in place without undue delay, following the receipt of an expression of interest from an Interested Appropriate Partner.

Saint Lucia put in place its exchange agreements without undue delay.

Recommendations:

No recommendations made.

SR 2.3 Jurisdictions should ensure that the exchange agreements in effect provide for the exchange of information in accordance with the requirements of the Model CAA.

Saint Lucia's exchange agreements provide for the exchange of information in accordance with the requirements of the Model CAA.

Recommendations:

No recommendations made.

Comments by the assessed jurisdiction

Saint Lucia notes the comments on the AEOI legal determination report and commits to making the necessary changes in adherence to the recommendations.

Saint Vincent and the Grenadines

Overall findings

Saint Vincent and the Grenadines' legal framework implementing the AEOI Standard is in place but needs improvement in order to be fully consistent with the requirements of the AEOI Terms of Reference. While Saint Vincent and the Grenadines' international legal framework to exchange the information with all of Saint Vincent and the Grenadines Interested Appropriate Partners (CR2) is consistent with the requirements, its domestic legislative framework requiring Reporting Financial Institutions to conduct the due diligence and reporting procedures (CR1) has two main deficiencies significant to the proper functioning of elements of the AEOI Standard. These are, firstly, Saint Vincent and the Grenadines' legislative framework provides for jurisdiction-specific Non-Reporting Financial Institutions that are not in accordance with the requirements and secondly, there is a deficiency in the enforcement framework in place.

The methodology used for the peer reviews and that therefore underpins this report is outlined in Chapter 2.

Overall determination on the legal framework: In Place But **Needs Improvement**

Conclusions on the legal framework

General context

Saint Vincent and the Grenadines commenced exchanges under the AEOI Standard in 2018.

In order to provide for Reporting Financial Institutions to collect and report the information to be exchanged, Saint Vincent and the Grenadines:

- enacted the Automatic Exchange of Information (Common reporting Standards) Act 2016; and
- introduced the Automatic Exchange of Information (Common reporting Standards) Regulations 2016.

Under this framework Reporting Financial Institutions were required to commence the due diligence procedures in relation to New Accounts from 1 January 2017. With respect to Preexisting Accounts, Reporting Financial Institutions were required to complete the due diligence procedures on High Value Individual Accounts by 31 December 2017 and on Lower Value Individual Accounts and Entity Accounts by 31 December 2018.

With respect to the exchange of information under the AEOI Standard, Saint Vincent and the Grenadines is a Party to the Convention on Mutual Administrative Assistance in Tax Matters and activated the associated CRS Multilateral Competent Authority Agreement in time for exchanges in 2018.

Detailed findings

The detailed findings for Saint Vincent and the Grenadines are below, organised per Core Requirement (CR) and sub-requirement (SR), as extracted from the AEOI Terms of Reference (www.oecd.org/tax/transparency/documents/aeoi-terms-of-reference.pdf).

CR1 Domestic legal framework: Jurisdictions should have a domestic legislative framework in place that requires all Reporting Financial Institutions to conduct the due diligence and reporting procedures in the CRS, and that provides for the effective implementation of the CRS as set out therein.

Determination: In Place But **Needs Improvement**

Saint Vincent and the Grenadines' domestic legislative framework is in place and contains most of the key aspects of the CRS and its Commentary requiring Reporting Financial Institutions to conduct the due diligence and reporting procedures, but it needs improvement in relation to the scope of Reporting Financial Institutions required to report information (SR 1.1) and the framework to enforce the requirements (SR 1.4). More specifically, Saint Vincent and the Grenadines provides for jurisdiction-specific Non-Reporting Financial Institutions that are not in accordance with the requirements and there is a deficiency in the enforcement framework in place.

SR 1.1 Jurisdictions should define the scope of Reporting Financial Institutions consistently with the CRS.

Saint Vincent and the Grenadines has defined the scope of Reporting Financial Institutions in its domestic legislative framework in a manner that is largely consistent with the CRS and its Commentary. However, certain specific deficiencies have been identified, namely Saint Vincent and the Grenadines provides for two jurisdiction-specific Non-Reporting Financial Institutions that are not in accordance with the requirements. The scope of Reporting Financial Institutions, including the provision of Non-Reporting Financial Institutions, is material to the proper functioning of the AEOI Standard.

Recommendations:

Saint Vincent and the Grenadines should amend its domestic legislative framework to remove Friendly Societies from its jurisdiction-specific list of Non-Reporting Financial Institutions as they do not meet the requirements of the AEOI Standard such as in relation to the purpose of the deposits and the restrictions on the contributions and withdrawals.

Saint Vincent and the Grenadines should amend its domestic legislative framework to remove Non-Profit Organisations from its jurisdiction-specific list of Non-Reporting Financial Institutions as they do not meet the requirements in the AEOI Standard.

SR 1.2 Jurisdictions should define the scope of Financial Accounts and Reportable Accounts consistently with the CRS and incorporate the due diligence procedures to identify them.

Saint Vincent and the Grenadines has defined the scope of the Financial Accounts that are required to be reported in its domestic legislative framework and incorporated the due diligence procedures that must be applied to identify them in accordance with the CRS and its Commentary.

Recommendations:

No Recommendations made.

SR 1.3 Jurisdictions should incorporate the reporting requirements contained in Section I of the CRS into their domestic legislative framework.

Saint Vincent and the Grenadines has incorporated the reporting requirements in its domestic legislative framework in accordance with the CRS and its Commentary.

Recommendations:

No recommendations made.

SR 1.4 Jurisdictions should have a legislative framework in place that allows for the enforcement of the requirements of the CRS in practice.

Saint Vincent and the Grenadines has a legislative framework in place to enforce the requirements in a manner that is largely consistent with the CRS and its Commentary. However, a deficiency has been identified. Saint Vincent and the Grenadines' legislative framework does not include sanctions on Reporting Financial Institutions for failing to apply due diligence procedures in accordance with the AEOI Standard. This is a key element of the required enforcement framework and is therefore material to the proper functioning of the AEOI Standard.

Recommendations:

Saint Vincent and the Grenadines should amend its domestic legislative framework to include sanctions for failure to apply the due diligence and reporting procedures, rather than being limited to failures leading to incorrect reporting.

CR2 International legal framework: Jurisdictions should have exchange relationships in effect with all Interested Appropriate Partners as committed to and that provide for the exchange of information in accordance with the Model CAA.

Determination: In Place

Saint Vincent and the Grenadines' international legal framework to exchange the information is in place, is consistent with the Model CAA and its Commentary and provides for exchange with all of Saint Vincent and the Grenadines' Interested Appropriate Partners (i.e. all jurisdictions that are interested in receiving information from Saint Vincent and the Grenadines and that meet the required standard in relation to confidentiality and data safeguards). (SRs 2.1 – 2.3)

SR 2.1 Jurisdictions should have exchange agreements in effect with all Interested Appropriate Partners that permit the automatic exchange of CRS information.

Saint Vincent and the Grenadines has exchange agreements that permit the automatic exchange of CRS information in effect with all its Interested Appropriate Partners.

Recommendations:

No recommendations made.

SR 2.2 Such an exchange agreement should be put in place without undue delay, following the receipt of an expression of interest from an Interested Appropriate Partner.

Saint Vincent and the Grenadines put in place its exchange agreements without undue delay.

Recommendations:

No recommendations made.

SR 2.3 Jurisdictions should ensure that the exchange agreements in effect provide for the exchange of information in accordance with the requirements of the Model CAA.

Saint Vincent and the Grenadines' exchange agreements provide for the exchange of information in accordance with the requirements of the Model CAA.

Recommendations:

No recommendations made.

Comments by the assessed jurisdiction

Saint Vincent and the Grenadines remains committed to ensuring that its legal framework for the implementation of the AEOI Standard is fully consistent with the requirements of the AEOI Terms of Reference.

Saint Vincent and the Grenadines notes the recommendations made and will work towards meeting these recommendations.

At the same time, Saint Vincent and the Grenadines wishes to record by way of comment, one matter arising from its present assessment. While Saint Vincent and the Grenadines immediately sees the necessity of removing Non-Profit Organizations from its List of Non-Reporting Financial Institutions, the country is obliged to indicate its view that the recommendation with respect to Friendly Societies does not properly reflect the facts in our jurisdiction with respect to this type of financial entity. A Friendly Society is an indigenous community driven, alternative savings association, developed to address a particular need of rural communities in relation to the affordability of burial expenses. Though the narrow purpose of the Friendly Society is a financial benefit upon the occurrence of death, one other incidental purpose has evolved along the years, in the form of very small savings brought about by any contribution in excess of the required contribution, being returned to the member once annually.

The authorities in Saint Vincent and the Grenadines are unable to refute the conclusion that based on the technical requirements of the Standard for Automatic Exchange of Financial Account Information in Tax Matters, a Friendly Society under the law of Saint Vincent and the Grenadines is precluded from being classified as a Broad Participation Retirement Fund, or strictly captured under Sub-Paragraph B(5)(1)(c). However, in the country's specific context, the authorities in Saint Vincent and the Grenadines wish to underscore that Friendly Societies are an example of a financial entity which fulfils the technical requirements of the Standards of being a Reporting Institution, however, its operational basis for AEOI is nil or negligible and likewise its financial account information will invariably have nil or negligible value to the country's AEOI partners.

The jurisdiction suggests that it may be worthwhile to consider whether it should be given an opportunity to bring Friendly Societies more in line with the requirements of a Non-Reporting Financial Institution as a more apposite treatment of this particular entity, rather than incurring an administrative burden on this type of low risk entity and causing a deluge of information to the country's AEOI partners, which the authorities are confident would serve no useful or relevant purpose in tackling tax evasion and avoidance.

Saint Vincent and the Grenadines reiterates its commitment to being a responsible, co-operative and accountable tax jurisdiction, as has been demonstrated by measures taken, both legislative and administrative, over the past several years.

Samoa

Overall findings

Samoa's legal framework implementing the AEOI Standard is in place and is consistent with the requirements of the AEOI Terms of Reference. This includes Samoa's domestic legislative framework requiring Reporting Financial Institutions to conduct the due diligence and reporting procedures (CR1) and its international legal framework to exchange the information with all of Samoa's Interested Appropriate Partners (CR2).

The methodology used for the peer reviews and that therefore underpins this report is outlined in Chapter 2.

Overall determination on the legal framework: In Place

Conclusions on the legal framework

General context

Samoa commenced exchanges under the AEOI Standard in 2018.

In order to provide for Reporting Financial Institutions to collect and report the information to be exchanged, Samoa enacted the Tax Information Exchange Amendment Act 2017, which is an amendment to the Tax Information Exchange Act 2012.

Under this framework Reporting Financial Institutions were required to commence the due diligence procedures in relation to New Accounts from 1 January 2017. With respect to Preexisting Accounts, Reporting Financial Institutions were required to complete the due diligence procedures on High Value Individual Accounts by 31 December 2017 and on Lower Value Individual Accounts and Entity Accounts by 31 December 2018.

With respect to the exchange of information under the AEOI Standard, Samoa is a Party to the Convention on Mutual Administrative Assistance in Tax Matters and activated the associated CRS Multilateral Competent Authority Agreement in time for exchanges in 2018.

Detailed findings

The detailed findings for Samoa are below, organised per Core Requirement (CR) and sub-requirement (SR), as extracted from the AEOI Terms of Reference (www.oecd.org/tax/transparency/documents/aeoi-terms-of-reference.pdf).

CR1 Domestic legal framework: Jurisdictions should have a domestic legislative framework in place that requires all Reporting Financial Institutions to conduct the due diligence and reporting procedures in the CRS, and that provides for the effective implementation of the CRS as set out therein.

Determination: In Place

Samoa's domestic legislative framework is in place and contains all of the key aspects of the CRS and its Commentary requiring Reporting Financial Institutions to conduct the due diligence and reporting procedures (SRs 1.1 – 1.3). It also provides for a framework to enforce the requirements (SR 1.4).

SR 1.1 Jurisdictions should define the scope of Reporting Financial Institutions consistently with the CRS.

Samoa has defined the scope of Reporting Financial Institutions in its domestic legislative framework in accordance with the CRS and its Commentary.

Recommendations:

No recommendations made.

SR 1.2 Jurisdictions should define the scope of Financial Accounts and Reportable Accounts consistently with the CRS and incorporate the due diligence procedures to identify them.

Samoa has defined the scope of the Financial Accounts that are required to be reported in its domestic legislative framework and incorporated the due diligence procedures that must be applied to identify them in accordance with the CRS and its Commentary.

Recommendations:

No recommendations made.

SR 1.3 Jurisdictions should incorporate the reporting requirements contained in Section I of the CRS into their domestic legislative framework.

Samoa has incorporated the reporting requirements in its domestic legislative framework in accordance with the CRS and its Commentary.

Recommendations:

No recommendations made.

SR 1.4 Jurisdictions should have a legislative framework in place that allows for the enforcement of the requirements of the CRS in practice.

Samoa has a legislative framework in place to enforce the requirements in accordance with the CRS and its Commentary.

Recommendations:

No recommendations made.

CR2 International legal framework: Jurisdictions should have exchange relationships in effect with all Interested Appropriate Partners as committed to and that provide for the exchange of information in accordance with the Model CAA.

Determination: In Place

Samoa's international legal framework to exchange the information is in place, is consistent with the Model CAA and its Commentary and provides for exchange with all of Samoa's Interested Appropriate Partners (i.e. all jurisdictions that are interested in receiving information from Samoa and that meet the required standard in relation to confidentiality and data safeguards). (SRs 2.1 – 2.3)

SR 2.1 Jurisdictions should have exchange agreements in effect with all Interested Appropriate Partners that permit the automatic exchange of CRS information.

Samoa has exchange agreements that permit the automatic exchange of CRS information in effect with all its Interested Appropriate Partners.

Recommendations:

No recommendations made.

SR 2.2 Such an exchange agreement should be put in place without undue delay, following the receipt of an expression of interest from an Interested Appropriate Partner.

Samoa put in place its exchange agreements without undue delay.

Recommendations:

No recommendations made.

SR 2.3 Jurisdictions should ensure that the exchange agreements in effect provide for the exchange of information in accordance with the requirements of the Model CAA.

Samoa's exchange agreements provide for the exchange of information in accordance with the requirements of the Model CAA.

Recommendations:

No recommendations made.

Comments by the assessed jurisdiction

No comments made.

San Marino

Overall findings

San Marino's legal framework implementing the AEOI Standard is in place and is consistent with the requirements of the AEOI Terms of Reference. This includes San Marino's domestic legislative framework requiring Reporting Financial Institutions to conduct the due diligence and reporting procedures (CR1) and its international legal framework to exchange the information with all of San Marino's Interested Appropriate Partners (CR2).

The methodology used for the peer reviews and that therefore underpins this report is outlined in Chapter 2.

Overall determination on the legal framework: In Place

Conclusions on the legal framework

General context

San Marino commenced exchanges under the AEOI Standard in 2017.

In order to provide for Reporting Financial Institutions to collect and report the information to be exchanged, San Marino:

- enacted Law no. 174 of 27 November 2015;
- introduced Regulation no. 20 of 30 December 2015 – Technical Regulations on the protection of personal data in application of exchange of information in tax matters; and
- issued further guidance, which is legally binding.

Under this framework Reporting Financial Institutions were required to commence the due diligence procedures in relation to New Accounts from 1 January 2016. With respect to Preexisting Accounts, Reporting Financial Institutions were required to complete the due diligence procedures on High Value Individual Accounts by 31 December 2016 and on Lower Value Individual Accounts and Entity Accounts by 31 December 2017.

With respect to the exchange of information under the AEOI Standard, San Marino:

- is a Party to the Convention on Mutual Administrative Assistance in Tax Matters and activated the associated CRS Multilateral Competent Authority Agreement in time for exchanges in 2017; and
- has in place an agreement with the European Union.

Detailed findings

The detailed findings for San Marino are below, organised per Core Requirement (CR) and sub-requirement (SR), as extracted from the AEOI Terms of Reference (www.oecd.org/tax/transparency/documents/aeoi-terms-of-reference.pdf).

CR1 Domestic legal framework: Jurisdictions should have a domestic legislative framework in place that requires all Reporting Financial Institutions to conduct the due diligence and reporting procedures in the CRS, and that provides for the effective implementation of the CRS as set out therein.

Determination: In Place

San Marino's domestic legislative framework is in place and contains all of the key aspects of the CRS and its Commentary requiring Reporting Financial Institutions to conduct the due diligence and reporting procedures (SRs 1.1 – 1.3). It also provides for a framework to enforce the requirements (SR 1.4).

SR 1.1 Jurisdictions should define the scope of Reporting Financial Institutions consistently with the CRS.

San Marino has defined the scope of Reporting Financial Institutions in its domestic legislative framework in accordance with the CRS and its Commentary.

Recommendations:

No recommendations made.

SR 1.2 Jurisdictions should define the scope of Financial Accounts and Reportable Accounts consistently with the CRS and incorporate the due diligence procedures to identify them.

San Marino has defined the scope of the Financial Accounts that are required to be reported in its domestic legislative framework and incorporated the due diligence procedures that must be applied to identify them in accordance with the CRS and its Commentary.

Recommendations:

No recommendations made.

SR 1.3 Jurisdictions should incorporate the reporting requirements contained in Section I of the CRS into their domestic legislative framework.

San Marino has incorporated the reporting requirements in its domestic legislative framework in accordance with the CRS and its Commentary.

Recommendations:

No recommendations made.

SR 1.4 Jurisdictions should have a legislative framework in place that allows for the enforcement of the requirements of the CRS in practice.

San Marino has a legislative framework in place to enforce the requirements in accordance with the CRS and its Commentary.

Recommendations:

No recommendations made.

CR2 International legal framework: Jurisdictions should have exchange relationships in effect with all Interested Appropriate Partners as committed to and that provide for the exchange of information in accordance with the Model CAA.

Determination: In Place

San Marino's international legal framework to exchange the information is in place, is consistent with the Model CAA and its Commentary and provides for exchange with all of San Marino's Interested Appropriate

Partners (i.e. all jurisdictions that are interested in receiving information from San Marino and that meet the required standard in relation to confidentiality and data safeguards). (SRs 2.1 – 2.3)

SR 2.1 Jurisdictions should have exchange agreements in effect with all Interested Appropriate Partners that permit the automatic exchange of CRS information.

San Marino has exchange agreements that permit the automatic exchange of CRS information in effect with all its Interested Appropriate Partners.

Recommendations:

No recommendations made.

SR 2.2 Such an exchange agreement should be put in place without undue delay, following the receipt of an expression of interest from an Interested Appropriate Partner.

San Marino put in place its exchange agreements without undue delay.

Recommendations:

No recommendations made.

SR 2.3 Jurisdictions should ensure that the exchange agreements in effect provide for the exchange of information in accordance with the requirements of the Model CAA.

San Marino's exchange agreements provide for the exchange of information in accordance with the requirements of the Model CAA.

Recommendations:

No recommendations made.

Comments by the assessed jurisdiction

No comments made.

Saudi Arabia

Overall findings

Saudi Arabia's legal framework implementing the AEOI Standard is in place and is consistent with the requirements of the AEOI Terms of Reference. This includes Saudi Arabia's domestic legislative framework requiring Reporting Financial Institutions to conduct the due diligence and reporting procedures (CR1) and its international legal framework to exchange the information with all of Saudi Arabia's Interested Appropriate Partners (CR2).

The methodology used for the peer reviews and that therefore underpins this report is outlined in Chapter 2.

Overall determination on the legal framework: In Place

Conclusions on the legal framework

General context

Saudi Arabia commenced exchanges under the AEOI Standard in 2018.

In order to provide for Reporting Financial Institutions to collect and report the information to be exchanged, Saudi Arabia enacted:

- the Decision of the Council of Ministers No. (705) Approving the joining of the Multilateral Competent Authority Agreement on Automatic Exchange of Financial Account Information, and the Annex of the Common Standard on Reporting and Due Diligence for Financial Account Information (the Agreement and the Common Standard);
- the Royal Decree No. M/125 ratifying the joining of the Agreement and the Common Standard;
- the Decision of the Council of Ministers No. (706) Approving of the Special Regulations for Addressing Failures to Report Information for Tax Purposes in Accordance with the Provisions of Conventions to which the Kingdom of Saudi Arabia is a Party (the Enforcement Regulations);
- the Decision of the Council of Ministers No. (108) Approving the application of the provisions of the Special Regulations on the Agreement and the Common Standard; and
- the Ministerial Decision No. (893) Approving the Administrative Rules and Procedures for the Implementation of the Agreement and the Common Standard (The Implementation Rules), amended by Ministerial Decision No. (4483).

Under this framework Reporting Financial Institutions were required to commence the due diligence procedures in relation to New Accounts from 8 September 2017. With respect to Preexisting Accounts, Reporting Financial Institutions were required to complete the due diligence procedures on High Value Individual Accounts by 28 February 2018 and on Lower Value Individual Accounts and Entity Accounts by 31 December 2018.

Following the initial Global Forum peer review, Saudi Arabia amended its legislative framework to address issues identified, effective from 27 June 2020.

With respect to the exchange of information under the AEOI Standard, Saudi Arabia is a Party to the Convention on Mutual Administrative Assistance in Tax Matters and activated the associated CRS Multilateral Competent Authority Agreement in time for exchanges in 2018.

Detailed findings

The detailed findings for Saudi Arabia are below, organised per Core Requirement (CR) and sub-requirement (SR), as extracted from the AEOI Terms of Reference (www.oecd.org/tax/transparency/documents/aeoi-terms-of-reference.pdf).

CR1 Domestic legal framework: Jurisdictions should have a domestic legislative framework in place that requires all Reporting Financial Institutions to conduct the due diligence and reporting procedures in the CRS, and that provides for the effective implementation of the CRS as set out therein.

Determination: In Place

Saudi Arabia's domestic legislative framework is in place and contains all of the key aspects of the CRS and its Commentary requiring Reporting Financial Institutions to conduct the due diligence and reporting procedures (SRs 1.1 – 1.3). It also provides for a framework to enforce the requirements (SR 1.4).

SR 1.1 Jurisdictions should define the scope of Reporting Financial Institutions consistently with the CRS.

Saudi Arabia has defined the scope of Reporting Financial Institutions in its domestic legislative framework in accordance with the CRS and its Commentary.

Recommendations:

No recommendations made.

SR 1.2 Jurisdictions should define the scope of Financial Accounts and Reportable Accounts consistently with the CRS and incorporate the due diligence procedures to identify them.

Saudi Arabia has defined the scope of the Financial Accounts that are required to be reported in its domestic legislative framework and incorporated the due diligence procedures that must be applied to identify them in accordance with the CRS and its Commentary.

Recommendations:

No recommendations made.

SR 1.3 Jurisdictions should incorporate the reporting requirements contained in Section I of the CRS into their domestic legislative framework.

Saudi Arabia has incorporated the reporting requirements in its domestic legislative framework in accordance with the CRS and its Commentary.

Recommendations:

No recommendations made.

SR 1.4 Jurisdictions should have a legislative framework in place that allows for the enforcement of the requirements of the CRS in practice.

Saudi Arabia has a legislative framework in place to enforce the requirements in accordance with the CRS and its Commentary.

Recommendations:

No recommendations made.

CR2 International legal framework: Jurisdictions should have exchange relationships in effect with all Interested Appropriate Partners as committed to and that provide for the exchange of information in accordance with the Model CAA.

Determination: In Place

Saudi Arabia's international legal framework to exchange the information is in place, is consistent with the Model CAA and its Commentary and provides for exchange with all of Saudi Arabia's Interested Appropriate Partners (i.e. all jurisdictions that are interested in receiving information from Saudi Arabia and that meet the required standard in relation to confidentiality and data safeguards). (SRs 2.1 – 2.3)

SR 2.1 Jurisdictions should have exchange agreements in effect with all Interested Appropriate Partners that permit the automatic exchange of CRS information.

Saudi Arabia has exchange agreements that permit the automatic exchange of CRS information in effect with all its Interested Appropriate Partners.

Recommendations:

No recommendations made.

SR 2.2 Such an exchange agreement should be put in place without undue delay, following the receipt of an expression of interest from an Interested Appropriate Partner.

Saudi Arabia put in place its exchange agreements without undue delay.

Recommendations:

No recommendations made.

SR 2.3 Jurisdictions should ensure that the exchange agreements in effect provide for the exchange of information in accordance with the requirements of the Model CAA.

Saudi Arabia's exchange agreements provide for the exchange of information in accordance with the requirements of the Model CAA.

Recommendations:

No recommendations made.

Comments by the assessed jurisdiction

No comments made.

Seychelles

Overall findings

The Seychelles' legal framework implementing the AEOI Standard is in place but needs improvement in order to be fully consistent with the requirements of the AEOI Terms of Reference. While the Seychelles' international legal framework to exchange the information with all of the Seychelles' Interested Appropriate Partners (CR2) is consistent with the requirements, the Seychelles domestic legislative framework requiring Reporting Financial Institutions to conduct the due diligence and reporting procedures (CR1) has deficiencies significant to the proper functioning of elements of the AEOI Standard. More specifically, deficiencies have been identified in the Seychelles' enforcement framework.

The methodology used for the peer reviews and that therefore underpins this report is outlined in Chapter 2.

Overall determination on the legal framework: In Place But **Needs Improvement**

Conclusions on the legal framework

General context

The Seychelles commenced exchanges under the AEOI Standard in 2017.

In order to provide for Reporting Financial Institutions to collect and report the information to be exchanged, the Seychelles amended its Revenue Administration Act of 2009 and SI 1 of 2015.

Under this framework Reporting Financial Institutions were required to commence the due diligence procedures in relation to New Accounts from 1 January 2016. With respect to Preexisting Accounts, Reporting Financial Institutions were required to complete the due diligence procedures on High Value Individual Accounts by 31 December 2016 and on Lower Value Individual Accounts and Entity Accounts by 31 December 2017.

Following the initial Global Forum peer review, the Seychelles amended its legislative framework to address issues identified, effective from June 2017.

With respect to the exchange of information under the AEOI Standard, the Seychelles is a Party to the Convention on Mutual Administrative Assistance in Tax Matters and activated the associated CRS Multilateral Competent Authority Agreement in time for exchanges in 2017.

Detailed findings

The detailed findings for the Seychelles are below, organised per Core Requirement (CR) and sub-requirement (SR), as extracted from the AEOI Terms of Reference (www.oecd.org/tax/transparency/documents/aeoi-terms-of-reference.pdf).

CR1 Domestic legal framework: Jurisdictions should have a domestic legislative framework in place that requires all Reporting Financial Institutions to conduct the due diligence and reporting procedures in the CRS, and that provides for the effective implementation of the CRS as set out therein.

Determination: In Place But **Needs Improvement**

The Seychelles' domestic legislative framework is in place and contains most of the key aspects of the CRS and its Commentary requiring Reporting Financial Institutions to conduct the due diligence and reporting procedures, but it needs improvement in relation to the framework to enforce the requirements (SR 1.4). Most significantly, the Seychelles' legislative framework does not impose sanctions on Account Holders and Controlling Persons for the provision of a false self-certification and does not include strong measures to ensure that valid self-certifications are always obtained for New Accounts.

SR 1.1 Jurisdictions should define the scope of Reporting Financial Institutions consistently with the CRS.

The Seychelles has defined the scope of Reporting Financial Institutions in its domestic legislative framework in accordance with the CRS and its Commentary.

Recommendations:

No Recommendations made.

SR 1.2 Jurisdictions should define the scope of Financial Accounts and Reportable Accounts consistently with the CRS and incorporate the due diligence procedures to identify them.

The Seychelles has defined the scope of the Financial Accounts that are required to be reported in its domestic legislative framework and incorporated the due diligence procedures that must be applied to identify them in accordance with the CRS and its Commentary.

Recommendations:

No Recommendations made.

SR 1.3 Jurisdictions should incorporate the reporting requirements contained in Section I of the CRS into their domestic legislative framework.

The Seychelles has incorporated the reporting requirements in its domestic legislative framework in accordance with the CRS and its Commentary.

Recommendations:

No recommendations made.

SR 1.4 Jurisdictions should have a legislative framework in place that allows for the enforcement of the requirements of the CRS in practice.

The Seychelles has a legislative framework in place to enforce the requirements in a manner that is largely consistent with the CRS and its Commentary. However, deficiencies have been identified. More specifically, the Seychelles' legislative framework:

- does not impose sanctions on Account Holders and Controlling Persons for the provision of a false self-certification; and
- does not permits accounts to be reported as undocumented when self-certifications are not obtained and/or validated in the limited circumstances where they are not obtained on the opening of the account, rather than including measures to ensure that valid self-certifications are always obtained as required.

These are key elements of the required enforcement framework and are therefore material to the proper functioning of the AEOI Standard.

Recommendations:

The Seychelles should amend its domestic legislative framework to include sanctions on Account Holders and Controlling Persons for the provision of a false self-certification.

The Seychelles should amend its domestic legislative framework to include strong measures to ensure that valid self-certifications are always obtained for New Accounts, rather than allowing accounts to be reported as undocumented in the limited circumstances a self-certification is permitted to be obtained after the opening of a New Account.

CR2 International legal framework: Jurisdictions should have exchange relationships in effect with all Interested Appropriate Partners as committed to and that provide for the exchange of information in accordance with the Model CAA.

Determination: In Place

The Seychelles' international legal framework to exchange the information is in place, is consistent with the Model CAA and its Commentary and provides for exchange with all of the Seychelles' Interested Appropriate Partners (i.e. all jurisdictions that are interested in receiving information from the Seychelles and that meet the required standard in relation to confidentiality and data safeguards). (SRs 2.1 – 2.3)

SR 2.1 Jurisdictions should have exchange agreements in effect with all Interested Appropriate Partners that permit the automatic exchange of CRS information.

The Seychelles has exchange agreements that permit the automatic exchange of CRS information in effect with all its Interested Appropriate Partners.

Recommendations:

No recommendations made.

SR 2.2 Such an exchange agreement should be put in place without undue delay, following the receipt of an expression of interest from an Interested Appropriate Partner.

The Seychelles put in place its exchange agreements without undue delay.

Recommendations:

No recommendations made.

SR 2.3 Jurisdictions should ensure that the exchange agreements in effect provide for the exchange of information in accordance with the requirements of the Model CAA.

The Seychelles' exchange agreements provide for the exchange of information in accordance with the requirements of the Model CAA.

Recommendations:

No recommendations made.

Comments by the assessed jurisdiction

General context: The Republic of Seychelles is in the process of amending Schedule 4 and 5 of the Revenue Administration (Common Reporting Standards) Regulation of 2015 to include the list of participating and reportable jurisdictions. We are encountering some delays due to the pandemic Covid-19. The Seychelles is also working on a proposal for amending the law to include very strong sanctions/measures so as to ensure that valid self-certifications are always obtained for New Accounts.

SR 1.4: The Republic of Seychelles have not developed their own guidance but we are using the one issued on the OECD's website.

Singapore

Overall findings

Singapore's legal framework implementing the AEOI Standard is in place and is consistent with the requirements of the AEOI Terms of Reference. This includes Singapore's domestic legislative framework requiring Reporting Financial Institutions to conduct the due diligence and reporting procedures (CR1) and its international legal framework to exchange the information with all of Singapore's Interested Appropriate Partners (CR2).

The methodology used for the peer reviews and that therefore underpins this report is outlined in Chapter 2.

Overall determination on the legal framework: In Place

Conclusions on the legal framework

General context

Singapore commenced exchanges under the AEOI Standard in 2018.

In order to provide for Reporting Financial Institutions to collect and report the information to be exchanged, Singapore:

- enacted Part XXB of the Income Tax Act;
- introduced the Income Tax (International Tax Compliance Agreements) (Common Reporting Standard) Regulations 2016; and
- issued Frequently Asked Questions, which are not legally binding.

Under this framework Reporting Financial Institutions were required to commence the due diligence procedures in relation to New Accounts from 1 January 2017. With respect to Preexisting Accounts, Reporting Financial Institutions were required to complete the due diligence procedures on High Value Individual Accounts by 31 December 2017 and on Lower Value Individual Accounts and Entity Accounts by 31 December 2018.

With respect to the exchange of information under the AEOI Standard, Singapore:

- is a Party to the Convention on Mutual Administrative Assistance in Tax Matters and activated the associated CRS Multilateral Competent Authority Agreement in time for exchanges in 2018; and
- put in place 19 bilateral agreements.[1]

Detailed findings

The detailed findings for Singapore are below, organised per Core Requirement (CR) and sub-requirement (SR), as extracted from the AEOI Terms of Reference (www.oecd.org/tax/transparency/documents/aeoi-terms-of-reference.pdf).

CR1 Domestic legal framework: Jurisdictions should have a domestic legislative framework in place that requires all Reporting Financial Institutions to conduct the due diligence and reporting procedures in the CRS, and that provides for the effective implementation of the CRS as set out therein.

Determination: In Place

Singapore's domestic legislative framework is in place and contains all of the key aspects of the CRS and its Commentary requiring Reporting Financial Institutions to conduct the due diligence and reporting procedures (SRs 1.1 – 1.3). It also provides for a framework to enforce the requirements (SR 1.4).

SR 1.1 Jurisdictions should define the scope of Reporting Financial Institutions consistently with the CRS.

Singapore has defined the scope of Reporting Financial Institutions in its domestic legislative framework in accordance with the CRS and its Commentary.

Recommendations:

No recommendations made.

SR 1.2 Jurisdictions should define the scope of Financial Accounts and Reportable Accounts consistently with the CRS and incorporate the due diligence procedures to identify them.

Singapore has defined the scope of the Financial Accounts that are required to be reported in its domestic legislative framework and incorporated the due diligence procedures that must be applied to identify them in accordance with the CRS and its Commentary.

Recommendations:

No recommendations made.

SR 1.3 Jurisdictions should incorporate the reporting requirements contained in Section I of the CRS into their domestic legislative framework.

Singapore has incorporated the reporting requirements in its domestic legislative framework in accordance with the CRS and its Commentary.

Recommendations:

No recommendations made.

SR 1.4 Jurisdictions should have a legislative framework in place that allows for the enforcement of the requirements of the CRS in practice.

Singapore has a legislative framework in place to enforce the requirements in accordance with the CRS and its Commentary.

Recommendations:

No recommendations made.

CR2 International legal framework: Jurisdictions should have exchange relationships in effect with all Interested Appropriate Partners as committed to and that provide for the exchange of information in accordance with the Model CAA.

Determination: In Place

Singapore's international legal framework to exchange the information is in place, is consistent with the Model CAA and its Commentary and provides for exchange with all of Singapore's Interested Appropriate

Partners (i.e. all jurisdictions that are interested in receiving information from Singapore and that meet the required standard in relation to confidentiality and data safeguards). (SRs 2.1 – 2.3)

SR 2.1 Jurisdictions should have exchange agreements in effect with all Interested Appropriate Partners that permit the automatic exchange of CRS information.

Singapore has exchange agreements that permit the automatic exchange of CRS information in effect with all its Interested Appropriate Partners.

Recommendations:

No recommendations made.

SR 2.2 Such an exchange agreement should be put in place without undue delay, following the receipt of an expression of interest from an Interested Appropriate Partner.

Singapore put in place its exchange agreements without undue delay.

Recommendations:

No recommendations made.

SR 2.3 Jurisdictions should ensure that the exchange agreements in effect provide for the exchange of information in accordance with the requirements of the Model CAA.

Singapore's exchange agreements provide for the exchange of information in accordance with the requirements of the Model CAA.

Recommendations:

No recommendations made.

Comments by the assessed jurisdiction

Singapore has been a member of the Global Forum on Transparency and Exchange of Information since its establishment as a self-standing body in 2009.

We are pleased with the overall determination of our legal framework to be "In Place" as assigned under the current review based on the AEOI Terms of Reference. It affirms the robustness of Singapore's Exchange of Information (EOI) regime, and that the regime is in line with the international AEOI Standard based on the Common Reporting Standard.

Singapore remains fully committed to the AEOI standard and will continue to ensure that our EOI regime continues to be in line with the international standard.

Note

[1] With Australia, Canada, Denmark, Estonia, Finland, Iceland, Ireland, Italy, Japan, Korea, Latvia, Lithuania, Malta, the Netherlands, New Zealand, Norway, South Africa, Switzerland and the United Kingdom. At the request of eight jurisdictions, namely Australia, Canada, Estonia, Italy, Japan, Korea, the Netherlands and New Zealand, Singapore has also activated relationships under the CRS MCAA with them.

Sint Maarten

Overall findings

Sint Maarten's legal framework to implement the AEOI Standard is not in place. This is because Sint Maarten has not put in place a domestic legislative framework requiring Reporting Financial Institutions to conduct the due diligence and reporting procedures (CR1) nor an international legal framework to exchange the information with all Interested Appropriate Partners (CR2).

The methodology used for the peer reviews and that therefore underpins this report is outlined in Chapter 2.

Overall determination on the legal framework: Not In Place

Conclusions on the legal framework

General context

Sint Maarten has not yet implemented the necessary legal frameworks.

Detailed findings

The detailed findings for Sint Maarten are below, organised per Core Requirement (CR) and sub-requirement (SR), as extracted from the AEOI Terms of Reference (www.oecd.org/tax/transparency/documents/aeoi-terms-of-reference.pdf).

CR1 Domestic legal framework: Jurisdictions should have a domestic legislative framework in place that requires all Reporting Financial Institutions to conduct the due diligence and reporting procedures in the CRS, and that provides for the effective implementation of the CRS as set out therein.

Determination: Not In Place

Sint Maarten has not put in place a domestic legislative framework requiring Reporting Financial Institutions to conduct the due diligence and reporting procedures, therefore the CR1 Domestic legal framework is determined to be not in place. As no such framework is in place a detailed analysis in relation to each SR has not been possible.

CR2 International legal framework: Jurisdictions should have exchange relationships in effect with all Interested Appropriate Partners as committed to and that provide for the exchange of information in accordance with the Model CAA.

Determination: Not In Place

Sint Maarten has not put in place the international legal framework to exchange the information with all of Sint Maarten's Interested Appropriate Partners, therefore the CR2 International legal framework is determined to be not in place. As no such framework is in place a detailed analysis in relation to each SR has not been possible.

Comments by the assessed jurisdiction

Notwithstanding the many setbacks that Sint Maarten has faced during the last few years, political instability and a major hurricane among others, Sint Maarten can announce that its primary legislation is finally in place and we are working diligently on having our secondary legislation put 'in place'. This is currently in the legislative process and our hopes are that this also can be finalized expeditiously. Only after this legislation is in place a notification to the Co-ordinating Body Secretariat pursuant to Section 7 of the Multilateral Competent Authority Agreement on Exchange of Financial Account Information, signed on behalf of the Competent Authority of Sint Maarten, can be considered in order to receive an 'In Place' determination regarding Sint Maarten's International legal framework.

Sint Maarten has started working on the Action Plan to meet the Confidentiality and Data safeguard requirements. The target date for this to be completed is September 2021.

Slovak Republic

Overall findings

The Slovak Republic's legal framework implementing the AEOI Standard is in place and is consistent with the requirements of the AEOI Terms of Reference. This includes the Slovak Republic's domestic legislative framework requiring Reporting Financial Institutions to conduct the due diligence and reporting procedures (CR1) and its international legal framework to exchange the information with all of the Slovak Republic's Interested Appropriate Partners (CR2).

The methodology used for the peer reviews and that therefore underpins this report is outlined in Chapter 2.

Overall determination on the legal framework: In Place

Conclusions on the legal framework

General context

The Slovak Republic commenced exchanges under the AEOI Standard in 2017.

In order to provide for Reporting Financial Institutions to collect and report the information to be exchanged, the Slovak Republic:

- enacted Act 359/2015 Coll., as amended by Act 300/2016 and Act 305/2019; and
- introduced Decree 446/2015 Coll., as amended by Decree 348/2018.

Under this framework Reporting Financial Institutions were required to commence the due diligence procedures in relation to New Accounts from 1 January 2016. With respect to Preexisting Accounts, Reporting Financial Institutions were required to complete the due diligence procedures on High Value Individual Accounts by 31 December 2016 and on Lower Value Individual Accounts and Entity Accounts by 31 December 2017.

Following the initial Global Forum peer review, the Slovak Republic made various amendments to its legislative framework to address issues identified, the last of which was effective from 1 January 2021.

With respect to the exchange of information under the AEOI Standard, the Slovak Republic:

- is a Party to the Convention on Mutual Administrative Assistance in Tax Matters and activated the associated CRS Multilateral Competent Authority Agreement in time for exchanges in 2017;
- has in place European Directive 2011/16/EU on Administrative Cooperation in the Field of Taxation as amended by Directive 2014/107/EU; and
- has in place European Union agreements with five European third countries.[1]

Detailed findings

The detailed findings for the Slovak Republic are below, organised per Core Requirement (CR) and sub-requirement (SR), as extracted from the AEOI Terms of Reference (www.oecd.org/tax/transparency/documents/aeoi-terms-of-reference.pdf).

CR1 Domestic legal framework: Jurisdictions should have a domestic legislative framework in place that requires all Reporting Financial Institutions to conduct the due diligence and reporting procedures in the CRS, and that provides for the effective implementation of the CRS as set out therein.

Determination: In Place

The Slovak Republic's domestic legislative framework is in place and contains all of the key aspects of the CRS and its Commentary requiring Reporting Financial Institutions to conduct the due diligence and reporting procedures (SRs 1.1 – 1.3). It also provides a framework to enforce the requirements (SR 1.4).

SR 1.1 Jurisdictions should define the scope of Reporting Financial Institutions consistently with the CRS.

The Slovak Republic has defined the scope of Reporting Financial Institutions in its domestic legislative framework in accordance with the CRS and its Commentary.

Recommendations:

No recommendations made.

SR 1.2 Jurisdictions should define the scope of Financial Accounts and Reportable Accounts consistently with the CRS and incorporate the due diligence procedures to identify them.

The Slovak Republic has defined the scope of the Financial Accounts that are required to be reported in its domestic legislative framework and incorporated the due diligence procedures that must be applied to identify them in accordance with the CRS and its Commentary.

Recommendations:

No recommendations made.

SR 1.3 Jurisdictions should incorporate the reporting requirements contained in Section I of the CRS into their domestic legislative framework.

The Slovak Republic has incorporated the reporting requirements in its domestic legislative framework in accordance with the CRS and its Commentary.

Recommendations:

No recommendations made.

SR 1.4 Jurisdictions should have a legislative framework in place that allows for the enforcement of the requirements of the CRS in practice.

The Slovak Republic has a legislative framework in place to enforce the requirements in accordance with the CRS and its Commentary.

Recommendations:

No recommendations made.

CR2 International legal framework: Jurisdictions should have exchange relationships in effect with all Interested Appropriate Partners as committed to and that provide for the exchange of information in accordance with the Model CAA.

Determination: In Place

The Slovak Republic's international legal framework to exchange the information is in place, is consistent with the Model CAA and its Commentary and provides for exchange with all of the Slovak Republic's

Interested Appropriate Partners (i.e. all jurisdictions that are interested in receiving information from the Slovak Republic and that meet the required standard in relation to confidentiality and data safeguards). (SRs 2.1 – 2.3)

SR 2.1 Jurisdictions should have exchange agreements in effect with all Interested Appropriate Partners that permit the automatic exchange of CRS information.

The Slovak Republic has exchange agreements that permit the automatic exchange of CRS information in effect with all its Interested Appropriate Partners.

Recommendations:

No recommendations made.

SR 2.2 Such an exchange agreement should be put in place without undue delay, following the receipt of an expression of interest from an Interested Appropriate Partner.

The Slovak Republic put in place its exchange agreements without undue delay.

Recommendations:

No recommendations made.

SR 2.3 Jurisdictions should ensure that the exchange agreements in effect provide for the exchange of information in accordance with the requirements of the Model CAA.

The Slovak Republic's exchange agreements provide for the exchange of information in accordance with the requirements of the Model CAA.

Recommendations:

No recommendations made.

Comments by the assessed jurisdiction

No comments made.

Note

[1] Andorra, Liechtenstein, Monaco, San Marino and Switzerland.

Slovenia

Overall findings

Slovenia's legal framework implementing the AEOI Standard is in place and is consistent with the requirements of the AEOI Terms of Reference. This includes Slovenia's domestic legislative framework requiring Reporting Financial Institutions to conduct the due diligence and reporting procedures (CR1) and its international legal framework to exchange the information with all of Slovenia's Interested Appropriate Partners (CR2).

The methodology used for the peer reviews and that therefore underpins this report is outlined in Chapter 2.

Overall determination on the legal framework: In Place

Conclusions on the legal framework

General context

Slovenia commenced exchanges under the AEOI Standard in 2017.

In order to provide for Reporting Financial Institutions to collect and report the information to be exchanged, Slovenia:

- amended the Tax Procedure Act (ZDavP-2I, as further amended in the OJ No. 69/2017 of 8 December 2017);
- amended the Rules on the implementation of the Tax Procedure Act; and
- issued further guidance, which is not legally binding.

Under this framework Reporting Financial Institutions were required to commence the due diligence procedures in relation to New Accounts from 1 January 2016. With respect to Preexisting Accounts, Reporting Financial Institutions were required to complete the due diligence procedures on High Value Individual Accounts by 31 December 2016 and on Lower Value Individual Accounts and Entity Accounts by 31 December 2017.

Following the initial peer review by the Global Forum, Slovenia amended its legislative framework to address issues identified, effective from 9 December 2017.

With respect to the exchange of information under the AEOI Standard, Slovenia:

- is a Party to the convention on Mutual Administrative Assistance in Tax Matters and activated the associated CRS Multilateral Competent Authority Agreement in time for exchanges in 2017;
- has implemented European Directive 2011/16/EU on Administrative Cooperation in the Field of Taxation, as amended by Directive 2014/107/EU; and
- has in place European Union agreements with five European third countries.[1]

Detailed findings

The detailed findings for Slovenia are below, organised per Core Requirement (CR) and sub-requirement (SR), as extracted from the AEOI Terms of Reference (www.oecd.org/tax/transparency/documents/aeoi-terms-of-reference.pdf).

CR1 Domestic legal framework: Jurisdictions should have a domestic legislative framework in place that requires all Reporting Financial Institutions to conduct the due diligence and reporting procedures in the CRS, and that provides for the effective implementation of the CRS as set out therein.

Determination: In Place

Slovenia's domestic legislative framework is in place and contains all of the key aspects of the CRS and its Commentary requiring Reporting Financial Institutions to conduct the due diligence and reporting procedures (SRs 1.1 – 1.3). It also provides for a framework to enforce the requirements (SR 1.4).

SR 1.1 Jurisdictions should define the scope of Reporting Financial Institutions consistently with the CRS.

Slovenia has defined the scope of Reporting Financial Institutions in its domestic legislative framework in accordance with the CRS and its Commentary.

Recommendations:

No recommendations made.

SR 1.2 Jurisdictions should define the scope of Financial Accounts and Reportable Accounts consistently with the CRS and incorporate the due diligence procedures to identify them.

Slovenia has defined the scope of the Financial Accounts that are required to be reported in its domestic legislative framework and incorporated the due diligence procedures that must be applied to identify them in accordance with the CRS and its Commentary.

Recommendations:

No recommendations made.

SR 1.3 Jurisdictions should incorporate the reporting requirements contained in Section I of the CRS into their domestic legislative framework.

Slovenia has incorporated the reporting requirements in its domestic legislative framework in accordance with the CRS and its Commentary.

Recommendations:

No recommendations made.

SR 1.4 Jurisdictions should have a legislative framework in place that allows for the enforcement of the requirements of the CRS in practice.

Slovenia has a legislative framework in place to enforce the requirements in accordance with the CRS and its Commentary.

Recommendations:

No recommendations made.

CR2 International legal framework: Jurisdictions should have exchange relationships in effect with all Interested Appropriate Partners as committed to and that provide for the exchange of information in accordance with the Model CAA.

Determination: In Place

Slovenia's international legal framework to exchange the information is in place, is consistent with the Model CAA and its Commentary and provides for exchange with all of Slovenia's Interested Appropriate

Partners (i.e. all jurisdictions that are interested in receiving information from Slovenia and that meet the required standard in relation to confidentiality and data safeguards). (SRs 2.1 – 2.3)

SR 2.1 Jurisdictions should have exchange agreements in effect with all Interested Appropriate Partners that permit the automatic exchange of CRS information.

Slovenia has exchange agreements that permit the automatic exchange of CRS information in effect with all its Interested Appropriate Partners.

Recommendations:

No recommendations made.

SR 2.2 Such an exchange agreement should be put in place without undue delay, following the receipt of an expression of interest from an Interested Appropriate Partner.

Slovenia put in place its exchange agreements without undue delay.

Recommendations:

No recommendations made.

SR 2.3 Jurisdictions should ensure that the exchange agreements in effect provide for the exchange of information in accordance with the requirements of the Model CAA.

Slovenia's exchange agreements provide for the exchange of information in accordance with the requirements of the Model CAA.

Recommendations:

No recommendations made.

Comments by the assessed jurisdiction

Slovenia wishes to express its gratitude and deep appreciation for the excellent work carried out by the Secretariat of the Global Forum and the AEOI Assessment Panel. Slovenia is confident that the AEOI legal determination report is a fair and accurate picture of the legal framework in force. We are satisfied with the conclusion that Slovenia's legal framework implementing the AEOI Standard is in place and is consistent with the requirements of the AEOI Terms of Reference and that there are no recommendations.

Note

[1] Andorra, Liechtenstein, Monaco, San Marino and Switzerland.

South Africa

Overall findings

South Africa's legal framework implementing the AEOI Standard is in place and is consistent with the requirements of the AEOI Terms of Reference. This includes South Africa's domestic legislative framework requiring Reporting Financial Institutions to conduct the due diligence and reporting procedures (CR1) and its international legal framework to exchange the information with all of South Africa's Interested Appropriate Partners (CR2).

The methodology used for the peer reviews and that therefore underpins this report is outlined in Chapter 2.

Overall determination on the legal framework: In Place

Conclusions on the legal framework

General context

South Africa commenced exchanges under the AEOI Standard in 2017.

In order to provide for Reporting Financial Institutions to collect and report the information to be exchanged, South Africa:

- enacted enabling provisions in the Tax Administration Act, 28 of 2011;
- introduced the CRS Regulations; and
- issued further guidance, which is not legally binding.

Under this framework Reporting Financial Institutions were required to commence the due diligence procedures in relation to New Accounts from 1 March 2016. With respect to Preexisting Accounts, Reporting Financial Institutions were required to complete the due diligence procedures on High Value Individual Accounts by 28 February 2017 and on Lower Value Individual Accounts and Entity Accounts by 28 February 2018.

Following the initial Global Forum peer review, South Africa amended its legislative framework to address issues identified, effective from 1 June 2021.

With respect to the exchange of information under the AEOI Standard, South Africa:

- is a Party to the Convention on Mutual Administrative Assistance in Tax Matters and activated the associated CRS Multilateral Competent Authority Agreement in time for exchanges in 2017; and
- put in place three bilateral agreements.[1]

Detailed findings

The detailed findings for South Africa are below, organised per Core Requirement (CR) and sub-requirement (SR), as extracted from the AEOI Terms of Reference (www.oecd.org/tax/transparency/documents/aeoi-terms-of-reference.pdf).

CR1 Domestic legal framework: Jurisdictions should have a domestic legislative framework in place that requires all Reporting Financial Institutions to conduct the due diligence and reporting procedures in the CRS, and that provides for the effective implementation of the CRS as set out therein.

Determination: In Place

South Africa's domestic legislative framework is in place and contains all of the key aspects of the CRS and its Commentary requiring Reporting Financial Institutions to conduct the due diligence and reporting procedures (SRs 1.1 – 1.3). It also provides a framework to enforce the requirements (SR 1.4).

SR 1.1 Jurisdictions should define the scope of Reporting Financial Institutions consistently with the CRS.

South Africa has defined the scope of Reporting Financial Institutions in its domestic legislative framework in accordance with the CRS and its Commentary.

Recommendations:

No recommendations made.

SR 1.2 Jurisdictions should define the scope of Financial Accounts and Reportable Accounts consistently with the CRS and incorporate the due diligence procedures to identify them.

South Africa has defined the scope of the Financial Accounts that are required to be reported in its domestic legislative framework and incorporated the due diligence procedures that must be applied to identify them in accordance with the CRS and its Commentary.

Recommendations:

No recommendations made.

SR 1.3 Jurisdictions should incorporate the reporting requirements contained in Section I of the CRS into their domestic legislative framework.

South Africa has incorporated the reporting requirements in its domestic legislative framework in accordance with the CRS and its Commentary.

Recommendations:

No recommendations made.

SR 1.4 Jurisdictions should have a legislative framework in place that allows for the enforcement of the requirements of the CRS in practice.

South Africa has a legislative framework in place to enforce the requirements in accordance with the CRS and its Commentary.

Recommendations:

No recommendations made.

CR2 International legal framework: Jurisdictions should have exchange relationships in effect with all Interested Appropriate Partners as committed to and that provide for the exchange of information in accordance with the Model CAA.

Determination: In Place

South Africa's international legal framework to exchange the information is in place, is consistent with the Model CAA and its Commentary and provides for exchange with all of South Africa's Interested Appropriate

Partners (i.e. all jurisdictions that are interested in receiving information from South Africa and that meet the required standard in relation to confidentiality and data safeguards). (SRs 2.1 – 2.3)

SR 2.1 Jurisdictions should have exchange agreements in effect with all Interested Appropriate Partners that permit the automatic exchange of CRS information.

South Africa has exchange agreements that permit the automatic exchange of CRS information in effect with all its Interested Appropriate Partners.

Recommendations:

No recommendations made.

SR 2.2 Such an exchange agreement should be put in place without undue delay, following the receipt of an expression of interest from an Interested Appropriate Partner.

South Africa put in place its exchange agreements without undue delay.

Recommendations:

No recommendations made.

SR 2.3 Jurisdictions should ensure that the exchange agreements in effect provide for the exchange of information in accordance with the requirements of the Model CAA.

South Africa's exchange agreements provide for the exchange of information in accordance with the requirements of the Model CAA.

Recommendations:

No recommendations made.

Comments by the assessed jurisdiction

No comments made.

Note

[1] With Hong Kong (China), Qatar and Singapore. South Africa has also activated a relationship under the CRS MCAA with Qatar.

Spain

Overall findings

Spain's legal framework implementing the AEOI Standard is in place and is consistent with the requirements of the AEOI Terms of Reference. This includes Spain's domestic legislative framework requiring Reporting Financial Institutions to conduct the due diligence and reporting procedures (CR1) and its international legal framework to exchange the information with all of Spain's Interested Appropriate Partners (CR2).

The methodology used for the peer reviews and that therefore underpins this report is outlined in Chapter 2.

Overall determination on the legal framework: In Place

Conclusions on the legal framework

General context

Spain commenced exchanges under the AEOI Standard in 2017.

In order to provide for Reporting Financial Institutions to collect and report the information to be exchanged, Spain:

- enacted the 22nd Additional Provision of General Taxation Law passed by Act 58/2003; and
- introduced the Royal Decree 1021/2015 that contains the requirement to determine the residence for tax purposes of Account Holders and those who have control over Financial Accounts and the requirement to report information pursuant to Mutual Assistance; and
- introduced the Order HAP/1695/2016 on FORM 289 on annual reporting on financial accounts in the field of mutual assistance.

Under this framework Reporting Financial Institutions were required to commence the due diligence procedures in relation to New Accounts from 1 January 2016. With respect to Preexisting Accounts, Reporting Financial Institutions were required to complete the due diligence procedures on High Value Individual Accounts by 31 December 2016 and on Lower Value Individual Accounts and Entity Accounts by 31 December 2017.

Following the initial Global Forum peer review, Spain amended its legislative framework to address issues identified, effective from 11 July 2021.

With respect to the exchange of information under the AEOI Standard, Spain:

- is a Party to the Convention on Mutual Administrative Assistance in Tax Matters and activated the associated CRS Multilateral Competent Authority Agreement in time for exchanges in 2017;
- has in place European Directive 2011/16/EU on Administrative Cooperation in the Field of Taxation as amended by Directive 2014/107/EU; and
- has in place European Union agreements with five European third countries.[1]

Detailed findings

The detailed findings for Spain are below, organised per Core Requirement (CR) and sub-requirement (SR), as extracted from the AEOI Terms of Reference (www.oecd.org/tax/transparency/documents/aeoi-terms-of-reference.pdf).

CR1 Domestic legal framework: Jurisdictions should have a domestic legislative framework in place that requires all Reporting Financial Institutions to conduct the due diligence and reporting procedures in the CRS, and that provides for the effective implementation of the CRS as set out therein.

Determination: In Place

Spain's domestic legislative framework is in place and contains all of the key aspects of the CRS and its Commentary requiring Reporting Financial Institutions to conduct the due diligence and reporting procedures (SRs 1.1 – 1.3). It also provides for a framework to enforce the requirements (SR 1.4).

SR 1.1 Jurisdictions should define the scope of Reporting Financial Institutions consistently with the CRS.

Spain has defined the scope of Reporting Financial Institutions in its domestic legislative framework in accordance with the CRS and its Commentary.

Recommendations:

No recommendations made.

SR 1.2 Jurisdictions should define the scope of Financial Accounts and Reportable Accounts consistently with the CRS and incorporate the due diligence procedures to identify them.

Spain has defined the scope of the Financial Accounts that are required to be reported in its domestic legislative framework and incorporated the due diligence procedures that must be applied to identify them in accordance with the CRS and its Commentary.

Recommendations:

No recommendations made.

SR 1.3 Jurisdictions should incorporate the reporting requirements contained in Section I of the CRS into their domestic legislative framework.

Spain has incorporated the reporting requirements in its domestic legislative framework in accordance with the CRS and its Commentary.

Recommendations:

No recommendations made.

SR 1.4 Jurisdictions should have a legislative framework in place that allows for the enforcement of the requirements of the CRS in practice.

Spain has a legislative framework in place to enforce the requirements in accordance with the CRS and its Commentary.

Recommendations:

No recommendations made.

CR2 International legal framework: Jurisdictions should have exchange relationships in effect with all Interested Appropriate Partners as committed to and that provide for the exchange of information in accordance with the Model CAA.

Determination: In Place

Spain's international legal framework to exchange the information is in place, is consistent with the Model CAA and its Commentary and provides for exchange with all of Spain's Interested Appropriate Partners (i.e. all jurisdictions that are interested in receiving information from Spain and that meet the required standard in relation to confidentiality and data safeguards). (SRs 2.1 – 2.3)

SR 2.1 Jurisdictions should have exchange agreements in effect with all Interested Appropriate Partners that permit the automatic exchange of CRS information.

Spain has exchange agreements that permit the automatic exchange of CRS information in effect with all its Interested Appropriate Partners.

Recommendations:

No recommendations made.

SR 2.2 Such an exchange agreement should be put in place without undue delay, following the receipt of an expression of interest from an Interested Appropriate Partner.

Spain put in place its exchange agreements without undue delay.

Recommendations:

No recommendations made.

SR 2.3 Jurisdictions should ensure that the exchange agreements in effect provide for the exchange of information in accordance with the requirements of the Model CAA.

Spain's exchange agreements provide for the exchange of information in accordance with the requirements of the Model CAA.

Recommendations:

No recommendations made.

Comments by the assessed jurisdiction

No comments made.

Note

[1] Andorra, Liechtenstein, Monaco, San Marino and Switzerland.

Sweden

Overall findings

Sweden's legal framework implementing the AEOI Standard is in place and is consistent with the requirements of the AEOI Terms of Reference. This includes Sweden's domestic legislative framework requiring Reporting Financial Institutions to conduct the due diligence and reporting procedures (CR1) and its international legal framework to exchange the information with all of Sweden's Interested Appropriate Partners (CR2).

The methodology used for the peer reviews and that therefore underpins this report is outlined in Chapter 2.

Overall determination on the legal framework: In Place

Conclusions on the legal framework

General context

Sweden commenced exchanges under the AEOI Standard in 2017.

In order to provide for Reporting Financial Institutions to collect and report the information to be exchanged, Sweden:

- amended its Tax Procedure Code (2011:1244) and the Tax Procedure Ordinance (2011:1261);
- enacted Act (2015:911) on the identification of reportable accounts with regard to automatic exchange of information on financial accounts;
- enacted Act (2015:912) on the automatic exchange of information on financial accounts; and
- introduced Ordinance (2015:921) on the identification of reportable accounts with regard to automatic exchange of information on financial accounts and Ordinance (2015:922) on the automatic exchange of information on financial accounts.

Under this framework Reporting Financial Institutions were required to commence the due diligence procedures in relation to New Accounts from 1 January 2016. With respect to Preexisting Accounts, Reporting Financial Institutions were required to complete the due diligence procedures on High Value Individual Accounts by 31 December 2016 and on Lower Value Individual Accounts and Entity Accounts by 31 December 2017.

Following the initial Global Forum peer review, Sweden amended its legislative framework to address issues identified, effective from 1 January 2019.

With respect to the exchange of information under the AEOI Standard, Sweden:

- is a Party to the Convention on Mutual Administrative Assistance in Tax Matters and activated the associated CRS Multilateral Competent Authority Agreement in time for exchanges in 2017;
- has in place European Directive 2011/16/EU on Administrative Cooperation in the Field of Taxation, as amended by Directive 2014/107/EU; and
- has in place European Union agreements with five European third countries.[1]

Detailed findings

The detailed findings for Sweden are below, organised per Core Requirement (CR) and sub-requirement (SR), as extracted from the AEOI Terms of Reference (www.oecd.org/tax/transparency/documents/aeoi-terms-of-reference.pdf).

CR1 Domestic legal framework: Jurisdictions should have a domestic legislative framework in place that requires all Reporting Financial Institutions to conduct the due diligence and reporting procedures in the CRS, and that provides for the effective implementation of the CRS as set out therein.

Determination: In Place

Sweden's domestic legislative framework is in place and contains all of the key aspects of the CRS and its Commentary requiring Reporting Financial Institutions to conduct the due diligence and reporting procedures (SRs 1.1 – 1.3). It also provides for a framework to enforce the requirements (SR 1.4).

SR 1.1 Jurisdictions should define the scope of Reporting Financial Institutions consistently with the CRS.

Sweden has defined the scope of Reporting Financial Institutions in its domestic legislative framework in accordance with the CRS and its Commentary.

Recommendations:

No recommendations made.

SR 1.2 Jurisdictions should define the scope of Financial Accounts and Reportable Accounts consistently with the CRS and incorporate the due diligence procedures to identify them.

Sweden has defined the scope of the Financial Accounts that are required to be reported in its domestic legislative framework and incorporated the due diligence procedures that must be applied to identify them in accordance with the CRS and its Commentary.

Recommendations:

No recommendations made.

SR 1.3 Jurisdictions should incorporate the reporting requirements contained in Section I of the CRS into their domestic legislative framework.

Sweden has incorporated the reporting requirements in its domestic legislative framework in accordance with the CRS and its Commentary.

Recommendations:

No recommendations made.

SR 1.4 Jurisdictions should have a legislative framework in place that allows for the enforcement of the requirements of the CRS in practice.

Sweden has a legislative framework in place to enforce the requirements in accordance with the CRS and its Commentary.

Recommendations:

No recommendations made.

CR2 International legal framework: Jurisdictions should have exchange relationships in effect with all Interested Appropriate Partners as committed to and that provide for the exchange of information in accordance with the Model CAA.

Determination: In Place

Sweden's international legal framework to exchange the information is in place, is consistent with the Model CAA and its Commentary and provides for exchange with all of Sweden's Interested Appropriate Partners (i.e. all jurisdictions that are interested in receiving information from Sweden and that meet the required standard in relation to confidentiality and data safeguards). (SRs 2.1 – 2.3)

SR 2.1 Jurisdictions should have exchange agreements in effect with all Interested Appropriate Partners that permit the automatic exchange of CRS information.

Sweden has exchange agreements that permit the automatic exchange of CRS information in effect with all its Interested Appropriate Partners.

Recommendations:

No recommendations made.

SR 2.2 Such an exchange agreement should be put in place without undue delay, following the receipt of an expression of interest from an Interested Appropriate Partner.

Sweden put in place its exchange agreements without undue delay.

Recommendations:

No recommendations made.

SR 2.3 Jurisdictions should ensure that the exchange agreements in effect provide for the exchange of information in accordance with the requirements of the Model CAA.

Sweden's exchange agreements provide for the exchange of information in accordance with the requirements of the Model CAA.

Recommendations:

No recommendations made.

Comments by the assessed jurisdiction

No comments made.

Note

[1] Andorra, Liechtenstein, Monaco, San Marino and Switzerland.

Switzerland

Overall findings

Switzerland's legal framework implementing the AEOI Standard is in place but needs improvement in order to be fully consistent with the requirements of the AEOI Terms of Reference. While Switzerland's international legal framework to exchange the information with all of Switzerland's Interested Appropriate Partners (CR2) is consistent with the requirements of the AEOI Terms of Reference, its domestic legislative framework requiring Reporting Financial Institutions to conduct the due diligence and reporting procedures (CR1) has deficiencies significant to the proper functioning of elements of the AEOI Standard. More specifically, Switzerland provides for jurisdiction-specific Non-Reporting Financial Institutions and Excluded Accounts that do not meet the requirements of the AEOI Standard.

The methodology used for the peer reviews and that therefore underpins this report is outlined in Chapter 2.

Overall determination on the legal framework: In Place But **Needs Improvement**

Conclusions on the legal framework

General context

Switzerland commenced exchanges under the AEOI Standard in 2018.

In order to provide for Reporting Financial Institutions to collect and report the information to be exchanged, Switzerland:

- enacted the Federal Act of 18 December 2015 on the International Automatic Exchange of Information in Tax Matters; as amended on 9 October 2020;
- introduced the Ordinance of 23 November 2016 on the International Automatic Exchange of Information in Tax Matters; as amended on 9 October 2020;
- issued further guidance, which is legally binding; and
- made reference to the Federal Act of 12 December 2014 on the Implementation of the Revised FATF Recommendations of 2012 for the purposes of the identification of Controlling Persons under the AEOI Standard.

Under this framework Reporting Financial Institutions were required to commence the due diligence procedures in relation to New Accounts from 1 January 2017. With respect to Preexisting Accounts, Reporting Financial Institutions were required to complete the due diligence procedures on High Value Individual Accounts by 31 December 2017 and on Lower Value Individual Accounts and Entity Accounts by 31 December 2018.

Following the initial Global Forum peer review, Switzerland made various amendments to its legislative framework to address issues identified, the last of which will be effective from 1 January 2021.

With respect to the exchange of information under the AEOI Standard, Switzerland:

- is a Party to the Convention on Mutual Administrative Assistance in Tax Matters and activated the associated CRS Multilateral Competent Authority Agreement in time for exchanges in 2018;
- has in place an agreement with the European Union; and
- put in place two bilateral agreements.[1]

Detailed findings

The detailed findings for Switzerland are below, organised per Core Requirement (CR) and sub-requirement (SR), as extracted from the AEOI Terms of Reference (www.oecd.org/tax/transparency/documents/aeoi-terms-of-reference.pdf).

CR1 Domestic legal framework: Jurisdictions should have a domestic legislative framework in place that requires all Reporting Financial Institutions to conduct the due diligence and reporting procedures in the CRS, and that provides for the effective implementation of the CRS as set out therein.

Determination: In Place But **Needs Improvement**

Switzerland's domestic legislative framework is in place and contains most of the key aspects of the CRS and its Commentary requiring Reporting Financial Institutions to conduct the due diligence and reporting procedures, but it needs improvement in relation to the scope of Reporting Financial Institutions required to report information (SR 1.1), and the scope of Financial Accounts required to be reported (SR 1.2).

More specifically, Switzerland provides for categories of jurisdiction-specific Non-Reporting Financial Institutions and Excluded Accounts that do not meet the requirements of the AEOI Standard.

SR 1.1 Jurisdictions should define the scope of Reporting Financial Institutions consistently with the CRS.

Switzerland has defined the scope of Reporting Financial Institutions in its domestic legislative framework in a manner that is largely consistent with the CRS and its Commentary. However, deficiencies have been identified. More specifically, Switzerland provides for two categories of jurisdiction-specific Non-Reporting Financial Institutions that do not correspond to any of the categories of Non-Reporting Financial Institutions foreseen in the AEOI Standard. The scope of Reporting Financial Institutions, including the provision on Non-Reporting Financial Institutions is material to the proper functioning of the AEOI Standard.

Recommendations:

Switzerland should amend its domestic legislative framework to remove two categories from its jurisdiction-specific list of Non-Reporting Financial Institutions as they do not correspond to any of the categories of Non-Reporting Financial Institutions foreseen in the AEOI Standard. The entries are: i) associations that pursue a non-commercial purpose, and ii) foundations that pursue a public, charitable or non-material purpose.

SR 1.2 Jurisdictions should define the scope of Financial Accounts and Reportable Accounts consistently with the CRS and incorporate the due diligence procedures to identify them.

Switzerland has defined the scope of the Financial Accounts that are required to be reported in its domestic legislative framework and incorporated the due diligence procedures that must be applied to them in a manner that is largely consistent with the CRS and its Commentary. However, deficiencies have been identified. More specifically, Switzerland provides for three jurisdiction-specific Excluded Accounts which are not in line with the requirements of the AEOI Standard. Two of the Excluded Accounts do not correspond to any of the categories of Excluded Accounts in the AEOI Standard. The capital contribution accounts have some similarity to escrow accounts, but do not relate to the sale, exchange or lease of real or personal property and do not have sufficiently similar characteristics to the requirements nor to ensure that these accounts pose a low risk of being used to evade tax. The scope of Financial Accounts, including the provision of Excluded Accounts, is material to the proper functioning of the AEOI Standard.

Recommendations:

Switzerland should amend its domestic legislative framework to remove three entries from its jurisdiction-specific list of Excluded Accounts as they do not meet the requirements. The entries are: i) accounts of associations that pursue a non-commercial purpose; ii) accounts of foundations that pursue a public, charitable or non-material purpose; and iii) capital contribution accounts.

SR 1.3 Jurisdictions should incorporate the reporting requirements contained in Section I of the CRS into their domestic legislative framework.

Switzerland has incorporated the reporting requirements in its domestic legislative framework in accordance with the CRS and its Commentary.

Recommendations:

No recommendations made.

SR 1.4 Jurisdictions should have a legislative framework in place that allows for the enforcement of the requirements of the CRS in practice.

Switzerland has a legislative framework in place to enforce the requirements in accordance with the CRS and its Commentary.

Recommendations:

No recommendations made.

CR2 International legal framework: Jurisdictions should have exchange relationships in effect with all Interested Appropriate Partners as committed to and that provide for the exchange of information in accordance with the Model CAA.

Determination: In Place

Switzerland's international legal framework to exchange the information is in place, is consistent with the Model CAA and its Commentary and provides for exchange with all of Switzerland's Interested Appropriate Partners (i.e. all jurisdictions that are interested in receiving information from Switzerland and that meet the required standard in relation to confidentiality and data safeguards). (SRs 2.1 – 2.3)

SR 2.1 Jurisdictions should have exchange agreements in effect with all Interested Appropriate Partners that permit the automatic exchange of CRS information.

Switzerland has exchange agreements that permit the automatic exchange of CRS information in effect with all its Interested Appropriate Partners.

Recommendations:

No recommendations made.

SR 2.2 Such an exchange agreement should be put in place without undue delay, following the receipt of an expression of interest from an Interested Appropriate Partner.

Switzerland put in place its exchange agreements without undue delay.

Recommendations:

No recommendations made.

SR 2.3 Jurisdictions should ensure that the exchange agreements in effect provide for the exchange of information in accordance with the requirements of the Model CAA.

Switzerland's exchange agreements provide for the exchange of information in accordance with the requirements of the Model CAA.

Recommendations:

No recommendations made.

Comments by the assessed jurisdiction

Switzerland would like to express its general appreciation for the work of the Global Forum and reiterates that it takes its commitment to implement the AEOI Standard according to the Global Forum's recommendations very seriously. Following the initial Global Forum peer review, Switzerland made various amendments to its legislative framework to address the issues identified.

Switzerland takes note of the remaining recommendations set out under SR 1.1. and 1.2., but is convinced that the entities and accounts concerned have a very low risk of being misused for tax evasion, especially as the legal framework contains strict requirements that significantly reduce or exclude the danger of abuse, which is therefore of a theoretical nature. Nonetheless, Switzerland understands the reasons for the recommendations in the context of the applicable standard.

Switzerland would like to highlight that the treatment of the concerned entities and accounts will be discussed as a part of the OECD's review of the AEOI Standard with first discussions starting in late October 2020. Regarding the treatment of non-profit entities, the OECD Secretariat has already submitted a specific proposal for the review of the AEOI Standard. This proposal reflects Switzerland's concerns and would take into account four recommendations on SR 1.1 and SR 1.2 regarding non-commercial associations and charitable foundations. As regards capital contribution accounts, it is necessary to await the outcome of the discussions.

As long as the discussions of the issues raised as part of the OECD's review of the AEOI Standard have not taken place, the question whether or not the entities and accounts aforementioned are exempt from the reporting requirements should be left open and should not prejudice Switzerland's legal determination.

Note

[1] With Hong Kong (China) and Singapore.

Trinidad and Tobago

Overall findings

Trinidad and Tobago's legal framework to implement the AEOI Standard is not in place. This is because Trinidad and Tobago has not put in place a domestic legislative framework requiring Reporting Financial Institutions to conduct the due diligence and reporting procedures (CR1) nor an international legal framework to exchange the information with all Interested Appropriate Partners (CR2).

The methodology used for the peer reviews and that therefore underpins this report is outlined in Chapter 2.

Overall determination on the legal framework: Not In Place

Conclusions on the legal framework

General context

Trinidad and Tobago has not yet implemented the necessary legal frameworks.

Detailed findings

The detailed findings for Trinidad and Tobago are below, organised per Core Requirement (CR) and sub-requirement (SR), as extracted from the AEOI Terms of Reference (www.oecd.org/tax/transparency/documents/aeoi-terms-of-reference.pdf).

CR1 Domestic legal framework: Jurisdictions should have a domestic legislative framework in place that requires all Reporting Financial Institutions to conduct the due diligence and reporting procedures in the CRS, and that provides for the effective implementation of the CRS as set out therein.

Determination: Not In Place

Trinidad and Tobago has not put in place a domestic legislative framework requiring Reporting Financial Institutions to conduct the due diligence and reporting procedures, therefore the CR1 Domestic legal framework is determined to be not in place. As no such framework is in place a detailed analysis in relation to each SR has not been possible.

CR2 International legal framework: Jurisdictions should have exchange relationships in effect with all Interested Appropriate Partners as committed to and that provide for the exchange of information in accordance with the Model CAA.

Determination: Not In Place

Trinidad and Tobago has not put in place the international legal framework to exchange the information with all of Trinidad and Tobago's Interested Appropriate Partners, therefore the CR2 International legal framework is determined to be not in place. As no such framework is in place a detailed analysis in relation to each SR has not been possible.

Comments by the assessed jurisdiction

No comments made.

Turkey

Overall findings

Turkey's legal framework implementing the AEOI Standard is in place and is consistent with the requirements of the AEOI Terms of Reference. This includes Turkey's domestic legislative framework requiring Reporting Financial Institutions to conduct the due diligence and reporting procedures (CR1) and its international legal framework to exchange the information with all of Turkey's Interested Appropriate Partners (CR2).

The methodology used for the peer reviews and that therefore underpins this report is outlined in Chapter 2.

Overall determination on the legal framework: In Place

Conclusions on the legal framework

General context

Turkey commenced exchanges under the AEOI Standard in 2018.

In order to provide for Reporting Financial Institutions to collect and report the information to be exchanged, Turkey:

- relies on Articles 148, 149 and 152/A of the Tax Procedure Law;
- issued the Official letter from the Turkish Revenue Administration dated 30/06/2017 and its attachment "Guidance on Residency and Due Diligence", that was amended in April 2020; and
- made reference to the Regulation on Prevention Measures Regarding Laundering Proceeds of Crime and Financing of Terrorism (reviewed for the definition of beneficial owner) implementing the FATF Recommendations for the purposes of the identification of Controlling Persons under the AEOI Standard.

Under this framework Reporting Financial Institutions were required to commence the due diligence procedures in relation to New Accounts from 1 July 2017. With respect to Preexisting Accounts, Reporting Financial Institutions were required to complete the due diligence procedures on High Value Individual Accounts by 30 June 2018 and on Lower Value Individual Accounts and Entity Accounts by 30 June 2019.

Following the initial Global Forum peer review, Turkey amended its legislative framework to address issues identified, effective from 1 April 2020.

With respect to the exchange of information under the AEOI Standard, Turkey:

- put in place two bilateral agreements in time for exchanges from 2018[1]; and
- is a Party to the Convention on Mutual Administrative Assistance in Tax Matters and activated the associated CRS Multilateral Competent Authority Agreement in time for exchanges in 2020.

Detailed findings

The detailed findings for Turkey are below, organised per Core Requirement (CR) and sub-requirement (SR), as extracted from the AEOI Terms of Reference (www.oecd.org/tax/transparency/documents/aeoi-terms-of-reference.pdf).

CR1 Domestic legal framework: Jurisdictions should have a domestic legislative framework in place that requires all Reporting Financial Institutions to conduct the due diligence and reporting procedures in the CRS, and that provides for the effective implementation of the CRS as set out therein.

Determination: In Place

Turkey's domestic legislative framework is in place and contains all of the key aspects of the CRS and its Commentary requiring Reporting Financial Institutions to conduct the due diligence and reporting procedures (SRs 1.1 – 1.3). It also provides for a framework to enforce the requirements (SR 1.4).

SR 1.1 Jurisdictions should define the scope of Reporting Financial Institutions consistently with the CRS.

Turkey has defined the scope of Reporting Financial Institutions in its domestic legislative framework in accordance with the CRS and its Commentary.

Recommendations:

No recommendations made.

SR 1.2 Jurisdictions should define the scope of Financial Accounts and Reportable Accounts consistently with the CRS and incorporate the due diligence procedures to identify them.

Turkey has defined the scope of the Financial Accounts that are required to be reported in its domestic legislative framework and incorporated the due diligence procedures that must be applied to identify them in accordance with the CRS and its Commentary.

Recommendations:

No recommendations made.

SR 1.3 Jurisdictions should incorporate the reporting requirements contained in Section I of the CRS into their domestic legislative framework.

Turkey has incorporated the reporting requirements in its domestic legislative framework in accordance with the CRS and its Commentary.

Recommendations:

No recommendations made.

SR 1.4 Jurisdictions should have a legislative framework in place that allows for the enforcement of the requirements of the CRS in practice.

Turkey has a legislative framework in place to enforce the requirements in accordance with the CRS and its Commentary.

Recommendations:

No recommendations made.

CR2 International legal framework: Jurisdictions should have exchange relationships in effect with all Interested Appropriate Partners as committed to and that provide for the exchange of information in accordance with the Model CAA.

Determination: In Place

Turkey's international legal framework to exchange the information is in place, is consistent with the Model CAA and its Commentary and provides for exchange with all of Turkey's Interested Appropriate Partners (i.e. all jurisdictions that are interested in receiving information from Turkey and that meet the required standard in relation to confidentiality and data safeguards). (SRs 2.1 – 2.3)

SR 2.1 Jurisdictions should have exchange agreements in effect with all Interested Appropriate Partners that permit the automatic exchange of CRS information.

Turkey has exchange agreements that permit the automatic exchange of CRS information in effect with all its Interested Appropriate Partners.

Recommendations:

No recommendations made.

SR 2.2 Such an exchange agreement should be put in place without undue delay, following the receipt of an expression of interest from an Interested Appropriate Partner.

Turkey put in place its exchange agreements without undue delay.

Recommendations:

No recommendations made.

SR 2.3 Jurisdictions should ensure that the exchange agreements in effect provide for the exchange of information in accordance with the requirements of the Model CAA.

Turkey's exchange agreements provide for the exchange of information in accordance with the requirements of the Model CAA.

Recommendations:

No recommendations made.

Comments by the assessed jurisdiction

No comments made.

Note

[1] With Latvia and Norway. Turkey has also activated relationships under the CRS MCAA with both jurisdictions.

Turks and Caicos Islands

Overall findings

The Turks and Caicos Islands' legal framework implementing the AEOI Standard is in place but needs improvement in order to be fully consistent with the requirements of the AEOI Terms of Reference. While the Turks and Caicos Islands' international legal framework to exchange the information with all of the Turks and Caicos Islands' Interested Appropriate Partners (CR2) is consistent with the requirements, its domestic legislative framework requiring Reporting Financial Institutions to conduct the due diligence and reporting procedures has deficiencies in areas significant to the proper functioning of elements of the AEOI Standard. More specifically, the Turks and Caicos Islands provides for a jurisdiction-specific Excluded Account that is not in accordance with the requirements and its legislative framework does not ensure that valid self-certifications are always obtained for New Accounts.

The methodology used for the peer reviews and that therefore underpins this report is outlined in Chapter 2.

Overall determination on the legal framework: In Place But **Needs Improvement**

Conclusions on the legal framework

General context

The Turks and Caicos Islands commenced exchanges under the AEOI Standard in 2018.

In order to provide for Reporting Financial Institutions to collect and report the information to be exchanged, the Turks and Caicos Islands:

- amended the Tax Information (Exchange and Mutual Administrative Assistance) Ordinance;
- introduced the Tax Information (Multilateral Competent Authority Agreement on Automatic Exchange of Financial Account Information and the Common Reporting Standard) Order 2016, as amended in 2017;
- introduced the International Tax Compliance Regulations 2016, as amended in May 2017; and
- issued further guidance, which is not legally binding.

Under this framework Reporting Financial Institutions were required to commence the due diligence procedures in relation to New Accounts from 1 January 2016. With respect to Preexisting Accounts, Reporting Financial Institutions were required to complete the due diligence procedures on High Value Individual Accounts by 31 December 2016 and on Lower Value Individual Accounts and Entity Accounts by 31 December 2017.

With respect to the exchange of information under the AEOI Standard, the Turks and Caicos Islands:

- has the Convention on Mutual Administrative Assistance in Tax Matters in place[1] and activated the associated CRS Multilateral Competent Authority Agreement in time for exchanges in 2018; and
- put in place two bilateral agreements.[2]

Detailed findings

The detailed findings for the Turks and Caicos Islands are below, organised per Core Requirement (CR) and sub-requirement (SR), as extracted from the AEOI Terms of Reference (www.oecd.org/tax/transparency/documents/aeoi-terms-of-reference.pdf).

CR1 Domestic legal framework: Jurisdictions should have a domestic legislative framework in place that requires all Reporting Financial Institutions to conduct the due diligence and reporting procedures in the CRS, and that provides for the effective implementation of the CRS as set out therein.

Determination: In Place But **Needs Improvement**

The Turks and Caicos Islands' domestic legislative framework is in place and contains most of the key aspects of the CRS and its Commentary requiring Reporting Financial Institutions to conduct the due diligence and reporting procedures, but it needs improvement in relation to the scope of Financial Accounts required to be reported (SR 1.2) and the framework to enforce the requirements (SR 1.4). More specifically, the Turks and Caicos Islands provides for a jurisdiction-specific Excluded Account that is not in accordance with the requirements and does not provide for specific measures to ensure that valid self-certifications are always obtained for New Accounts.

SR 1.1 Jurisdictions should define the scope of Reporting Financial Institutions consistently with the CRS.

The Turks and Caicos Islands has defined the scope of Reporting Financial Institutions in its domestic legislative framework in accordance with the CRS and its Commentary.

Recommendations:

No recommendations made.

SR 1.2 Jurisdictions should define the scope of Financial Accounts and Reportable Accounts consistently with the CRS and incorporate the due diligence procedures to identify them.

The Turks and Caicos Islands has defined the scope of the Financial Accounts that are required to be reported in its domestic legislative framework and incorporated the due diligence procedures that must be applied to identify them in a manner that is largely consistent with the CRS and its Commentary. However, a deficiency has been identified. More specifically the Turks and Caicos Islands has provided for a jurisdiction-specific Excluded Account that does not meet the requirements. The cope of Financial Accounts, including the provision of Excluded Accounts, is material to the proper functioning of the AEOI Standard.

Recommendations:

The Turks and Caicos Islands should amend its domestic legislative framework to remove Dormant Accounts from its jurisdiction-specific list of Excluded Accounts as they do not meet the requirements of the AEOI Standard, as no threshold for the exclusion has been set as required.

SR 1.3 Jurisdictions should incorporate the reporting requirements contained in Section I of the CRS into their domestic legislative framework.

The Turks and Caicos Islands has incorporated the reporting requirements in its domestic legislative framework in accordance with the CRS and its Commentary.

Recommendations:

No recommendations made.

SR 1.4 Jurisdictions should have a legislative framework in place that allows for the enforcement of the requirements of the CRS in practice.

The Turks and Caicos Islands has a legislative framework in place to enforce the requirements in a manner that is largely consistent with the CRS and its Commentary. However, a deficiency has been identified. More specifically, the Turks and Caicos Islands' legislative framework permits accounts to be reported as undocumented when self-certifications are not obtained and/or validated after the opening of the account, rather than include measures to ensure valid self-certifications are always obtained as required. This is a key element of the required enforcement framework and is therefore material to the proper functioning of the AEOI Standard.

Recommendations:

The Turks and Caicos Islands should amend its domestic legislative framework to include strong measures to ensure that valid self-certifications are always obtained for New Accounts and, more specifically, in the limited circumstances where a valid self-certification is permitted to be obtained after the opening of a New Account.

CR2 International legal framework: Jurisdictions should have exchange relationships in effect with all Interested Appropriate Partners as committed to and that provide for the exchange of information in accordance with the Model CAA.

Determination: In Place

The Turks and Caicos Islands' international legal framework to exchange the information is in place, is consistent with the Model CAA and its Commentary and provides for exchange with all of the Turks and Caicos Islands' Interested Appropriate Partners (i.e. all jurisdictions that are interested in receiving information from the Turks and Caicos Islands and that meet the required standard in relation to confidentiality and data safeguards). (SRs 2.1 – 2.3)

SR 2.1 Jurisdictions should have exchange agreements in effect with all Interested Appropriate Partners that permit the automatic exchange of CRS information.

The Turks and Caicos Islands has exchange agreements that permit the automatic exchange of CRS information in effect with all its Interested Appropriate Partners.

Recommendations:

No recommendations made.

SR 2.2 Such an exchange agreement should be put in place without undue delay, following the receipt of an expression of interest from an Interested Appropriate Partner.

The Turks and Caicos Islands put in place its exchange agreements without undue delay.

Recommendations:

No recommendations made.

SR 2.3 Jurisdictions should ensure that the exchange agreements in effect provide for the exchange of information in accordance with the requirements of the Model CAA.

The Turks and Caicos Islands' exchange agreements provide for the exchange of information in accordance with the requirements of the Model CAA.

Recommendations:

No recommendations made.

Comments by the assessed jurisdiction

The Turks and Caicos Islands wishes to acknowledge the work of the Assessment Team and Experts reviewing the AEOI standard for compliance, and thank them for their assistance and cooperation. It was not a simple exercise and proved to be quite costly for a small jurisdiction to implement in terms of administration, technology and legislation. The capacity in terms of resources is still expanding with continuous efforts being made to fall within the boundaries of the standard.

Turks and Caicos Islands has recently implemented a new AEOI Reporting Tool with greater efficiency and reporting capabilities. For those partner jurisdictions that had some difficulty with previous years' submissions, we will happily review the files and re-submit.

Notes

[1] Through a territorial extension by the United Kingdom.

[2] With the Isle of Man and the United Kingdom.

United Arab Emirates

Overall findings

The United Arab Emirates' legal framework implementing the AEOI Standard is in place and is consistent with the requirements of the AEOI Terms of Reference. This includes the United Arab Emirates' domestic legislative framework requiring Reporting Financial Institutions to conduct the due diligence and reporting procedures (CR1) and its international legal framework to exchange the information with all of the United Arab Emirates' Interested Appropriate Partners (CR2).

The methodology used for the peer reviews and that therefore underpins this report is outlined in Chapter 2.

Overall determination on the legal framework: In Place

Conclusions on the legal framework

General context

The United Arab Emirates commenced exchanges under the AEOI Standard in 2018.

The United Arab Emirates has a decentralised regulatory system to provide for Reporting Financial Institutions to collect and report the information to be exchanged. There are now six Regulatory Authorities specified by Cabinet Resolution No. (5/11) of 2020, with each Regulatory Authority of the United Arab Emirates having enacted rules to cover the entities they regulate. These are:

- The Central Bank (CB)- Notice No. 404/2016, amended on 20 August 2020;
- The Securities and Commodities Authority (SCA) - Decision of the Chairman of the SCA Board of Directors No. (25 / R.M) of 2017 Concerning the Issuance of Regulation for Common Standards to Prepare the Tax Reports, amended on 3 August 2020;
- The Insurance Authority (IA) - Insurance Authority Circular No. 34 issued on 9 September 2020;
- The Dubai International Finance Centre (DIFC) - Common Reporting Standard Law No. (2) of 2018 and the CRS Regulations of the Board of Directors of the DIFCA, amended on 30 July 2020;
- The Abu Dhabi Global Market (ADGM) - Common Reporting Standard Regulations 2017, amended on 24 June 2020; and
- Ministry of Finance (MoF) – CRS Guidance Notes issued in 2016, revised and reissued on 3 August 2020.

The United Arab Emirates also made reference to Federal Decree-law No. 20 of 2018 relating to anti-money laundering for the purposes of the identification of Controlling Persons under the AEOI Standard.

Centralised guidance was also issued by the Ministry of Finance. The Guidance and the aforementioned rules enacted by Regulatory Authorities are legally binding.

Under this framework Reporting Financial Institutions were required to commence the due diligence procedures in relation to New Accounts from 1 January 2017. With respect to Preexisting Accounts, Reporting Financial Institutions were required to complete the due diligence procedures on High Value Individual Accounts by 31 December 2017 and on Lower Value Individual Accounts and Entity Accounts by 31 December 2018.

Following the initial Global Forum peer review, the United Arab Emirates amended its legislative framework to address issues identified, the last of which was effective from 20 August 2020.

With respect to the exchange of information under the AEOI Standard, the United Arab Emirates is a Party to the Convention on Mutual Administrative Assistance in Tax Matters and activated the associated CRS Multilateral Competent Authority Agreement in time for exchanges in 2018.

Detailed findings

The detailed findings for the United Arab Emirates are below, organised per Core Requirement (CR) and sub-requirement (SR), as extracted from the AEOI Terms of Reference (www.oecd.org/tax/transparency/documents/aeoi-terms-of-reference.pdf).

CR1 Domestic legal framework: Jurisdictions should have a domestic legislative framework in place that requires all Reporting Financial Institutions to conduct the due diligence and reporting procedures in the CRS, and that provides for the effective implementation of the CRS as set out therein.

Determination: In Place

The United Arab Emirates' domestic legislative framework is in place and contains all of the key aspects of the CRS and its Commentary requiring Reporting Financial Institutions to conduct the due diligence and reporting procedures (SRs 1.1 – 1.3). It also provides for a framework to enforce the requirements (SR 1.4).

SR 1.1 Jurisdictions should define the scope of Reporting Financial Institutions consistently with the CRS.

The United Arab Emirates has defined the scope of Reporting Financial Institutions in its domestic legislative framework in a manner that is consistent with the CRS and its Commentary.

Recommendations:

No recommendations made.

SR 1.2 Jurisdictions should define the scope of Financial Accounts and Reportable Accounts consistently with the CRS and incorporate the due diligence procedures to identify them.

The United Arab Emirates has defined the scope of the Financial Accounts that are required to be reported in its domestic legislative framework and incorporated the due diligence procedures that must be applied to identify them in accordance with the CRS and its Commentary.

Recommendations:

No recommendations made.

SR 1.3 Jurisdictions should incorporate the reporting requirements contained in Section I of the CRS into their domestic legislative framework.

The United Arab Emirates has incorporated the reporting requirements in its domestic legislative framework in accordance with the CRS and its Commentary.

Recommendations:

No recommendations made.

SR 1.4 Jurisdictions should have a legislative framework in place that allows for the enforcement of the requirements of the CRS in practice.

The United Arab Emirates has a legislative framework in place to enforce the requirements in accordance with the CRS and its Commentary.

Recommendations:

No recommendations made.

CR2 International legal framework: Jurisdictions should have exchange relationships in effect with all Interested Appropriate Partners as committed to and that provide for the exchange of information in accordance with the Model CAA.

Determination: In Place

The United Arab Emirates' international legal framework to exchange the information is in place, is consistent with the Model CAA and its Commentary and provides for exchange with all of the United Arab Emirates' Interested Appropriate Partners (i.e. all jurisdictions that are interested in receiving information from the United Arab Emirates and that meet the required standard in relation to confidentiality and data safeguards). (SRs 2.1 – 2.3)

SR 2.1 Jurisdictions should have exchange agreements in effect with all Interested Appropriate Partners that permit the automatic exchange of CRS information.

The United Arab Emirates has exchange agreements that permit the automatic exchange of CRS information in effect with all its Interested Appropriate Partners.

Recommendations:

No recommendations made.

SR 2.2 Such an exchange agreement should be put in place without undue delay, following the receipt of an expression of interest from an Interested Appropriate Partner.

The United Arab Emirates put in place its exchange agreements without undue delay.

Recommendations:

No recommendations made.

SR 2.3 Jurisdictions should ensure that the exchange agreements in effect provide for the exchange of information in accordance with the requirements of the Model CAA.

The United Arab Emirates' exchange agreements provide for the exchange of information in accordance with the requirements of the Model CAA.

Recommendations:

No recommendations made.

Comments by the assessed jurisdiction

No comments made.

United Kingdom

Overall findings

The United Kingdom's legal framework implementing the AEOI Standard is in place and is consistent with the requirements of the AEOI Terms of Reference. This includes the United Kingdom's domestic legislative framework requiring Reporting Financial Institutions to conduct the due diligence and reporting procedures (CR1) and its international legal framework to exchange the information with all of the United Kingdom's Interested Appropriate Partners (CR2).

The methodology used for the peer reviews and that therefore underpins this report is outlined in Chapter 2.

Overall determination on the legal framework: In Place

Conclusions on the legal framework

General context

The United Kingdom commenced exchanges under the AEOI Standard in 2017.

In order to provide for Reporting Financial Institutions to collect and report the information to be exchanged, the United Kingdom:

- enacted Section 222 of the Finance Act 2013;
- introduced the International Tax Compliance Regulations 2015 as amended by Statutory Instruments 1839 of 2015, 899 of 2016, 598 of 2017, 490 of 2018, 881 of 2019 and 438 of 2020; and
- issued further guidance, which is not legally binding.

Under this framework Reporting Financial Institutions were required to commence the due diligence procedures in relation to New Accounts from 1 January 2016. With respect to Preexisting Accounts, Reporting Financial Institutions were required to complete the due diligence procedures on High Value Individual Accounts by 31 December 2016 and on Lower Value Individual Accounts and Entity Accounts by 31 December 2017.

Following the initial Global Forum peer review, the United Kingdom made various amendments to its legislative framework to address issues identified, the last of which was effective from 13 May 2020.

With respect to the exchange of information under the AEOI Standard, the United Kingdom:

- is a Party to the Convention on Mutual Administrative Assistance in Tax Matters and activated the associated CRS Multilateral Competent Authority Agreement in time for exchanges in 2017; and
- put in place 12 bilateral agreements.[1]

Detailed findings

The detailed findings for the United Kingdom are below, organised per Core Requirement (CR) and sub-requirement (SR), as extracted from the AEOI Terms of Reference (www.oecd.org/tax/transparency/documents/aeoi-terms-of-reference.pdf).

CR1 Domestic legal framework: Jurisdictions should have a domestic legislative framework in place that requires all Reporting Financial Institutions to conduct the due diligence and reporting procedures in the CRS, and that provides for the effective implementation of the CRS as set out therein.

Determination: In Place

The United Kingdom's domestic legislative framework is in place and contains all of the key aspects of the CRS and its Commentary requiring Reporting Financial Institutions to conduct the due diligence and reporting procedures (SRs 1.1 – 1.3). It also provides for a framework to enforce the requirements (SR 1.4).

SR 1.1 Jurisdictions should define the scope of Reporting Financial Institutions consistently with the CRS.

The United Kingdom has defined the scope of Reporting Financial Institutions in its domestic legislative framework in accordance with the CRS and its Commentary.

Recommendations:

No recommendations made.

SR 1.2 Jurisdictions should define the scope of Financial Accounts and Reportable Accounts consistently with the CRS and incorporate the due diligence procedures to identify them.

The United Kingdom has defined the scope of the Financial Accounts that are required to be reported in its domestic legislative framework and incorporated the due diligence procedures that must be applied to identify them in accordance with the CRS and its Commentary.

Recommendations:

No recommendations made.

SR 1.3 Jurisdictions should incorporate the reporting requirements contained in Section I of the CRS into their domestic legislative framework.

The United Kingdom has incorporated the reporting requirements in its domestic legislative framework in accordance with the CRS and its Commentary.

Recommendations:

No recommendations made.

SR 1.4 Jurisdictions should have a legislative framework in place that allows for the enforcement of the requirements of the CRS in practice.

The United Kingdom has a legislative framework in place to enforce the requirements in accordance with the CRS and its Commentary.

Recommendations:

No recommendations made.

CR2 International legal framework: Jurisdictions should have exchange relationships in effect with all Interested Appropriate Partners as committed to and that provide for the exchange of information in accordance with the Model CAA.

Determination: In Place

The United Kingdom's international legal framework to exchange the information is in place, is consistent with the Model CAA and its Commentary and provides for exchange with all of the United Kingdom's

Interested Appropriate Partners (i.e. all jurisdictions that are interested in receiving information from the United Kingdom and that meet the required standard in relation to confidentiality and data safeguards). (SRs 2.1 – 2.3)

SR 2.1 Jurisdictions should have exchange agreements in effect with all Interested Appropriate Partners that permit the automatic exchange of CRS information.

The United Kingdom has exchange agreements that permit the automatic exchange of CRS information in effect with all its Interested Appropriate Partners.

Recommendations:

No recommendations made.

SR 2.2 Such an exchange agreement should be put in place without undue delay, following the receipt of an expression of interest from an Interested Appropriate Partner.

The United Kingdom put in place its exchange agreements without undue delay.

Recommendations:

No recommendations made.

SR 2.3 Jurisdictions should ensure that the exchange agreements in effect provide for the exchange of information in accordance with the requirements of the Model CAA.

The United Kingdom's exchange agreements provide for the exchange of information in accordance with the requirements of the Model CAA.

Recommendations:

No recommendations made.

Comments by the assessed jurisdiction

No comments made.

Note

[1] With Anguilla, Bermuda, the British Virgin Islands, the Cayman Islands, Guernsey, Hong Kong (China), the Isle of Man, Jersey, Montserrat, Qatar, Singapore and the Turks and Caicos Islands. The United Kingdom has also activated a relationship under the CRS MCAA with Qatar.

Uruguay

Overall findings

Uruguay's legal framework implementing the AEOI Standard is in place but needs improvement in order to be fully consistent with the requirements of the AEOI Terms of Reference. While Uruguay's international legal framework to exchange the information with all of Uruguay's Interested Appropriate Partners (CR2) is consistent with the requirements, its domestic legislative framework requiring Reporting Financial Institutions to conduct the due diligence and reporting procedures (CR1) has deficiencies significant to the proper functioning of elements of the AEOI Standard. More specifically, some definitions necessary to define Reportable Financial Institutions and Financial Accounts are incomplete, and there are no rules to prevent the circumvention of the due diligence and reporting procedures.

The methodology used for the peer reviews and that therefore underpins this report is outlined in Chapter 2.

Overall determination on the legal framework: In Place But **Needs Improvement**

Conclusions on the legal framework

General context

Uruguay commenced exchanges under the AEOI Standard in 2018.

In order to provide for Reporting Financial Institutions to collect and report the information to be exchanged, Uruguay:

- enacted Decree 77/017, as amended by Decree Nº 243/2018;
- enacted DGI Resolution Nº 6396/2017 of 25 September, 2017;
- published Frequently Asked Questions, which are not legally binding; and
- made reference to Law 19.484 for purposes of the identification of Controlling Persons under the AEOI Standard.

Under this framework Reporting Financial Institutions were required to commence the due diligence procedures in relation to New Accounts from 1 January 2017. With respect to Preexisting Accounts, Reporting Financial Institutions were required to complete the due diligence procedures on High Value Individual Accounts by 31 December 2017 and on Lower Value Individual Accounts and Entity Accounts by 31 December 2018.

With respect to the exchange of information under the AEOI Standard, Uruguay is a Party to the Convention on Mutual Administrative Assistance in Tax Matters and activated the associated CRS Multilateral Competent Authority Agreement in time for exchanges in 2018.

Detailed findings

The detailed findings for Uruguay are below, organised per Core Requirement (CR) and sub-requirement (SR), as extracted from the AEOI Terms of Reference (www.oecd.org/tax/transparency/documents/aeoi-terms-of-reference.pdf).

CR1 Domestic legal framework: Jurisdictions should have a domestic legislative framework in place that requires all Reporting Financial Institutions to conduct the due diligence and reporting procedures in the CRS, and that provides for the effective implementation of the CRS as set out therein.

Determination: In Place But **Needs Improvement**

Uruguay's domestic legislative framework is in place and contains most of the key aspects of the CRS and its Commentary requiring Reporting Financial Institutions to conduct the due diligence and reporting procedures, but it needs improvement in relation to the scope of Reporting Financial Institutions required to report information (SR 1.1), the scope of Financial Accounts required to be reported (SR 1.2) and the framework to enforce the requirements (SR 1.4). Most significantly, it is not clear that fiscally transparent Reporting Financial Institutions are fully in scope, certain definitions related to Reportable Accounts are incomplete, and Uruguay's enforcement framework does not contain rules to prevent circumvention of due diligence and reporting obligations.

SR 1.1 Jurisdictions should define the scope of Reporting Financial Institutions consistently with the CRS.

Uruguay has defined the scope of Reporting Financial Institutions in its domestic legislative framework in a manner that is largely consistent with the CRS and its Commentary. However, deficiencies have been identified. Most significantly, Uruguay's legislative framework does not specify how the residence of a fiscally transparent Reporting Financial Institution is to be determined. The scope of Reporting Financial Institutions is material to the proper functioning of the AEOI Standard.

Recommendations:

Uruguay should amend its domestic legislative framework to ensure that the residency of a fiscally transparent Financial Institution is determined in accordance with the AEOI Standard.

Uruguay should amend its domestic legislative framework to require the term Investment Entity to be interpreted in accordance with similar language defining "financial institution" in the FATF Recommendations.

Uruguay should amend its domestic legislative framework to remove Health Insurance Companies from its jurisdiction-specific list of categories of Non-Reporting Financial Institutions as their characteristics are not substantially similar to those set out in the AEOI Standard.

SR 1.2 Jurisdictions should define the scope of Financial Accounts and Reportable Accounts consistently with the CRS and incorporate the due diligence procedures to identify them.

Uruguay has defined the scope of the Financial Accounts that are required to be reported in its domestic legislative framework and incorporated the due diligence procedures that must be applied to identify them in a manner that is largely consistent with the CRS and its Commentary. However, deficiencies have been identified. Most significantly, Uruguay's domestic legal framework does not fully incorporate the definitions of Entity, Equity Interest and Annuity Contract. The scope of Financial Accounts and the due diligence procedures are material to the proper functioning of the AEOI Standard.

Recommendations:

Uruguay should amend its domestic legislative framework to define Entity in accordance with the AEOI Standard.

Uruguay should amend its domestic legislative framework to define the term Equity Interest in the case of partnerships, in accordance with the AEOI Standard.

Uruguay should amend its domestic legislative framework to include the complete definition of the term Annuity Contract in accordance with the AEOI Standard.

Uruguay should amend its domestic legislative framework to remove three entries from its jurisdiction-specific list of categories of Excluded Accounts as they do not meet the requirements. These are: i) insurance contracts and ii) retirement account policies held by Uruguayan residents, and iii) Dormant Accounts.

SR 1.3 Jurisdictions should incorporate the reporting requirements contained in Section I of the CRS into their domestic legislative framework.

Uruguay has incorporated the reporting requirements in its domestic legislative framework in accordance with the CRS and its Commentary.

Recommendations:

No recommendations made.

SR 1.4 Jurisdictions should have a legislative framework in place that allows for the enforcement of the requirements of the CRS in practice.

Uruguay has a legislative framework in place to enforce the requirements in a manner that is largely consistent with the CRS and its Commentary. However, deficiencies have been identified. Most significantly, Uruguay's legislative framework does not include rules to prevent Financial Institutions, persons or intermediaries from adopting practices intended to circumvent the reporting and due diligence procedures as required. This is a key element to the required enforcement framework and is therefore material to the proper functioning of the AEOI Standard.

Recommendations:

Uruguay should amend its domestic legislative framework to introduce rules to prevent Financial Institutions, persons and intermediaries from adopting practices intended to circumvent the due diligence and reporting procedures.

Uruguay should amend its domestic legislative framework to require Reporting Financial Institutions to maintain records for at least five years from the deadline to report the information, rather than from when they file the report.

CR2 International legal framework: Jurisdictions should have exchange relationships in effect with all Interested Appropriate Partners as committed to and that provide for the exchange of information in accordance with the Model CAA.

Determination: In Place

Uruguay's international legal framework to exchange the information is in place, is consistent with the Model CAA and its Commentary and provides for exchange with all of Uruguay's Interested Appropriate Partners (i.e. all jurisdictions that are interested in receiving information from Uruguay and that meet the required standard in relation to confidentiality and data safeguards). (SRs 2.1 – 2.3)

SR 2.1 Jurisdictions should have exchange agreements in effect with all Interested Appropriate Partners that permit the automatic exchange of CRS information.

Uruguay has exchange agreements that permit the automatic exchange of CRS information in effect with all its Interested Appropriate Partners.

Recommendations:

No recommendations made.

SR 2.2 Such an exchange agreement should be put in place without undue delay, following the receipt of an expression of interest from an Interested Appropriate Partner.

Uruguay put in place its exchange agreements without undue delay.

Recommendations:

No recommendations made.

SR 2.3 Jurisdictions should ensure that the exchange agreements in effect provide for the exchange of information in accordance with the requirements of the Model CAA.

Uruguay's exchange agreements provide for the exchange of information in accordance with the requirements of the Model CAA.

Recommendations:

No recommendations made.

Comments by the assessed jurisdiction

No comments made.

Vanuatu

Overall findings

Vanuatu's legal framework implementing the AEOI Standard is in place and is consistent with the requirements of the AEOI Terms of Reference. This includes Vanuatu's domestic legislative framework requiring Reporting Financial Institutions to conduct the due diligence and reporting procedures (CR1) and its international legal framework to exchange the information with all of Vanuatu's Interested Appropriate Partners (CR2).

The methodology used for the peer reviews and that therefore underpins this report is outlined in Chapter 2.

Overall determination on the legal framework: In Place

Conclusions on the legal framework

General context

Vanuatu commenced exchanges under the AEOI Standard in 2018.

In order to provide for Reporting Financial Institutions to collect and report the information to be exchanged, Vanuatu:

- enacted International Tax Cooperation Act No. 7 of 2016 that was subsequently replaced by Tax Administration Act No. 37 of 2018 (with full effect from 1 January 2020);
- introduced Automatic Exchange of Information Regulations Order No. 76 of 2017 that was subsequently replaced by the Tax Administration Regulation Order No. 154 of 2019 (with full effect from 1 January 2020), as amended with effect from 14 September 2020; and
- issued further guidance, which is not legally binding.

Under this framework Reporting Financial Institutions were required to commence the due diligence procedures in relation to New Accounts from 30 June 2017. With respect to Preexisting Accounts, Reporting Financial Institutions were required to complete the due diligence procedures on High Value Individual Accounts by 31 December 2017 and on Lower Value Individual Accounts and Entity Accounts by 31 December 2018.

Following the initial Global Forum peer review, Vanuatu made various amendments to its legislative framework to address issues identified, the last of which was effective from 14 September 2020.

With respect to the exchange of information under the AEOI Standard, Vanuatu is a Party to the Convention on Mutual Administrative Assistance in Tax Matters and activated the associated CRS Multilateral Competent Authority Agreement in time for exchanges in 2018.

Detailed findings

The detailed findings for Vanuatu are below, organised per Core Requirement (CR) and sub-requirement (SR), as extracted from the AEOI Terms of Reference (www.oecd.org/tax/transparency/documents/aeoi-terms-of-reference.pdf).

CR1 Domestic legal framework: Jurisdictions should have a domestic legislative framework in place that requires all Reporting Financial Institutions to conduct the due diligence and reporting procedures in the CRS, and that provides for the effective implementation of the CRS as set out therein.

Determination: In Place

Vanuatu's domestic legislative framework is in place and contains all of the key aspects of the CRS and its Commentary requiring Reporting Financial Institutions to conduct the due diligence and reporting procedures (SRs 1.1 – 1.3). It also provides for a framework to enforce the requirements (SR 1.4).

SR 1.1 Jurisdictions should define the scope of Reporting Financial Institutions consistently with the CRS.

Vanuatu has defined the scope of Reporting Financial Institutions in its domestic legislative framework in accordance with the CRS and its Commentary.

Recommendations:

No recommendations made.

SR 1.2 Jurisdictions should define the scope of Financial Accounts and Reportable Accounts consistently with the CRS and incorporate the due diligence procedures to identify them.

Vanuatu has defined the scope of the Financial Accounts that are required to be reported in its domestic legislative framework and incorporated the due diligence procedures that must be applied to identify them in accordance with the CRS and its Commentary.

Recommendations:

No recommendations made.

SR 1.3 Jurisdictions should incorporate the reporting requirements contained in Section I of the CRS into their domestic legislative framework.

Vanuatu has incorporated the reporting requirements in its domestic legislative framework in accordance with the CRS and its Commentary.

Recommendations:

No recommendations made.

SR 1.4 Jurisdictions should have a legislative framework in place that allows for the enforcement of the requirements of the CRS in practice.

Vanuatu has a legislative framework in place to enforce the requirements in accordance with the CRS and its Commentary.

Recommendations:

No recommendations made.

CR2 International legal framework: Jurisdictions should have exchange relationships in effect with all Interested Appropriate Partners as committed to and that provide for the exchange of information in accordance with the Model CAA.

Determination: In Place

Vanuatu's international legal framework to exchange the information is in place, is consistent with the Model CAA and its Commentary and provides for exchange with all of Vanuatu's Interested Appropriate

Partners (i.e. all jurisdictions that are interested in receiving information from Vanuatu and that meet the required standard in relation to confidentiality and data safeguards). (SRs 2.1 – 2.3)

SR 2.1 Jurisdictions should have exchange agreements in effect with all Interested Appropriate Partners that permit the automatic exchange of CRS information.

Vanuatu has exchange agreements that permit the automatic exchange of CRS information in effect with all its Interested Appropriate Partners.

Recommendations:

No recommendations made.

SR 2.2 Such an exchange agreement should be put in place without undue delay, following the receipt of an expression of interest from an Interested Appropriate Partner.

Vanuatu put in place its exchange agreements without undue delay.

Recommendations:

No recommendations made.

SR 2.3 Jurisdictions should ensure that the exchange agreements in effect provide for the exchange of information in accordance with the requirements of the Model CAA.

Vanuatu's exchange agreements provide for the exchange of information in accordance with the requirements of the Model CAA.

Recommendations:

No recommendations made.

Comments by the assessed jurisdiction

Vanuatu thanks the Global Forum and its staff for the assistance and support given to us to ensure that Vanuatu's legal framework is in place.

Vanuatu is committed to meeting our international obligations and will work with the Global Forum into the future to ensure our framework stays compliant with international best practice.

Annex A. Assessments carried out under the Staged Approach

For all of the requirements of the AEOI Standard to be properly assessed, the peer reviews would have to be delayed until the exchanges had been routinely taking place for some time. The Global Forum therefore put in place a "Staged Approach" to monitor, assess and assist in the implementation of the AEOI Standard, while it was being implemented.

Of central importance to the approach was the concept that, by looking early in the implementation process at the areas that could be assessed in advance of exchanges taking place, any issues with respect to key areas of implementation could be quickly identified and addressed. This was to help ensure the effective implementation of the AEOI Standard from the start.

Recent years have therefore seen various monitoring and assistance activities being carried out by the Global Forum, with the peer review elements being separated into modules. The diagram below depicts each module of the Staged Approach, including the timings with respect to the jurisdictions committed to commence exchanges from 2017 or 2018. The individual modules are described in more detail below.

Figure A A.1. The Staged Approach to the AEOI assessment process

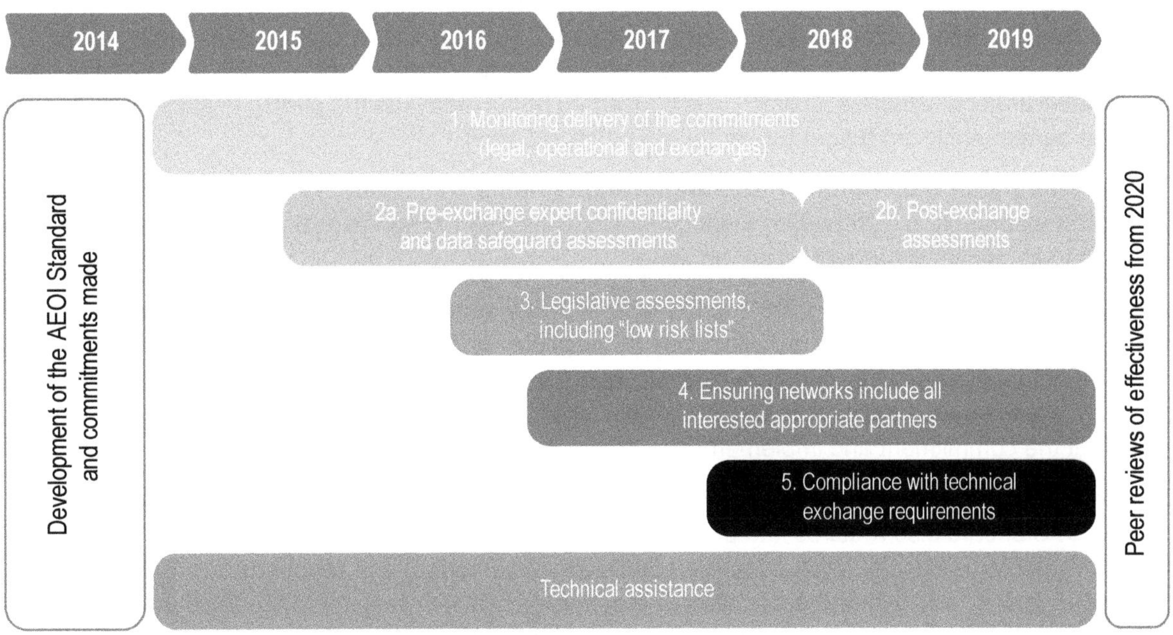

Source: Secretariat of the Global Forum on Transparency and Exchange of Information for Tax Purposes.

Individual modules of the Staged Approach

1. Commitments and monitoring implementation: Every jurisdiction that commits to implement the AEOI Standard are tracked with respect to all of the key implementation milestones, with jurisdictions providing regular updates to the Global Forum on their progress. The results of this process have been used to provide regular internal monitoring reports to Global Forum members and to the G20, as well as to produce this report. The tracking of key milestones also allows the identification of assistance needs, such as on domestic legislation, international agreements, information technology systems and administrative infrastructure.

2. Expert confidentiality and data safeguard assessments: Vital to the exchange of information is the security of the information being exchange. Legal and operational frameworks must therefore be in place to keep the information exchanged confidential and properly safeguarded. An expert panel from member jurisdictions conduct pre-exchange assessments to ensure jurisdictions meet the confidentiality and data safeguard requirements, prior to them exchanging information. The Global Forum provides assistance where issues are identified. Post-exchange reviews, including of the operational frameworks actually used for the exchanges, are also underway for all jurisdictions exchanging information, to provide assurance that the requirements continue to be met.

3. Legislative assessments, including low-risk lists: Every jurisdiction must also introduce a legislative framework to ensure Reporting Financial Institutions conduct the required due diligence and reporting procedures, as well as a framework for enforcement. Each jurisdiction's domestic legislative framework is therefore peer reviewed once it is put in place (i.e. even before exchanges commence). This includes a legislative gap analysis to ensure all of the key elements of the AEOI Standard are incorporated and an assessment of each jurisdiction's lists of Non-Reporting Financial Institutions and Excluded Accounts to ensure their conformity with the AEOI Standard. Where gaps are found, recommendations are made.

4. Ensuring networks include all interested appropriate partners: Reviewing the exchange agreements being put in place is also a key component of the monitoring and review processes. This ensures the delivery by each jurisdiction of its commitment to exchange information with "all Interested Appropriate Partners". Where a jurisdiction is concerned about delays to the putting in place of a particular exchange agreement it can trigger a peer review of the situation.

5. Compliance with the technical exchange requirements: Ultimately, jurisdictions must collect the actual information from the Reporting Financial Institutions and exchange it. Each jurisdiction's technical readiness to exchange is therefore also monitored.

Technical assistance: Realising the full benefits of AEOI requires as many jurisdictions as possible implementing the AEOI Standard as effectively as possible. This requires assistance to be given where needed. Ensuring developing countries can access the benefits the AEOI Standard has to offer, in particular, often requires significant support. The Global Forum therefore provides technical assistance throughout the commitment and implementation process.

Reviews of the effectiveness of the implementation of the AEOI Standard: Securing the full benefits of the AEOI Standard also requires it to be operating effectively in practice, including that jurisdictions are ensuring Reporting Financial Institutions are effectively implementing the requirements. With exchanges now fully underway, and with the publication of the conclusions with respect to the legal frameworks, the peer reviews with respect to the effectiveness of the implementation of the AEOI Standard in practice have commenced. The first results are expected to be published in 2022.

Annex B. Details of the exchange agreements in place

The table below presents information on all of the exchange agreements in place with respect to the AEOI Standard by the Assessed Jurisdictions. This includes agreements activated through multilateral frameworks (such as the CRS Multilateral Competent Authority Agreement or in a European Union context) as well as bilateral agreements.

Jurisdiction	Exchange agreements in place:
Albania (88)	Andorra, Anguilla, Antigua and Barbuda, Argentina, Australia, Austria, Azerbaijan, Belgium, Brazil, British Virgin Islands, Bulgaria, Cayman Islands, Chile, China, Colombia, Cook Islands, Costa Rica, Croatia, Curaçao, Cyprus, Czech Republic, Denmark, Dominica, Ecuador, Estonia, Faroe Islands, Finland, France, Germany, Ghana, Gibraltar, Greece, Greenland, Grenada, Guernsey, Hong Kong, China, Hungary, Iceland, India, Indonesia, Ireland, Isle of Man, Israel, Italy, Japan, Jersey, Korea, Kuwait, Latvia, Liechtenstein, Lithuania, Luxembourg, Macau, China, Malaysia, Malta, Mauritius, Mexico, Montserrat, Nauru, Netherlands, New Caledonia, New Zealand, Nigeria, Norway, Pakistan, Peru, Poland, Portugal, Romania, Russia, Saint Lucia, Saint Vincent and the Grenadines, San Marino, Saudi Arabia, Seychelles, Singapore, Slovak Republic, Slovenia, South Africa, Spain, Sweden, Switzerland, Turkey, Turks and Caicos Islands, United Arab Emirates, United Kingdom, Uruguay, Vanuatu
Andorra (86)	Albania, Anguilla, Antigua and Barbuda, Argentina, Australia, Austria, Azerbaijan, Belgium, Bermuda, Brazil, British Virgin Islands, Bulgaria, Canada, Cayman Islands, Chile, China, Colombia, Cook Islands, Costa Rica, Croatia, Curaçao, Cyprus, Czech Republic, Denmark, Estonia, Faroe Islands, Finland, France, Germany, Ghana, Gibraltar, Greece, Greenland, Grenada, Guernsey, Hong Kong, China, Hungary, Iceland, India, Indonesia, Ireland, Isle of Man, Israel, Italy, Japan, Jersey, Korea, Kuwait, Latvia, Liechtenstein, Lithuania, Luxembourg, Malaysia, Malta, Mauritius, Mexico, Monaco, Montserrat, Nauru, Netherlands, New Zealand, Nigeria, Norway, Pakistan, Panama, Poland, Portugal, Romania, Russia, Saint Lucia, Saint Vincent and the Grenadines, San Marino, Saudi Arabia, Seychelles, Singapore, Slovak Republic, Slovenia, South Africa, Spain, Sweden, Switzerland, Turkey, Turks and Caicos Islands, United Arab Emirates, United Kingdom, Uruguay
Anguilla (58)	Albania, Andorra, Argentina, Australia, Austria, Belgium, Brazil, Canada, Chile, China, Colombia, Croatia, Curaçao, Cyprus, Czech Republic, Denmark, Estonia, Faroe Islands, Finland, France, Germany, Greece, Greenland, Hungary, Iceland, India, Indonesia, Ireland, Italy, Japan, Korea, Latvia, Liechtenstein, Lithuania, Luxembourg, Malaysia, Malta, Mauritius, Mexico, Monaco, Netherlands, New Zealand, Norway, Pakistan, Poland, Portugal, San Marino, Saudi Arabia, Seychelles, Singapore, Slovak Republic, Slovenia, South Africa, Spain, Sweden, Switzerland, United Kingdom, Uruguay
Antigua and Barbuda (86)	Albania, Andorra, Argentina, Aruba, Australia, Austria, Bahamas, Bahrain, Barbados, Belgium, Belize, Bermuda, Brazil, British Virgin Islands, Brunei Darussalam, Bulgaria, Canada, Cayman Islands, Chile, China, Colombia, Cook Islands, Costa Rica, Croatia, Curaçao, Cyprus, Czech Republic, Denmark, Dominica, Estonia, Faroe Islands, Finland, France, Germany, Gibraltar, Greece, Greenland, Grenada, Guernsey, Hong Kong, China, Hungary, Iceland, India, Indonesia, Ireland, Isle of Man, Israel, Italy, Japan, Jersey, Korea, Kuwait, Latvia, Liechtenstein, Lithuania, Luxembourg, Malaysia, Malta, Mauritius, Mexico, Montserrat, Nauru, Netherlands, New Zealand, Norway, Panama, Poland, Portugal, Romania, Russia, Saint Lucia, Saint Vincent and the Grenadines, San Marino, Saudi Arabia, Seychelles, Singapore, Slovak Republic, Slovenia, South Africa, Spain, Sweden, Switzerland, Turks and Caicos Islands, United Arab Emirates, United Kingdom, Uruguay
Argentina (103)	Albania, Andorra, Anguilla, Antigua and Barbuda, Aruba, Australia, Austria, Azerbaijan, Bahamas, Bahrain, Barbados, Belgium, Belize, Bermuda, Brazil, British Virgin Islands, Brunei Darussalam, Bulgaria, Canada, Cayman Islands, Chile, China, Colombia, Cook Islands, Costa Rica, Croatia, Curaçao, Cyprus, Czech Republic, Denmark, Dominica, Ecuador, Estonia, Faroe Islands, Finland, France, Germany, Ghana, Gibraltar, Greece, Greenland, Grenada, Guernsey, Hong Kong, China, Hungary, Iceland, India, Indonesia, Ireland, Isle of Man, Israel, Italy, Japan, Jersey, Korea, Kuwait, Latvia, Lebanon, Liechtenstein, Lithuania, Luxembourg, Macau, China, Malaysia, Malta, Marshall Islands, Mauritius, Mexico, Monaco, Montserrat, Nauru, Netherlands, New Caledonia, New Zealand, Nigeria, Norway, Pakistan, Panama, Peru, Poland, Portugal, Qatar, Romania, Russia, Saint Kitts and Nevis, Saint Lucia, Saint Vincent and the Grenadines, Samoa, San Marino, Saudi Arabia, Seychelles, Singapore, Slovak Republic, Slovenia, South Africa, Spain, Sweden, Switzerland, Turkey, Turks and Caicos Islands, United Arab Emirates, United Kingdom, Uruguay, Vanuatu
Aruba (66)	Antigua and Barbuda, Argentina, Australia, Austria, Azerbaijan, Barbados, Belgium, Brazil, Canada, Chile, China, Colombia, Cook Islands, Croatia, Czech Republic, Denmark, Estonia, Faroe Islands, Finland, France, Germany, Gibraltar,

Jurisdiction	Exchange agreements in place:
	Greece, Greenland, Guernsey, Hungary, Iceland, India, Indonesia, Ireland, Isle of Man, Israel, Italy, Japan, Jersey, Korea, Latvia, Liechtenstein, Lithuania, Luxembourg, Malaysia, Malta, Mauritius, Mexico, Monaco, New Zealand, Norway, Pakistan, Panama, Poland, Portugal, Russia, Saint Lucia, San Marino, Saudi Arabia, Seychelles, Singapore, Slovak Republic, Slovenia, South Africa, Spain, Sweden, Switzerland, Turkey, United Kingdom, Uruguay
Australia (103)	Albania, Andorra, Anguilla, Antigua and Barbuda, Argentina, Aruba, Austria, Azerbaijan, Bahamas, Bahrain, Barbados, Belgium, Belize, Bermuda, Brazil, British Virgin Islands, Brunei Darussalam, Bulgaria, Canada, Cayman Islands, Chile, China, Colombia, Cook Islands, Costa Rica, Croatia, Curaçao, Cyprus, Czech Republic, Denmark, Dominica, Ecuador, Estonia, Faroe Islands, Finland, France, Germany, Ghana, Gibraltar, Greece, Greenland, Grenada, Guernsey, Hong Kong, China, Hungary, Iceland, India, Indonesia, Ireland, Isle of Man, Israel, Italy, Japan, Jersey, Korea, Kuwait, Latvia, Lebanon, Liechtenstein, Lithuania, Luxembourg, Macau, China, Malaysia, Malta, Marshall Islands, Mauritius, Mexico, Monaco, Montserrat, Nauru, Netherlands, New Caledonia, New Zealand, Nigeria, Norway, Pakistan, Panama, Peru, Poland, Portugal, Qatar, Romania, Russia, Saint Kitts and Nevis, Saint Lucia, Saint Vincent and the Grenadines, Samoa, San Marino, Saudi Arabia, Seychelles, Singapore, Slovak Republic, Slovenia, South Africa, Spain, Sweden, Switzerland, Turkey, Turks and Caicos Islands, United Arab Emirates, United Kingdom, Uruguay, Vanuatu
Austria (102)	Albania, Andorra, Anguilla, Antigua and Barbuda, Argentina, Aruba, Australia, Azerbaijan, Bahamas, Bahrain, Barbados, Belgium, Belize, Bermuda, Brazil, British Virgin Islands, Brunei Darussalam, Bulgaria, Canada, Cayman Islands, Chile, China, Colombia, Cook Islands, Costa Rica, Croatia, Curaçao, Cyprus, Czech Republic, Denmark, Dominica, Ecuador, Estonia, Faroe Islands, Finland, France, Germany, Ghana, Gibraltar, Greece, Greenland, Grenada, Guernsey, Hong Kong, China, Hungary, Iceland, India, Indonesia, Ireland, Isle of Man, Israel, Italy, Japan, Jersey, Korea, Kuwait, Latvia, Lebanon, Liechtenstein, Lithuania, Luxembourg, Macau, China, Malaysia, Malta, Marshall Islands, Mauritius, Mexico, Monaco, Montserrat, Nauru, Netherlands, New Zealand, Nigeria, Niue, Norway, Pakistan, Panama, Poland, Portugal, Qatar, Romania, Russia, Saint Kitts and Nevis, Saint Lucia, Saint Vincent and the Grenadines, Samoa, San Marino, Saudi Arabia, Seychelles, Singapore, Slovak Republic, Slovenia, South Africa, Spain, Sweden, Switzerland, Turkey, Turks and Caicos Islands, United Arab Emirates, United Kingdom, Uruguay, Vanuatu
Azerbaijan (93)	Albania, Andorra, Argentina, Aruba, Australia, Austria, Bahamas, Bahrain, Belgium, Belize, Bermuda, Brazil, British Virgin Islands, Bulgaria, Canada, Cayman Islands, Chile, China, Colombia, Cook Islands, Costa Rica, Croatia, Curaçao, Cyprus, Czech Republic, Denmark, Estonia, Faroe Islands, Finland, France, Germany, Ghana, Gibraltar, Greece, Greenland, Grenada, Guernsey, Hong Kong, China, Hungary, Iceland, India, Indonesia, Ireland, Isle of Man, Israel, Italy, Japan, Jersey, Korea, Kuwait, Latvia, Lebanon, Liechtenstein, Lithuania, Luxembourg, Macau, China, Malaysia, Malta, Marshall Islands, Mauritius, Mexico, Monaco, Nauru, Netherlands, New Zealand, Nigeria, Norway, Pakistan, Panama, Poland, Portugal, Qatar, Romania, Russia, Saint Kitts and Nevis, Saint Lucia, Saint Vincent and the Grenadines, Samoa, San Marino, Saudi Arabia, Seychelles, Singapore, Slovak Republic, Slovenia, South Africa, Spain, Sweden, Switzerland, Turkey, Turks and Caicos Islands, United Arab Emirates, United Kingdom, Uruguay
Bahamas (65)	Antigua and Barbuda, Argentina, Australia, Austria, Azerbaijan, Belgium, Brazil, Canada, Chile, China, Colombia, Costa Rica, Croatia, Cyprus, Czech Republic, Denmark, Estonia, Faroe Islands, Finland, France, Germany, Gibraltar, Greece, Greenland, Grenada, Guernsey, Hong Kong, China, Hungary, Iceland, India, Indonesia, Ireland, Isle of Man, Israel, Italy, Japan, Jersey, Korea, Latvia, Liechtenstein, Lithuania, Luxembourg, Malaysia, Malta, Mauritius, Mexico, Monaco, Netherlands, New Zealand, Norway, Panama, Poland, Portugal, Russia, Saudi Arabia, Seychelles, Singapore, Slovak Republic, Slovenia, South Africa, Spain, Sweden, Switzerland, United Kingdom, Uruguay
Bahrain (64)	Antigua and Barbuda, Argentina, Australia, Austria, Azerbaijan, Barbados, Belgium, Brazil, Canada, Chile, China, Colombia, Cook Islands, Costa Rica, Croatia, Curaçao, Cyprus, Czech Republic, Denmark, Estonia, Faroe Islands, Finland, France, Germany, Gibraltar, Greece, Greenland, Grenada, Guernsey, Hungary, Iceland, India, Indonesia, Ireland, Isle of Man, Italy, Japan, Jersey, Korea, Latvia, Lithuania, Luxembourg, Malaysia, Malta, Mauritius, Mexico, Netherlands, New Zealand, Norway, Pakistan, Poland, Portugal, Russia, Saudi Arabia, Seychelles, Singapore, Slovak Republic, Slovenia, South Africa, Spain, Sweden, Switzerland, United Kingdom, Uruguay
Barbados (79)	Antigua and Barbuda, Argentina, Aruba, Australia, Austria, Bahrain, Belgium, Belize, Bermuda, Brazil, British Virgin Islands, Bulgaria, Canada, Cayman Islands, Chile, China, Colombia, Cook Islands, Costa Rica, Croatia, Curaçao, Cyprus, Czech Republic, Denmark, Dominica, Estonia, Faroe Islands, Finland, France, Germany, Gibraltar, Greece, Greenland, Guernsey, Hungary, Iceland, India, Indonesia, Ireland, Isle of Man, Israel, Italy, Japan, Jersey, Korea, Kuwait, Latvia, Lithuania, Luxembourg, Malaysia, Malta, Mauritius, Mexico, Montserrat, Netherlands, New Zealand, Norway, Panama, Poland, Portugal, Qatar, Romania, Russia, Saint Kitts and Nevis, Saint Lucia, Saint Vincent and the Grenadines, San Marino, Saudi Arabia, Seychelles, Singapore, Slovak Republic, Slovenia, South Africa, Spain, Sweden, Switzerland, United Kingdom, Uruguay, Vanuatu
Belgium (105)	Albania, Andorra, Anguilla, Antigua and Barbuda, Argentina, Aruba, Australia, Austria, Azerbaijan, Bahamas, Bahrain, Barbados, Belize, Bermuda, Brazil, British Virgin Islands, Brunei Darussalam, Bulgaria, Canada, Cayman Islands, Chile, China, Colombia, Cook Islands, Costa Rica, Croatia, Curaçao, Cyprus, Czech Republic, Denmark, Dominica, Ecuador, Estonia, Faroe Islands, Finland, France, Germany, Ghana, Gibraltar, Greece, Greenland, Grenada, Guernsey, Hong Kong, China, Hungary, Iceland, India, Indonesia, Ireland, Isle of Man, Israel, Italy, Japan, Jersey, Korea, Kuwait, Latvia, Lebanon, Liechtenstein, Lithuania, Luxembourg, Macau, China, Malaysia, Malta, Marshall Islands, Mauritius, Mexico, Monaco, Montserrat, Nauru, Netherlands, New Caledonia, New Zealand, Nigeria, Niue, Norway, Oman, Pakistan, Panama, Peru, Poland, Portugal, Qatar, Romania, Russia, Saint Kitts and Nevis, Saint Lucia, Saint Vincent and the Grenadines, Samoa, San Marino, Saudi Arabia, Seychelles, Singapore, Slovak Republic, Slovenia, South Africa, Spain, Sweden, Switzerland,

Jurisdiction	Exchange agreements in place:
	Turkey, Turks and Caicos Islands, United Arab Emirates, United Kingdom, Uruguay, Vanuatu
Belize (69)	Antigua and Barbuda, Argentina, Australia, Austria, Azerbaijan, Barbados, Belgium, Brazil, Canada, Chile, China, Colombia, Cook Islands, Costa Rica, Croatia, Curaçao, Cyprus, Czech Republic, Denmark, Estonia, Faroe Islands, Finland, France, Germany, Gibraltar, Greece, Greenland, Grenada, Guernsey, Hungary, Iceland, India, Indonesia, Ireland, Isle of Man, Israel, Italy, Japan, Jersey, Korea, Latvia, Liechtenstein, Lithuania, Luxembourg, Malaysia, Malta, Mauritius, Mexico, Netherlands, New Zealand, Norway, Pakistan, Panama, Poland, Portugal, Russia, Saint Lucia, San Marino, Saudi Arabia, Seychelles, Singapore, Slovak Republic, Slovenia, South Africa, Spain, Sweden, Switzerland, United Kingdom, Uruguay
Bermuda (68)	Andorra, Antigua and Barbuda, Argentina, Australia, Austria, Azerbaijan, Barbados, Belgium, Brazil, Canada, Chile, China, Colombia, Cook Islands, Croatia, Cyprus, Czech Republic, Denmark, Estonia, Faroe Islands, Finland, France, Germany, Greece, Greenland, Guernsey, Hong Kong, China, Hungary, Iceland, India, Indonesia, Ireland, Israel, Italy, Japan, Jersey, Korea, Latvia, Liechtenstein, Lithuania, Luxembourg, Malaysia, Malta, Mauritius, Mexico, Monaco, Netherlands, New Zealand, Norway, Pakistan, Panama, Poland, Portugal, Russia, Saint Lucia, San Marino, Saudi Arabia, Seychelles, Singapore, Slovak Republic, Slovenia, South Africa, Spain, Sweden, Switzerland, Turkey, United Kingdom, Uruguay
Brazil (102)	Albania, Andorra, Anguilla, Antigua and Barbuda, Argentina, Aruba, Australia, Austria, Azerbaijan, Bahamas, Bahrain, Barbados, Belgium, Belize, Bermuda, British Virgin Islands, Brunei Darussalam, Bulgaria, Canada, Cayman Islands, Chile, China, Colombia, Cook Islands, Costa Rica, Croatia, Curaçao, Cyprus, Czech Republic, Denmark, Dominica, Ecuador, Estonia, Faroe Islands, Finland, France, Germany, Ghana, Gibraltar, Greece, Greenland, Grenada, Guernsey, Hong Kong, China, Hungary, Iceland, India, Indonesia, Ireland, Isle of Man, Israel, Italy, Japan, Jersey, Korea, Kuwait, Latvia, Lebanon, Liechtenstein, Lithuania, Luxembourg, Macau, China, Malaysia, Malta, Marshall Islands, Mauritius, Mexico, Monaco, Montserrat, Nauru, Netherlands, New Zealand, Nigeria, Norway, Pakistan, Panama, Peru, Poland, Portugal, Qatar, Romania, Russia, Saint Kitts and Nevis, Saint Lucia, Saint Vincent and the Grenadines, Samoa, San Marino, Saudi Arabia, Seychelles, Singapore, Slovak Republic, Slovenia, South Africa, Spain, Sweden, Switzerland, Turkey, Turks and Caicos Islands, United Arab Emirates, United Kingdom, Uruguay, Vanuatu
British Virgin Islands (72)	Albania, Andorra, Antigua and Barbuda, Argentina, Australia, Austria, Azerbaijan, Barbados, Belgium, Brazil, Canada, Chile, China, Colombia, Cook Islands, Costa Rica, Croatia, Curaçao, Cyprus, Czech Republic, Denmark, Ecuador, Estonia, Faroe Islands, Finland, France, Germany, Greece, Greenland, Grenada, Guernsey, Hong Kong, China, Hungary, Iceland, India, Indonesia, Ireland, Israel, Italy, Japan, Korea, Latvia, Liechtenstein, Lithuania, Luxembourg, Malaysia, Malta, Mauritius, Mexico, Monaco, Netherlands, New Zealand, Norway, Pakistan, Panama, Poland, Portugal, Russia, Saint Lucia, San Marino, Saudi Arabia, Seychelles, Singapore, Slovak Republic, Slovenia, South Africa, Spain, Sweden, Switzerland, Turkey, United Kingdom, Uruguay
Brunei Darussalam (52)	Antigua and Barbuda, Argentina, Australia, Austria, Belgium, Brazil, Chile, China, Colombia, Costa Rica, Croatia, Cyprus, Czech Republic, Denmark, Estonia, Faroe Islands, Finland, France, Germany, Gibraltar, Greece, Guernsey, Hong Kong, China, Hungary, Indonesia, Ireland, Isle of Man, Italy, Japan, Jersey, Korea, Liechtenstein, Luxembourg, Malta, Netherlands, New Zealand, Norway, Poland, Portugal, Saint Lucia, San Marino, Saudi Arabia, Singapore, Slovak Republic, Slovenia, South Africa, Spain, Sweden, Switzerland, Turkey, United Kingdom, Uruguay
Bulgaria (76)	Albania, Andorra, Antigua and Barbuda, Argentina, Australia, Austria, Azerbaijan, Barbados, Belgium, Brazil, Canada, Chile, China, Colombia, Cook Islands, Costa Rica, Croatia, Curaçao, Cyprus, Czech Republic, Denmark, Estonia, Faroe Islands, Finland, France, Germany, Gibraltar, Greece, Greenland, Grenada, Guernsey, Hong Kong, China, Hungary, Iceland, India, Indonesia, Ireland, Isle of Man, Israel, Italy, Japan, Jersey, Korea, Latvia, Liechtenstein, Lithuania, Luxembourg, Malaysia, Malta, Mauritius, Mexico, Monaco, Netherlands, New Zealand, Norway, Pakistan, Panama, Peru, Poland, Portugal, Romania, Russia, Saint Lucia, San Marino, Saudi Arabia, Seychelles, Singapore, Slovak Republic, Slovenia, South Africa, Spain, Sweden, Switzerland, Turkey, United Kingdom, Uruguay
Canada (91)	Andorra, Anguilla, Antigua and Barbuda, Argentina, Aruba, Australia, Austria, Azerbaijan, Bahamas, Bahrain, Barbados, Belgium, Belize, Bermuda, Brazil, British Virgin Islands, Bulgaria, Cayman Islands, Chile, China, Colombia, Cook Islands, Costa Rica, Croatia, Curaçao, Cyprus, Czech Republic, Denmark, Estonia, Faroe Islands, Finland, France, Germany, Gibraltar, Greece, Greenland, Grenada, Guernsey, Hong Kong, China, Hungary, Iceland, India, Indonesia, Ireland, Isle of Man, Israel, Italy, Japan, Jersey, Korea, Kuwait, Latvia, Lebanon, Liechtenstein, Lithuania, Luxembourg, Macau, China, Malaysia, Malta, Marshall Islands, Mauritius, Mexico, Monaco, Montserrat, Nauru, Netherlands, New Zealand, Norway, Panama, Poland, Portugal, Romania, Saint Kitts and Nevis, Saint Lucia, Saint Vincent and the Grenadines, Samoa, San Marino, Seychelles, Singapore, Slovak Republic, Slovenia, South Africa, Spain, Sweden, Switzerland, Turkey, Turks and Caicos Islands, United Arab Emirates, United Kingdom, Uruguay, Vanuatu
Cayman Islands (74)	Albania, Andorra, Antigua and Barbuda, Argentina, Australia, Austria, Azerbaijan, Barbados, Belgium, Brazil, Canada, Chile, China, Colombia, Cook Islands, Costa Rica, Croatia, Curaçao, Cyprus, Czech Republic, Denmark, Ecuador, Estonia, Faroe Islands, Finland, France, Germany, Greece, Greenland, Grenada, Guernsey, Hong Kong, China, Hungary, Iceland, India, Indonesia, Ireland, Isle of Man, Israel, Italy, Japan, Korea, Latvia, Liechtenstein, Lithuania, Luxembourg, Malaysia, Malta, Mauritius, Mexico, Monaco, Netherlands, New Zealand, Norway, Pakistan, Panama, Peru, Poland, Portugal, Russia, Saint Lucia, San Marino, Saudi Arabia, Seychelles, Singapore, Slovak Republic, Slovenia, South Africa, Spain, Sweden, Switzerland, Turkey, United Kingdom, Uruguay
Chile (103)	Albania, Andorra, Anguilla, Antigua and Barbuda, Argentina, Aruba, Australia, Austria, Azerbaijan, Bahamas, Bahrain, Barbados, Belgium, Belize, Bermuda, Brazil, British Virgin Islands, Brunei Darussalam, Bulgaria, Canada, Cayman Islands,

Jurisdiction	Exchange agreements in place:
	China, Colombia, Cook Islands, Costa Rica, Croatia, Curaçao, Cyprus, Czech Republic, Denmark, Dominica, Ecuador, Estonia, Faroe Islands, Finland, France, Germany, Ghana, Gibraltar, Greece, Greenland, Grenada, Guernsey, Hong Kong, China, Hungary, Iceland, India, Indonesia, Ireland, Isle of Man, Israel, Italy, Japan, Jersey, Korea, Kuwait, Latvia, Lebanon, Liechtenstein, Lithuania, Luxembourg, Macau, China, Malaysia, Malta, Marshall Islands, Mauritius, Mexico, Monaco, Montserrat, Nauru, Netherlands, New Caledonia, New Zealand, Nigeria, Norway, Pakistan, Panama, Peru, Poland, Portugal, Qatar, Romania, Russia, Saint Kitts and Nevis, Saint Lucia, Saint Vincent and the Grenadines, Samoa, San Marino, Saudi Arabia, Seychelles, Singapore, Slovak Republic, Slovenia, South Africa, Spain, Sweden, Switzerland, Turkey, Turks and Caicos Islands, United Arab Emirates, United Kingdom, Uruguay, Vanuatu
China (101)	Albania, Andorra, Anguilla, Antigua and Barbuda, Argentina, Aruba, Australia, Austria, Azerbaijan, Bahamas, Bahrain, Barbados, Belgium, Belize, Bermuda, Brazil, British Virgin Islands, Brunei Darussalam, Bulgaria, Canada, Cayman Islands, Chile, Colombia, Cook Islands, Costa Rica, Croatia, Curaçao, Cyprus, Czech Republic, Denmark, Dominica, Ecuador, Estonia, Faroe Islands, Finland, France, Germany, Ghana, Gibraltar, Greece, Greenland, Grenada, Guernsey, Hong Kong, China, Hungary, Iceland, India, Indonesia, Ireland, Isle of Man, Israel, Italy, Japan, Jersey, Korea, Kuwait, Latvia, Lebanon, Liechtenstein, Lithuania, Luxembourg, Malaysia, Malta, Marshall Islands, Mauritius, Mexico, Monaco, Montserrat, Nauru, Netherlands, New Zealand, Nigeria, Norway, Oman, Pakistan, Panama, Poland, Portugal, Qatar, Romania, Russia, Saint Kitts and Nevis, Saint Lucia, Saint Vincent and the Grenadines, Samoa, San Marino, Saudi Arabia, Seychelles, Singapore, Slovak Republic, Slovenia, South Africa, Spain, Sweden, Switzerland, Turkey, Turks and Caicos Islands, United Arab Emirates, United Kingdom, Uruguay, Vanuatu
Colombia (103)	Albania, Andorra, Anguilla, Antigua and Barbuda, Argentina, Aruba, Australia, Austria, Azerbaijan, Bahamas, Bahrain, Barbados, Belgium, Belize, Bermuda, Brazil, British Virgin Islands, Brunei Darussalam, Bulgaria, Canada, Cayman Islands, Chile, China, Cook Islands, Costa Rica, Croatia, Curaçao, Cyprus, Czech Republic, Denmark, Dominica, Ecuador, Estonia, Faroe Islands, Finland, France, Germany, Ghana, Gibraltar, Greece, Greenland, Grenada, Guernsey, Hong Kong, China, Hungary, Iceland, India, Indonesia, Ireland, Isle of Man, Israel, Italy, Japan, Jersey, Korea, Kuwait, Latvia, Lebanon, Liechtenstein, Lithuania, Luxembourg, Macau, China, Malaysia, Malta, Marshall Islands, Mauritius, Mexico, Monaco, Montserrat, Nauru, Netherlands, New Caledonia, New Zealand, Nigeria, Norway, Pakistan, Panama, Peru, Poland, Portugal, Qatar, Romania, Russia, Saint Kitts and Nevis, Saint Lucia, Saint Vincent and the Grenadines, Samoa, San Marino, Saudi Arabia, Seychelles, Singapore, Slovak Republic, Slovenia, South Africa, Spain, Sweden, Switzerland, Turkey, Turks and Caicos Islands, United Arab Emirates, United Kingdom, Uruguay, Vanuatu
Cook Islands (90)	Albania, Andorra, Antigua and Barbuda, Argentina, Aruba, Australia, Austria, Azerbaijan, Bahrain, Barbados, Belgium, Belize, Bermuda, Brazil, British Virgin Islands, Bulgaria, Canada, Cayman Islands, Chile, China, Colombia, Costa Rica, Croatia, Curaçao, Cyprus, Czech Republic, Denmark, Estonia, Faroe Islands, Finland, France, Germany, Ghana, Gibraltar, Greece, Greenland, Grenada, Guernsey, Hong Kong, China, Hungary, Iceland, India, Indonesia, Ireland, Isle of Man, Israel, Italy, Japan, Jersey, Korea, Kuwait, Latvia, Liechtenstein, Lithuania, Luxembourg, Macau, China, Malaysia, Malta, Marshall Islands, Mauritius, Mexico, Nauru, Netherlands, New Zealand, Norway, Pakistan, Panama, Poland, Portugal, Romania, Russia, Saint Lucia, Saint Vincent and the Grenadines, Samoa, San Marino, Saudi Arabia, Seychelles, Singapore, Slovak Republic, Slovenia, South Africa, Spain, Sweden, Switzerland, Turkey, Turks and Caicos Islands, United Arab Emirates, United Kingdom, Uruguay, Vanuatu
Costa Rica (92)	Albania, Andorra, Antigua and Barbuda, Argentina, Australia, Austria, Azerbaijan, Bahamas, Bahrain, Barbados, Belgium, Belize, Brazil, British Virgin Islands, Brunei Darussalam, Bulgaria, Canada, Cayman Islands, Chile, China, Colombia, Cook Islands, Croatia, Curaçao, Cyprus, Czech Republic, Denmark, Dominica, Estonia, Faroe Islands, Finland, France, Germany, Ghana, Gibraltar, Greece, Greenland, Grenada, Guernsey, Hong Kong, China, Hungary, Iceland, India, Indonesia, Ireland, Isle of Man, Israel, Italy, Japan, Jersey, Korea, Kuwait, Latvia, Lebanon, Liechtenstein, Lithuania, Luxembourg, Malaysia, Malta, Mauritius, Mexico, Montserrat, Nauru, Netherlands, New Zealand, Nigeria, Norway, Pakistan, Panama, Poland, Portugal, Romania, Russia, Saint Lucia, Saint Vincent and the Grenadines, Samoa, San Marino, Saudi Arabia, Seychelles, Singapore, Slovak Republic, Slovenia, South Africa, Spain, Sweden, Switzerland, Turkey, Turks and Caicos Islands, United Arab Emirates, United Kingdom, Uruguay, Vanuatu
Croatia (105)	Albania, Andorra, Anguilla, Antigua and Barbuda, Argentina, Aruba, Australia, Austria, Azerbaijan, Bahamas, Bahrain, Barbados, Belgium, Belize, Bermuda, Brazil, British Virgin Islands, Brunei Darussalam, Bulgaria, Canada, Cayman Islands, Chile, China, Colombia, Cook Islands, Costa Rica, Curaçao, Cyprus, Czech Republic, Denmark, Dominica, Ecuador, Estonia, Faroe Islands, Finland, France, Germany, Ghana, Gibraltar, Greece, Greenland, Grenada, Guernsey, Hong Kong, China, Hungary, Iceland, India, Indonesia, Ireland, Isle of Man, Israel, Italy, Japan, Jersey, Korea, Kuwait, Latvia, Lebanon, Liechtenstein, Lithuania, Luxembourg, Macau, China, Malaysia, Malta, Marshall Islands, Mauritius, Mexico, Monaco, Montserrat, Nauru, Netherlands, New Caledonia, New Zealand, Nigeria, Niue, Norway, Oman, Pakistan, Panama, Peru, Poland, Portugal, Qatar, Romania, Russia, Saint Kitts and Nevis, Saint Lucia, Saint Vincent and the Grenadines, Samoa, San Marino, Saudi Arabia, Seychelles, Singapore, Slovak Republic, Slovenia, South Africa, Spain, Sweden, Switzerland, Turkey, Turks and Caicos Islands, United Arab Emirates, United Kingdom, Uruguay, Vanuatu
Curaçao (87)	Albania, Andorra, Anguilla, Antigua and Barbuda, Argentina, Australia, Austria, Azerbaijan, Bahrain, Barbados, Belgium, Belize, Brazil, British Virgin Islands, Bulgaria, Canada, Cayman Islands, Chile, China, Colombia, Cook Islands, Costa Rica, Croatia, Cyprus, Czech Republic, Denmark, Estonia, Faroe Islands, Finland, France, Germany, Ghana, Gibraltar, Greece, Greenland, Grenada, Guernsey, Hungary, Iceland, India, Indonesia, Ireland, Isle of Man, Israel, Italy, Japan, Jersey, Korea, Kuwait, Latvia, Lebanon, Liechtenstein, Lithuania, Luxembourg, Malaysia, Malta, Marshall Islands, Mauritius, Mexico, Monaco, Montserrat, Nauru, New Zealand, Nigeria, Norway, Pakistan, Poland, Portugal, Romania, Russia, Saint Lucia,

Jurisdiction	Exchange agreements in place:
	Saint Vincent and the Grenadines, Samoa, San Marino, Saudi Arabia, Seychelles, Singapore, Slovak Republic, Slovenia, South Africa, Spain, Sweden, Switzerland, Turks and Caicos Islands, United Arab Emirates, United Kingdom, Uruguay
Cyprus (101)	Albania, Andorra, Anguilla, Antigua and Barbuda, Argentina, Australia, Austria, Azerbaijan, Bahamas, Bahrain, Barbados, Belgium, Belize, Bermuda, Brazil, British Virgin Islands, Brunei Darussalam, Bulgaria, Canada, Cayman Islands, Chile, China, Colombia, Cook Islands, Costa Rica, Croatia, Curaçao, Czech Republic, Denmark, Dominica, Estonia, Faroe Islands, Finland, France, Germany, Ghana, Gibraltar, Greece, Greenland, Grenada, Guernsey, Hong Kong, China, Hungary, Iceland, India, Indonesia, Ireland, Isle of Man, Israel, Italy, Japan, Jersey, Korea, Kuwait, Latvia, Lebanon, Liechtenstein, Lithuania, Luxembourg, Macau, China, Malaysia, Malta, Marshall Islands, Mauritius, Mexico, Monaco, Montserrat, Nauru, Netherlands, New Caledonia, New Zealand, Nigeria, Niue, Norway, Oman, Pakistan, Panama, Peru, Poland, Portugal, Qatar, Romania, Russia, Saint Lucia, Saint Vincent and the Grenadines, Samoa, San Marino, Saudi Arabia, Seychelles, Singapore, Slovak Republic, Slovenia, South Africa, Spain, Sweden, Switzerland, Turks and Caicos Islands, United Arab Emirates, United Kingdom, Uruguay, Vanuatu
Czech Republic (105)	Albania, Andorra, Anguilla, Antigua and Barbuda, Argentina, Aruba, Australia, Austria, Azerbaijan, Bahamas, Bahrain, Barbados, Belgium, Belize, Bermuda, Brazil, British Virgin Islands, Brunei Darussalam, Bulgaria, Canada, Cayman Islands, Chile, China, Colombia, Cook Islands, Costa Rica, Croatia, Curaçao, Cyprus, Denmark, Dominica, Ecuador, Estonia, Faroe Islands, Finland, France, Germany, Ghana, Gibraltar, Greece, Greenland, Grenada, Guernsey, Hong Kong, China, Hungary, Iceland, India, Indonesia, Ireland, Isle of Man, Israel, Italy, Japan, Jersey, Korea, Kuwait, Latvia, Lebanon, Liechtenstein, Lithuania, Luxembourg, Macau, China, Malaysia, Malta, Marshall Islands, Mauritius, Mexico, Monaco, Montserrat, Nauru, Netherlands, New Caledonia, New Zealand, Nigeria, Niue, Norway, Oman, Pakistan, Panama, Peru, Poland, Portugal, Qatar, Romania, Russia, Saint Kitts and Nevis, Saint Lucia, Saint Vincent and the Grenadines, Samoa, San Marino, Saudi Arabia, Seychelles, Singapore, Slovak Republic, Slovenia, South Africa, Spain, Sweden, Switzerland, Turkey, Turks and Caicos Islands, United Arab Emirates, United Kingdom, Uruguay, Vanuatu
Denmark (105)	Albania, Andorra, Anguilla, Antigua and Barbuda, Argentina, Aruba, Australia, Austria, Azerbaijan, Bahamas, Bahrain, Barbados, Belgium, Belize, Bermuda, Brazil, British Virgin Islands, Brunei Darussalam, Bulgaria, Canada, Cayman Islands, Chile, China, Colombia, Cook Islands, Costa Rica, Croatia, Curaçao, Cyprus, Czech Republic, Dominica, Ecuador, Estonia, Faroe Islands, Finland, France, Germany, Ghana, Gibraltar, Greece, Greenland, Grenada, Guernsey, Hong Kong, China, Hungary, Iceland, India, Indonesia, Ireland, Isle of Man, Israel, Italy, Japan, Jersey, Korea, Kuwait, Latvia, Lebanon, Liechtenstein, Lithuania, Luxembourg, Macau, China, Malaysia, Malta, Marshall Islands, Mauritius, Mexico, Monaco, Montserrat, Nauru, Netherlands, New Caledonia, New Zealand, Nigeria, Niue, Norway, Oman, Pakistan, Panama, Peru, Poland, Portugal, Qatar, Romania, Russia, Saint Kitts and Nevis, Saint Lucia, Saint Vincent and the Grenadines, Samoa, San Marino, Saudi Arabia, Seychelles, Singapore, Slovak Republic, Slovenia, South Africa, Spain, Sweden, Switzerland, Turkey, Turks and Caicos Islands, United Arab Emirates, United Kingdom, Uruguay, Vanuatu
Dominica (63)	Albania, Antigua and Barbuda, Argentina, Australia, Austria, Barbados, Belgium, Brazil, Chile, China, Colombia, Costa Rica, Croatia, Cyprus, Czech Republic, Denmark, Ecuador, Estonia, Faroe Islands, Finland, France, Germany, Gibraltar, Greece, Greenland, Grenada, Guernsey, Hong Kong, China, Hungary, India, Indonesia, Ireland, Isle of Man, Israel, Italy, Japan, Jersey, Korea, Latvia, Liechtenstein, Lithuania, Luxembourg, Malta, Mexico, Netherlands, New Zealand, Norway, Poland, Portugal, Russia, Saint Lucia, San Marino, Saudi Arabia, Singapore, Slovak Republic, Slovenia, South Africa, Spain, Sweden, Switzerland, Turkey, United Kingdom, Uruguay
Estonia (105)	Albania, Andorra, Anguilla, Antigua and Barbuda, Argentina, Aruba, Australia, Austria, Azerbaijan, Bahamas, Bahrain, Barbados, Belgium, Belize, Bermuda, Brazil, British Virgin Islands, Brunei Darussalam, Bulgaria, Canada, Cayman Islands, Chile, China, Colombia, Cook Islands, Costa Rica, Croatia, Curaçao, Cyprus, Czech Republic, Denmark, Dominica, Ecuador, Faroe Islands, Finland, France, Germany, Ghana, Gibraltar, Greece, Greenland, Grenada, Guernsey, Hong Kong, China, Hungary, Iceland, India, Indonesia, Ireland, Isle of Man, Israel, Italy, Japan, Jersey, Korea, Kuwait, Latvia, Lebanon, Liechtenstein, Lithuania, Luxembourg, Macau, China, Malaysia, Malta, Marshall Islands, Mauritius, Mexico, Monaco, Montserrat, Nauru, Netherlands, New Caledonia, New Zealand, Nigeria, Niue, Norway, Oman, Pakistan, Panama, Peru, Poland, Portugal, Qatar, Romania, Russia, Saint Kitts and Nevis, Saint Lucia, Saint Vincent and the Grenadines, Samoa, San Marino, Saudi Arabia, Seychelles, Singapore, Slovak Republic, Slovenia, South Africa, Spain, Sweden, Switzerland, Turkey, Turks and Caicos Islands, United Arab Emirates, United Kingdom, Uruguay, Vanuatu
Faroe Islands (100)	Albania, Andorra, Anguilla, Antigua and Barbuda, Argentina, Aruba, Australia, Austria, Azerbaijan, Bahamas, Bahrain, Barbados, Belgium, Belize, Bermuda, Brazil, British Virgin Islands, Brunei Darussalam, Bulgaria, Canada, Cayman Islands, Chile, China, Colombia, Cook Islands, Costa Rica, Croatia, Curaçao, Cyprus, Czech Republic, Denmark, Dominica, Ecuador, Estonia, Finland, France, Germany, Ghana, Gibraltar, Greece, Greenland, Grenada, Guernsey, Hong Kong, China, Hungary, Iceland, India, Indonesia, Ireland, Isle of Man, Israel, Italy, Japan, Jersey, Korea, Kuwait, Latvia, Lebanon, Liechtenstein, Lithuania, Luxembourg, Macau, China, Malaysia, Malta, Marshall Islands, Mauritius, Mexico, Monaco, Montserrat, Nauru, Netherlands, New Zealand, Norway, Pakistan, Panama, Poland, Portugal, Qatar, Romania, Russia, Saint Kitts and Nevis, Saint Lucia, Saint Vincent and the Grenadines, Samoa, San Marino, Saudi Arabia, Seychelles, Singapore, Slovak Republic, Slovenia, South Africa, Spain, Sweden, Switzerland, Turkey, Turks and Caicos Islands, United Arab Emirates, United Kingdom, Uruguay, Vanuatu
Finland (104)	Albania, Andorra, Anguilla, Antigua and Barbuda, Argentina, Aruba, Australia, Austria, Azerbaijan, Bahamas, Bahrain, Barbados, Belgium, Belize, Bermuda, Brazil, British Virgin Islands, Brunei Darussalam, Bulgaria, Canada, Cayman Islands, Chile, China, Colombia, Cook Islands, Costa Rica, Croatia, Curaçao, Cyprus, Czech Republic, Denmark, Dominica, Ecuador, Estonia, Faroe Islands, France, Germany, Ghana, Gibraltar, Greece, Greenland, Grenada, Guernsey, Hong

Jurisdiction	Exchange agreements in place:
	Kong, China, Hungary, Iceland, India, Indonesia, Ireland, Isle of Man, Israel, Italy, Japan, Jersey, Korea, Kuwait, Latvia, Lebanon, Liechtenstein, Lithuania, Luxembourg, Macau, China, Malaysia, Malta, Marshall Islands, Mauritius, Mexico, Monaco, Montserrat, Nauru, Netherlands, New Caledonia, New Zealand, Nigeria, Niue, Norway, Oman, Pakistan, Panama, Poland, Portugal, Qatar, Romania, Russia, Saint Kitts and Nevis, Saint Lucia, Saint Vincent and the Grenadines, Samoa, San Marino, Saudi Arabia, Seychelles, Singapore, Slovak Republic, Slovenia, South Africa, Spain, Sweden, Switzerland, Turkey, Turks and Caicos Islands, United Arab Emirates, United Kingdom, Uruguay, Vanuatu
France (104)	Albania, Andorra, Anguilla, Antigua and Barbuda, Argentina, Aruba, Australia, Austria, Azerbaijan, Bahamas, Bahrain, Barbados, Belgium, Belize, Bermuda, Brazil, British Virgin Islands, Brunei Darussalam, Bulgaria, Canada, Cayman Islands, Chile, China, Colombia, Cook Islands, Costa Rica, Croatia, Curaçao, Cyprus, Czech Republic, Denmark, Dominica, Ecuador, Estonia, Faroe Islands, Finland, Germany, Ghana, Gibraltar, Greece, Greenland, Grenada, Guernsey, Hong Kong, China, Hungary, Iceland, India, Indonesia, Ireland, Isle of Man, Israel, Italy, Japan, Jersey, Korea, Kuwait, Latvia, Lebanon, Liechtenstein, Lithuania, Luxembourg, Macau, China, Malaysia, Malta, Marshall Islands, Mauritius, Mexico, Monaco, Montserrat, Nauru, Netherlands, New Zealand, Nigeria, Niue, Norway, Oman, Pakistan, Panama, Peru, Poland, Portugal, Qatar, Romania, Russia, Saint Kitts and Nevis, Saint Lucia, Saint Vincent and the Grenadines, Samoa, San Marino, Saudi Arabia, Seychelles, Singapore, Slovak Republic, Slovenia, South Africa, Spain, Sweden, Switzerland, Turkey, Turks and Caicos Islands, United Arab Emirates, United Kingdom, Uruguay, Vanuatu
Germany (105)	Albania, Andorra, Anguilla, Antigua and Barbuda, Argentina, Aruba, Australia, Austria, Azerbaijan, Bahamas, Bahrain, Barbados, Belgium, Belize, Bermuda, Brazil, British Virgin Islands, Brunei Darussalam, Bulgaria, Canada, Cayman Islands, Chile, China, Colombia, Cook Islands, Costa Rica, Croatia, Curaçao, Cyprus, Czech Republic, Denmark, Dominica, Ecuador, Estonia, Faroe Islands, Finland, France, Ghana, Gibraltar, Greece, Greenland, Grenada, Guernsey, Hong Kong, China, Hungary, Iceland, India, Indonesia, Ireland, Isle of Man, Israel, Italy, Japan, Jersey, Korea, Kuwait, Latvia, Lebanon, Liechtenstein, Lithuania, Luxembourg, Macau, China, Malaysia, Malta, Marshall Islands, Mauritius, Mexico, Monaco, Montserrat, Nauru, Netherlands, New Caledonia, New Zealand, Nigeria, Niue, Norway, Oman, Pakistan, Panama, Peru, Poland, Portugal, Qatar, Romania, Russia, Saint Kitts and Nevis, Saint Lucia, Saint Vincent and the Grenadines, Samoa, San Marino, Saudi Arabia, Seychelles, Singapore, Slovak Republic, Slovenia, South Africa, Spain, Sweden, Switzerland, Turkey, Turks and Caicos Islands, United Arab Emirates, United Kingdom, Uruguay, Vanuatu
Ghana (70)	Albania, Andorra, Argentina, Australia, Austria, Azerbaijan, Belgium, Brazil, Chile, China, Colombia, Cook Islands, Costa Rica, Croatia, Curaçao, Cyprus, Czech Republic, Denmark, Ecuador, Estonia, Faroe Islands, Finland, France, Germany, Gibraltar, Greece, Greenland, Grenada, Guernsey, Hong Kong, China, Hungary, Iceland, India, Indonesia, Ireland, Isle of Man, Israel, Italy, Japan, Jersey, Korea, Latvia, Liechtenstein, Lithuania, Luxembourg, Malaysia, Malta, Mauritius, Mexico, Netherlands, New Zealand, Norway, Pakistan, Poland, Portugal, Russia, Saint Lucia, San Marino, Saudi Arabia, Seychelles, Singapore, Slovak Republic, Slovenia, South Africa, Spain, Sweden, Switzerland, Turkey, United Kingdom, Uruguay
Gibraltar (96)	Albania, Andorra, Antigua and Barbuda, Argentina, Aruba, Australia, Austria, Azerbaijan, Bahamas, Bahrain, Barbados, Belgium, Belize, Brazil, Brunei Darussalam, Bulgaria, Canada, Chile, China, Colombia, Cook Islands, Costa Rica, Croatia, Curaçao, Cyprus, Czech Republic, Denmark, Dominica, Ecuador, Estonia, Faroe Islands, Finland, France, Germany, Ghana, Greece, Greenland, Grenada, Guernsey, Hong Kong, China, Hungary, Iceland, India, Indonesia, Ireland, Isle of Man, Israel, Italy, Japan, Korea, Kuwait, Latvia, Lebanon, Liechtenstein, Lithuania, Luxembourg, Macau, China, Malaysia, Malta, Marshall Islands, Mauritius, Mexico, Monaco, Nauru, Netherlands, New Caledonia, New Zealand, Nigeria, Norway, Pakistan, Panama, Peru, Poland, Portugal, Qatar, Romania, Russia, Saint Kitts and Nevis, Saint Lucia, Saint Vincent and the Grenadines, Samoa, San Marino, Saudi Arabia, Seychelles, Singapore, Slovak Republic, Slovenia, South Africa, Spain, Sweden, Switzerland, Turkey, United Arab Emirates, United Kingdom, Uruguay, Vanuatu
Greece (105)	Albania, Andorra, Anguilla, Antigua and Barbuda, Argentina, Aruba, Australia, Austria, Azerbaijan, Bahamas, Bahrain, Barbados, Belgium, Belize, Bermuda, Brazil, British Virgin Islands, Brunei Darussalam, Bulgaria, Canada, Cayman Islands, Chile, China, Colombia, Cook Islands, Costa Rica, Croatia, Curaçao, Cyprus, Czech Republic, Denmark, Dominica, Ecuador, Estonia, Faroe Islands, Finland, France, Germany, Ghana, Gibraltar, Greenland, Grenada, Guernsey, Hong Kong, China, Hungary, Iceland, India, Indonesia, Ireland, Isle of Man, Israel, Italy, Japan, Jersey, Korea, Kuwait, Latvia, Lebanon, Liechtenstein, Lithuania, Luxembourg, Macau, China, Malaysia, Malta, Marshall Islands, Mauritius, Mexico, Monaco, Montserrat, Nauru, Netherlands, New Caledonia, New Zealand, Nigeria, Niue, Norway, Oman, Pakistan, Panama, Peru, Poland, Portugal, Qatar, Romania, Russia, Saint Kitts and Nevis, Saint Lucia, Saint Vincent and the Grenadines, Samoa, San Marino, Saudi Arabia, Seychelles, Singapore, Slovak Republic, Slovenia, South Africa, Spain, Sweden, Switzerland, Turkey, Turks and Caicos Islands, United Arab Emirates, United Kingdom, Uruguay, Vanuatu
Greenland (101)	Albania, Andorra, Anguilla, Antigua and Barbuda, Argentina, Aruba, Australia, Austria, Azerbaijan, Bahamas, Bahrain, Barbados, Belgium, Belize, Bermuda, Brazil, British Virgin Islands, Bulgaria, Canada, Cayman Islands, Chile, China, Colombia, Cook Islands, Costa Rica, Croatia, Curaçao, Cyprus, Czech Republic, Denmark, Dominica, Ecuador, Estonia, Faroe Islands, Finland, France, Germany, Ghana, Gibraltar, Greece, Grenada, Guernsey, Hong Kong, China, Hungary, Iceland, India, Indonesia, Ireland, Isle of Man, Israel, Italy, Japan, Jersey, Korea, Kuwait, Latvia, Lebanon, Liechtenstein, Lithuania, Luxembourg, Macau, China, Malaysia, Malta, Marshall Islands, Mauritius, Mexico, Monaco, Montserrat, Nauru, Netherlands, New Zealand, Nigeria, Norway, Pakistan, Panama, Peru, Poland, Portugal, Qatar, Romania, Russia, Saint Kitts and Nevis, Saint Lucia, Saint Vincent and the Grenadines, Samoa, San Marino, Saudi Arabia, Seychelles, Singapore, Slovak Republic, Slovenia, South Africa, Spain, Sweden, Switzerland, Turkey, Turks and Caicos Islands, United Arab Emirates, United Kingdom, Uruguay, Vanuatu

Jurisdiction	Exchange agreements in place:
Grenada (91)	Albania, Andorra, Antigua and Barbuda, Argentina, Australia, Austria, Azerbaijan, Bahamas, Bahrain, Belgium, Belize, Brazil, British Virgin Islands, Bulgaria, Canada, Cayman Islands, Chile, China, Colombia, Cook Islands, Costa Rica, Croatia, Curaçao, Cyprus, Czech Republic, Denmark, Dominica, Estonia, Faroe Islands, Finland, France, Germany, Ghana, Gibraltar, Greece, Greenland, Guernsey, Hong Kong, China, Hungary, Iceland, India, Indonesia, Ireland, Isle of Man, Israel, Italy, Japan, Jersey, Korea, Kuwait, Latvia, Lebanon, Liechtenstein, Lithuania, Luxembourg, Macau, China, Malaysia, Malta, Marshall Islands, Mauritius, Mexico, Montserrat, Nauru, Netherlands, New Zealand, Nigeria, Norway, Pakistan, Panama, Poland, Portugal, Romania, Russia, Saint Lucia, Saint Vincent and the Grenadines, Samoa, San Marino, Saudi Arabia, Seychelles, Singapore, Slovak Republic, Slovenia, South Africa, Spain, Sweden, Switzerland, Turkey, United Arab Emirates, United Kingdom, Uruguay, Vanuatu
Guernsey (99)	Albania, Andorra, Antigua and Barbuda, Argentina, Aruba, Australia, Austria, Azerbaijan, Bahamas, Bahrain, Barbados, Belgium, Belize, Bermuda, Brazil, British Virgin Islands, Brunei Darussalam, Bulgaria, Canada, Cayman Islands, Chile, China, Colombia, Cook Islands, Costa Rica, Croatia, Curaçao, Cyprus, Czech Republic, Denmark, Dominica, Ecuador, Estonia, Faroe Islands, Finland, France, Germany, Ghana, Gibraltar, Greece, Greenland, Grenada, Hong Kong, China, Hungary, Iceland, India, Indonesia, Ireland, Isle of Man, Israel, Italy, Japan, Jersey, Korea, Kuwait, Latvia, Lebanon, Liechtenstein, Lithuania, Luxembourg, Macau, China, Malaysia, Malta, Marshall Islands, Mauritius, Mexico, Monaco, Nauru, Netherlands, New Caledonia, New Zealand, Nigeria, Norway, Pakistan, Panama, Peru, Poland, Portugal, Qatar, Romania, Russia, Saint Kitts and Nevis, Saint Lucia, Saint Vincent and the Grenadines, Samoa, San Marino, Saudi Arabia, Seychelles, Singapore, Slovak Republic, Slovenia, South Africa, Spain, Sweden, Switzerland, Turkey, United Arab Emirates, United Kingdom, Uruguay
Hong Kong, China (83)	Albania, Andorra, Antigua and Barbuda, Argentina, Australia, Austria, Azerbaijan, Bahamas, Belgium, Bermuda, Brazil, British Virgin Islands, Brunei Darussalam, Bulgaria, Canada, Cayman Islands, Chile, China, Colombia, Cook Islands, Costa Rica, Croatia, Cyprus, Czech Republic, Denmark, Dominica, Estonia, Faroe Islands, Finland, France, Germany, Ghana, Gibraltar, Greece, Greenland, Grenada, Guernsey, Hungary, Iceland, India, Indonesia, Ireland, Isle of Man, Israel, Italy, Japan, Jersey, Korea, Kuwait, Latvia, Lebanon, Liechtenstein, Lithuania, Luxembourg, Malaysia, Malta, Mauritius, Mexico, Netherlands, New Zealand, Nigeria, Norway, Peru, Poland, Portugal, Qatar, Romania, Russia, Saint Lucia, San Marino, Saudi Arabia, Singapore, Slovak Republic, Slovenia, South Africa, Spain, Sweden, Switzerland, Turkey, Turks and Caicos Islands, United Arab Emirates, United Kingdom, Uruguay
Hungary (103)	Albania, Andorra, Anguilla, Antigua and Barbuda, Argentina, Aruba, Australia, Austria, Azerbaijan, Bahamas, Bahrain, Barbados, Belgium, Belize, Bermuda, Brazil, British Virgin Islands, Brunei Darussalam, Bulgaria, Canada, Cayman Islands, Chile, China, Colombia, Cook Islands, Costa Rica, Croatia, Curaçao, Cyprus, Czech Republic, Denmark, Dominica, Ecuador, Estonia, Faroe Islands, Finland, France, Germany, Ghana, Gibraltar, Greece, Greenland, Grenada, Guernsey, Hong Kong, China, Iceland, India, Indonesia, Ireland, Isle of Man, Israel, Italy, Japan, Jersey, Korea, Kuwait, Latvia, Liechtenstein, Lithuania, Luxembourg, Macau, China, Malaysia, Malta, Marshall Islands, Mauritius, Mexico, Monaco, Montserrat, Nauru, Netherlands, New Caledonia, New Zealand, Nigeria, Niue, Norway, Oman, Pakistan, Panama, Poland, Portugal, Qatar, Romania, Russia, Saint Kitts and Nevis, Saint Lucia, Saint Vincent and the Grenadines, Samoa, San Marino, Saudi Arabia, Seychelles, Singapore, Slovak Republic, Slovenia, South Africa, Spain, Sweden, Switzerland, Turkey, Turks and Caicos Islands, United Arab Emirates, United Kingdom, Uruguay, Vanuatu
Iceland (97)	Albania, Andorra, Anguilla, Antigua and Barbuda, Argentina, Aruba, Australia, Austria, Azerbaijan, Bahamas, Bahrain, Barbados, Belgium, Belize, Bermuda, Brazil, British Virgin Islands, Bulgaria, Canada, Cayman Islands, Chile, China, Colombia, Cook Islands, Costa Rica, Croatia, Curaçao, Cyprus, Czech Republic, Denmark, Estonia, Faroe Islands, Finland, France, Germany, Ghana, Gibraltar, Greece, Greenland, Grenada, Guernsey, Hong Kong, China, Hungary, India, Indonesia, Ireland, Isle of Man, Israel, Italy, Japan, Jersey, Korea, Kuwait, Latvia, Lebanon, Liechtenstein, Lithuania, Luxembourg, Macau, China, Malaysia, Malta, Marshall Islands, Mauritius, Mexico, Monaco, Montserrat, Nauru, Netherlands, New Zealand, Nigeria, Norway, Pakistan, Panama, Poland, Portugal, Qatar, Romania, Russia, Saint Kitts and Nevis, Saint Lucia, Saint Vincent and the Grenadines, Samoa, San Marino, Saudi Arabia, Seychelles, Singapore, Slovak Republic, Slovenia, South Africa, Spain, Sweden, Switzerland, Turkey, Turks and Caicos Islands, United Arab Emirates, United Kingdom, Uruguay
India (100)	Albania, Andorra, Anguilla, Antigua and Barbuda, Argentina, Aruba, Australia, Austria, Azerbaijan, Bahamas, Bahrain, Barbados, Belgium, Belize, Bermuda, Brazil, British Virgin Islands, Bulgaria, Canada, Cayman Islands, Chile, China, Colombia, Cook Islands, Costa Rica, Croatia, Curaçao, Cyprus, Czech Republic, Denmark, Dominica, Ecuador, Estonia, Faroe Islands, Finland, France, Germany, Ghana, Gibraltar, Greece, Greenland, Grenada, Guernsey, Hong Kong, China, Hungary, Iceland, Indonesia, Ireland, Isle of Man, Israel, Italy, Japan, Jersey, Korea, Kuwait, Latvia, Lebanon, Liechtenstein, Lithuania, Luxembourg, Macau, China, Malaysia, Malta, Marshall Islands, Mauritius, Mexico, Monaco, Montserrat, Nauru, Netherlands, New Zealand, Nigeria, Norway, Pakistan, Panama, Poland, Portugal, Qatar, Romania, Russia, Saint Kitts and Nevis, Saint Lucia, Saint Vincent and the Grenadines, Samoa, San Marino, Saudi Arabia, Seychelles, Singapore, Slovak Republic, Slovenia, South Africa, Spain, Sweden, Switzerland, Turkey, Turks and Caicos Islands, United Arab Emirates, United Kingdom, Uruguay, Vanuatu
Indonesia (102)	Albania, Andorra, Anguilla, Antigua and Barbuda, Argentina, Aruba, Australia, Austria, Azerbaijan, Bahamas, Bahrain, Barbados, Belgium, Belize, Bermuda, Brazil, British Virgin Islands, Brunei Darussalam, Bulgaria, Canada, Cayman Islands, Chile, China, Colombia, Cook Islands, Costa Rica, Croatia, Curaçao, Cyprus, Czech Republic, Denmark, Dominica, Ecuador, Estonia, Faroe Islands, Finland, France, Germany, Ghana, Gibraltar, Greece, Greenland, Grenada, Guernsey, Hong Kong, China, Hungary, Iceland, India, Ireland, Isle of Man, Italy, Japan, Jersey, Korea, Kuwait, Latvia, Lebanon,

Jurisdiction	Exchange agreements in place:
	Liechtenstein, Lithuania, Luxembourg, Macau, China, Malaysia, Malta, Marshall Islands, Mauritius, Mexico, Monaco, Montserrat, Nauru, Netherlands, New Caledonia, New Zealand, Nigeria, Norway, Pakistan, Panama, Peru, Poland, Portugal, Qatar, Romania, Russia, Saint Kitts and Nevis, Saint Lucia, Saint Vincent and the Grenadines, Samoa, San Marino, Saudi Arabia, Seychelles, Singapore, Slovak Republic, Slovenia, South Africa, Spain, Sweden, Switzerland, Turkey, Turks and Caicos Islands, United Arab Emirates, United Kingdom, Uruguay, Vanuatu
Ireland (104)	Albania, Andorra, Anguilla, Antigua and Barbuda, Argentina, Aruba, Australia, Austria, Azerbaijan, Bahamas, Bahrain, Barbados, Belgium, Belize, Bermuda, Brazil, British Virgin Islands, Brunei Darussalam, Bulgaria, Canada, Cayman Islands, Chile, China, Colombia, Cook Islands, Costa Rica, Croatia, Curaçao, Cyprus, Czech Republic, Denmark, Dominica, Ecuador, Estonia, Faroe Islands, Finland, France, Germany, Ghana, Gibraltar, Greece, Greenland, Grenada, Guernsey, Hong Kong, China, Hungary, Iceland, India, Indonesia, Isle of Man, Israel, Italy, Japan, Jersey, Korea, Kuwait, Latvia, Lebanon, Liechtenstein, Lithuania, Luxembourg, Macau, China, Malaysia, Malta, Marshall Islands, Mauritius, Mexico, Monaco, Montserrat, Nauru, Netherlands, New Zealand, Nigeria, Niue, Norway, Oman, Pakistan, Panama, Peru, Poland, Portugal, Qatar, Romania, Russia, Saint Kitts and Nevis, Saint Lucia, Saint Vincent and the Grenadines, Samoa, San Marino, Saudi Arabia, Seychelles, Singapore, Slovak Republic, Slovenia, South Africa, Spain, Sweden, Switzerland, Turkey, Turks and Caicos Islands, United Arab Emirates, United Kingdom, Uruguay, Vanuatu
Isle of Man (98)	Albania, Andorra, Antigua and Barbuda, Argentina, Aruba, Australia, Austria, Azerbaijan, Bahamas, Bahrain, Barbados, Belgium, Belize, Brazil, Brunei Darussalam, Bulgaria, Canada, Cayman Islands, Chile, China, Colombia, Cook Islands, Costa Rica, Croatia, Curaçao, Cyprus, Czech Republic, Denmark, Dominica, Ecuador, Estonia, Faroe Islands, Finland, France, Germany, Ghana, Gibraltar, Greece, Greenland, Grenada, Guernsey, Hong Kong, China, Hungary, Iceland, India, Indonesia, Ireland, Israel, Italy, Japan, Jersey, Korea, Kuwait, Latvia, Lebanon, Liechtenstein, Lithuania, Luxembourg, Macau, China, Malaysia, Malta, Marshall Islands, Mauritius, Mexico, Monaco, Nauru, Netherlands, New Caledonia, New Zealand, Nigeria, Norway, Pakistan, Panama, Peru, Poland, Portugal, Qatar, Romania, Russia, Saint Kitts and Nevis, Saint Lucia, Saint Vincent and the Grenadines, Samoa, San Marino, Saudi Arabia, Seychelles, Singapore, Slovak Republic, Slovenia, South Africa, Spain, Sweden, Switzerland, Turkey, United Arab Emirates, United Kingdom, Uruguay, Vanuatu
Israel (90)	Albania, Andorra, Antigua and Barbuda, Argentina, Aruba, Australia, Austria, Azerbaijan, Bahamas, Barbados, Belgium, Belize, Bermuda, Brazil, British Virgin Islands, Bulgaria, Canada, Cayman Islands, Chile, China, Colombia, Cook Islands, Costa Rica, Croatia, Curaçao, Cyprus, Czech Republic, Denmark, Dominica, Ecuador, Estonia, Faroe Islands, Finland, France, Germany, Ghana, Gibraltar, Greece, Greenland, Grenada, Guernsey, Hong Kong, China, Hungary, Iceland, India, Ireland, Isle of Man, Italy, Japan, Jersey, Korea, Latvia, Liechtenstein, Lithuania, Luxembourg, Macau, China, Malta, Mauritius, Mexico, Monaco, Montserrat, Nauru, Netherlands, New Zealand, Nigeria, Norway, Panama, Poland, Portugal, Romania, Russia, Saint Kitts and Nevis, Saint Lucia, Saint Vincent and the Grenadines, Samoa, San Marino, Seychelles, Singapore, Slovak Republic, Slovenia, South Africa, Spain, Sweden, Switzerland, Turkey, Turks and Caicos Islands, United Arab Emirates, United Kingdom, Uruguay, Vanuatu
Italy (105)	Albania, Andorra, Anguilla, Antigua and Barbuda, Argentina, Aruba, Australia, Austria, Azerbaijan, Bahamas, Bahrain, Barbados, Belgium, Belize, Bermuda, Brazil, British Virgin Islands, Brunei Darussalam, Bulgaria, Canada, Cayman Islands, Chile, China, Colombia, Cook Islands, Costa Rica, Croatia, Curaçao, Cyprus, Czech Republic, Denmark, Dominica, Ecuador, Estonia, Faroe Islands, Finland, France, Germany, Ghana, Gibraltar, Greece, Greenland, Grenada, Guernsey, Hong Kong, China, Hungary, Iceland, India, Indonesia, Ireland, Isle of Man, Israel, Japan, Jersey, Korea, Kuwait, Latvia, Lebanon, Liechtenstein, Lithuania, Luxembourg, Macau, China, Malaysia, Malta, Marshall Islands, Mauritius, Mexico, Monaco, Montserrat, Nauru, Netherlands, New Caledonia, New Zealand, Nigeria, Niue, Norway, Oman, Pakistan, Panama, Peru, Poland, Portugal, Qatar, Romania, Russia, Saint Kitts and Nevis, Saint Lucia, Saint Vincent and the Grenadines, Samoa, San Marino, Saudi Arabia, Seychelles, Singapore, Slovak Republic, Slovenia, South Africa, Spain, Sweden, Switzerland, Turkey, Turks and Caicos Islands, United Arab Emirates, United Kingdom, Uruguay, Vanuatu
Japan (104)	Albania, Andorra, Anguilla, Antigua and Barbuda, Argentina, Aruba, Australia, Austria, Azerbaijan, Bahamas, Bahrain, Barbados, Belgium, Belize, Bermuda, Brazil, British Virgin Islands, Brunei Darussalam, Bulgaria, Canada, Cayman Islands, Chile, China, Colombia, Cook Islands, Costa Rica, Croatia, Curaçao, Cyprus, Czech Republic, Denmark, Dominica, Ecuador, Estonia, Faroe Islands, Finland, France, Germany, Ghana, Gibraltar, Greece, Greenland, Grenada, Guernsey, Hong Kong, China, Hungary, Iceland, India, Indonesia, Ireland, Isle of Man, Israel, Italy, Jersey, Korea, Kuwait, Latvia, Lebanon, Liechtenstein, Lithuania, Luxembourg, Macau, China, Malaysia, Malta, Marshall Islands, Mauritius, Mexico, Monaco, Montserrat, Nauru, Netherlands, New Caledonia, New Zealand, Nigeria, Norway, Oman, Pakistan, Panama, Peru, Poland, Portugal, Qatar, Romania, Russia, Saint Kitts and Nevis, Saint Lucia, Saint Vincent and the Grenadines, Samoa, San Marino, Saudi Arabia, Seychelles, Singapore, Slovak Republic, Slovenia, South Africa, Spain, Sweden, Switzerland, Turkey, Turks and Caicos Islands, United Arab Emirates, United Kingdom, Uruguay, Vanuatu
Jersey (97)	Albania, Andorra, Antigua and Barbuda, Argentina, Aruba, Australia, Austria, Azerbaijan, Bahamas, Bahrain, Barbados, Belgium, Belize, Bermuda, Brazil, Brunei Darussalam, Bulgaria, Canada, Chile, China, Colombia, Cook Islands, Costa Rica, Croatia, Curaçao, Cyprus, Czech Republic, Denmark, Dominica, Ecuador, Estonia, Faroe Islands, Finland, France, Germany, Ghana, Greece, Greenland, Grenada, Guernsey, Hong Kong, China, Hungary, Iceland, India, Indonesia, Ireland, Isle of Man, Israel, Italy, Japan, Korea, Kuwait, Latvia, Lebanon, Liechtenstein, Lithuania, Luxembourg, Macau, China, Malaysia, Malta, Marshall Islands, Mauritius, Mexico, Monaco, Nauru, Netherlands, New Caledonia, New Zealand, Nigeria, Norway, Pakistan, Panama, Peru, Poland, Portugal, Qatar, Romania, Russia, Saint Kitts and Nevis, Saint Lucia, Saint Vincent and the Grenadines, Samoa, San Marino, Saudi Arabia, Seychelles, Singapore, Slovak Republic, Slovenia, South Africa, Spain, Sweden, Switzerland, Turkey, United Arab Emirates, United Kingdom, Uruguay, Vanuatu

Jurisdiction	Exchange agreements in place:
Korea (103)	Albania, Andorra, Anguilla, Antigua and Barbuda, Argentina, Aruba, Australia, Austria, Azerbaijan, Bahamas, Bahrain, Barbados, Belgium, Belize, Bermuda, Brazil, British Virgin Islands, Brunei Darussalam, Bulgaria, Canada, Cayman Islands, Chile, China, Colombia, Cook Islands, Costa Rica, Croatia, Curaçao, Cyprus, Czech Republic, Denmark, Dominica, Ecuador, Estonia, Faroe Islands, Finland, France, Germany, Ghana, Gibraltar, Greece, Greenland, Grenada, Guernsey, Hong Kong, China, Hungary, Iceland, India, Indonesia, Ireland, Isle of Man, Israel, Italy, Japan, Jersey, Kuwait, Latvia, Lebanon, Liechtenstein, Lithuania, Luxembourg, Macau, China, Malaysia, Malta, Marshall Islands, Mauritius, Mexico, Monaco, Montserrat, Nauru, Netherlands, New Caledonia, New Zealand, Nigeria, Norway, Pakistan, Panama, Peru, Poland, Portugal, Qatar, Romania, Russia, Saint Kitts and Nevis, Saint Lucia, Saint Vincent and the Grenadines, Samoa, San Marino, Saudi Arabia, Seychelles, Singapore, Slovak Republic, Slovenia, South Africa, Spain, Sweden, Switzerland, Turkey, Turks and Caicos Islands, United Arab Emirates, United Kingdom, Uruguay, Vanuatu
Kuwait (71)	Albania, Andorra, Antigua and Barbuda, Argentina, Australia, Austria, Azerbaijan, Barbados, Belgium, Brazil, Canada, Chile, China, Colombia, Cook Islands, Costa Rica, Croatia, Curaçao, Cyprus, Czech Republic, Denmark, Estonia, Faroe Islands, Finland, France, Germany, Gibraltar, Greece, Greenland, Grenada, Guernsey, Hong Kong, China, Hungary, Iceland, India, Indonesia, Ireland, Isle of Man, Italy, Japan, Jersey, Korea, Latvia, Liechtenstein, Lithuania, Luxembourg, Malaysia, Malta, Mauritius, Mexico, Netherlands, New Zealand, Norway, Pakistan, Panama, Poland, Portugal, Russia, Saint Lucia, San Marino, Saudi Arabia, Seychelles, Singapore, Slovak Republic, Slovenia, South Africa, Spain, Sweden, Switzerland, United Kingdom, Uruguay
Latvia (104)	Albania, Andorra, Anguilla, Antigua and Barbuda, Argentina, Aruba, Australia, Austria, Azerbaijan, Bahamas, Bahrain, Barbados, Belgium, Belize, Bermuda, Brazil, British Virgin Islands, Bulgaria, Canada, Cayman Islands, Chile, China, Colombia, Cook Islands, Costa Rica, Croatia, Curaçao, Cyprus, Czech Republic, Denmark, Dominica, Ecuador, Estonia, Faroe Islands, Finland, France, Germany, Ghana, Gibraltar, Greece, Greenland, Grenada, Guernsey, Hong Kong, China, Hungary, Iceland, India, Indonesia, Ireland, Isle of Man, Israel, Italy, Japan, Jersey, Korea, Kuwait, Lebanon, Liechtenstein, Lithuania, Luxembourg, Macau, China, Malaysia, Malta, Marshall Islands, Mauritius, Mexico, Monaco, Montserrat, Nauru, Netherlands, New Caledonia, New Zealand, Nigeria, Niue, Norway, Oman, Pakistan, Panama, Peru, Poland, Portugal, Qatar, Romania, Russia, Saint Kitts and Nevis, Saint Lucia, Saint Vincent and the Grenadines, Samoa, San Marino, Saudi Arabia, Seychelles, Singapore, Slovak Republic, Slovenia, South Africa, Spain, Sweden, Switzerland, Turkey, Turks and Caicos Islands, United Arab Emirates, United Kingdom, Uruguay, Vanuatu
Lebanon (67)	Argentina, Australia, Austria, Azerbaijan, Belgium, Brazil, Canada, Chile, China, Colombia, Costa Rica, Croatia, Curaçao, Cyprus, Czech Republic, Denmark, Estonia, Faroe Islands, Finland, France, Germany, Gibraltar, Greece, Greenland, Grenada, Guernsey, Hong Kong, China, Iceland, India, Indonesia, Ireland, Isle of Man, Italy, Japan, Jersey, Korea, Latvia, Liechtenstein, Lithuania, Luxembourg, Malaysia, Malta, Mauritius, Mexico, Monaco, Netherlands, New Zealand, Norway, Pakistan, Panama, Poland, Portugal, Russia, Saint Lucia, San Marino, Saudi Arabia, Seychelles, Singapore, Slovak Republic, Slovenia, South Africa, Spain, Sweden, Switzerland, Turkey, United Kingdom, Uruguay
Liechtenstein (100)	Albania, Andorra, Anguilla, Antigua and Barbuda, Argentina, Aruba, Australia, Austria, Azerbaijan, Bahamas, Belgium, Belize, Bermuda, Brazil, British Virgin Islands, Brunei Darussalam, Bulgaria, Canada, Cayman Islands, Chile, China, Colombia, Cook Islands, Costa Rica, Croatia, Curaçao, Cyprus, Czech Republic, Denmark, Dominica, Ecuador, Estonia, Faroe Islands, Finland, France, Germany, Ghana, Gibraltar, Greece, Greenland, Grenada, Guernsey, Hong Kong, China, Hungary, Iceland, India, Indonesia, Ireland, Isle of Man, Israel, Italy, Japan, Jersey, Korea, Kuwait, Latvia, Lebanon, Lithuania, Luxembourg, Macau, China, Malaysia, Malta, Marshall Islands, Mauritius, Mexico, Monaco, Montserrat, Nauru, Netherlands, New Caledonia, New Zealand, Nigeria, Norway, Pakistan, Panama, Peru, Poland, Portugal, Romania, Russia, Saint Kitts and Nevis, Saint Lucia, Saint Vincent and the Grenadines, Samoa, San Marino, Saudi Arabia, Seychelles, Singapore, Slovak Republic, Slovenia, South Africa, Spain, Sweden, Switzerland, Turkey, Turks and Caicos Islands, United Arab Emirates, United Kingdom, Uruguay, Vanuatu
Lithuania (103)	Albania, Andorra, Anguilla, Antigua and Barbuda, Argentina, Aruba, Australia, Austria, Azerbaijan, Bahamas, Bahrain, Barbados, Belgium, Belize, Bermuda, Brazil, British Virgin Islands, Bulgaria, Canada, Cayman Islands, Chile, China, Colombia, Cook Islands, Costa Rica, Croatia, Curaçao, Cyprus, Czech Republic, Denmark, Dominica, Estonia, Faroe Islands, Finland, France, Germany, Ghana, Gibraltar, Greece, Greenland, Grenada, Guernsey, Hong Kong, China, Hungary, Iceland, India, Indonesia, Ireland, Isle of Man, Israel, Italy, Japan, Jersey, Korea, Kuwait, Latvia, Lebanon, Liechtenstein, Luxembourg, Macau, China, Malaysia, Malta, Marshall Islands, Mauritius, Mexico, Monaco, Montserrat, Nauru, Netherlands, New Caledonia, New Zealand, Nigeria, Niue, Norway, Oman, Pakistan, Panama, Peru, Poland, Portugal, Qatar, Romania, Russia, Saint Kitts and Nevis, Saint Lucia, Saint Vincent and the Grenadines, Samoa, San Marino, Saudi Arabia, Seychelles, Singapore, Slovak Republic, Slovenia, South Africa, Spain, Sweden, Switzerland, Turkey, Turks and Caicos Islands, United Arab Emirates, United Kingdom, Uruguay, Vanuatu
Luxembourg (105)	Albania, Andorra, Anguilla, Antigua and Barbuda, Argentina, Aruba, Australia, Austria, Azerbaijan, Bahamas, Bahrain, Barbados, Belgium, Belize, Bermuda, Brazil, British Virgin Islands, Brunei Darussalam, Bulgaria, Canada, Cayman Islands, Chile, China, Colombia, Cook Islands, Costa Rica, Croatia, Curaçao, Cyprus, Czech Republic, Denmark, Dominica, Ecuador, Estonia, Faroe Islands, Finland, France, Germany, Ghana, Gibraltar, Greece, Greenland, Grenada, Guernsey, Hong Kong, China, Hungary, Iceland, India, Indonesia, Ireland, Isle of Man, Israel, Italy, Japan, Jersey, Korea, Kuwait, Latvia, Lebanon, Liechtenstein, Lithuania, Macau, China, Malaysia, Malta, Marshall Islands, Mauritius, Mexico, Monaco, Montserrat, Nauru, Netherlands, New Caledonia, New Zealand, Nigeria, Niue, Norway, Oman, Pakistan, Panama, Peru, Poland, Portugal, Qatar, Romania, Russia, Saint Kitts and Nevis, Saint Lucia, Saint Vincent and the Grenadines, Samoa, San Marino, Saudi Arabia, Seychelles, Singapore, Slovak Republic, Slovenia, South Africa, Spain, Sweden, Switzerland,

Jurisdiction	Exchange agreements in place:
	Turkey, Turks and Caicos Islands, United Arab Emirates, United Kingdom, Uruguay, Vanuatu
Macau, China (66)	Albania, Argentina, Australia, Austria, Azerbaijan, Belgium, Brazil, Canada, Chile, Colombia, Cook Islands, Croatia, Cyprus, Czech Republic, Denmark, Ecuador, Estonia, Faroe Islands, Finland, France, Germany, Gibraltar, Greece, Greenland, Grenada, Guernsey, Hungary, Iceland, India, Indonesia, Ireland, Isle of Man, Israel, Italy, Japan, Jersey, Korea, Latvia, Liechtenstein, Lithuania, Luxembourg, Malaysia, Malta, Mauritius, Mexico, Netherlands, New Zealand, Norway, Panama, Peru, Poland, Portugal, Russia, Saint Lucia, San Marino, Saudi Arabia, Singapore, Slovak Republic, Slovenia, South Africa, Spain, Sweden, Switzerland, Turkey, United Kingdom, Uruguay
Malaysia (97)	Albania, Andorra, Anguilla, Antigua and Barbuda, Argentina, Aruba, Australia, Austria, Azerbaijan, Bahamas, Bahrain, Barbados, Belgium, Belize, Bermuda, Brazil, British Virgin Islands, Bulgaria, Canada, Cayman Islands, Chile, China, Colombia, Cook Islands, Costa Rica, Croatia, Curaçao, Cyprus, Czech Republic, Denmark, Estonia, Faroe Islands, Finland, France, Germany, Ghana, Gibraltar, Greece, Greenland, Grenada, Guernsey, Hong Kong, China, Hungary, Iceland, India, Indonesia, Ireland, Isle of Man, Italy, Japan, Jersey, Korea, Kuwait, Latvia, Lebanon, Liechtenstein, Lithuania, Luxembourg, Macau, China, Malta, Marshall Islands, Mauritius, Mexico, Monaco, Montserrat, Nauru, Netherlands, New Zealand, Nigeria, Norway, Pakistan, Panama, Poland, Portugal, Qatar, Romania, Russia, Saint Kitts and Nevis, Saint Lucia, Saint Vincent and the Grenadines, Samoa, San Marino, Saudi Arabia, Seychelles, Singapore, Slovak Republic, Slovenia, South Africa, Spain, Sweden, Switzerland, Turkey, Turks and Caicos Islands, United Arab Emirates, United Kingdom, Uruguay, Vanuatu
Malta (104)	Albania, Andorra, Anguilla, Antigua and Barbuda, Argentina, Aruba, Australia, Austria, Azerbaijan, Bahamas, Bahrain, Barbados, Belgium, Belize, Bermuda, Brazil, British Virgin Islands, Brunei Darussalam, Bulgaria, Canada, Cayman Islands, Chile, China, Colombia, Cook Islands, Costa Rica, Croatia, Curaçao, Cyprus, Czech Republic, Denmark, Dominica, Ecuador, Estonia, Faroe Islands, Finland, France, Germany, Ghana, Gibraltar, Greece, Greenland, Grenada, Guernsey, Hong Kong, China, Hungary, Iceland, India, Indonesia, Ireland, Isle of Man, Israel, Italy, Japan, Jersey, Korea, Kuwait, Latvia, Lebanon, Liechtenstein, Lithuania, Luxembourg, Macau, China, Malaysia, Marshall Islands, Mauritius, Mexico, Monaco, Montserrat, Nauru, Netherlands, New Zealand, Nigeria, Niue, Norway, Oman, Pakistan, Panama, Peru, Poland, Portugal, Qatar, Romania, Russia, Saint Kitts and Nevis, Saint Lucia, Saint Vincent and the Grenadines, Samoa, San Marino, Saudi Arabia, Seychelles, Singapore, Slovak Republic, Slovenia, South Africa, Spain, Sweden, Switzerland, Turkey, Turks and Caicos Islands, United Arab Emirates, United Kingdom, Uruguay, Vanuatu
Marshall Islands (60)	Argentina, Australia, Austria, Azerbaijan, Belgium, Brazil, Canada, Chile, China, Colombia, Cook Islands, Croatia, Curaçao, Cyprus, Czech Republic, Denmark, Estonia, Faroe Islands, Finland, France, Germany, Gibraltar, Greece, Greenland, Grenada, Guernsey, Hungary, Iceland, India, Indonesia, Ireland, Isle of Man, Italy, Japan, Jersey, Korea, Latvia, Liechtenstein, Lithuania, Luxembourg, Malaysia, Malta, Mauritius, Mexico, Netherlands, Norway, Pakistan, Poland, Portugal, Russia, Saudi Arabia, Seychelles, Slovak Republic, Slovenia, South Africa, Spain, Sweden, Switzerland, United Kingdom, Uruguay
Mauritius (97)	Albania, Andorra, Anguilla, Antigua and Barbuda, Argentina, Aruba, Australia, Austria, Azerbaijan, Bahamas, Bahrain, Barbados, Belgium, Belize, Bermuda, Brazil, British Virgin Islands, Bulgaria, Canada, Cayman Islands, Chile, China, Colombia, Cook Islands, Costa Rica, Croatia, Curaçao, Cyprus, Czech Republic, Denmark, Estonia, Faroe Islands, Finland, France, Germany, Ghana, Gibraltar, Greece, Greenland, Grenada, Guernsey, Hong Kong, China, Hungary, Iceland, India, Indonesia, Ireland, Isle of Man, Israel, Italy, Japan, Jersey, Korea, Kuwait, Latvia, Lebanon, Liechtenstein, Lithuania, Luxembourg, Macau, China, Malaysia, Malta, Marshall Islands, Mexico, Monaco, Montserrat, Nauru, Netherlands, New Zealand, Norway, Pakistan, Panama, Poland, Portugal, Qatar, Romania, Russia, Saint Kitts and Nevis, Saint Lucia, Saint Vincent and the Grenadines, Samoa, San Marino, Saudi Arabia, Seychelles, Singapore, Slovak Republic, Slovenia, South Africa, Spain, Sweden, Switzerland, Turkey, Turks and Caicos Islands, United Arab Emirates, United Kingdom, Uruguay, Vanuatu
Mexico (99)	Albania, Andorra, Anguilla, Antigua and Barbuda, Argentina, Aruba, Australia, Austria, Azerbaijan, Bahamas, Bahrain, Barbados, Belgium, Belize, Bermuda, Brazil, British Virgin Islands, Bulgaria, Canada, Cayman Islands, Chile, China, Colombia, Cook Islands, Costa Rica, Croatia, Curaçao, Cyprus, Czech Republic, Denmark, Dominica, Estonia, Faroe Islands, Finland, France, Germany, Ghana, Gibraltar, Greece, Greenland, Grenada, Guernsey, Hong Kong, China, Hungary, Iceland, India, Indonesia, Ireland, Isle of Man, Israel, Italy, Japan, Jersey, Korea, Kuwait, Latvia, Lebanon, Liechtenstein, Lithuania, Luxembourg, Macau, China, Malaysia, Malta, Marshall Islands, Mauritius, Monaco, Montserrat, Nauru, Netherlands, New Zealand, Nigeria, Norway, Pakistan, Panama, Poland, Portugal, Qatar, Romania, Russia, Saint Kitts and Nevis, Saint Lucia, Saint Vincent and the Grenadines, Samoa, San Marino, Saudi Arabia, Seychelles, Singapore, Slovak Republic, Slovenia, South Africa, Spain, Sweden, Switzerland, Turkey, Turks and Caicos Islands, United Arab Emirates, United Kingdom, Uruguay, Vanuatu
Monaco (78)	Andorra, Anguilla, Argentina, Aruba, Australia, Austria, Azerbaijan, Bahamas, Belgium, Bermuda, Brazil, British Virgin Islands, Bulgaria, Canada, Cayman Islands, Chile, China, Colombia, Croatia, Curaçao, Cyprus, Czech Republic, Denmark, Estonia, Faroe Islands, Finland, France, Germany, Gibraltar, Greece, Greenland, Guernsey, Hungary, Iceland, India, Indonesia, Ireland, Isle of Man, Israel, Italy, Japan, Jersey, Korea, Latvia, Lebanon, Liechtenstein, Lithuania, Luxembourg, Malaysia, Malta, Mauritius, Mexico, Montserrat, Nauru, Netherlands, New Zealand, Norway, Panama, Poland, Portugal, Romania, Russia, Saint Kitts and Nevis, Samoa, San Marino, Saudi Arabia, Seychelles, Singapore, Slovak Republic, Slovenia, South Africa, Spain, Sweden, Switzerland, Turks and Caicos Islands, United Arab Emirates, United Kingdom, Uruguay

Jurisdiction	Exchange agreements in place:
Montserrat (64)	Albania, Andorra, Antigua and Barbuda, Argentina, Australia, Austria, Barbados, Belgium, Brazil, Canada, Chile, China, Colombia, Costa Rica, Croatia, Curaçao, Cyprus, Czech Republic, Denmark, Estonia, Faroe Islands, Finland, France, Germany, Greece, Greenland, Grenada, Hungary, Iceland, India, Indonesia, Ireland, Israel, Italy, Japan, Korea, Latvia, Liechtenstein, Lithuania, Luxembourg, Malaysia, Malta, Mauritius, Mexico, Monaco, Netherlands, New Zealand, Norway, Poland, Portugal, Russia, Saint Lucia, San Marino, Saudi Arabia, Seychelles, Singapore, Slovak Republic, Slovenia, South Africa, Spain, Sweden, Switzerland, United Kingdom, Uruguay
Nauru (72)	Albania, Andorra, Antigua and Barbuda, Argentina, Australia, Austria, Azerbaijan, Belgium, Brazil, Canada, Chile, China, Colombia, Cook Islands, Costa Rica, Croatia, Curaçao, Cyprus, Czech Republic, Denmark, Estonia, Faroe Islands, Finland, France, Germany, Gibraltar, Greece, Greenland, Grenada, Guernsey, Hungary, Iceland, India, Indonesia, Ireland, Isle of Man, Israel, Italy, Japan, Jersey, Korea, Latvia, Liechtenstein, Lithuania, Luxembourg, Malaysia, Malta, Mauritius, Mexico, Monaco, Netherlands, New Zealand, Norway, Pakistan, Panama, Poland, Portugal, Russia, Saint Lucia, San Marino, Saudi Arabia, Seychelles, Singapore, Slovak Republic, Slovenia, South Africa, Spain, Sweden, Switzerland, Turkey, United Kingdom, Uruguay
Netherlands (103)	Albania, Andorra, Anguilla, Antigua and Barbuda, Argentina, Australia, Austria, Azerbaijan, Bahamas, Bahrain, Barbados, Belgium, Belize, Bermuda, Brazil, British Virgin Islands, Brunei Darussalam, Bulgaria, Canada, Cayman Islands, Chile, China, Colombia, Cook Islands, Costa Rica, Croatia, Cyprus, Czech Republic, Denmark, Dominica, Ecuador, Estonia, Faroe Islands, Finland, France, Germany, Ghana, Gibraltar, Greece, Greenland, Grenada, Guernsey, Hong Kong, China, Hungary, Iceland, India, Indonesia, Ireland, Isle of Man, Israel, Italy, Japan, Jersey, Korea, Kuwait, Latvia, Lebanon, Liechtenstein, Lithuania, Luxembourg, Macau, China, Malaysia, Malta, Marshall Islands, Mauritius, Mexico, Monaco, Montserrat, Nauru, New Caledonia, New Zealand, Nigeria, Niue, Norway, Oman, Pakistan, Panama, Peru, Poland, Portugal, Qatar, Romania, Russia, Saint Kitts and Nevis, Saint Lucia, Saint Vincent and the Grenadines, Samoa, San Marino, Saudi Arabia, Seychelles, Singapore, Slovak Republic, Slovenia, South Africa, Spain, Sweden, Switzerland, Turkey, Turks and Caicos Islands, United Arab Emirates, United Kingdom, Uruguay, Vanuatu
New Zealand (102)	Albania, Andorra, Anguilla, Antigua and Barbuda, Argentina, Aruba, Australia, Austria, Azerbaijan, Bahamas, Bahrain, Barbados, Belgium, Belize, Bermuda, Brazil, British Virgin Islands, Brunei Darussalam, Bulgaria, Canada, Cayman Islands, Chile, China, Colombia, Cook Islands, Costa Rica, Croatia, Curaçao, Cyprus, Czech Republic, Denmark, Dominica, Ecuador, Estonia, Faroe Islands, Finland, France, Germany, Ghana, Gibraltar, Greece, Greenland, Grenada, Guernsey, Hong Kong, China, Hungary, Iceland, India, Indonesia, Ireland, Isle of Man, Israel, Italy, Japan, Jersey, Korea, Kuwait, Latvia, Lebanon, Liechtenstein, Lithuania, Luxembourg, Macau, China, Malaysia, Malta, Mauritius, Mexico, Monaco, Montserrat, Nauru, Netherlands, New Caledonia, Nigeria, Norway, Pakistan, Panama, Peru, Poland, Portugal, Qatar, Romania, Russia, Saint Kitts and Nevis, Saint Lucia, Saint Vincent and the Grenadines, Samoa, San Marino, Saudi Arabia, Seychelles, Singapore, Slovak Republic, Slovenia, South Africa, Spain, Sweden, Switzerland, Turkey, Turks and Caicos Islands, United Arab Emirates, United Kingdom, Uruguay, Vanuatu
Niue (26)	Austria, Belgium, Croatia, Cyprus, Czech Republic, Denmark, Estonia, Finland, France, Germany, Greece, Hungary, Ireland, Italy, Latvia, Lithuania, Luxembourg, Malta, Netherlands, Poland, Portugal, Slovak Republic, Slovenia, Spain, Sweden, United Kingdom
Norway (103)	Albania, Andorra, Anguilla, Antigua and Barbuda, Argentina, Aruba, Australia, Austria, Azerbaijan, Bahamas, Bahrain, Barbados, Belgium, Belize, Bermuda, Brazil, British Virgin Islands, Brunei Darussalam, Bulgaria, Canada, Cayman Islands, Chile, China, Colombia, Cook Islands, Costa Rica, Croatia, Curaçao, Cyprus, Czech Republic, Denmark, Dominica, Ecuador, Estonia, Faroe Islands, Finland, France, Germany, Ghana, Gibraltar, Greece, Greenland, Grenada, Guernsey, Hong Kong, China, Hungary, Iceland, India, Indonesia, Ireland, Isle of Man, Israel, Italy, Japan, Jersey, Korea, Kuwait, Latvia, Lebanon, Liechtenstein, Lithuania, Luxembourg, Macau, China, Malaysia, Malta, Marshall Islands, Mauritius, Mexico, Monaco, Montserrat, Nauru, Netherlands, New Caledonia, New Zealand, Nigeria, Pakistan, Panama, Peru, Poland, Portugal, Qatar, Romania, Russia, Saint Kitts and Nevis, Saint Lucia, Saint Vincent and the Grenadines, Samoa, San Marino, Saudi Arabia, Seychelles, Singapore, Slovak Republic, Slovenia, South Africa, Spain, Sweden, Switzerland, Turkey, Turks and Caicos Islands, United Arab Emirates, United Kingdom, Uruguay, Vanuatu
Pakistan (86)	Albania, Andorra, Anguilla, Argentina, Aruba, Australia, Austria, Azerbaijan, Bahrain, Belgium, Belize, Bermuda, Brazil, British Virgin Islands, Bulgaria, Cayman Islands, Chile, China, Colombia, Cook Islands, Costa Rica, Croatia, Curaçao, Cyprus, Czech Republic, Denmark, Estonia, Faroe Islands, Finland, France, Germany, Ghana, Gibraltar, Greece, Greenland, Grenada, Guernsey, Hungary, Iceland, India, Indonesia, Ireland, Isle of Man, Italy, Japan, Jersey, Korea, Kuwait, Latvia, Lebanon, Liechtenstein, Lithuania, Luxembourg, Malaysia, Malta, Marshall Islands, Mauritius, Mexico, Nauru, Netherlands, New Zealand, Nigeria, Norway, Poland, Portugal, Romania, Russia, Saint Kitts and Nevis, Saint Lucia, Saint Vincent and the Grenadines, Samoa, San Marino, Saudi Arabia, Seychelles, Singapore, Slovak Republic, Slovenia, South Africa, Spain, Sweden, Switzerland, Turkey, Turks and Caicos Islands, United Arab Emirates, United Kingdom, Uruguay
Panama (83)	Andorra, Antigua and Barbuda, Argentina, Aruba, Australia, Austria, Azerbaijan, Bahamas, Barbados, Belgium, Belize, Bermuda, Brazil, British Virgin Islands, Bulgaria, Canada, Cayman Islands, Chile, China, Colombia, Cook Islands, Costa Rica, Croatia, Cyprus, Czech Republic, Denmark, Estonia, Faroe Islands, Finland, France, Germany, Gibraltar, Greece, Greenland, Grenada, Guernsey, Hungary, Iceland, India, Indonesia, Ireland, Isle of Man, Israel, Italy, Japan, Jersey, Korea, Kuwait, Latvia, Lebanon, Liechtenstein, Lithuania, Luxembourg, Macau, China, Malaysia, Malta, Mauritius, Mexico, Monaco, Nauru, Netherlands, New Zealand, Norway, Poland, Portugal, Romania, Russia, Saint Kitts and Nevis, Saint Vincent and the Grenadines, San Marino, Saudi Arabia, Seychelles, Singapore, Slovak Republic, Slovenia, South Africa,

Jurisdiction	Exchange agreements in place:
	Spain, Sweden, Switzerland, Turks and Caicos Islands, United Arab Emirates, United Kingdom, Uruguay
Poland (104)	Albania, Andorra, Anguilla, Antigua and Barbuda, Argentina, Aruba, Australia, Austria, Azerbaijan, Bahamas, Bahrain, Barbados, Belgium, Belize, Bermuda, Brazil, British Virgin Islands, Brunei Darussalam, Bulgaria, Canada, Cayman Islands, Chile, China, Colombia, Cook Islands, Costa Rica, Croatia, Curaçao, Cyprus, Czech Republic, Denmark, Dominica, Ecuador, Estonia, Faroe Islands, Finland, France, Germany, Ghana, Gibraltar, Greece, Greenland, Grenada, Guernsey, Hong Kong, China, Hungary, Iceland, India, Indonesia, Ireland, Isle of Man, Israel, Italy, Japan, Jersey, Korea, Kuwait, Latvia, Lebanon, Liechtenstein, Lithuania, Luxembourg, Macau, China, Malaysia, Malta, Marshall Islands, Mauritius, Mexico, Monaco, Montserrat, Nauru, Netherlands, New Caledonia, New Zealand, Nigeria, Niue, Norway, Oman, Pakistan, Panama, Portugal, Qatar, Romania, Russia, Saint Kitts and Nevis, Saint Lucia, Saint Vincent and the Grenadines, Samoa, San Marino, Saudi Arabia, Seychelles, Singapore, Slovak Republic, Slovenia, South Africa, Spain, Sweden, Switzerland, Turkey, Turks and Caicos Islands, United Arab Emirates, United Kingdom, Uruguay, Vanuatu
Portugal (104)	Albania, Andorra, Anguilla, Antigua and Barbuda, Argentina, Aruba, Australia, Austria, Azerbaijan, Bahamas, Bahrain, Barbados, Belgium, Belize, Bermuda, Brazil, British Virgin Islands, Brunei Darussalam, Bulgaria, Canada, Cayman Islands, Chile, China, Colombia, Cook Islands, Costa Rica, Croatia, Curaçao, Cyprus, Czech Republic, Denmark, Dominica, Estonia, Faroe Islands, Finland, France, Germany, Ghana, Gibraltar, Greece, Greenland, Grenada, Guernsey, Hong Kong, China, Hungary, Iceland, India, Indonesia, Ireland, Isle of Man, Israel, Italy, Japan, Jersey, Korea, Kuwait, Latvia, Lebanon, Liechtenstein, Lithuania, Luxembourg, Macau, China, Malaysia, Malta, Marshall Islands, Mauritius, Mexico, Monaco, Montserrat, Nauru, Netherlands, New Caledonia, New Zealand, Nigeria, Niue, Norway, Oman, Pakistan, Panama, Peru, Poland, Qatar, Romania, Russia, Saint Kitts and Nevis, Saint Lucia, Saint Vincent and the Grenadines, Samoa, San Marino, Saudi Arabia, Seychelles, Singapore, Slovak Republic, Slovenia, South Africa, Spain, Sweden, Switzerland, Turkey, Turks and Caicos Islands, United Arab Emirates, United Kingdom, Uruguay, Vanuatu
Qatar (59)	Argentina, Australia, Austria, Azerbaijan, Barbados, Belgium, Brazil, Chile, China, Colombia, Croatia, Cyprus, Czech Republic, Denmark, Estonia, Faroe Islands, Finland, France, Germany, Gibraltar, Greece, Greenland, Guernsey, Hong Kong, China, Hungary, Iceland, India, Indonesia, Ireland, Isle of Man, Italy, Japan, Jersey, Korea, Latvia, Lithuania, Luxembourg, Malaysia, Malta, Mauritius, Mexico, Netherlands, New Zealand, Norway, Poland, Portugal, Russia, San Marino, Seychelles, Singapore, Slovak Republic, Slovenia, South Africa, Spain, Sweden, Switzerland, Turkey, United Kingdom, Uruguay
Romania (77)	Albania, Andorra, Antigua and Barbuda, Argentina, Australia, Austria, Azerbaijan, Barbados, Belgium, Brazil, Bulgaria, Canada, Chile, China, Colombia, Cook Islands, Costa Rica, Croatia, Curaçao, Cyprus, Czech Republic, Denmark, Ecuador, Estonia, Faroe Islands, Finland, France, Germany, Gibraltar, Greece, Greenland, Grenada, Guernsey, Hong Kong, China, Hungary, Iceland, India, Indonesia, Ireland, Isle of Man, Israel, Italy, Japan, Jersey, Korea, Latvia, Liechtenstein, Lithuania, Luxembourg, Malaysia, Malta, Mauritius, Mexico, Monaco, Netherlands, New Zealand, Norway, Pakistan, Panama, Peru, Poland, Portugal, Russia, Saint Lucia, San Marino, Saudi Arabia, Seychelles, Singapore, Slovak Republic, Slovenia, South Africa, Spain, Sweden, Switzerland, Turkey, United Kingdom, Uruguay
Russia (98)	Albania, Andorra, Antigua and Barbuda, Argentina, Aruba, Australia, Austria, Azerbaijan, Bahamas, Bahrain, Barbados, Belgium, Belize, Bermuda, Brazil, British Virgin Islands, Bulgaria, Cayman Islands, Chile, China, Colombia, Cook Islands, Costa Rica, Croatia, Curaçao, Cyprus, Czech Republic, Denmark, Dominica, Ecuador, Estonia, Faroe Islands, Finland, France, Germany, Ghana, Gibraltar, Greece, Greenland, Grenada, Guernsey, Hong Kong, China, Hungary, Iceland, India, Indonesia, Ireland, Isle of Man, Israel, Italy, Japan, Jersey, Korea, Kuwait, Latvia, Lebanon, Liechtenstein, Lithuania, Luxembourg, Macau, China, Malaysia, Malta, Marshall Islands, Mauritius, Mexico, Monaco, Montserrat, Nauru, Netherlands, New Zealand, Nigeria, Norway, Pakistan, Panama, Poland, Portugal, Qatar, Romania, Saint Kitts and Nevis, Saint Lucia, Saint Vincent and the Grenadines, Samoa, San Marino, Saudi Arabia, Seychelles, Singapore, Slovak Republic, Slovenia, South Africa, Spain, Sweden, Switzerland, Turkey, Turks and Caicos Islands, United Arab Emirates, United Kingdom, Uruguay, Vanuatu
Saint Kitts and Nevis (62)	Argentina, Australia, Austria, Azerbaijan, Barbados, Belgium, Brazil, Canada, Chile, China, Colombia, Croatia, Czech Republic, Denmark, Estonia, Faroe Islands, Finland, France, Germany, Gibraltar, Greece, Greenland, Guernsey, Hungary, Iceland, India, Indonesia, Ireland, Isle of Man, Israel, Italy, Japan, Jersey, Korea, Latvia, Liechtenstein, Lithuania, Luxembourg, Malaysia, Malta, Mauritius, Mexico, Monaco, Netherlands, New Zealand, Norway, Pakistan, Panama, Poland, Portugal, Russia, San Marino, Saudi Arabia, Seychelles, Slovak Republic, Slovenia, South Africa, Spain, Sweden, Switzerland, United Kingdom, Uruguay
Saint Lucia (91)	Albania, Andorra, Antigua and Barbuda, Argentina, Aruba, Australia, Austria, Azerbaijan, Barbados, Belgium, Belize, Bermuda, Brazil, British Virgin Islands, Brunei Darussalam, Bulgaria, Canada, Cayman Islands, Chile, China, Colombia, Cook Islands, Costa Rica, Croatia, Curaçao, Cyprus, Czech Republic, Denmark, Dominica, Estonia, Faroe Islands, Finland, France, Germany, Ghana, Gibraltar, Greece, Greenland, Grenada, Guernsey, Hong Kong, China, Hungary, Iceland, India, Indonesia, Ireland, Isle of Man, Israel, Italy, Japan, Jersey, Korea, Kuwait, Latvia, Lebanon, Liechtenstein, Lithuania, Luxembourg, Macau, China, Malaysia, Malta, Mauritius, Mexico, Montserrat, Nauru, Netherlands, New Zealand, Nigeria, Norway, Pakistan, Poland, Portugal, Romania, Russia, Saint Vincent and the Grenadines, San Marino, Saudi Arabia, Seychelles, Singapore, Slovak Republic, Slovenia, South Africa, Spain, Sweden, Switzerland, Turkey, Turks and Caicos Islands, United Arab Emirates, United Kingdom, Uruguay, Vanuatu

Jurisdiction	Exchange agreements in place:
Saint Vincent and the Grenadines (73)	Albania, Andorra, Antigua and Barbuda, Argentina, Australia, Austria, Azerbaijan, Barbados, Belgium, Brazil, Canada, Chile, China, Colombia, Cook Islands, Costa Rica, Croatia, Curaçao, Cyprus, Czech Republic, Denmark, Estonia, Faroe Islands, Finland, France, Germany, Gibraltar, Greece, Greenland, Grenada, Guernsey, Hungary, Iceland, India, Indonesia, Ireland, Isle of Man, Israel, Italy, Japan, Jersey, Korea, Latvia, Liechtenstein, Lithuania, Luxembourg, Malaysia, Malta, Mauritius, Mexico, Netherlands, New Zealand, Norway, Pakistan, Panama, Peru, Poland, Portugal, Russia, Saint Lucia, San Marino, Saudi Arabia, Seychelles, Singapore, Slovak Republic, Slovenia, South Africa, Spain, Sweden, Switzerland, Turkey, United Kingdom, Uruguay
Samoa (66)	Argentina, Australia, Austria, Azerbaijan, Belgium, Brazil, Canada, Chile, China, Colombia, Cook Islands, Costa Rica, Croatia, Curaçao, Cyprus, Czech Republic, Denmark, Ecuador, Estonia, Faroe Islands, Finland, France, Germany, Gibraltar, Greece, Greenland, Grenada, Guernsey, Hungary, Iceland, India, Indonesia, Ireland, Isle of Man, Israel, Italy, Japan, Jersey, Korea, Latvia, Liechtenstein, Lithuania, Luxembourg, Malaysia, Malta, Mauritius, Mexico, Monaco, Netherlands, New Zealand, Norway, Pakistan, Poland, Portugal, Russia, San Marino, Saudi Arabia, Seychelles, Slovak Republic, Slovenia, South Africa, Spain, Sweden, Switzerland, United Kingdom, Uruguay
San Marino (99)	Albania, Andorra, Anguilla, Antigua and Barbuda, Argentina, Aruba, Australia, Austria, Azerbaijan, Barbados, Belgium, Belize, Bermuda, Brazil, British Virgin Islands, Brunei Darussalam, Bulgaria, Canada, Cayman Islands, Chile, China, Colombia, Cook Islands, Costa Rica, Croatia, Curaçao, Cyprus, Czech Republic, Denmark, Dominica, Ecuador, Estonia, Faroe Islands, Finland, France, Germany, Ghana, Gibraltar, Greece, Greenland, Grenada, Guernsey, Hong Kong, China, Hungary, Iceland, India, Indonesia, Ireland, Isle of Man, Israel, Italy, Japan, Jersey, Korea, Kuwait, Latvia, Lebanon, Liechtenstein, Lithuania, Luxembourg, Macau, China, Malaysia, Malta, Mauritius, Mexico, Monaco, Montserrat, Nauru, Netherlands, New Caledonia, New Zealand, Nigeria, Norway, Pakistan, Panama, Peru, Poland, Portugal, Qatar, Romania, Russia, Saint Kitts and Nevis, Saint Lucia, Saint Vincent and the Grenadines, Samoa, Saudi Arabia, Seychelles, Singapore, Slovak Republic, Slovenia, South Africa, Spain, Sweden, Switzerland, Turkey, Turks and Caicos Islands, United Arab Emirates, United Kingdom, Uruguay
Saudi Arabia (98)	Albania, Andorra, Anguilla, Antigua and Barbuda, Argentina, Aruba, Australia, Austria, Azerbaijan, Bahamas, Bahrain, Barbados, Belgium, Belize, Bermuda, Brazil, British Virgin Islands, Brunei Darussalam, Bulgaria, Cayman Islands, Chile, China, Colombia, Cook Islands, Costa Rica, Croatia, Curaçao, Cyprus, Czech Republic, Denmark, Dominica, Ecuador, Estonia, Faroe Islands, Finland, France, Germany, Ghana, Gibraltar, Greece, Greenland, Grenada, Guernsey, Hong Kong, China, Hungary, Iceland, India, Indonesia, Ireland, Isle of Man, Italy, Japan, Jersey, Korea, Kuwait, Latvia, Lebanon, Liechtenstein, Lithuania, Luxembourg, Macau, China, Malaysia, Malta, Marshall Islands, Mauritius, Mexico, Monaco, Montserrat, Nauru, Netherlands, New Zealand, Nigeria, Norway, Pakistan, Panama, Poland, Portugal, Romania, Russia, Saint Kitts and Nevis, Saint Lucia, Saint Vincent and the Grenadines, Samoa, San Marino, Seychelles, Singapore, Slovak Republic, Slovenia, South Africa, Spain, Sweden, Switzerland, Turkey, Turks and Caicos Islands, United Arab Emirates, United Kingdom, Uruguay, Vanuatu
Seychelles (95)	Albania, Andorra, Anguilla, Antigua and Barbuda, Argentina, Aruba, Australia, Austria, Azerbaijan, Bahamas, Bahrain, Barbados, Belgium, Belize, Bermuda, Brazil, British Virgin Islands, Bulgaria, Canada, Cayman Islands, Chile, China, Colombia, Cook Islands, Costa Rica, Croatia, Curaçao, Cyprus, Czech Republic, Denmark, Estonia, Faroe Islands, Finland, France, Germany, Ghana, Gibraltar, Greece, Greenland, Grenada, Guernsey, Hungary, Iceland, India, Indonesia, Ireland, Isle of Man, Israel, Italy, Japan, Jersey, Korea, Kuwait, Latvia, Lebanon, Liechtenstein, Lithuania, Luxembourg, Malaysia, Malta, Marshall Islands, Mauritius, Mexico, Monaco, Montserrat, Nauru, Netherlands, New Zealand, Nigeria, Norway, Pakistan, Panama, Poland, Portugal, Qatar, Romania, Russia, Saint Kitts and Nevis, Saint Lucia, Saint Vincent and the Grenadines, Samoa, San Marino, Saudi Arabia, Singapore, Slovak Republic, Slovenia, South Africa, Spain, Sweden, Switzerland, Turkey, Turks and Caicos Islands, United Arab Emirates, United Kingdom, Uruguay
Singapore (100)	Albania, Andorra, Anguilla, Antigua and Barbuda, Argentina, Aruba, Australia, Austria, Azerbaijan, Bahamas, Bahrain, Barbados, Belgium, Belize, Bermuda, Brazil, British Virgin Islands, Brunei Darussalam, Bulgaria, Canada, Cayman Islands, Chile, China, Colombia, Cook Islands, Costa Rica, Croatia, Curaçao, Cyprus, Czech Republic, Denmark, Dominica, Ecuador, Estonia, Faroe Islands, Finland, France, Germany, Ghana, Gibraltar, Greece, Greenland, Grenada, Guernsey, Hong Kong, China, Hungary, Iceland, India, Indonesia, Ireland, Isle of Man, Israel, Italy, Japan, Jersey, Korea, Kuwait, Latvia, Lebanon, Liechtenstein, Lithuania, Luxembourg, Macau, China, Malaysia, Malta, Mauritius, Mexico, Monaco, Montserrat, Nauru, Netherlands, New Zealand, Nigeria, Norway, Oman, Pakistan, Panama, Peru, Poland, Portugal, Qatar, Romania, Russia, Saint Lucia, Saint Vincent and the Grenadines, San Marino, Saudi Arabia, Seychelles, Slovak Republic, Slovenia, South Africa, Spain, Sweden, Switzerland, Turkey, Turks and Caicos Islands, United Arab Emirates, United Kingdom, Uruguay, Vanuatu
Sint Maarten (0)	
Slovak Republic (105)	Albania, Andorra, Anguilla, Antigua and Barbuda, Argentina, Aruba, Australia, Austria, Azerbaijan, Bahamas, Bahrain, Barbados, Belgium, Belize, Bermuda, Brazil, British Virgin Islands, Brunei Darussalam, Bulgaria, Canada, Cayman Islands, Chile, China, Colombia, Cook Islands, Costa Rica, Croatia, Curaçao, Cyprus, Czech Republic, Denmark, Dominica, Ecuador, Estonia, Faroe Islands, Finland, France, Germany, Ghana, Gibraltar, Greece, Greenland, Grenada, Guernsey, Hong Kong, China, Hungary, Iceland, India, Indonesia, Ireland, Isle of Man, Israel, Italy, Japan, Jersey, Korea, Kuwait, Latvia, Lebanon, Liechtenstein, Lithuania, Luxembourg, Macau, China, Malaysia, Malta, Marshall Islands, Mauritius, Mexico, Monaco, Montserrat, Nauru, Netherlands, New Caledonia, New Zealand, Nigeria, Niue, Norway, Oman, Pakistan, Panama, Peru, Poland, Portugal, Qatar, Romania, Russia, Saint Kitts and Nevis, Saint Lucia, Saint Vincent and the Grenadines, Samoa, San Marino, Saudi Arabia, Seychelles, Singapore, Slovenia, South Africa, Spain, Sweden,

Jurisdiction	Exchange agreements in place:
	Switzerland, Turkey, Turks and Caicos Islands, United Arab Emirates, United Kingdom, Uruguay, Vanuatu
Slovenia (105)	Albania, Andorra, Anguilla, Antigua and Barbuda, Argentina, Aruba, Australia, Austria, Azerbaijan, Bahamas, Bahrain, Barbados, Belgium, Belize, Bermuda, Brazil, British Virgin Islands, Brunei Darussalam, Bulgaria, Canada, Cayman Islands, Chile, China, Colombia, Cook Islands, Costa Rica, Croatia, Curaçao, Cyprus, Czech Republic, Denmark, Dominica, Ecuador, Estonia, Faroe Islands, Finland, France, Germany, Ghana, Gibraltar, Greece, Greenland, Grenada, Guernsey, Hong Kong, China, Hungary, Iceland, India, Indonesia, Ireland, Isle of Man, Israel, Italy, Japan, Jersey, Korea, Kuwait, Latvia, Lebanon, Liechtenstein, Lithuania, Luxembourg, Macau, China, Malaysia, Malta, Marshall Islands, Mauritius, Mexico, Monaco, Montserrat, Nauru, Netherlands, New Caledonia, New Zealand, Nigeria, Niue, Norway, Oman, Pakistan, Panama, Peru, Poland, Portugal, Qatar, Romania, Russia, Saint Kitts and Nevis, Saint Lucia, Saint Vincent and the Grenadines, Samoa, San Marino, Saudi Arabia, Seychelles, Singapore, Slovak Republic, South Africa, Spain, Sweden, Switzerland, Turkey, Turks and Caicos Islands, United Arab Emirates, United Kingdom, Uruguay, Vanuatu
South Africa (102)	Albania, Andorra, Anguilla, Antigua and Barbuda, Argentina, Aruba, Australia, Austria, Azerbaijan, Bahamas, Bahrain, Barbados, Belgium, Belize, Bermuda, Brazil, British Virgin Islands, Brunei Darussalam, Bulgaria, Canada, Cayman Islands, Chile, China, Colombia, Cook Islands, Costa Rica, Croatia, Curaçao, Cyprus, Czech Republic, Denmark, Dominica, Ecuador, Estonia, Faroe Islands, Finland, France, Germany, Ghana, Gibraltar, Greece, Greenland, Grenada, Guernsey, Hong Kong, China, Hungary, Iceland, India, Indonesia, Ireland, Isle of Man, Israel, Italy, Japan, Jersey, Korea, Kuwait, Latvia, Lebanon, Liechtenstein, Lithuania, Luxembourg, Macau, China, Malaysia, Malta, Marshall Islands, Mauritius, Mexico, Monaco, Montserrat, Nauru, Netherlands, New Zealand, Nigeria, Norway, Pakistan, Panama, Peru, Poland, Portugal, Qatar, Romania, Russia, Saint Kitts and Nevis, Saint Lucia, Saint Vincent and the Grenadines, Samoa, San Marino, Saudi Arabia, Seychelles, Singapore, Slovak Republic, Slovenia, Spain, Sweden, Switzerland, Turkey, Turks and Caicos Islands, United Arab Emirates, United Kingdom, Uruguay, Vanuatu
Spain (105)	Albania, Andorra, Anguilla, Antigua and Barbuda, Argentina, Aruba, Australia, Austria, Azerbaijan, Bahamas, Bahrain, Barbados, Belgium, Belize, Bermuda, Brazil, British Virgin Islands, Brunei Darussalam, Bulgaria, Canada, Cayman Islands, Chile, China, Colombia, Cook Islands, Costa Rica, Croatia, Curaçao, Cyprus, Czech Republic, Denmark, Dominica, Ecuador, Estonia, Faroe Islands, Finland, France, Germany, Ghana, Gibraltar, Greece, Greenland, Grenada, Guernsey, Hong Kong, China, Hungary, Iceland, India, Indonesia, Ireland, Isle of Man, Israel, Italy, Japan, Jersey, Korea, Kuwait, Latvia, Lebanon, Liechtenstein, Lithuania, Luxembourg, Macau, China, Malaysia, Malta, Marshall Islands, Mauritius, Mexico, Monaco, Montserrat, Nauru, Netherlands, New Caledonia, New Zealand, Nigeria, Niue, Norway, Oman, Pakistan, Panama, Peru, Poland, Portugal, Qatar, Romania, Russia, Saint Kitts and Nevis, Saint Lucia, Saint Vincent and the Grenadines, Samoa, San Marino, Saudi Arabia, Seychelles, Singapore, Slovak Republic, Slovenia, South Africa, Sweden, Switzerland, Turkey, Turks and Caicos Islands, United Arab Emirates, United Kingdom, Uruguay, Vanuatu
Sweden (104)	Albania, Andorra, Anguilla, Antigua and Barbuda, Argentina, Aruba, Australia, Austria, Azerbaijan, Bahamas, Bahrain, Barbados, Belgium, Belize, Bermuda, Brazil, British Virgin Islands, Brunei Darussalam, Bulgaria, Canada, Cayman Islands, Chile, China, Colombia, Cook Islands, Costa Rica, Croatia, Curaçao, Cyprus, Czech Republic, Denmark, Dominica, Estonia, Faroe Islands, Finland, France, Germany, Ghana, Gibraltar, Greece, Greenland, Grenada, Guernsey, Hong Kong, China, Hungary, Iceland, India, Indonesia, Ireland, Isle of Man, Israel, Italy, Japan, Jersey, Korea, Kuwait, Latvia, Lebanon, Liechtenstein, Lithuania, Luxembourg, Macau, China, Malaysia, Malta, Marshall Islands, Mauritius, Mexico, Monaco, Montserrat, Nauru, Netherlands, New Caledonia, New Zealand, Nigeria, Niue, Norway, Oman, Pakistan, Panama, Peru, Poland, Portugal, Qatar, Romania, Russia, Saint Kitts and Nevis, Saint Lucia, Saint Vincent and the Grenadines, Samoa, San Marino, Saudi Arabia, Seychelles, Singapore, Slovak Republic, Slovenia, South Africa, Spain, Switzerland, Turkey, Turks and Caicos Islands, United Arab Emirates, United Kingdom, Uruguay, Vanuatu
Switzerland (101)	Albania, Andorra, Anguilla, Antigua and Barbuda, Argentina, Aruba, Australia, Austria, Azerbaijan, Bahamas, Bahrain, Barbados, Belgium, Belize, Bermuda, Brazil, British Virgin Islands, Brunei Darussalam, Bulgaria, Canada, Cayman Islands, Chile, China, Colombia, Cook Islands, Costa Rica, Croatia, Curaçao, Cyprus, Czech Republic, Denmark, Dominica, Estonia, Faroe Islands, Finland, France, Germany, Ghana, Gibraltar, Greece, Greenland, Grenada, Guernsey, Hong Kong, China, Hungary, Iceland, India, Indonesia, Ireland, Isle of Man, Israel, Italy, Japan, Jersey, Korea, Kuwait, Latvia, Lebanon, Liechtenstein, Lithuania, Luxembourg, Macau, China, Malaysia, Malta, Marshall Islands, Mauritius, Mexico, Monaco, Montserrat, Nauru, Netherlands, New Zealand, Nigeria, Norway, Pakistan, Panama, Peru, Poland, Portugal, Qatar, Romania, Russia, Saint Kitts and Nevis, Saint Lucia, Saint Vincent and the Grenadines, Samoa, San Marino, Saudi Arabia, Seychelles, Singapore, Slovak Republic, Slovenia, South Africa, Spain, Sweden, Turkey, Turks and Caicos Islands, United Arab Emirates, United Kingdom, Uruguay, Vanuatu
Trinidad and Tobago (0)	
Turkey (86)	Albania, Andorra, Argentina, Aruba, Australia, Austria, Azerbaijan, Belgium, Bermuda, Brazil, British Virgin Islands, Brunei Darussalam, Bulgaria, Canada, Cayman Islands, Chile, China, Colombia, Cook Islands, Costa Rica, Croatia, Czech Republic, Denmark, Dominica, Ecuador, Estonia, Faroe Islands, Finland, France, Germany, Ghana, Gibraltar, Greece, Greenland, Grenada, Guernsey, Hong Kong, China, Hungary, Iceland, India, Indonesia, Ireland, Isle of Man, Israel, Italy, Japan, Jersey, Korea, Latvia, Lebanon, Liechtenstein, Lithuania, Luxembourg, Macau, China, Malaysia, Malta, Mauritius, Mexico, Nauru, Netherlands, New Zealand, Nigeria, Norway, Pakistan, Poland, Portugal, Qatar, Romania, Russia, Saint Lucia, Saint Vincent and the Grenadines, San Marino, Saudi Arabia, Seychelles, Singapore, Slovak Republic, Slovenia, South Africa, Spain, Sweden, Switzerland, Turks and Caicos Islands, United Arab Emirates, United Kingdom, Uruguay,

Jurisdiction	Exchange agreements in place:
	Vanuatu
Turks and Caicos Islands (68)	Albania, Andorra, Antigua and Barbuda, Argentina, Australia, Austria, Azerbaijan, Belgium, Brazil, Canada, Chile, China, Colombia, Cook Islands, Costa Rica, Croatia, Curaçao, Cyprus, Czech Republic, Denmark, Estonia, Faroe Islands, Finland, France, Germany, Greece, Greenland, Hong Kong, China, Hungary, Iceland, India, Indonesia, Ireland, Israel, Italy, Japan, Korea, Latvia, Liechtenstein, Lithuania, Luxembourg, Malaysia, Malta, Mauritius, Mexico, Monaco, Netherlands, New Zealand, Norway, Pakistan, Panama, Poland, Portugal, Russia, Saint Lucia, San Marino, Saudi Arabia, Seychelles, Singapore, Slovak Republic, Slovenia, South Africa, Spain, Sweden, Switzerland, Turkey, United Kingdom, Uruguay
United Arab Emirates (74)	Albania, Andorra, Antigua and Barbuda, Argentina, Australia, Austria, Azerbaijan, Belgium, Brazil, Canada, Chile, China, Colombia, Cook Islands, Costa Rica, Croatia, Curaçao, Cyprus, Czech Republic, Denmark, Ecuador, Estonia, Faroe Islands, Finland, France, Germany, Gibraltar, Greece, Greenland, Grenada, Guernsey, Hong Kong, China, Hungary, Iceland, India, Indonesia, Ireland, Isle of Man, Israel, Italy, Japan, Jersey, Korea, Latvia, Liechtenstein, Lithuania, Luxembourg, Malaysia, Malta, Mauritius, Mexico, Monaco, Netherlands, New Zealand, Norway, Pakistan, Panama, Poland, Portugal, Russia, Saint Lucia, San Marino, Saudi Arabia, Seychelles, Singapore, Slovak Republic, Slovenia, South Africa, Spain, Sweden, Switzerland, Turkey, United Kingdom, Uruguay
United Kingdom (104)	Albania, Andorra, Anguilla, Antigua and Barbuda, Argentina, Aruba, Australia, Austria, Azerbaijan, Bahamas, Bahrain, Barbados, Belgium, Belize, Bermuda, Brazil, British Virgin Islands, Brunei Darussalam, Bulgaria, Canada, Cayman Islands, Chile, China, Colombia, Cook Islands, Costa Rica, Croatia, Curaçao, Cyprus, Czech Republic, Denmark, Dominica, Ecuador, Estonia, Faroe Islands, Finland, France, Germany, Ghana, Gibraltar, Greece, Greenland, Grenada, Guernsey, Hong Kong, China, Hungary, Iceland, India, Indonesia, Ireland, Isle of Man, Israel, Italy, Japan, Jersey, Korea, Kuwait, Latvia, Lebanon, Liechtenstein, Lithuania, Luxembourg, Macau, China, Malaysia, Malta, Marshall Islands, Mauritius, Mexico, Monaco, Montserrat, Nauru, Netherlands, New Zealand, Nigeria, Niue, Norway, Oman, Pakistan, Panama, Peru, Poland, Portugal, Qatar, Romania, Russia, Saint Kitts and Nevis, Saint Lucia, Saint Vincent and the Grenadines, Samoa, San Marino, Saudi Arabia, Seychelles, Singapore, Slovak Republic, Slovenia, South Africa, Spain, Sweden, Switzerland, Turkey, Turks and Caicos Islands, United Arab Emirates, Uruguay, Vanuatu
Uruguay (103)	Albania, Andorra, Anguilla, Antigua and Barbuda, Argentina, Aruba, Australia, Austria, Azerbaijan, Bahamas, Bahrain, Barbados, Belgium, Belize, Bermuda, Brazil, British Virgin Islands, Brunei Darussalam, Bulgaria, Canada, Cayman Islands, Chile, China, Colombia, Cook Islands, Costa Rica, Croatia, Curaçao, Cyprus, Czech Republic, Denmark, Dominica, Ecuador, Estonia, Faroe Islands, Finland, France, Germany, Ghana, Gibraltar, Greece, Greenland, Grenada, Guernsey, Hong Kong, China, Hungary, Iceland, India, Indonesia, Ireland, Isle of Man, Israel, Italy, Japan, Jersey, Korea, Kuwait, Latvia, Lebanon, Liechtenstein, Lithuania, Luxembourg, Macau, China, Malaysia, Malta, Marshall Islands, Mauritius, Mexico, Monaco, Montserrat, Nauru, Netherlands, New Caledonia, New Zealand, Nigeria, Norway, Pakistan, Panama, Peru, Poland, Portugal, Qatar, Romania, Russia, Saint Kitts and Nevis, Saint Lucia, Saint Vincent and the Grenadines, Samoa, San Marino, Saudi Arabia, Seychelles, Singapore, Slovak Republic, Slovenia, South Africa, Spain, Sweden, Switzerland, Turkey, Turks and Caicos Islands, United Arab Emirates, United Kingdom, Vanuatu
Vanuatu (63)	Albania, Argentina, Australia, Austria, Barbados, Belgium, Brazil, Canada, Chile, China, Colombia, Cook Islands, Costa Rica, Croatia, Cyprus, Czech Republic, Denmark, Ecuador, Estonia, Faroe Islands, Finland, France, Germany, Gibraltar, Greece, Greenland, Grenada, Hungary, India, Indonesia, Ireland, Isle of Man, Israel, Italy, Japan, Jersey, Korea, Latvia, Liechtenstein, Lithuania, Luxembourg, Malaysia, Malta, Mauritius, Mexico, Netherlands, New Zealand, Norway, Poland, Portugal, Russia, Saint Lucia, Saudi Arabia, Singapore, Slovak Republic, Slovenia, South Africa, Spain, Sweden, Switzerland, Turkey, United Kingdom, Uruguay

Annex C. The AEOI Terms of Reference

Below are the Core Requirements and Sub-Requirements of the AEOI Terms of Reference with respect to the implementation of the AEOI Standard.

CR 1 Legal framework: Jurisdictions should have a domestic legislative framework in place that requires all Reporting Financial Institutions to conduct the due diligence and reporting procedures in the CRS, and that provides for the effective implementation of the CRS as set out therein

Defining Reporting Financial Institutions

SR 1.1 Jurisdictions should define the scope of Reporting Financial Institutions consistently with the CRS, in particular by:

a) incorporating the definitions contained in paragraph A of Section VIII of the CRS into their domestic legislative framework; and

b) ensuring that any Financial Institution or category of Financial Institutions defined domestically as a Non-Reporting Financial Institution meets the requirements for its status as a Non-Reporting Financial Institution as set out in paragraph B of Section VIII of the CRS.

Defining the Financial Accounts to be reported and incorporating the due diligence procedures to identify them

SR 1.2 Jurisdictions should define the scope of Financial Accounts and Reportable Accounts consistently with the CRS and incorporate the due diligence procedures to identify them, in particular by:

a) incorporating the definitions contained in subparagraphs C. 1 to 16, and paragraphs D and E of Section VIII of the CRS into their domestic legislative framework.

b) defining New Accounts as those opened from the first day of the calendar year (or other appropriate reporting period) prior to the year of first exchange and Preexisting Accounts as those that are open on the last day of the preceding calendar year (or other appropriate reporting period).

c) incorporating the due diligence procedures contained in Sections II to VII of the CRS into their domestic legislative framework.[1]

d) ensuring that any Financial Account or category of Financial Accounts defined in their domestic legislative framework as an Excluded Account meets the requirements for its status as an Excluded Account as set out in subparagraph C. 17 of Section VIII of the CRS.

Reporting the information

SR 1.3 Jurisdictions should incorporate the reporting requirements contained in Section I of the CRS into their domestic legislative framework.[2]

Enforcement

SR 1.4 Jurisdictions should have a legislative framework in place that allows for the enforcement of the requirements of the CRS in practice, including through rules to:

a) prevent Financial Institutions, persons or intermediaries from adopting practices intended to circumvent the due diligence and reporting procedures;

b) require Reporting Financial Institutions to keep records of the steps undertaken and any evidence relied upon for the due diligence procedures for at least five years following the end of the period within which the Reporting Financial Institution must report the information required to be reported under Section I of the CRS;

c) ensure that valid self-certifications are always obtained for New Accounts; and

d) address non-compliance with the requirements of the CRS.

CR 1 Effectiveness in practice: Jurisdictions should ensure that in practice Reporting Financial Institutions correctly implement the due diligence and reporting procedures, which includes a requirement for jurisdictions to have in place an administrative framework to ensure the effective implementation of the CRS

Ensuring effectiveness domestically

SR 1.5 Jurisdictions should ensure that in practice Reporting Financial Institutions identify the Financial Accounts they maintain, identify the Reportable Accounts among those Financial Accounts, as well as their Account Holders, and where relevant Controlling Persons, by correctly conducting the due diligence procedures and collect and report the required information with respect to each Reportable Account. This includes having in place:

a) an effective administrative compliance framework to ensure the effective implementation of, and compliance with, the CRS. This framework should:

   i. be based on a strategy that facilitates compliance by Reporting Financial Institutions and which is informed by a risk assessment in respect of the effective implementation of the CRS that takes into account relevant information sources (including third party sources);

   ii. include procedures to ensure that Financial Institutions correctly apply the definitions of Reporting Financial Institutions and Non-Reporting Financial Institutions;

   iii. include procedures to periodically verify Reporting Financial Institutions' compliance,[3] conducted by authorities that have adequate powers with respect to the reviewed Reporting Financial Institutions, with procedures to access the records they maintain;[4] and

b) effective procedures to ensure that Financial Institutions, persons or intermediaries do not circumvent the due diligence and reporting procedures;

c) effective enforcement mechanisms to address non-compliance by Reporting Financial Institutions;

d) strong measures to ensure that valid self-certifications are always obtained for New Accounts;[5]

e) effective procedures to ensure that each, or each type of, jurisdiction-specific Non-Reporting Financial Institution and Excluded Account continue to present a low risk of being used to evade tax;[6] and

f) effective procedures to follow up with a Reporting Financial Institution when undocumented accounts are reported in order to establish the reasons why such information is being reported.[7]

International collaboration to ensure effectiveness

SR 1.6 Jurisdictions should collaborate on compliance and enforcement. This requires jurisdictions to:

a) use all appropriate measures available under the jurisdiction's domestic law to address errors or non-compliance notified to the jurisdiction by an exchange partner;[8] and

b) have in place effective procedures to notify an exchange partner of errors that may have led to incomplete or incorrect information reporting or non-compliance with the due diligence or reporting procedures by a Reporting Financial Institution in the jurisdiction of the exchange partner.[9]

CR2 Legal framework: Jurisdictions should have exchange relationships in effect with all Interested Appropriate Partners as committed to and that provide for the exchange of information in accordance with the Model CAA

Putting in place the exchange agreements on time

SR 2.1 Jurisdictions should have exchange agreements in effect with all Interested Appropriate Partners that permit the automatic exchange of CRS information.

SR 2.2 Such an exchange agreement should be put in place without undue delay, following the receipt of an expression of interest from an Interested Appropriate Partner.[10]

The contents of the agreements

SR 2.3 Jurisdictions should ensure that the exchange agreements in effect provide for the exchange of information in accordance with the requirements of the Model CAA,[11] including with respect to:

a) the categories of information to be exchanged;[12]

b) the timing of the exchange of information;[13]

c) the notifying of an exchange partner when the jurisdiction has reason to believe that an error may have led to incomplete or incorrect information reporting or there is non-compliance with the due diligence or reporting procedures by a Reporting Financial Institution, located in the exchange partner;[14] and

d) taking all appropriate measures available under the jurisdiction's domestic law to address errors or non-compliance notified to it.[15]

CR2 Effectiveness in practice: Jurisdictions should exchange the information effectively in practice, in a timely manner, including by sorting, preparing, validating and transmitting it in accordance with the AEOI Standard

Preparing and validating the information

SR 2.4 Jurisdictions should sort, prepare and validate the information in accordance with the CRS XML Schema and the associated requirements in the CRS XML Schema User Guide[16] and the File Error and Correction-related validations in the Status Message User Guide (i.e. the 50000 and 80000 range).[17]

Transmitting the information

SR 2.5 Jurisdictions should agree and use, with each exchange partner, transmission methods that meet appropriate minimum standards to ensure the confidentiality and integrity of the data throughout the transmission, including its encryption to a minimum secure standard.[18]

SR 2.6 Jurisdictions should carry out all exchanges annually within nine months of the end of the calendar year to which the information relates.[19]

SR 2.7 Jurisdictions should send the information in accordance with the agreed transmission methods and encryption standards.[20]

SR 2.8 Jurisdictions should have the systems in place to receive information and, once it has been received, should send a status message to the sending jurisdictions in accordance with the CRS Status Message XML Schema and the related User Guide.

Providing corrections, amendments or additions

SR 2.9 Jurisdictions should respond to a notification from an exchange partner as referred to in Section 4 of the Model CAA (which may include Status Messages) in accordance with the timelines set out in the Commentary to Section 4 of the Model CAA. In all other cases, jurisdictions should send corrected, amended or additional information received from a Reporting Financial Institution as soon as possible after it has been received.[21]

Core Requirement 3: Jurisdictions should keep the information exchanged confidential and properly safeguarded, and use it in accordance with the exchange agreement under which it was exchanged SR

SR 3.1 Jurisdictions should meet the confidentiality and data safeguard requirements, including on the use of the information, referred to in Section 5 of the Model CAA to be able to receive information under the AEOI Standard.

Notes

[1] Sections II to VII of the CRS set out the General Due Diligence Requirements, the Due Diligence for Preexisting Individual Accounts, the Due Diligence for New Individual Accounts, the Due Diligence for Preexisting Entity Accounts, the Due Diligence for New Entity Accounts, the Special Due Diligence Rules and the Defined Terms respectively. Paragraphs D and E of 3 Section VIII of the CRS set out the definitions relevant to the due diligence procedures.

[2] Section I of the CRS sets out the General Reporting Requirements, specifying the information that must be reported with respect to each Reportable Account.

[3] Paragraph A. 3 of Section IX of the CRS

[4] Paragraph A. 2 of Section IX of the CRS

[5] Paragraph 18 of the Commentary on Section IX of the CRS

[6] Paragraph A. 4 of Section IX of the CRS

[7] Paragraph A. 3 of Section IX of the CRS

[8] Section 4 of the Model CAA

[9] Section 4 of the Model CAA

[10] Exchange agreements are expected to be put in place in time for exchanges from the date committed to unless the expression of interest indicates a later date for the commencement of exchanges or the expression of interest is not received in time. Whether the expression of interest is received in time for exchanges to commence in a particular year will depend on the specific circumstances, including the approach to the implementation of the AEOI Standard taken by the potential exchange partners.

[11] Note that the agreements can take various forms. What is key is that both exchange partners are satisfied that the arrangement in place delivers the outcomes specified in the requirements.

[12] Section 2 of the Model CAA

[13] Section 3 of the Model CAA

[14] Section 4 of the Model CAA

[15] Section 4 of the Model CAA

[16] Paragraph 5 of Section 3 of the Model CAA

[17] If using the Common Transmission System, the information should be prepared in accordance with the File Preparation and Encryption User Guide.

[18] Paragraph 6 of Section 3 of the Model CAA and the File Preparation and Encryption User Guide

[19] Paragraph 3 of Section 3 of the Model CAA also states that information is only required to be exchanged with respect to a calendar year if both jurisdictions have in effect legislation that requires reporting with respect to such calendar year that is consistent with the scope of exchange required (Section 2 of the Model CAA) and the reporting and due diligence procedures contained in the CRS.

[20] Paragraph 6 of Section 3 of the Model CAA and the File Preparation and Encryption User Guide

[21] Commentary on Section 2 of the Model CAA

www.ingramcontent.com/pod-product-compliance
Ingram Content Group UK Ltd.
Pitfield, Milton Keynes, MK11 3LW, UK
UKHW051456290926
15471UKWH00008B/1238

9 789264 352889